A
DICTIONARY
of SEA TERMS

BY

A. ANSTED

———

FULLY ILLUSTRATED

———

Revised by
PETER CLISSOLD

GLASGOW
BROWN, SON & FERGUSON, LTD., Nautical Publishers
4–10 Darnley Street
G41 2SD

First Edition	- -	1920
Second Edition	- -	1928
Third Edition	- -	1985

ISBN 0 85174 481 8

© 1985 Brown, Son & Ferguson, Limited, Glasgow, G41 2SD

Printed and Made in Great Britain

PREFACE TO THE FIRST EDITION

I AM anxious to make it clear that this little Dictionary is intended as a help to beginners. I do not profess to teach those who may be already experienced in yachting and the art of boat-sailing, and still less those acquainted with the sea. For these there are various nautical dictionaries; but so far as I am aware, there is no such work exclusively devoted to those who start in entire ignorance of their subject; and to supply this apparent want the present work is an attempt.

Such a work presents some difficulties, and is, therefore, naturally open to criticism. Nautical terms are essentially technical; many are used in various senses, while sometimes several may have but one meaning. And besides these we have a list of expressions which, while they cannot be regarded as sea terms, have direct reference to boat-building and boat-sailing.

It is to be feared, too, that some of those phrases now commonly met with in the sporting journals may have been overlooked. Numerous as are the terms in daily use among seafaring men, their number has been considerably enlarged of late years, not only in consequence of recent improvements in yacht-building, which require new names for parts and fittings hitherto unknown, but chiefly in consequence of that tendency in a certain class of sporting scriveners so to expand the technicality and the volubility of their nautical language that it has been found impossible to keep pace with them.

True maritime terms may generally be traced back to very simple derivations. To understand the derivation of a word is to understand it in its fullest meaning. For this reason, wherever the origin of an expression is known, I have taken the opportunity of inserting it.

The principal works of reference used in this compilation are: Falconer's "Dictionary of the Marine" (1768); Smyth's "Sailor's Word-Book" (c. 1830); "Dictionary of Science, Literature and Art" (Brande and Cox) (1875); "The Boating-man's Vade-Mecum" (Winn); "Boat-sailing for Amateurs" (Davies). To these and other authorities I must acknowledge my indebtedness. And, in conclusion, I must fulfil a promise in dedicating my work to my two children, who, at the age of seven and eight, are already handy in a boat and familiar with a great number of the terms I have endeavoured to explain.

A.A.   Southend. September 1897

PREFACE TO THE NEW EDITION

Sea terms are mostly of ancient origin, but since the turn of the century, when the first edition of this Dictionary was compiled, many new materials and techniques have come into use; for example, Glass Re-enforced Plastic for building, and the internal-combustion engine for propelling vessels. Nearly all the sailing craft mentioned in the Dictionary may, and probably will, be fitted with motors and, as likely as not, their rig will be modified in consequence. Regulations, too, have been altered; for instance, the Regulations for Preventing Collisions at Sea and the International Code of Signals have been revised more than once, while Helm Orders have been changed to Steering Orders, which resulted in the spoken orders being reversed in meaning. Our knowledge of ships and seafaring in earlier times has also increased.

Ansted dealt thoroughly with the craft and customs of his time and I have not altered his style, but it has been necessary to add more than 260 entries to bring his work up to date.

The twelve drawings which appear over the initials C.H.W. are by Commander C. H. Williams, R.D., R.N.R. (who served in the *Hugomont*, one of the vessels he illustrates) and are reproduced, by kind permission, from *The Mariner's Mirror*, the Journal of the Society for Nautical Research, in which they originally appeared.

Ansted acknowledges his debt to earlier writers of dictionaries and I have been glad to consult C. W. F. Layton's *Dictionary of Nautical Words & Terms*, and P. Kemp's *The Oxford Companion to Ships & the Sea*, besides many other standard works.

While certainly not exhaustive, it is hoped that this enlarged edition will be sufficient to meet the needs of those first encountering the sea, either in person or in literature, while others already familiar with nautical matters, may find interest in the description of things no longer often encountered.

P.C.

A

DICTIONARY OF SEA TERMS

A

A.—The highest class under which vessels are registered at Lloyd's. It is sub-divided into A1 and A2.

a'.—An Anglo-Saxonism for "on" or "in." It is in constant use at sea.

A.B.—The initial letters of the words *able-bodied*. A full or first-class seaman, commonly called an able seaman, is classed A.B.

Aback.—Spoken of the sails when laid flat against a mast, either by a sudden change of wind, or, in some instances, they may be *laid aback* for some special purpose. (*See* BACK.)

Abaft.—Behind or towards the stern of a vessel. Thus, "abaft the funnel," so frequently seen on board pleasure steam boats, will mean "behind the funnel."

Abeam.—On the side of a vessel, amidships. Thus "wind abeam," or "wind on the beam," will mean wind at right angles to the vessel. (*See* WIND.)

Aboard, or **on board.**—On, or in, a vessel.

About.—A turning round.

To *go about.*—To turn a vessel round, in sailing, on to another tack or direction. (*See* TACK.)

Above board.—Above deck. Hence the expression in everyday use, meaning "honest," "fair," or "in the light of day."

Abox.—An old term used in *wearing* a ship. It means to lay the ship aback, and thus to *box her off*.

Abreast.—On the beam. At right angles to the vessel's fore and aft line.

Accul (old term).—Spoken of a deep bight or bay which ends as a *cul de sac*.

Acker.—An eddy or rising tide. (*See* EAGRE and BORE.)

Ackmen.—An old name for freshwater thieves.

Acock-bill.—Spoken of a ship's anchor, when hanging out with the flukes extended in a position ready for dropping: of a yard when one yardarm is topped up and the other bowsed down; once a sign of mourning.

Acorn.—An ornament at the head of a mast fashioned in the shape of an acorn.

Adrift.—Anything which floats unfastened, as a boat or a spar, which may have broken away, or a ship which has parted from her anchor. Anything loose or untied, and thus, of a person, absent or late.

Afloat.—Floating on the water. Off the ground.

Aft.—Behind: towards the *after* or stern part of a vessel, or it may be behind the vessel itself: thus a boat may be said to be towed *aft*.

After-part.—The hinder part. Thus a steersman may, according to the position of the wheel, stand amidships, or in the *after* part of the vessel. So also the *after* cabin will be the cabin nearest the stern. (*See also* ABAFT.)

Aground.—Resting on the ground, often spoken of a vessel which has accidentally run aground, or as it is sometimes said, *taken the ground*. (*See* GROUND.)

Ahead.—In front of. Before.

Wind ahead.—Wind directly against the course of a vessel.

Ahull.—"The situation of a ship when all her sails are furled, and her helm lashed on the lee-side; she then lies nearly with her side to the wind and sea, her head somewhat turned towards the direction of the wind." (Falconer's Dictionary.) (*See also* under TRYING.)

Ahoy.—An interjection, which, preceded by a vessel's name, is the customary way to hail a vessel.

Aldis.—A powerful electric signalling lamp.

Alee.—The situation of the helm when pushed close down to the lee-side of the ship, in order to put the ship about, or to lay her head to the windward.

All hands. All hands ahoy ("*tout le monde en haut:*" Fr.) (at sea).—The call by which all hands are ordered on deck whether it be, as in a ship, to execute some necessary change, or, as with fishermen, to haul a net.

All in the wind.—An expression used to describe the position of a vessel when head to wind (*i.e.,* pointing directly against the wind), with all her sails flapping. (*See also* "in irons," under IRON, "in stays," etc., under TACK.) The term is also sometimes used in everyday conversation, meaning "all in a flurry."

Allotment.—That part of a seaman's wages which he wishes to be paid each month to a relative or savings bank.

All standing.—To be brought up all standing is to come to a sudden and unexpected stop.

All told.—Every person counted. The term has usual references to a ship's crew, when it will include the *idlers,* etc., but not passengers. Thus a ship may have a crew of 20, but be 23 all told—that is including cook, carpenter, and steward.

Aloft (*Loffter,* Dan.).—Up in the tops: overhead. In the upper rigging, or on the yards, etc.

Lay aloft.—The order to go aloft, as "lay aloft and furl the royals."

Alongside.—By the side of.

Aloof (old term).—To keep aloof, *i.e.*, to keep the *luff*—*i.e.*, up to the wind. (*See* LUFF.)

Alow.—Low down. Below, or below deck.

Amain.—Suddenly: forcibly. To *let go amain,* to let go suddenly.

Amateur.—In sporting language one who takes up an occupation for pleasure—not for money. In rowing the meaning is somewhat restricted. (*See also* under CORINTHIAN.) At Henley, 1879, the following definition of an amateur was adopted. "No person shall be considered an amateur oarsman or sculler:—1. Who has ever competed in any open competition for a stake, money, or entrance fee; 2. Who has ever competed with or against a professional for any prize; 3. Who has ever taught, pursued, or assisted in the practice of athletic exercises of any kind as a means of gaining a livelihood; 4. Who has been employed in or about boats for money or wages; 5. Who is, or has been by trade or employment for wages, a mechanic, artisan, or labourer."

America's Cup.—Yacht race trophy, first presented by the Royal Yacht Squadron in 1851 and won by the schooner *America*. Held by the U.S.A. until 1983, when the Australian yacht *Australia II* beat the United States' *Liberty*.

Amidships.—Generally speaking, the middle portion of a vessel. The point of intersection of two lines, one drawn from stem to stern, the other across the beam (or widest part), will be the actual midships.

Anchor.—The form and parts of an anchor are as follows:—A is the *shank*, B the *arms,* terminating in the *flukes* (C), the extremities of which (D) are called the *bills* or *peaks,* while the smooth flat side of the fluke (E) is the *palm.* F is the *crown,* and G the *throat.* The *stock* or *beam* (H) crosses the lower part of the shank at right angles, and in a plane at right angles to the plane of the arms: J is the *shoulder* of the stock. K is the ring, to which the cable is bent or the chain shackled (L). (For the manner of bending— *i.e.*, attaching a rope to this ring, see KNOTS.) The ring hangs in the *eye.* The stock of an anchor is the agent which brings the flukes into a position to hold the ground. In doing this it has often to sustain great strains, and is therefore, the part most liable to injury.

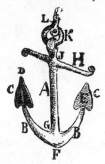

ANCHOR

For this reason a stout stock is to be recommended. It has been said that the sectional area at the smallest part of an anchor should be three times that of the cable.

To *drop, let go,* or *cast* anchor, are terms equivalent to *coming to an anchor.*

To *weigh anchor* is to get the anchor up preparatory to getting under sail. This is done by first *heaving short*—*i.e.,* hauling upon the cable until the vessel is nearly over her anchor, which brings the anchor *apeak*—that is standing on its crown. When the anchor is once lifted from the ground it is said to be *aweigh, weighed* or *atrip*: when it reaches the surface of the water it is *awash*. The ship being now free is said to be *under weigh* (not under *way,* for *way* means *momentum*), and the vessel may be *under weigh* without having *way*: she is, in point of fact, *under weigh* from the moment her anchor is weighed. (*See also* under WAY and WEIGH.)

Catting the anchor is getting it up to the *cathead*. When it has been stowed on the *bill-board* it is said to be *fished,* and the tackle by which this is done is called the *fish-tackle*.

Anchor apeak denotes that the cable has been drawn in so short as to bring the ship directly over it.

Anchor acock-bill is a term used to signify that the anchor hangs, merely by its cable, over the vessel's side, with the stock or flukes extended, just above the water. This, in the London river and in many other havens, is prohibited by law.

If the anchor holds the ground well it is said to *bite*. Should it drag it is said to *come home*. But at the same time to *fetch home* or *bring home* the anchor is to draw the ship closer up to it, for the purpose, perhaps, of weighing it.

When the cable becomes twisted round the shank or stock, or entangled with it in any way, it is called *fouling*.

To *shoe the anchor* "is to cover the flukes with a broad triangular piece of thick plank, whose area is greater than that of the flukes, in order to give the anchor a stronger hold in soft ground."

To *back an anchor,* "to carry out a small anchor, as the stream or kedge, ahead of the large one by which the ship usually rides, in order to support it, and prevent it from loosening, or *coming home,* in bad ground. In this situation the latter is confined by the former, in the same manner that the ship is restrained by the latter." (Falconer's Dictionary.) A weight is sometimes used as a substitute for the smaller anchor.

Large vessels carry several anchors, often one on each bow, called, in consequence, *bower* anchors. Other large ones are known as *sheet, stream, stern, waist* and *spare* anchors, and besides these they have small ones called *kedges* (or *kedge anchors*), *killicks* or *mudhooks*. The sheet-anchor, the largest and most powerful carried by a ship, is popularly supposed to be used only in emergency or as a last resource; and hence the use of the term in this sense in general conversation. Kedges are smaller anchors carried by a ship and used by her for various purposes, such as when swinging her, or when moving from one station to another only a short distance away: they are also valuable in case of the vessel taking the ground.

The first type of anchor illustrated is known as the *Admiralty Pattern* or *Fisherman's Anchor* and has been in use for some 2000 years, but when of a size and weight necessary to hold large ships it is awkward to handle and stow, and so has been superceded by the *Stockless Anchor* which can be hove right up and secured in the hawse-pipe. The arms of a *stockless anchor* hinge on the shank and have *Tripping palms* which cause the flukes to bite into the ground when a pull is exerted on the anchor. The *Danforth Anchor* has a light stock at the crown extending beyond the flukes to ensure that both flukes lie flat and bite into the ground. *The Plough, Ploughshare or CQR* anchor is the type now usually carried by small craft. The flukes, shaped like ploughshares, turn on the shank and dig into the ground when the vessel pulls upon her anchor. (*See* BECUEING.)

STOCKLESS
AND TRIPLE-GRIP

The mushroom anchor—so named on account of its shape (see fig.)—is employed on mud or other soft bottoms, where it obtains a hold far more secure than any other form.

The objects in all these anchors (beyond the system of gripping) are to lessen the risks of fouling, and to present no fluke above ground against which, in shallow places, a vessel might strike. The usual method of working the anchor cable in small craft is to take two or three turns with it round the windlass (*i.e.,* just sufficient to get a certain bite), and then to pass the rest of the chain through an aperture in the deck, made for the purpose, and thus down to the chain locker.

MUSHROOM ANCHOR

Anchorage.—The ground in which the anchor is cast. Thus one may find good anchorage or bad, the good being that in which the vessel will ride safely, the bad that in which the anchor will be likely to drag. Yet it is not always the nature of the soil which constitutes good anchorage; currents or the run of the tide always have much to do with it. Land-locked bays, therefore, and positions well out of the tide, will form the best anchorage. The term anchorage is also occasionally used to denote those dues which are paid by vessels for the privilege of casting anchor in certain harbours.

Anchor Buoy.—A small buoy whose rope is attached to the crown of an anchor to show the position of the anchor on the bottom.

Anemometer.—An instrument for measuring the force or velocity of the wind. The anemometer most generally used is one devised by Dr. Robinson, and made by Casella, who also elaborated and modified Robinson's instrument and produced one of great accuracy.

Aneroid.—An instrument answering to the mercury barometer, but acting by the pressure of the atmosphere upon thin metallic plates. Its general form resembles that of a watch. The aneroid is frequently used at sea to obtain meteorological readings, although amongst scientific men it is hardly considered sufficiently sensitive. Yachtsmen are seldom without an aneroid.

Antifouling.—Paint applied to the underwater part of a vessel's hull to kill marine organisations which would otherwise attach themselves there.

Antiscorbutics.—Medicine or food, such as lime-juice, fresh vegetables and fruit, taken as a prevention against scurvy.

Apeak.—Spoken of the position of an anchor when a vessel is *hove-short* above it. (*See* ANCHOR.)

Apparently · drowned.—For directions for restoring. (*See* DROWNED.)

Apron, stemson, or **stomach-piece.**—1. (In shipbuilding.) A backing or strengthening timber behind the stem-post of a vessel. (*See* diagram under FRAME.) 2. (In hydraulic engineering.) The enclosure of timber, brick, or stone at the down side of a lock is sometimes called the *apron wall*.

Arching.—Another name for *hogging* (*which see*).

Ardent.—A vessel is described as ardent when, her tendency being to run up into the wind, she carries a good *weather helm* (*which see*).

Arming. The tallow or soap placed in the base of a *sounding lead*. Its object is so that the nature of the ground over which the ship is passing can be ascertained from the particles which adhere.

Ashore.—On *terra firma*. A vessel aground is sometimes spoken of as "ashore." (*See* GROUND.)

Astay.—In line with a stay, or with the fore stay.

Astern.—Behind. In the after part of a vessel; behind the vessel; in her wake.

Go astern.—Go sternwards: or, with a steam boat, an order to work her backwards.

Athwart, athwartships.—Across. Hence the rowers' seats in an open boat are called "thwarts" because they lie athwart, or across the boat.

To *drop athwart* anything.—To come across it; to find it.

Athwart hawse.—Within the length of a vessel's cable. (The term is explained under HAWSE.)

Atrip.—1. Spoken of an anchor when it is just off the ground or *aweigh*. (*See* ANCHOR.) 2. (Of sails.) When the sails are ready for trimming.

At the dip.—A flag or signal not hoisted to its full height. The Answering Pennant at the dip signifies: "Your signal is seen, but is not understood."

Austral.—Southern.

Avast.—The order to stop or pause in any exercise; as "avast heaving."

Awash.—Being under or washed over by water, as the lee gunwale of a yacht or decked sailing boat may be when she lies much over.

Anchor awash.—When, in weighing the anchor, it reaches the surface of the water, it is said to be awash.

Away.—Gone: having let anything go: free.

Carried away.—Broken away; as to carry away a topmast—*i.e.*, to suffer the loss of the topmast.

Aweather.—Towards the weather side—*i.e.*, the side upon which the wind blows.

Helm aweather.—The helm put up. (*See* HELM.)

Aweigh.—Spoken of an anchor when it has been lifted from the ground.

Awheft.—Said of a flag when *stopped* so as to represent a *wheft*.

Awning.—A canvas covering acting as a roof or tent.

Aye (*adv.*, perhaps from *ajo,* Lat. (defective verb), to say yes).— Yes, and is always used in lieu thereof at sea, with a repetition, "Aye, aye, sir," meaning "I understand; and will execute the order."

Azimuth.—The bearing of a celestial object.

B

Back.—With *sailing ships.*—To back is to haul the sails over to windward. In square rigged vessels this is only done on special occasions, when it is called *laying the sails aback.* In small craft the practice is more frequent, and especially with boats which are slow in stays, (*i.e.,* in coming round, in tacking), as those of much length often are. By holding a foresail or a jib over to the weather side (the side upon which the wind is blowing) the boat's head will be thrown off, or away from the wind, and she will often come round; this is called *boxing off her head.* But by holding the boom of the main or mizzen sail to windward, her stern will be thrown off; and this, properly speaking, is back-sailing, which is, as it were, the opposite to boxing off; although, in many instances, it answers the same purpose. (*See* BOXING OFF.)

With *steam vessels.*—"Back her" is an order to reverse engines, so that the ship may be suddenly stopped or made to *go astern.*

In *rowing,* to *back,* or *backwater,* is to stop the progress of a boat suddenly, or to drive her backwards, by pushing the oars in the direction contrary to that employed in ordinary rowing.

Back and fill.—A term used of a vessel when, in a narrow channel, with the wind against her, but with a favourable tide, she allows herself to be carried on the tide, keeping in the stream by alternately filling her sails and laying them aback.

To *back an anchor.*—To add a smaller anchor, or a weight, to a large one to prevent its coming home, *i.e.,* dragging. (*See* ANCHOR.)

Back-board or *backrail.*—In skiffs, the framing or rail round the after thwart, making this a comfortable seat for coxswain and passengers. It is sometimes of iron, and sometimes of mahogany and cane work.

Back-rope (in ships).—The rope which stays the *dolphin striker.* It is, properly speaking, the *pendant* of the *tackle* which sets up the dolphin striker, and it is usually of chain.

Back-stays.—Ropes stretched from a mast or topmast head to the sides of a vessel—some way aft of the mast—to give extra support to the masts against going forward. In smaller craft they are usually passed over the head of the mast, above the shrouds, and terminate with tackles. There are back-stays and topmast back-stays, named according to the mast they support, the term "back-stays" without further specification usually meaning those of the lower mast. The topmast back-stays are so arranged that they may be slackened off as the boom swings over; for their position is such that unless slackened the boom and sail would foul them. It is evident, therefore, that if the boat be tacking about, these topmast back-stays must be continually shifted, for which reason they are often called *shifting back-stays*; or that if she be running before the wind they must be run right out, so as to let the boom lay over; and consequently these shifting stays may just as well be, and often are, called *runners,* and sometimes *travellers.* In small boats, however, and those to be worked single-handed, this continual shifting of stays is found to be very awkward, while the mast is so short as hardly to require their support, except in the case of racing; and on this account they are generally dispensed with. In ships, the back-stays being more numerous, the forward ones are called *breast back-stays,* and sustain the mast when the wind is before the beam, while the after ones may be shifted from side to side, as required, and constitute the travellers.

Backing of the wind.—The veering of the wind in the direction opposite to that of the sun's circuit. Winds may continue veering in the direction of the sun for several days together, circling the compass several times; but the opposite to this, in an anti-clockwise direction called backing, seldom, if ever, completes the circle. Backing generally prognosticates unsettled weather.

Backspring.—A hawser used in mooring a ship, put out forward and leading aft, or put out aft and leading forward.

Backwater. (In rowing, *see* BACK.)—A *backwater* is a small stream or ditch behind a river wall; it takes the drainage of the country round, which has been cut off from the natural drainage of the river by the construction of the wall. The backwater therefore communicates with the river, either by pipes or at certain intervals by sluices.

Baffle.—To baffle with the wind is to contend against it, as when beating to windward in very foul weather. (*See* TACK.)

Baffling winds are those which frequently shift.

Baggy Rinkle.—Sennit used for chafing gear to prevent one rope from chafing another.

Bag-reef (in square sails).—An extra reef band (band of canvas) on a sail, the most general use of which is to prevent the sail from bagging.

Balance-lug.—(*See* LUG.)

Balance-reef (of a gaff-sail).—A reef *band* (that is a band of canvas) sewed diagonally across the sail from the highest reef cringle of the after leech to the throat earing. It allows the sail to be so reefed that either the peak or the lower half only may be set. But it is rarely seen.

Baldheaded.—Said of a square-rigged vessel which carries no sail above top gallant sail, or a schooner with no topsails.

Bale, baler.—To *bale* or *bale out* is to remove water from an open boat by means of a *baler,* which may be any small vessel capable of holding water, such as a hand bowl or an old tin pot. The baler is occasionally dignified by the name of the *kit*.

Ball, or **ball off.**—To twist rope yarns into balls.

Ballast.—"Weight deposited in a ship's hold when she has no cargo, or too little to bring her sufficiently low in the water. It is used to counterbalance the effect of the wind upon the masts, and give the ship a proper stability, that she may be enabled to carry sail without danger of upsetting. To ballast a ship, therefore, is the art of disposing those materials so that she may be duly poised and maintain a proper equilibrium on the water, so as neither to be too *stiff* nor too *crank,* qualities equally pernicious: as in the first, although the ship may be fitted to carry a great sail, yet her velocity will not be proportionately increased, whilst her masts are more endangered by her sudden jerks and excessive labouring: and, in the last, she will be incapable of carrying sail without the risk of upsetting. Stiffness in ballasting is occasioned by disposing a great quantity of heavy ballast, as lead, iron, etc., in the bottom, which naturally places the centre of gravity very near the keel; and that being the centre about which the vibrations are made, the lower it is placed the more violent will be the motion of rolling. Crankness, on the other hand, is occasioned by lading so as to raise the centre of gravity too high; which also endangers the mast in carrying sail when it blows hard: for when the masts lose their perpendicular height, they strain on the shrouds in the nature of a lever, which increases the size of their obliquity; and a ship that loses her masts is in great danger of being lost. The whole art of ballasting, therefore, consists in placing the centre of gravity to correspond with the trim and shape of the vessel, so as neither to be too high nor too low, too far forward nor too far aft; and to lade the ship so deep, that the surface of the water may nearly rise to the extreme breadth amidships; and thus she will be enabled to carry a good sail, incline but little, and ply well to the windward." (Falconer's "Dictionary of the Marine.")

Ballast.—"Weighty material placed in the bottom of a ship or vessel, to give her *stiffness;* that is, to increase her tendency to return to the upright position when inclined or *heeled over* by the force of the wind or other cause." (Brande and Cox.) Small craft may be ballasted with either iron (usually cast), lead, zinc, or bags of shot. Beaching boats often carry bags which are filled with shingle or sand as may be required: the sand is found, by absorbing a great quantity of water, to swell sometimes to so great an extent as to burst the bags, which should not therefore be too full of this material. Certain boats, more particularly those belonging to the Navy, are fitted with tanks filled with fresh water; and as this fresh water is withdrawn for use, salt water can take its place in the tank. The cheapest form of ballast for boats (next to shingle) is cast iron, which should be painted; the most expensive, and best, is shot in bags, which lies flat, and absorbs no moisture. A free waterway should be left under all ballast. In modern ships water ballast is always used and is carried in double-bottom tanks, in fore and after peaks, or in deep-tanks with a higher centre of gravity than the bottom tanks, the water being pumped out as required.

Balloon canvas, or **press canvas.**—The extra spread of canvas (*i.e.*, sail) used by yachts in racing. Thus a large cutter may carry, besides her ordinary sails, *balloon jib, balloon foresail, spinnaker, ringsail* (or *studsail*), *big topsail*, according to the weather and the courses she makes. (*See* diagram).

Bank (of oars).—*Single and double.*—(From the French word *banc,* a bench.) The origin of this word will indicate the meaning of the terms *single banked* and *double banked*. A single banked boat is one in which only one rower sits on each thwart

BALLOON CANVAS

A. REACHING   B. RUNNING
1. Balloon jib   5. Mainsail
2. Balloon foresail 6. Ringsail
3. Mainsail   7. Big topsail
4. Jack topsail   8. Spinnaker

(seat); a double banked boat one in which two men occupy each seat with an oar out each side, as is often the case in the Royal Navy.

Bank.—An elevation of the bottom of the sea.

Banker.—A vessel employed in the cod fishery, on the Banks of Newfoundland.

Bar (of a harbour).—A shoal or bank of sand, gravel, etc.; thrown up by the opposite action of the sea and river at the mouth of a river.

Barepoles.—The masts, yards, etc., of a vessel without the sails.

Sailing or *scudding under bare poles.*—Sailing or running before a gale without any sails set. (*See* SCUD.)

Barge.—"A general name given to flat-bottomed craft." In ancient times the name was also given to large boats of state or pleasure, and in later days to one of the boats of a man-of-war. The barges of today are of various descriptions, being either sea-going, river, or canal. But *lighters, hoys,* and other carrying craft on rivers are also indiscriminately comprehended under the name of barge. The sailing barge is particularly to be distinguished from other craft by being *sprit* rigged—*i.e.,* by having a sprit-sail as a mainsail (*see* SPRIT), and by a very small mizzen sail, sometimes called the *jigger,* the mast and sheet of which are often fixed to the rudder, and the use of which sail is to aid the action of the rudder (with which it works)

in getting the long hull about when *tacking*. The hull is very long, *wall-sided,* flat-bottomed, and lies very deep in the water; and, almost the whole of the interior being devoted to cargo, the mast is sometimes fixed on deck in a framework called the *tabernacle*. The class is subdivided into two rigs, viz.:—
1. The *topsail barge*—that is one carrying a topsail, and this is the sea-going barge; and 2. The *river* or *Medway barge,* which carries no topsail and is therefore rigged with only a pole main mast. Both of these carry the sprit-main-sail and the small mizzen either attached to or working with the rudder, the principle of which is well worthy of study, and which has sometimes been applied to pleasure boats. These vessels, in common with other flat-bottomed craft, have lee-boards (*which see*); they sail rapidly in a fresh breeze, very close to the wind, and can face almost any weather, with the seas washing over them from end to end.

Barges are today usually propelled by diesel engines.

3. In the Royal Navy, the boat of a Flag Officer.

Barge-pole.—A long pole used on board a barge, for pushing any object off her, or for holding on by, to a quay or wharf, for which latter purpose it is sometimes furnished with a hook. (*See* QUANT.)

TOPSAIL BARGES

RIVER BARGE

CANAL BARGE

Barque/Bark.—*Bark.*—Generally speaking a three-masted vessel square-rigged on the fore and main masts and fore-and-aft rigged on the mizzen. The following definition is given by Denham Robinson:— "*Bark* or *barque* (Low Lat., *barca*). A term applied rather vaguely to square-rigged merchant vessels. A bark has three masts which do not rake; but beyond this there appears·to be no special mark to distinguish it from any other large merchantman. A bark, however, is never a steamer." (*See* FOUR-MASTED BARQUE.)

FOUR-MASTED BARQUE, ABOUT 1890

Barquentine/Barkentine.—A vessel having three masts, the foremast square-rigged like the bark, but the main and mizzen masts fore-and-aft rigged. These are occasionally called three-masted schooners or jackass rig; but here again a distinction must be made, the barkentine having a brig foremast (*i.e.*, foremast, fore-topmast, and fore-topgallant), while the three-masted schooner has the schooner foremast (foremast and fore-top-mast only). (*See also* under SCHOONER.)

BARQUENTINE, ABOUT 1914

Barnacles.—"Most probably from the late Latin pernacula, diminutive of perna, *a ham,* from a supposed resemblance to a leg of pork." (Brande and Cox.) A general term amongst sea-faring men for any of those shelled animals of the division mollusca which fix themselves to the bottoms of boats, the piles of piers, quays, etc., under water, and more especially at the water line or between high and low water marks. It is found that there are certain metals, copper in particular, to which these creatures have an objection to fix themselves, in consequence of which fact wooden vessels are copper-bottomed. (*See* COPPER.) There are also certain paints which profess to answer the same purpose as copper.

Barometer.—A well-known instrument, invented by Torricelli, for measuring the weight or pressure of the atmosphere. Whatever tends to increase or diminish this pressure will cause the barometer to rise or fall. Hence the barometer is a foreteller of wind rather than of wet or dry. A rapid fall in pressure, in particular, indicates an increase in wind force. (*See* ANEROID.)

Barratry.—Fraudulent claim. Usually applied in cases where a ship has been deliberately lost, with the object of obtaining the insurance money.

Basin.—A dock in which vessels float at any state of the tide.

Batten.—Battens are long strips of wood, or other material, used for various purposes.

To *batten down.*—To cover up and fix down—usually spoken of hatches when they are covered over with canvas, and this canvas is held down with long battens.

Battened sails.—Sails across which light battens (often of bamboo) are laid. Their use may be said to be three-fold—Firstly, they assist in keeping sails flat, thereby increasing the speed of a boat; secondly, they simplify the process of reefing; and thirdly, they enable sail to be struck (dropped) with considerable rapidity. (*See* fig. under CANOE.) In England, battens are applied, as a rule, only to the sails of boats or small craft; but in the east, where the practice appears to have originated, they are employed in large sailing ships, and are found to be of great service where squalls come down very suddenly and with great severity. Various systems of reefing these sails have been tried of late years, some consisting of elaborate systems of tackles for drawing the battens together. These, however, are things rather of play: their great drawback lies in their liability to entanglement and as it is always possible that such an event might take place at a critical moment, beginners are recommended to have but little to do with them until sufficiently experienced to take the consequence of mishap.

Battleship.—The heaviest and most powerful type of warship.

Battle-cruiser.—A warship as powerfully armed as a battleship, but, in order to increase her speed, less heavily armoured.

Baulks.—Heavy pieces of timber, such as piles before erection, etc. Brackets, in almost any position, holding two or more timbers together, or preventing them from slipping.

Bawley.—The name given to a class of fishing smack once common to the Thames below Gravesend. These craft were often *clincher built* with *bluff-bows*; *cutter rigged*, with a *trysail* (mainsail without boom), and very generally carried a *jib-topsail*. They were exceedingly stiff; good weather boats; and were employed in the whitebait, sprat, and shrimp fisheries, etc.

Beach.—The margin of the land exposed to tidal action.

Beaching boats.—The act of running them up on a beach: when up

THAMES BAWLEY

they are said to be *beached*. It is not an easy matter to beach a boat in a heavy sea, the rudder becoming, as the boat approaches the shore, of less and less use: everything depends, therefore, upon the oars. It is accepted good practice to turn the boat's head to seaward (unless the boat is double-ended) before entering the surf, unshipping the rudder and using an oar over the stern to assist steering. Slight headway is given the boat each time an exceptionally heavy breaker approaches. As a rule it is dangerous to go in on a big wave: experience will soon convince the beginner that the advice to do so (except it comes from a "long-shore" man) may, if blindly followed, lead to unpleasant consequences. The small waves float the boat longest and more evenly, and are better to come in upon. Pull hard as the boat descends, lighter in the hollow of the wave, and easy on the top.

Beach boats are those which are kept on the beach. They are built to take the beach, and are far more useful in their situation than any strange ones can be. A *good beach boat* is one which takes the beach well and is easily got off it. Beaching boats, when their form admits of it, is a good practice; it increases their length of life. When beached for any length of time, however, they should occasionally be half filled with water to keep their strakes swelled.

On the beach.—Retired from sea service.

Beachcomber.—A seaman, or other person, particularly in the Pacific, who prefers to loaf, rather than seek employment.

Beacon.—A landmark put up to steer by. A pole marking out a shoal or a channel.

Beak, beak-head.—The beak is the extreme fore-part of a vessel. "The beak-head, in large vessels with figure-heads, is the small platform between the figure-head and the bulwarks of the forecastle. It is secluded from the view of the deck, and contains the latrines of the crew." This will be recognised on old ships.

Beam.—The width of a vessel, at her widest part: the term is derived from the *beams,* strong timbers extending across the ship, supporting the decks and strengthening the sides, and the widest of these will, of course, be the width of the vessel inside. But by the beam, meaning width, is now always understood to be the outside measurement. In nautical language, a wide vessel is said to have *more beam* than a narrow one; and, in like manner, a boat with *plenty of beam* (width) is described as *beamy.*

Beam ends.—A ship thrown completely upon her side is said to be *on her beam ends,* when her masts may have to be cut away before she can be righted. Hence, a person who, either in posture or in business, has very nearly over-reached the centre of gravity, may be said to be on his beam ends.

Abeam.—An object seen across the middle of the ship is spoken of as *abeam.* If the wind blows directly upon the side of the ship she is sailing with the *wind abeam:* if it lies in a direction between the beam and the quarter, she has the wind *abaft the beam* and is said to be *sailing free,* or *large* or *going free.*

"Beak-arm, or *fork-beam.*—A forked piece of timber, nearly of the depth of the beam, scarfed, tabled, and bolted, for additional security, to the sides of beams athwart large openings in decks, as the main hatchway and the mast-rooms.

"*Breast-beams* are those beams at the forepart of the quarter-deck and round-house, and after-part of the forecastle. They are sided larger than the rest, as they have an ornamental rail in the front, formed from the solid, and a rabbet one inch broader than its depth, which must be sufficient to bury the deals of the deck, and one inch above for a spurn-water. To prevent splitting the beam in the rabbet, the nails of the deck should be crossed, or so placed, alternately, as to form a sort of zigzag line.

"*Cat-beam,* or *beak-head beam.*—This is the broadest beam in a ship, generally made in two breadths, tabled and bolted together. The foreside is placed far enough forward to receive the heads of the stanchions of the beak-head bulk-head.

"The *collar-beam* is the beam upon which the stanchions of the beak-head bulk-head stand. The upper side of it is kept well with the upper side of the upper deck port-sills, and lets down upon the spirketing at the side. But its casting over the bowsprit in the middle giving it a form which in timber is not to be obtained without difficulty, a framing of two large carlings and a stanchion on each side of the bowsprit is now generally substituted in its place.

"*Half-beams* are short beams introduced to support the deck where there is no framing, as in those places where the beams are kept asunder by hatchways, ladder-ways, etc. They are let down on the clamp at the side, and near midships into fore-and-aft carlings. On some decks they are, abaft the mizzenmast, generally of fir, let into the side tier of carlings.

"The *midship-beam* is the longest beam of the ship, lodged in the midship frame, or between the widest frame of timbers.

"*Palleting-beams* are those beams under the flat of the magazine, bread-room, and powder-room, where there is a double palleting. The upper tier are of fir, and rabbets are taken out of their edge to form scuttles." (James Greenwood, B.A., "Rudimentary Treatise on Navigation," 1850.)

"*Orlop-beams.*—Those beams which support the orlop-deck, but are chiefly intended to fortify the hold."

Beam of an anchor.—The stock. (*See* ANCHOR.)

Bear.—*Bear away, bear up.*—If, after being close-hauled, the helm of the vessel be put *up* (*i.e.,* towards the windward side) and the sheets be eased off, by which actions the vessel will be made to sail more or less before the wind, she is said to be bearing away. Orders to *bear up,* or to *bear away,* mean practically, therefore, the same thing, viz., to put the helm up. (*See* under HELM.)

Bear down.—To go towards. This term has not of necessity any reference to the direction in which the tiller is to be thrust. It is understood, however, that the vessel which *bears down upon* another, or upon some object, is situated to windward of that object, and, therefore, has the advantage of it. If, for instance, we are told that a large ship is *bearing down* upon us, we instinctively look to the windward side.

Bear off.—Usually an order, as "bear off that cask"—meaning keep it off.

Bear a hand.—Usually an appeal for assistance, and that quickly.

Bearding.—The fore-part of a rudder. (*See* RUDDER.)

Bearers.—(*See* FLAT-FLOORS.)

Bearings.—The word "bearing" properly belongs to the art of navigation, in which it signifies "the direction, or angular distance from the meridian, in which an object is seen." Roughly speaking, it is the direction in which an object is seen from a vessel, as to say that, "the point of land bore N.E.," meaning that it was seen from the vessel in a north-easterly direction. Bearings may be also given with reference to the ship's head, thus: "Four points on the port bow," or "Red four five" is 45° to the left of the ship's head. "Fine on the starboard bow," or "green two (zer)o," about 20° to the right of her course. Thus to *keep one's bearings* is to keep a certain point in view in the same direction. To be *out of one's bearings*, to be travelling in a wrong direction. To *lose one's bearings*, to lose one's way, as it were, upon the waters.

Beat (in sailing).—*Beating, beating up, beating to windward*; also called *working to windward, pegging to windward*, and sometimes *tacking*, is making progress against the wind (and, therefore, close-hauled) by a zigzag course, with the wind first on one bow and then on the other.

Becalmed.—To be becalmed is to be left without a wind, and therefore, in a sailing ship, to be without power of moving. But we hear of vessels of considerable burden making habitual use of sweeps (large oars), when becalmed, so lately as the early part of the last century; and with some foreigners it is still the practice.

Beaufort Notation.—A code by which weather conditions may be tersely expressed by letters of the alphabet—*e.g.*, C = cloudy, O = overcast. (*See* ABBREVIATIONS, page 345.)

Beaufort Wind Scale.—(*See* WIND.)

Becket.—An eye in the end of a rope: it is often used in connection with a toggle. (*See* TOGGLE AND BECKET.) Falconer gives the following definition of *beckets*: "Anything used to confine loose ropes, tackles, oars, or spars, in a convenient place: hence, beckets are either large hooks, or short pieces of rope, with a knot on one end and an eye in the other, or formed like a circular wreath; or they are wooden brackets, and, probably, from a corruption and misapplication of this last term, arose the word becket, which seems often to be confounded with bracket." The word beckets, in naval phraseology, is sometimes used for pockets, thus, "Hands out of beckets, sir!"

To *becket the helm.*—To lash down the tiller of a boat so that it may not sway about when she is at anchor, or at her moorings. (*See also* LASH THE TILLER.)

Becueing.—A method of attaching a line to a small anchor or grapnel, so that in case the grapnel should become fixed under some rock, a strong pull will break the seizing (called the *stopper*), and enable the flukes to be drawn upwards. The manner in which this becueing is done will best be understood by reference to the engraving. It is much employed by crabmen and others working on rocky parts of the coast.

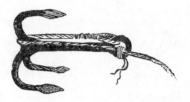

GRAPNEL BECUED

PLOUGH ANCHOR BECUED

Bed of the bowsprit.—That part of the beak of a large vessel, or the deck on a small one, in which the lower part of the bowsprit lies.

Bees.—Pieces of plank bolted to the upper end of the wooden bowsprit in a large vessel to take the fore topmast stay.

Before.—Forward, or in front of; more usually expressed *afore*.

Before the mast.—The lodgment of working seamen on shipboard, as distinguishing them from the officers, who lodge aft. Hence a man who goes as seaman is said to go before the mast.

Belay.—To make fast a rope (that rope being, generally, part of the running rigging, as a *fall*), by twisting it round (in the manner of a figure of 8) a *cleat, kevel* or *belaying-pin,* without tying it into a knot. Also used to mean "Stop, or cancel," as in "Belay that," *i.e.,* "Don't do it."

Belaying pin.—A pin or bolt of wood, galvanised iron, or of gun metal, placed in a convenient spot for the belaying of a halyard. In sailing ships the principal belaying pins are just by the shrouds, as all halyards lead here, but in small fore-and-aft rigged vessels they are placed around the masts.

Bellows.—*A fresh hand at the bellows.*—An expression often made use of to express that the wind has become fresher.

Bells.—On shipboard, bells express the time, and are struck by the officer of the watch. The bells are struck every half-hour. The day of 12 hours is divided into three, thus:—1. Noon to four o'clock. 2. Four o'clock to eight o'clock. 3. Eight o'clock to midnight—and the same at night. Thus in every four hours there will be 8 bells—viz., at noon, four o'clock, eight o'clock, and midnight; but in the *dog watches,* these being only of two hours' duration each, there will be but 4 bells.

Fog bells.—Every sailing ship and steam vessel is obliged to supply itself with a bell, called the fog bell, to be sounded while the ship lies at anchor in a fog, at intervals of not less than one minute.

Bell buoys.—Buoys placed at the entrance to certain harbours to mark the bar, or some shoal, and furnished with a bell.

Belly (of sails).—(*See* BUNT.)

Belly bands (of sails).—Strips or bands of canvas sewed across large sails about half way between the close-reef and the foot, to prevent them from bellying; for it is found that, after a time, all sails will belly, partly on account of the canvas stretching, but mainly because the edges, being strengthened with extra stuff and bolt ropes, are stiffer than the bunt.

Belly guy.—A guy (rope) or support in the middle, or belly of anything.

Below.—Low down; below deck; or under water.

Benches.—The after thwarts, or seats, in large open boats are sometimes called the *benches,* and those extending along the sides, *side-benches.*

Bend.—1. (Of a rope).—The bent portion (*see* BIGHT), and hence the name of a knot, as the carrick bend, common bend, etc. (*See* KNOTS.) From this—*To bend* becomes a general sea term for fastening anything, as to bend one rope to another, a sail to a yard or gaff, the anchor to its cable, etc.

2. To *bend* (in sailing) is to lie over under press of canvas.

Bends or *wales,* in ship building, are the thickest planks in the sides of a wooden ship, giving to it its chief strength. They are reckoned from the water upwards, being distinguished as the first, second or third bend, and they have the *beams* and upper *futtocks* bolted to them.

Bent timbers or *bent heads.*—These, in a small boat, correspond to the ribs in a larger vessel. Each is usually of one piece, steamed and bent into the shape of the boat; and the strakes (or planking) are secured to them. They are also called *heads,* meaning *bent-heads.*

Bent on a splice.—A sailor's manner of expressing that some person is bent upon getting married.

Beneap.—If a vessel should run aground towards high water, during the last of the *spring,* or big tides, she may possibly have to lie there until the following spring tides float her off: in this condition she is said to be beneaped, because the *neap* tides are not high enough to float her. The situation may be serious, since, during a whole fortnight, there is time for any changes in the weather, and in the event of a gale rising, the vessel might become a wreck. No vessel will allow herself, therefore, to become beneaped, if by any means she can be got off.

Bermuda rig.—This rig is now common and is made use of for most yachts, when it consists of one or more tall masts carrying triangular sails. The origin of the rig may be found in those

BERMUDA-RIGGED CYPRIOT
TRADING SCHOONER, 1930

"three-masted schooners built at Bermuda during the war of 1814. They went through the waves without rising to them, and consequently were too ticklish for northern stations." (Smyth.) (*See also* under MUDIAN.)

Berth.—On ship board, a cabin. Sometimes a bed, or any space for the swinging of a hammock, is so called. A ship's berth is the place in which she lies, or is anchored; thus, with good anchorage and in a sheltered situation, she is said to have come to a comfortable berth.

Berth.—A position or employment to be secured, in which case the term becomes synonymous with the word *billet*.

Best.—*Best and best, best boat.*—The expression "best and best" is often met with in reports of sculling matches about to be arranged—the competitors agreeing to row a match in best and best boats. This actually implies that each may choose the best boat he can find; and as it is customary to have special boats built for the occasion, on the most approved principles, these have become known as *best boats*. They may also be called *wager* boats, because wagers are usually laid on the result of the race. A *best boat* is, then, a racing boat of the most approved type. It is of the lightest possible material, very long and very narrow, with only just the room, in fact, in which a man can sit. It has no keel, being often semi-circular in section, and fitted with a small fin some way aft of the sculler which takes the place of keel; and the interior, except where the sculler sits, is covered in by oiled silk. It is fitted with sliding seats and long outriggers, and the well is protected by a wash-board, or coaming, some inches in height. The whole thing sometimes weighs no more than 17 lbs. These boats, it may well be imagined, are only suited to smooth waters, though it is astonishing to see what waves they will sometimes live through. It is no uncommon occurrence, however, for them to be swamped, and to render them less liable to such an accident an invention has lately been brought out, the principle of which is to cover them entirely in, placing the sculler on top. The principal, among other objections, to this method is that the sculler, being placed very high up, offers considerably more resistance to the wind than when low down. It remains to be seen whether this departure will materially influence the designs of future racing boats. A recent development is to have a fixed seat but a stretcher and outriggers linked and sliding together, so that the weight of the oarsman is not constantly shifting fore and aft and the boat runs more smoothly.

Between decks, or **'tween decks.**—In a vessel of more than one deck, to be between the upper and the lower.

Betwixt wind and water.—About the load water line. A vulnerable point in which to be struck, and hence its use in everyday conversation.

Bibbs.—Brackets or *bolsters* near the head of a mast upon which rest the trestle-trees. Bibbs are also called *hounds*. (*See* fig. under MAST.)

Big topsail.—(*See* TOPSAILS.)

Bight (Saxon, bygan, *to bend*: preterperfect *bent*).—1. Of a rope. The double part when it is folded, in contradistinction to the end. It is, in fact, the bend or loop in a rope (*see* KNOTS): hence the origin of the term "to bend on." (*See* BEND.) 2. Bight. A small inlet or bay on the line of a coast, or in the bank of a river.

Bilge (often pronounced *billidge*).—The bilge is the lower part of a vessel, upon which she rests when aground.

Bilge boards.—(*See* FLOOR BOARDS under FLOOR.)

Bilge pieces, or *bilge keels,* are strips fitted like keels on the outside of the bilges, and serving both as a cradle for her to rest upon, and, to a certain extent, as keels when she heels over in sailing. In steamers they minimise the rolling. (*See* diagram under FRAME.)

Bilge water.—The water that collects in the bottom of a vessel. It is said on board ship that when the bilge water pumps up clear, the vessel is leaky, while in a tight ship it comes up black and smelling. From this we have the popular expression, "as foul as bilge water." A little water is generally allowed to remain at the bottom of open boats for the purpose of keeping their lower boards swelled; but this cannot be looked upon as bilge water.

Bilge ways.—The timbers upon which a vessel is launched.

Bill (of an anchor).—The extremity of the fluke. (*See* ANCHOR.)

Bill of health.—"A certificate or instrument, signed by proper authorities, delivered to the masters of ships at the time of their clearing out from all ports or places suspected of being infected by particular disorders, certifying the state of health at the time that such ship sailed. Bills of health are of three kinds—*clean, foul,* and *suspected,* which are self-explanatory terms." (Brande and Cox.)

Bill of lading.—"A document, subscribed by the master of a ship, acknowledging the receipt of goods intrusted to him for transportation, and binding himself (under certain exceptions) to deliver them to the person to whom they are addressed, in good condition, for a certain remuneration or freightage. Of bills of lading there are usually triplicate copies: one for the party transmitting the goods, another for the person to whom the goods are addressed, and the third for the master." (Brande and Cox.)

Bi-lander (By-lander, or coaster).—"A small merchant vessel, with two masts. It is particularly distinguished from other vessels of two masts by the form of her mainsail, which is bent to the whole length of a yard hanging fore and aft, and inclined to the horizontal in an angle of about 45 degrees, and hanging immediately over the stern, while the fore end slopes downward, and comes as far forward as the middle of the ship; the foremost lower corner, called the tack, being secured to a ring-bolt in the deck, and the aftmost, or sheet, to another in the taffrail. At present there are few vessels of this description." (Falconer's Dictionary.) The vessel, common in the 16th and 17th century, has now become extinct.

Bill board.—On ships, a support upon which the bills, or flukes, of the anchor rest when it is on deck.

Billet.—A berth or position to be secured. The origin of the term is probably connected with the "billet" or letter introducing one person to another.

Billyboy.—A class of coasting vessels once sailing from the Humber ports, from which circumstance they are frequently called *Yorkshire* billyboys. The old billyboy was built with round and bluff stem and stern, and presented that which may be called a Dutch appearance. It was usually *ketch* rigged, carrying square sail, occasionally a square topsail, and sometimes, even, a mizzen staysail. But it was also rigged otherwise, as schooner or brigantine. These vessels are no longer to be seen.

BILLYBOY

Bind.—To wind around, as binding the end of a rope with yarn. Also an iron band, as the binding of a *dead-eye.*

Binnacle.—The fixed case and stand in which the compass in any vessel is set.

Bireme.—Warship in classical Greek and Roman times with two banks (or tiers) of oars on each side.

Bite.—Spoken of an anchor when it holds the ground—it then bites. (This must not be confounded with the word BIGHT.)

Bits.—Small posts or timber heads fixed through the deck of a vessel, either round masts or at the foot of the bowsprit. There are various bitts in a ship, but in small craft the term is generally understood to mean the *bowsprit bitts,* which supports the stock of the bow-sprit and frequently serve as kevels, or cleats, around which to "bitt" or wind the cable, so that it shall remain fast. (*See* fig. under BOWSPRIT.) In large vessels we find *riding bitts,* which are stout heads rising considerably from the deck expressly for the purpose of "bitting" the cable.

To *bitt the cable.*—To put it round the bitts in order to fasten it or slacken it gradually, which last is called *veering away.*

Bitter.—A ship stopped by her cable is said to be *brought up to a bitter.*

Blackbirder.—A vessel employed in transporting slaves, especially negroes or Pacific Islanders.

Blackgang.—Stokers, firemen and trimmers in a steamship.

Blacklead.—The bottom of a racing yacht is sometimes payed with (rubbed over with) blacklead to reduce the friction of the water with the hull.

Black-strake.—The strake on a vessel's side which is made black. "A range of planks immediately above the wales in a ship's side; they are always covered with a mixture of tar and lamp-black, which preserves the plank itself and forms an agreeable variety with the white bottom beneath, and the scraped planks of the side, covered with melted turpentine, or varnish of pine, alone." (Falconer.)

Blackwall hitch.—A hitch (or half-knot) for loosely attaching a rope to a hook. (*See* KNOTS.)

Blade.—The flat part of an oar, scull, or sweep; also of a paddle, though this last is more properly called the *fan*.

Blanket.—To take the wind of a vessel to leeward.

Bleed the monkey.—To steal from the grog kid.

Blind-pulley.—A hole or block without a sheave in it. (*See* BLOCK.)

Block.—The instrument generally described on shore as a "pulley"; but this latter term has little or no meaning among seafaring men, who invariably speak of a *block*. When two or more blocks are employed to move a single weight, they, with their ropes, constitute a *tackle*. (*See* TACKLE.) A block is a machine made up of several parts, and with the utmost nicety; and it may be regarded as among the most important parts of a vessel's rigging. The parts are as follows (*see* fig.):—The *block* is the piece (or block) of wood which constitutes the main body of the machine. The *shell* is the outside casing, the upper portion of which is called the *head*. This shell consists of two parts which encase the block and which are bound together, or *seized,* with a band called a *strop*; and to prevent this strop from slipping off they have grooves cut in them, above and below: the grooves are called *scores.* The scores do not meet at the head of the block, but at the bottom they do, forming a continuous groove called the *ass.* The *sheave* is the wheel of the pulley, and it fits into the *sheave-hole* or swallow, which is the slot, or

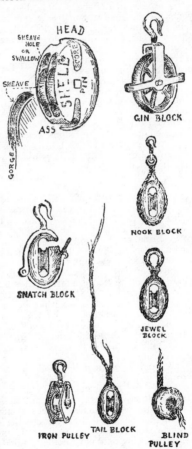

BLOCKS

mortise-hole, cut through the block to receive it. Blocks may be *double-sheaved, triple-sheaved,* or *fourfold-sheaved,* according to the number of sheaves they carry. Sheaves are of some hard wood (such as *lignum vitæ*) or of metal, sometimes of both; and they are fitted with a centre-piece called the *bouch,* which travels upon the *axle.* They are set in the sheave-hole, below the middle, so as to allow room for the rope to run freely through. The axle has, or should have, a square head. All blocks, however, are not furnished with sheaves. Those usually employed in standing rigging are blind or dead—*i.e.,* merely pierced with holes. Such are *deadeyes,* by which shrouds are hauled taut, and *blind pulleys,* often found on small craft, for leading ropes aft.

Blocks are of various descriptions, according to the uses to which they are turned. Some of them are as follows:—*Gin block.*—An iron block with a hook, to swing from a gin (a hoisting machine). *Hook block.*—A block to which a hook is attached. Such are blocks which are attached to a mast or any other spar. Small iron hook blocks are also used on various occasions. *Jewel block.*—A block which may be fitted to a yard-arm. Such blocks in a square rigged ship take the halyards of the studding-sails, while in fore-and-aft rig a jewel block may be fitted to the end of the gaff for the flag-halyard. *Snatch block.*—A block of one sheave into which the bight of a rope can be slipped. This is useful when the end of a rope cannot be got at. *Tail block.*—A block with rope strop, the ends of which are left long, so that they may be tied round anything; these ends forming what is called the "tail". *Blind pulleys* are wooden blocks having a hole pierced through them, but no sheave (above mentioned). *Deadeyes.*—Blind blocks connecting shrouds with channel plates, and serving to set up the shrouds. (*See* DEADEYES, under DEAD.) The use of iron blocks is becoming more common than formerly. They are employed on various occasions, as, for instance, for chains; and where they occur they are often called *iron pulleys.*

To *fleet* blocks in a tackle is to shift the moving block from one place of attachment to another place further along, ready for another pull. When the blocks of a tackle have been hauled close together it is said to be *Chock a block,* or *Two blocks.* To *strop* a block is to bind on its *strop* (the band by which it is attached to some other object, and which also holds the casing together). Strops may be of rope or iron.

The principle of the pulley is a subject outside the scope of such a work as the present; it will be found fully explained in any work on mechanics. But it may not be out of place to remind the reader that a fixed block serves merely to change the direction of a force, while with one or more movable blocks a mechanical advantage is obtained. This mechanical advantage, or "acquisition," is called the *purchase,* and hence it is that the rope upon which men pull to lift a weight is, in nautical phraseology, called the *purchase* of a tackle (a perfectly correct term), while the tackle itself also often goes by the same name.

Blocks are measured by their length over all, expressed in inches: *e.g.*, a 6 in. block is one which measures 6 in. in length over the entire wood-work. A block is generally supposed to take a rope of a circumference one-third its length: thus a 6 in. block will take a 2 in. rope; but the rule is not always followed. The best blocks are those in which the grain of the wood runs diagonally across the flat surface, for then they are less liable to split, and if they should it will be across the strop, which will still hold them together.

Blockade.—In international law, a prevention of exit or entrance from or to any port of an enemy in war, and an exlusion (under certain terms) of neutrals.

Blockship.—An old naval term. A ship engaged in blockading. "A large vessel employed on coast duty for the protection of a specified district."

Blow the gaff (old naval term).—To inform against any person or persons. To let out some secret.

Blue.—*Blue peter.*—The flag denoting the departure of a vessel, hoisted at the fore part of the rigging, either on the bowsprit, fore-stay, etc. It is a blue flag, with a white square in centre.

Blue-jacket.—A seaman of the Royal Navy (from the short jacket he used to wear).

Blue light.—A signal for a pilot at night.

Blue-nose.—A nautical appellative applied to any Nova Scotian ship, or sailor.

To *look blue.*—To look astonished or foolish.

Till all is blue.—Till the end of all things.

To *blue* (probably "to blow," or "blow away").—To squander a sum of money. In other words to make it look blue.

Bluff.—Abrupt. A cliff or highland projecting into the sea almost perpendicularly is called a bluff.

Bluff-bow, bluff-head.—A vessel is said to be *bluff-bowed* when she has broad and flat bows, and when her stem has but little or no rake (inclination) she may also be called bluff-headed. (*See* fig. under SQUARE STEM.)

Board.—1. *Board.* An expression signifying the *side* of a ship. Hence:—*aboard,* inside or on the ship.

By the board.—Over the ship's side. Therefore to *slip by the board* is to slip down by her side.

Board and board.—An expression signifying that two vessels come so near each other as to touch; but it is also used to describe the position of two ships which lie side by side.

To *board.*—Boarding is the act of going on board a vessel, but it is often understood to mean going on board by force, as in battle, piracy, or for the purpose of arresting some person or persons on board.

Boarders (in old warfare).—"Sailors appointed to make an attack by boarding, or to repel such an attempt by the enemy."

Boarding-pike.—A defensive weapon used by sailors in boarding an enemy's vessel. The practice of boarding an enemy has, of course, become extinct since the introduction of the modern type of ship.

Board in the smoke.—To take advantage or get the better of some person when they are not expecting it. The term is, of course, derived from the custom, in old warfare, of boarding an enemy when concealed by the smoke of guns.

2. *Board* (in sailing) is the distance a vessel travels between each tack (that is, without turning), so that to make *a good board* or *stretch* is to travel straight and make good progress against the wind; to make a *long board,* to keep for a long time on the same tack; to make *short boards,* to tack frequently; while to make a *stern board* is to fall back again from a point already gained, which may be the result of a strong head tide or any other accident. (*See* STERN BOARD.)

3. *Board of Trade.*—The Committee of the Privy Council for the Affairs of Trade. "The Board of Trade have certain powers in respect of passenger steamers on the Thames in common with other passenger steamboats, etc. This is also the department of the Government to which, under the Acts relating to the Conservancy Board and Trinity House, certain questions arising under these Acts are referred." *The Board of Trade* became the *Department of Trade and Industry* in 1970.

4. *Board Sailing.*—(*See* SAILBOARD.)

Boat.—The forms of boats are innumerable. They vary with locality, each district giving its own name as it does its own form. Reference must, therefore, be made under such heads as PETER-BOAT, WAGER-BOAT, etc.

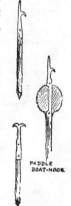

PADDLE
BOAT-HOOK.

BOAT-HOOKS

To *boat oars*—more commonly called *unshipping oars*—is to bring them into the boat, generally after rowing.

Boatboom.—A spar projecting from a ship's side in harbour to which boats may be secured and manned.

Boat-hook.—A most useful implement in the form of a hook or spike at the end of a pole. It has an infinite number of uses, as for instance, to hold on to a chain or rope, or a grassy bank; to keep a boat's head or stern away from a wall; to prevent collision with any other craft, etc.; and, in a sailing boat, to pick up a mooring. There are various forms of boat-hooks. One is a mere spike; another a hook and spike; a third a double hook. Sometimes a paddle-blade is combined with the boat-hook; and sometimes for sailing boats, the pole is marked in feet, and used in shallow water instead of the lead line. A person situated in the middle of a boat has more power to keep her straight with the boat-hook than if he were in the bow or stern. Seated amidships he can, by thrusting out the stern of the boat, get her head in, or, by pulling on the stern, get her away from any object.

Boat-skids "are long square pieces of fir, extending across the ship from the gang-board, and on which the boats, spare masts, etc., are laid." (Falconer's Dictionary.)

Boatswain (pronounced bo'sun).—"The second of the three warrant officers of a man-of-war; he has charge of the boats, rigging, anchors, and cables. It is his duty to *turn the hands up,* or summon the whole crew, whenever they are required for duty. He should, from the nature of his duties, be an active man, and a thorough seaman. The *boatswain's mates* assist the boatswain, summon the watches or other portions of the crew to duty, and inflict punishments." (Brande and Cox, 1865.) The chief Petty Officer of a merchant ship.

Boatswain's Call.—A whistle somewhat resembling a smoker's pipe, which is used to attract attention before a command is given.

Boatswain's chair.—A contrivance resembling the seat of a swing, which is suspended from a single rope, and used in working aloft.

Bob-stay.—A stay (or rope) made fast to the stem post of a boat, at the cutwater, and leading to the nose of the bowsprit, where it is taken up by a tackle sometimes called the *bob-stay purchase.* The *bob-stay fall* (*i.e.,* the rope leading from the tackle) serves to taughten the bob-stay; it leads inboard along the bowsprit and, in boats, belays to the bowsprit *bitts.* The act of hauling on this purchase is called *bowsing down the bowsprit.* (*See* diagram under BOWSPRIT.) The bob-stay may be of rope, wire-rope, or of chain. To it, in small craft, about one-third from the stem, is generally attached a rope leading on deck. This is the bob-stay *tricing-line*: its use is to *trice* up the bob-stay when at anchor—*i.e.,* to pull it up close to the stem-post, so as to prevent its chafing against the anchor or mooring chain. The office of the bob-stay is to prevent the bowsprit from *topping up.* It acts in opposition to the fore or fore topmast stays, and takes much of the strain of the head sails. It is not unusual, in yacht racing, to hear of its breaking; such an accident is fatal, as without a bob-stay the whole forward gear of the boat might be carried away, and the time required to rig a new one would upset any chance she might have. The yacht *Ailsa* broke her bob-stay at the start of the Royal Harwich Yacht Club Ocean Match in 1895, and was immediately brought to and taken back to Gravesend.

Body.—The hull of a vessel, without fittings.

Body-plan. (*See* LINE.)

Boejer.—A Dutch craft, with rounded ends and leeboards, cutter-rigged with a short curved gaff and Boom mainsail.

Bollards.—An old name, though one still in use, for those posts of timber frequently seen on the sides of docks, quays, piers, etc., on which hawsers or springs (ropes) are thrown for hauling vessels alongside.

BOLLARDS

Bollard timbers.—Otherwise called knight-heads (*which see*).

Bollocks.—Blocks secured to the middle of the topsail yards in large ships; the topsail *ties* pass through them, and thereby gain an increase of power in lifting the yards.

Bolster.—Generally speaking, a pad; often a piece of timber, either used to "bolster up" anything requiring slight alteration or support, or upon masts, to bear some part of the standing rigging. Thus the brackets on a mast which support the trestle trees, or those carrying shrouds or stays, are called bolsters or *bibbs*.

Bolt.—The appearance of a bolt is well known to everyone, whether ashore or afloat; it is a short rod, usually of iron or other metal (though occasionally of wood, when it is known as a trennel), holding two members together. On shipboard there are various bolts, besides those which hold the timbers; as, for instance—*bolt-eyes,* or *screw-eyes* (sometimes called *eye-bolts*), the heads of which form an eye, and which may be screwed into almost any part of a boat to lead ropes through or to make them fast; *ring-bolts,* into the heads of which are fitted a loose ring. (*See* also under these headings.)

Bolt-ropes.—The ropes along the borders or edges of a sail, for the purpose of strengthening those parts. Each bolt-rope takes its name from its position on a sail; thus there are the head, the foot and the leach ropes. (*See* SAIL.)

Bonaventure.—The fourth mast of a 16th century ship, carrying a lateen sail.

Bone in her teeth.—A vessel travelling at a good speed, seen from ahead, makes the white breaking wave from her stern look like a bone.

Bonnet.—An additional part made to fasten with latchings or *laskets* to the foot of the sails of small vessels in moderate winds. It is exactly similar to the foot of the sail it is intended for. Buttons are also sometimes used in fastening it. Bonnets were in constant use in the wherries of Norfolk and Suffolk (*see* fig. 1 under NORFOLK WHERRY), also in some of the Cornish fishing-craft. They were also originally employed on square sails.

BOOBY HATCH

2. A small cover or hood used to cover or protect a small fitting or opening.

Booby hatch.—A raised cabin head with sliding hatch. (*See* page 27.)

Boom.—A boom is a pole extending *outboard* (*i.e.,* outwards from a vessel); and from this, anything extending outwards is said to be boomed out, as a lug sail, which may be described as boomed out if only held outward by an oar; and the shrouds of a bowsprit, which are said to be boomed out on its whiskers. Sail booms take their names from the sails they extend, as the main, mizzen, or spinnaker booms. They constitute the only means whereby such sails can be taken beyond the sides, or taffrail; and they moreover help to stand the sails flat. As an example, for the fittings of a boom we may take that of the mainsail of a cutter. It is held to the mast either by a joint called the *gooseneck and shaffle* (*which see*), or, otherwise, it has jaws which partially encircle the mast, these jaws resting on a stout ring round the lower portion of the mast, called the *saddle* or *bolster*. The entire fitting constitutes that which is known as the *boom stays*. At the after end of the boom is generally to be found a member known as the *clamp* or *cleat*. This consists of a flat piece projecting on each side and perforated with various holes: it forms a sort of cleat, through the holes of which the *reef pendants* can be passed and tied down

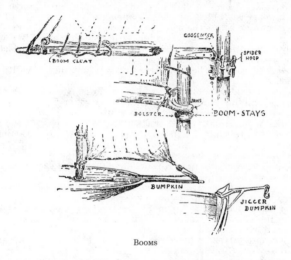

BOOMS

when the sail is reefed. This clamp is sometimes, however, dispensed with, and a *traveller*, or an *outhaul*, used in its place. Over the end of the boom the *grommet* of the *topping-lift* is passed; this latter is a rope used for lifting, or *topping*, the boom when taking in a reef, or *tricing* up the sail, it being necessary at such times to take the weight of the boom off the halyards. The boom rests, when the boat is at anchor, on a crutch—sometimes called a *mitchboard*—which may be either a simple pair of trestle legs, or, in the latter case, a flat board with a half circle cut out of the top, this also being to take the weight of the spar. (*See* CRUTCH.) And it is usually covered, when the sail is furled, by a water-proof sail cloth, which encloses boom, sail, and gaff—the gaff-halyards being unshackled and attached to slings

B

which pass under the boom. (*See* under SLING.) The tendency of a boom being to bend upwards it is made somewhat thicker in the middle than at the ends. In large racing yachts the mainsail is laced to the boom; but in *cruisers* the foot is generally tacked down at each end and, if fastened to the boom at all, merely lashed to it by short ropes, so as to be readily let go. A boom is not a necessary adjunct to the mainsail of a single-masted boat. Many, more especially fishing craft, carry sails which merely hang from the gaff, and may be brailed up by a clew-line, at any moment: these sails are called *trysails,* and are sometimes rigged to yachts for winter work; the fact that they are without the boom rendering them very handy in variable weather. Other booms, apart from the main, are as follow:—

Spinnaker boom.—A very long and light spar, often longer than the lower mast, which extends a *spinnaker*—*i.e.,* a racing sail, set, when running before the wind, on the side opposite to that on which the mainsail stands. When no longer in use, this boom is usually topped up to the mast, or, being run out forward of the shrouds, it may be laid forward by the bowsprit.

Lug sail boom.—The lower yard of a balance-lug is called the boom.

Jigger-boom.—The bumpkin which, in yawls, is often set out and fixed beyond the taffrail is sometimes known as the *jigger-boom.*

Boomkin (pronounced and often written "bumpkin").—This is a small boom, usually fixed, and serving to work a sail extending beyond the taffrail of a boat. If very small it may be called a *jigger.*

A *jib-boom* is a species of extra bowsprit supported by and extended beyond that spar: it is only found on large yachts, and not often there; belonging, mostly, to trading vessels.

A *flying jib-boom* is a prolongation of the jib-boom, carrying a flying jib: it belongs only to large vessels.

A sprit, which passes diagonally across a fore and aft sail, is not a boom; nor must it be confounded with it, as the office of each is very different from the other. (*See* SPRIT.)

Boom foresail (in a schooner).—The foresail; that is the gaff sail on the foremast. (*See* SCHOONER.) It is so called because it carries a boom, but principally to distinguish it from the fore stay-sail, which is often called the foresail. (*See* under FORE.) On occasions we hear seamen speak of "the two mainsails" or "both mainsails" of a schooner, meaning the mainsail and the boom foresail.

Boom-iron (in ships).—An iron implement composed of two rings, formed into one piece, so as nearly to resemble the figure 8. It is employed to connect two cylindrical pieces of wood together, such as the jib-boom to the bowsprit, studding sail booms to the yards, etc.

Boom square sail.—In old vessels one of the *courses* (usually the fore-course), the foot of which is extended on a boom so that it may be topped over the fore or main stay when the ship comes round.

Boom-stays.—The fittings of a boom to its mast. They may consist either of a *shaffle and gooseneck* joint, or of a saddle for the

jaws of the boom, when it has them. (*See* GOOSENECK AND SHAFFLE.)
2. *Boom.*—(*See* DHOW.)

Boot-topping.—Scraping a ship's bottom and paying it over with a mixture of tallow, sulphur, resin, etc. 2. The painted band round a ship at her waterline of special composition to prevent the growth of marine organisms there.

Bore.—"A word used to express the sudden rise of the tide in certain estuaries, as in the Severn."

To *bore.*—When down by the head a vessel is said to bore.

Both sheets aft.—An expression used with respect to a square rigged vessel, signifying that she is running before the wind, in doing which the sheets of her square sails will be drawn aft equally.

Bottlescrew.—A screw used for setting up rigging. It consists of a central part at each end of which a screw eye is fitted. On the central part being turned with a spike both eyes are screwed towards each other thus making the rope taut.

Bottom.—Of a ship, that part of her which is under the water line. As used by commercial men, the term sometimes refers to the ship itself, as, for instance, in the phrase, "a trade in foreign bottoms."

Bottomry.—Pledging a ship or the freight she earns to raise money necessary for the completion of the voyage. Repayment is contingent on the safe arrival of the vessel. Originally, signified marine insurance. (*See also* RESPONDENTIA.)

Bound.—Tightly held (of a ship).

Outward bound.—Leaving home.

Homeward bound.—Returning home.

Tide bound.—Unable to make progress because of a head tide.

Wind bound.—At anchor because unable to make progress in consequence of contrary winds.

Bow (Bows of a ship).—The sides at the fore-part of a vessel, distinguished one from the other by the right and left hand, the first being the *starboard-bow,* the second the *port-bow* (fig. 1).

FIG. 1.—
SAILING

(In rowing) *Bow.*—The headmost rower (nearest the bow): he is No. 1 (fig. 2, p. 32). All the rowers count from him; thus, the composition of an eight-oar boat will be as follows:—*Bow* (1), 2, 3, 4, 5, 6, 7, *stroke* (8), *coxswain.* In pair-oar or double-sculling the rowers are known as bow and stroke, and their oars are numbered 1 and 2.

Bow side.—The side upon which the bow-man puts out his oar; that is on his left-hand side. The terms starboard and port are never used in rowing, the *bow-side* and *stroke-side* being spoken of instead. The bow-side is therefore the starboard side.

Bow-board, in a pleasure skiff.—A board fitting the bows of a boat and forming a back upon which a person may recline.

Bowline.—(*See* BOWLINE.)

Bow-sprit (anciently *bolt-sprit*).—One of the main spars in a vessel. It is a pole or "sprit" projecting forward from the stem and taking the forestays and bobstays. Its office is to enable a vessel to carry an increased spread of canvas in the form of head-sails, and to furnish a forward support to the topmast, though this latter object could actually be obtained without its use. The methods of fitting a bowsprit and keeping it in place are as follow: Some little distance aft of the stempost and on the deck of the vessel are fitted two stout timber heads called the *bowsprit bitts*; between these bitts the bowsprit is *stepped* (or placed). It is kept from rising by a cross piece called the *crossbitt,* and from sliding inwards by a *fid* at the heel. At the stem are the *knightheads,* and the bowsprit runs between these also, and in large vessels is supported by them. But in small craft the bowsprit lies on the deck and does not require the support of the knight-

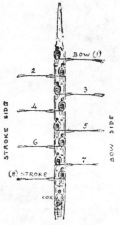

Fig. 2.—Rowing

heads, which are, therefore, of a different form. (*See* under KNIGHT-HEADS.) The bowsprit must, nevertheless, have some support at the stem, and this is obtained by a stout ring, called the *gammoning-iron,* through which it is passed; this gammoning iron is usually bolted to

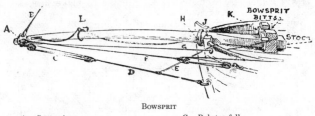

BOWSPRIT

A. Cranse-iron
B. Topmast forestay
C. Bobstay purchase
D. Bobstay
E. Rising line
F. Bowsprit shrouds
G. Bobstay fall
H. Gammoning iron
J. Knighthead
K. Crossbitt
L. Traveller with jib outhaul

the stem on its port, or left-hand side. The bowsprit, like the mast, requires *staying,* for it has to sustain almost as great a strain. At its forward end it is fitted with a metal cap, called the *cranse-iron,* which is made with several rings upon it to take the standing ends of the stays. The most important of these is the *bob-*

stay, for it holds the bowsprit down against the strain of the *topmast-forestay,* which leads from the topmast head to the nose of the bowsprit. Laterally, the bowsprit is stayed by shrouds, and if the boat is very narrow or the spar very long, these *bowsprit-shrouds* are *boomed out—i.e.,* extended on small cross-trees called *whiskers* (*which see*). The shrouds lead to the bows and are set up (or tightened) by means of a *purchase,* which leads in board, or in small boats sometimes by *screw-tighteners.* The angle which the bowsprit of a ship makes with the horizontal is called the *steeve*; this is seldom seen in small craft. The act of hauling it inboard is called *reeving it,* and that of hauling on the bobstay to tighten before making sail is *bowsing down* the bowsprit. The method of fixing the bowsprit constitutes the main difference between the cutter and sloop rig. In the sloop it is a standing spar, taking the tack of the foresail; in a cutter it is a reeving spar and the foresail is secured at the stemhead. (*See* under both CUTTER and SLOOP.)

Bower.—One of the large anchors of a ship which hold her by the *bows,* hence the name. (*See* ANCHOR.)

Bowgrace.—A name given, in ships sailing in frozen regions, to a framework of old rope or junk laid round the bows, stem and sides of a vessel to protect her from floating ice.

Bowline. 1.—A loop in a rope, tied in a peculiar manner and often used to throw over a post. (*See* KNOTS.) 2. A rope fastened to a square sail near the middle of the leech by three or four shorter ropes called *bridles.* Bowlines are employed on the principal sails in a square-rigged vessel to keep the weather edges forward and steady, for without some such tension the sails would be continuously shivering. Hence to be sailing with a *taut bowline* is to be close-hauled (*which see*). To *check the bowlines* is to slacken them as the ship falls off from the wind.

Bowse down.—To haul down taut. The act of tightening a bobstay by hauling on its fall (*i.e.,* its running end) is called *bowsing down the bowsprit.*

Box.—*Boxing the compass.*—Repeating the points of the compass in order, starting from any point. (*See* COMPASS.) Though this accomplishment may be unnecessary to amateur sailors a thorough familiarity with the compass cannot fail to prove of the utmost service on many occasions.

Boxing off.—Generally speaking, throwing a vessel's head off from the wind. There are many occasions in a sailing boat when this may be done, as, for instance, at starting, when unable to get round in tacking, or if there be danger of running aground. In the last case the plan formerly called *box hauling* may be resorted to, which, should the boat refuse to come round, will bring her back upon the same tack as she was before.

Box hauling (an obsolete term) is a method of "bringing a ship, when close-hauled, round upon the other tack, when she refuses to tack and there is not room to wear. By throwing the head sails aback she gets stern way; the helm thereupon being put a-lee, the ship's head falls rapidly off from the wind (this, because when a vessel is moving backwards the rudder acts the reverse way), which she soon brings aft; she is then speedily rounded to with but little loss of ground." (Brande and Cox.)

Brace.—A rope communicating with a boom or yard-arm for the purpose of trimming the sail to which such a spar may be attached. In square rigged ships the braces trim the yards horizontally. Hence the orders *brace back, brace in, brace* or *round up sharp,* etc.

Rudder braces.—The eyes in which a rudder swings are sometimes called braces. (*See* RUDDER.)

Brace of shakes.—A slang expression signifying "quickly". (Its origin is explained under the heading SHAKE.)

Brackish.—Spoken of water in a river when half salt and half fresh.

Brail.—A rope encircling a sail for the purpose of gathering it up to a mast or yard. Brails are used on square rigged vessels to assist in furling the sails. In fore-and-aft rig they are usually employed where no boom exists. They are common in fishing craft and almost

BARGE SAIL BRAILED UP

invariable in sea-going barges. When brails are hauled taut, the sail is said to be *brailed up*. (*See* fig.)

Break.—1. (Of the anchor.)—To out anchor.

2. (Of a sail.)—To *stop* a sail. (*See* STOP.)

3. (Of a flag.)—Flags are often broken, *i.e.,* hoisted to the mast-head, rolled up in a bunt, and set by jerking on the *downhaul* of the *halyard*. Ensigns, though, are always hoisted flying.

4. (*To break bulk.*)—"To take part of the ship's cargo out of the hold." (Bailey.)

Breaker.—1. A small water barrel.

2. *Breakers.*—Waves which, in consequence of the shallowness of the water, curl over and "break" as seen upon any beach. The breaking seas in deep waters, in high winds, or when the tide comes up against the wind, are not breakers. These have sometimes been called "white horses"; they are dangerous to small boats.

Breakwater.—An artificial bank or wall, of any material, set up either outside a harbour or along a coast to break the violence of the sea and create a smooth shelter. The small so-called breakwaters, or properly speaking *groynes,* often met with along a beach have been usually placed there for the formation, by the action of the sea, of an artificial beach, when the sea is washing away the land.

Breaming.—The cleansing of the bottom of a vessel by fire (this melts the pitch or other composition with which she has been covered) and scraping.

Breast-hook.—A stout knee in the extreme bow of a vessel holding the parts together. (*See* diagram under FRAME.)

Breast rope.—A mooring line from bow or quarter leading about right angles to the ship's fore and aft line.

Breeches buoy.—A lifebuoy fitted with canvas breeches, used with a rocket apparatus, (*see* ROCKET), to haul ashore persons from a wreck.

Breechings (*vulgo* britchings).—Back ropes or stays. 2.—Ropes fitted to the breeches of guns to limit their recoil when fired.

Bridge.—A superstructure having a clear view forward and on either side, from which a ship is conned and navigated.

Bridles.—Small ropes connecting some object with a larger rope. In square rigged ships, short ropes connecting the leech of a sail with the bowline. (*See* BOWLINE.)

Trawl bridles.—The ropes connecting the beam of a trawl to its warp or main rope.

BRIG

Brig.—A vessel with two masts (fore and main), both of them square rigged, but having a gaff mainsail. The brig is becoming a rare vessel, the brigantine and schooner having taken its place to a great extent, for reasons explained under the heading RIG. The vessel once known as the *snow* may be classed under brigs.

Hermaphrodite brig.—A combination of the brig and schooner rigs from which we get the modern brigantine (*which see*). It is square rigged on the foremast and fore-and-aft on the main mast.

Brig-mast.—The name given to a mast which carries a *top-gallant mast,* in contradistinction to the *schooner-mast,* which has no top-gallant, but only lower and top-mast. The brig-mast is the distinguishing difference between the brigantine and the schooner, and between the barkentine and the three-masted schooner (both of which see).

BRIGANTINE

Brigantine.—(A small or lesser brig.) A vessel with two masts (fore and main), the foremast brig rigged with square fore course, and the main mast schooner rigged. The rig, however, may vary slightly.

Bring-to.—*Bring up, bring up to the wind.*—The act of stopping the course of a sailing vessel by bringing her head up into the wind.

Bristol fashion.—"Shipshape and Bristol fashion," *i.e.,* smart and seamanlike.

Broach.—*Broaching to.*—A slewing round when running before the wind. This must often be the result of carelessness; the boat's head will run away to windward, with the result that she turns her back upon her proper course. Broaching to in a heavy following sea may result in a sailing vessel being dismasted and of a boat being thrown on its beam ends or *knocked down.*

Broad reach.—With the wind abaft the beam, between reaching and running.

Broadside.—To come up to a vessel broadside, is to approach her side foremost, as a dinghy or boat often comes up to a yacht.

Broadside.—A British broadside, in the old days of the wooden walls, was the reception often given to a too venturesome enemy; it consisted in firing all the cannon on one side of the ship at the same moment.

Broken-backed.—A vessel is said to have broken her back if her ends fall apart, as from running on a rock. (*See* HOGGING.)

Broom at the mast head.—A sign that a boat is for sale. (*See* fig.)

Brow.—A substantial gangway from ship to shore.

FOR SALE

Buccaneer.—Literally, "a smoker of meat or fish", who not infrequently became a pirate of the West Indies and South America during the seventeenth and eighteenth centuries: they are some-times called *filibustiers* by French writers. For a description of these freebooters see Burney's "History of the Buccaneers of America."

Bucklers.—Pieces of wood caulking the hawse holes.

Bucko.—A bully.

Bugalet.—"A small vessel with two masts, used on the coast of Brittany. The foremast is very short; and on each mast is carried a square sail, and, sometimes, a topsail over the mainsail. They have a bowsprit, and set one or two jibs." (Falconer's Dictionary.)

Build.—There are three methods, in boat building, of disposing

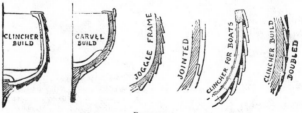

BUILDING

the planks of the sides. 1. *Clincher,* clinker, clench, or lapstrake. 2. *Carvel.* 3. *Diagonal.* A *clincher-built* boat is one in which the strakes overlap. This is the style most generally in vogue for small boats. In a *carvel-built* boat all the planks being flush with each other, a smooth surface is presented to the eye. This class of building is the most popular for yachts, and is even superseding clincher, to a small extent, for skiffs; but though more convenient, perhaps, on large hulls, it is hardly likely to take the place of clincher for open boats where any rough wear is required of them. As, in carvel building, the planks can only be secured at the timbers (or ribs) they require

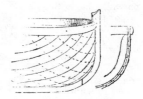

DIAGONAL BUILD

caulking to ensure water-tightness. In *diagonal-building* the planks are laid diagonally across the timbers, and most usually a second casing is laid over these running in the contrary direction. This method of building ensures great strength, though at the expense (unless very light-built) of some extra weight. The best wooden yachts are now built in this way, while such vessels as barges have for a long time been so where great durability is looked for.

Bulgeways, or **bilgeways.**—Timbers placed beneath a vessel while building. (*See also* under BILGE.)

Bulk.—Cargo or loose material.

Laden in bulk.—A vessel laden with loose cargo, as grain, ice, salt, etc.

Bulkhead.—A partition. Bulkheads may be of almost any material, as wood, canvas, or iron; and sometimes their office is to render a vessel additionally secure by dividing it into water-tight compartments.

Bull's-eye.—A round window in a cabin. Sometimes the central part of a port-hole light.

Bull rope.—A rope lead from a mooring buoy to the boatsprit end to keep the buoy clear of the vessel's stem. Any rope used to free or keep clear one thing from another.

Bulwarks.—A parapet round the deck of a vessel to protect persons or goods from being washed overboard, and the decks from the sea. In old battle ships they were very high and solid, thereby affording protection from an enemy's musketry; and during the day the hammocks of the crew were generally stowed beneath them.

Bum-boat.—An old term for a boat allowed to attend upon a ship in port, and supply the sailors with various small articles.

Bumpkin (probably correctly named *boom-kin,* a little boom).—A small fixed boom or short pole. It is usually seen, either as an extension aft to hold the block by which a mizzen sail is worked, or as a diminutive bowsprit for an open sailing boat. In the latter case, it is often of iron and fits over the stem-post, being fitted with a hook at the forward end, to take a foresail or the tack of a dipping lug. (*See* diagram under Boom.)

Certain yachts have a short thick bumpkin running out under, and partially supporting the bowsprit, as a jib-boom is supported in a large vessel. The object of this is to increase the size of the fore-sail by taking it beyond the stem-head, and a boat thus rigged is, in America, called a sloop, though not answering to our meaning of that word.

Bung.—1. The cork which stops the hole at the bottom of a boat. (*See* PLUG.) 2. In boat racing it used to be, and occasionally is, in some districts, the practice to start the competitors from moored buoys which were held by the coxswain and let go when the signal to go was given: at these times the buoy was called the "bung".

Bunk.—A bed on board ship. The word is used in contradistinction to hammock. A bunk is fixed, a hammock swung.

Bunker.—A compartment in which coal is carried. *Bunkers* often refers to the fuel itself, either coal or oil.

Bunt, or **belly.**—It is difficult to define the exact meaning of this term. Generally speaking, the bunt is the main body of a sail, exclusive of such parts as are named (as the luff and leech, the head, foot clew, etc.). In square sails the bunt has been thus described:—"That portion nearest the central perpendicular line. If a sail be divided into four equal portions, from side to side, the bunt would comprise the two centre strips."

Bunt lines.—Lines for gathering up the bunt of square sails to their yards. They are fastened to *cringles* in the *foot-rope* of a sail.

Bunting.—A thin woollen material used for making flags. *Bunting Tosser*, a naval signalman, often abbreviated to *Bunts*.

Buoy.—A floating object moored over a certain spot, either to mark a shoal or a course for vessels; or to which vessels may make fast; or for various other purposes. Buoys are of various shapes; *conical* or *nun, cylindrical* or *can,* or *spherical.* A *dan buoy* is a spar kept vertical by a weight at one end and a buoyant unit in the middle. They are also painted different colours to distinguish one class from another, and some carry *topmarks* of various shape to further distinguish them. Important positions are marked with *pillar buoys,* with a tall central structure, *light buoys* or *bell buoys.*

There are two systems of buoyage: in the *lateral* system buoys mark the port and starboard sides of a channel, etc., in the *cardinal* system buoys may be placed to the north, east, south or west of the danger to be avoided. From 1982 the previously different national systems have been replaced by the international (IALA) system, (*see* fig.), devised by the International Association of Lighthouse Authorities, but it should be remarked that in the Old World port-hand buoys should be left to port and starboard-hand buoys to starboard when *entering* harbour or proceeding in the same direction as the flood tide, in the New World port-hand buoys should be left to port and starboard-hand buoys to starboard when *leaving* harbour or proceeding in the same direction as the ebb tide.

Buoyancy.—That capacity of floating lightly which a vessel should possess. It is dependent upon form.

Centre of buoyancy.—The centre of gravity of the water displaced by any vessel.

Burden.—1. The capacity of a vessel, as 100 tons burden, etc.

2. *Burdens* (in shipbuilding).—Timbers laid over the floors to prevent cargo or ballast from injuring the lining. In boats the burdens are the *footwalings* (*which see*).

Burgee.—A small flag ending in a point or a swallow tail. If it is long and ends in a point it is, in mercantile language, a *pennant*; but among yacht clubs, each of which adopts one as a distinguishing mark, the burgee is almost always pointed, those of a commodore, rear, and vice being swallow-tailed. The different devices to be seen on yacht's burgees are very numerous. Those clubs which are Royal may, with very few exceptions, be distinguished by a regal crown surmounting their charge; thus the Royal Squadron displays, by privilege, the cross of St. George, over which is the crown; the Royal London, the arms of London on a blue field, above which is the crown; but the Royal Harwich—a lion rampant, or, on a blue field—is without the crown. It is the practice in large yacht clubs to register and number both its members and the boats belonging to its fleet, each having their own particular flag, or *number,* as it is usually called. By this means both boats and members are known separately, and it is possible to tell, by signal, not only what boat has come to a berth, but also who may be on board. The burgee marks the club to which a yacht belongs; numbers (flags) hoisted *over* the burgee indicate the boat's number (and therefore her name); numbers hoisted *under* the burgee indicate members' numbers (and therefore their names). Certain yacht clubs have the privilege granted to them of using certain ensigns. When a yacht flies a particular ensign the burgee of the same club is displayed with it. A yacht may belong to several clubs, but she never flies the burgee of one with the ensign of another. And when she comes to the head-

SWALLOW TAIL

R. Y. SQUADRON

ROYAL
ST. GEORGE Y. C.

ROYAL LONDON
Y. C.

quarters of a club to which she belongs, she always flies its burgee. On festive occasions, such as regattas, a yacht flies all the colours to which her owner has a right, in order of precedence, with those of the local club usually at the head, or if he be an officer of any club the ensign and burgee of that club have precedence. On Sundays the burgee may be hoisted and flown together with any colours that may have been won during the season, and the ensign over the taffrail.

ROYAL HARWICH Y. C.

Burgoo.—Porridge. First mentioned in Edward Coxere's "Adventures by Sea" (1656).

Bush, or **coak.**—The centre piece (usually of gun-metal) of a wooden sheave in a block. It is, in fact, the bearing of the pin on which the sheave runs. (For a description of its shape *see* under COAK.)

Buss.—"A two-masted vessel used by the Dutch and English in the herring fishery. It is nearly obsolete now; but when employed is from fifty to seventy tons in burden." (Brande and Cox.) Falconer describes it as having been "furnished with two small sheds or cabins, one at the prow and the other at the stern; the forward one being employed as the kitchen." These houses on deck may still be seen on many Dutch craft.

Butt.—The butt is the lower end of a yard or sprit.

Buttock.—The convexity of the under portion of the stern of a vessel; in other words, that part between the counter (or the transom) and the bilge. Its actual extent is from the after end of the sheer strake to the keel, in a curved and forward direction. From this we have what is called a *buttock line,* which, in the lines of a boat, is a longitudinal vertical section through one of the buttocks. On the breadth plan, therefore, it appears as a straight line parallel to the keel; from thence it is projected to the body plan, where it becomes a vertical line; and from thence again being projected to the sheer plan, it will be found to assume a curved form. (*See* LINE.)

By.—*By the head.*—Another manner of expressing the term "down by the head", that is,—the head depressed, as in the figure.

By and large.—Sailing with the wind before the beam, and sailing with the wind abaft the beam; that is, on the whole, everything considered.

By the lee.—Sailing with the wind nearly aft and

BY THE HEAD

the mainboom on the side from which the wind is blowing.

By the wind (in sailing).—Sailing with the wind *ahead* of the beam. (*See* under CLOSE-HAULED.)

C

Cab.—A shelter at the wing of a ship's bridge.

Cabin.—A habitable apartment on ship-board.

Cable.—The rope or chain by which a ship's anchor is held. Cables were formerly of hemp, but to-day chain cables are in almost universal use. The advantages of the latter are manifold: they neither chafe nor become rotten; "and by reason of their greater weight the strain is exerted on the cable rather than on the ship." A chain with a sectional diameter of 1 in. is said to be equivalent to a 10 in. cable, nearly.

"A *cable's length*—the tenth of a nautical mile; or approximately, 100 fathoms or 200 yards." (Lloyd's Almanac.) Chain cable is made in lengths of 15 fathoms. A cable is, or should be, fastened at the end to some strong part of the vessel. The lengths of chain are joined by shackles, and thus the cable may be shortened or lengthened without interfering either with the anchor or fixed end; these shackles have their pins countersunk, so as to offer no impediment to the free run of the cable, and they are placed lug forward for the same reason. Swivels may be placed at certain intervals (generally at every other length of chain) so that the chain by turning them may be prevented from *knitting,* that is, from twisting, the technical name for a twist in chain being *knit.* In very deep water it may sometimes be necessary to employ more than one length of cable; every additional length is termed a *shot* according to its number, thus *single-shot* indicates that one length has been added, *double-shot* two lengths, and so on. A cable is sometimes marked in fathoms; and one of the links is generally marked to show when it has gone out as far as its length and the necessary bite on the windlass will allow.

To *pay out, veer away,* or *slacken* are all synonymous terms for letting out a cable to a greater or less distance. To pay it out *cheap* is to slacken out quickly or throw the cable over-board in bulk.

To *slip the cable* is to let it go from the ship, an operation which may sometimes be necessary in emergency.

Cable laid, cablet. (*See* under ROPE.)

Caboose.—A cooking house on the deck of a ship.

Cackling.—(*See* KECKLING.)

Cadet (Naval).—A youth who, having been duly nominated to the Navy, holds a preparatory appointment thereto.

Caique.—A boat used in the Bosphorus. Elsewhere in the Mediterranean a small cargo or fishing vessel.

Caisson.—A steel floating structure which can be flooded and sunk to close the entrance to a dry dock. 2. A watertight casing in which men can work under water.

Call.—The small pipe (sometimes of silver) used by the boatswain of a ship in piping orders.

Camber.—1. A curvature upwards. A boat's deck, if curving upwards from side to side, or from stem to stern, is said to be cambered, and also her keel, if it be rounded. 2. A small dock, for boats or timber, is also sometimes called a camber.

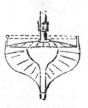

CAMBERED DECK

Camel.—A large hollow structure, that is filled with water and sunk under a vessel. When pumped out the buoyancy of the camel raises the ship.

Can Buoy.—A buoy showing a flat top above water.

Canal.—An artificial ditch or channel filled with water for purposes of inland navigation. It usually has a pathway on one or both sides, called the tow path. Canals may be said to intersect the whole surface of England.

CAN BUOY

Canoe.—The native American name for a dugout boat made out of a single trunk of a tree; but as we understand the term in England it means any boat propelled by paddles, of which there are various sorts, such as the *Canadian canoe* and the Eskimo *kayak,* with covered ends.

Canoe rig.—Sailing canoes are generally rigged with main, mizzen, and foresail; and their sails are often *battened*—that is, have battens, or splines, sewn in across them, both to keep them flat and to help in reefing them. Many fantastic devices may be indulged in with canoes, and some have a complete system of tiny blocks

CANOE RIG WITH BATTENED SAILS

on their main and mizzen sails, so arranged that by pulling on a thin lanyard led aft to the helmsman a reef may be taken in without his moving from his place in the well.

Cant.—To turn or lean over or round; the term is somewhat vaguely applied. A piece of wood used for the support of some part of a construction is also called a cant.

"*Cant* is a term used to express the position of any piece of timber that does not stand square, and then it is said to be on the cant."

Cantling.—The act of turning plank or timber to see the opposite side.

Cant-pieces.—Pieces of timber inserted and annexed to the angles of fishes and side-trees, so as to supply any part that may prove sappy or rotten.

Cant timbers.—"Those timbers which are situated at the two ends of a ship. They derive their name from being canted or raised obliquely from the keel, in contradistinction to those whose planes are perpendicular to it." (Falconer's Dictionary.)

Cant to.—To turn with the tide, as a vessel at anchor swings when the tide changes.

Canvas.—The material of which the sails of a ship are made. But the word has another meaning in its general application to all or any of the sails set; as to say, for instance, that a boat spreads "all her canvas", or that she sails under "racing canvas", press canvas, shortened canvas, etc.

Cap.—Generally speaking, a ring at the end of a spar.

Upper and lower cap.—The fittings to the head of a mast, through which an upper or top mast travels. The upper ring is called the cap; the lower, the yoke or lower cap. (*See* MAST.)

To *cap a rope.*—To cover the end of it with tarred canvas and *whip* it with yarn or twine.

Capful of wind.—A slight breeze.

Cape.—The extreme point of a promontory. When high and terminating at an acute angle, it is called a point. When low and of small projection it becomes a ness, or in Scotland a mull. Thus we have Morte Point, Orford Ness, Mull of Galloway. The word Naze may also be regarded as ness.

Cape Horn Fever.—Feigned illness of a seaman in cold and stormy weather.

Cappanus.—"The worm which adheres to and gnaws the bottom of a ship." (Falconer.)

Capsize (of a boat).—To turn it completely over in the water, as it might be if caught on the head of a breaker, or in smooth water, if those in it insist in sitting all on one side.

CAPSTAN

To *capsize a rope.*—to turn it over. Coils are capsized after being made so that the rope shall run out from the top of the coil.

Capstan.—A "wheel and axle", usually revolving in a horizontal position, that is, the axle being placed upright, and worked by long levers, *the capstan bars,* inserted into the head. Its use is to obtain great power in hauling, and thus it may be found in a ship for hauling in a cable, etc., or on a quay or dock; and in these days it is often worked by steam or electricity.

Caravel.—A Spanish or Portuguese vessel of the 15th and 16th centuries, rigged with lateen sails, *caravela latina*, or square-rigged on the fore and mainmast with a lateen sail on the after masts, *caravela redonda*.

CARAVELA LATINA

Cardinal points (of the compass).—The four main points, North, South, East, and West. (*See* COMPASS.)

Careen.—To *heel* or make to lie over on one side. The operation of heaving the ship down to one side, by the application of a strong purchase to her masts, so that she may be *breamed*. But copper sheathing has superseded the necessity for this. A vessel is also said to careen when she inclines under press of canvas, at sea.

Carley float.—A life-raft, like a large oval lifebuoy with a grating within it, capable of supporting a large number of persons.

Carlings, or **carlines** (in ship-building).—Short beams running fore and aft between the great transverse beams, which they bind securely together. They also aid in supporting the deck. (*See* diagrams under FRAME.)

Carrack.—The largest type of ship from the 14th to the 17th century, with very high fore and after castles. Square rigged on fore and main masts and with a lateen sail on the after mast or masts.

CARRACK, c. 1520

Carrick bend.—A peculiar form of knot.

Carronade.—A peculiar, short piece of ordnance, so called from Carron, the town in Scotland in which it was first made, of great destructive power but short range.

Carry away.—To break or lose any part of the rigging of a vessel, as a spar which may be snapped or a sail blown out. Thus it may be said of a yacht that she "carried away her topmast"—meaning that it broke.

Carry on.—To spread the utmost extent of canvas possible, as a yacht may do in racing. But the term is usually understood to mean that she is crowding it on at a risk. 2. An order to proceed.

Carvel.—A method of boat building in which the strakes are flush one with another and present a smooth surface. (*See* BUILD.)

Carving Note.—A form filled in by the owner of a ship being built, stating particulars of tonnage, name, port of registry etc. the tonnage being carved on the main beam.

Case.—The outer layer of planking on a boat. This name, however, only exists where there is a double layer, as in diagonally built craft. The inner layer is then called the case, and that outside it the *skin.*

Cast.—*Casting off* a boat's head is to pay it off when she has come on the proper tack.

To *cast anchor.*—To let go anchor. (*See* ANCHOR.)

Cast away.—Lost.

To cast off a rope.—To unfasten it.

Castor and Pollux.—"The name given to an electric meteor which sometimes appears at sea, attached to the extremities of the masts of ships under the form of balls of fire. When one light only is seen, it is called Helena. The meteor is generally supposed to indicate the cessation of a storm or a future calm; but Helena, or one ball only, to portend bad weather." (Brande and Cox.) More usually known as a *corposant* or *St. Elmo's Fire.*

Cat.—A name at one time given to a ship of peculiar build, and used, commonly, in the coal trade. Falconer describes its form as built without a beakhead and founded upon the Norwegian model, having a narrow *stern,* projecting *quarters,* and deep waist. "These vessels," he says, "are generally built remarkably strong, and carry from four to six hundred tons; or, in the language of their own mariners, from twenty to thirty *keels* of coal." Vessels answering tolerably well to such a description may still be seen in the North Sea.

The *cat,* on shipboard, is that part which has to do with the anchor and weighing it. Thus we have the *cathead,* a timber projecting from the bow, to which the anchor is secured.

Cat block, a block which is attached to the anchor when it reaches the cat-heads.

Cat hook, the hook by which the cat block is attached.

Cat fall, the rope, passing through the cat block, by which the anchor is hauled inwards, and all of these constitute the *cat tackle.*

Cat holes, in the stern of a ship, are holes through which a cable passes when it may be necessary to heave the ship astern.

Cat harpings, in the rigging of a ship, are ropes used to draw in the shrouds of masts or bowsprits that they may not interfere with the yards, etc.

CATHEAD

Cat rig, with sailing boats, etc., is a rig of one sail, the peculiarity of which consists in the manner in which the sail is hoisted. The mast is stepped very far forward, and a yard considerably longer than the masts runs along it, carrying a sail which is supposed to represent both the main and top-sail of other rigs. It is claimed for the cat-rig that it possesses great advantages in reefing. An improvement on it, consisting chiefly in the introduction of a reefing boom, was brought in by a Mr. Forbes, of America, some years ago; the description of this improved rig is quoted in Mr. Davies' "Boat Sailing for Amateurs". A modern version of this rig has two masts with wrap-round sails and wish-bone booms.

Cat's paw.—1. A name sometimes given to a light wind which sweeps gently over the surface of the sea in a calm, and then dies away. It is seen coming from a distance, and often in a triangular form. 2. Of a rope.—A peculiar turn given to a rope in order to hook a tackle to it is also called a *cat's paw*.

Catamaran.—A species of sailing raft used in the Indies. Its motions are controlled by two drop-boards let down, one from the fore part, the other astern, through the raft, and by means of these it may not only be steered to a nicety, but made to sail on the wind, tack and turn, just in the same manner as a boat. This raft is described in a most interesting manner by Captain Basil Hall in the "Lieutenant and Commander". More commonly, a native catamaran is a canoe whose stability is obtained by having a log held parallel to and at a distance from the main craft. 2. A yacht with twin hulls.

Catch (in rowing).—The *grip* (the more proper term) which an oar gets of the water at the commencement of a stroke. It should be firm and continuous, taken quickly, but without excitement; and there is no doubt that thus performed it produces great speed.

Catching a crab.—The art is described under the word CRAB.

Catch a turn.—Take a turn with a rope round a pin or cleat.

Caulking.—The operation performed upon wooden vessels to prevent leakage, and assist in fixing the whole frame of the hull. It consists of stuffing the seams (the spaces between the planks) with oakum, and then *paying* them with hot pitch.

Cavil.—(*See* CLEAT.)

Cay.—(*See* KEY.)

Centre-board, centre-keel or **drop-keel.**—A heavy, movable plate of iron, lead, or timber let down below the keel of a sailing boat, about midships. It serves a two-fold purpose, acting at once as a leeboard—enabling the boat to carry more sail than she otherwise could—and as a lifting keel which, in case of her running aground, can be raised immediately, thereby reducing the

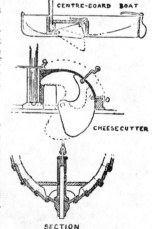

CENTRE-BOARD BOAT

CHEESECUTTER

SECTION

draught of the boat and enabling her to float again. In running before the wind a centre-board is raised, so that as small a resistance as possible may be presented to the water; in sailing close hauled it is let down to its fullest: and according to the spread of canvas carried and the direction of the wind, its depth between these extremes may be varied.

But the accumulation of all the weight and depth of a keel into one place may be carried to excess; and should the movable keel be made heavier than a light hull can well bear, its tendency is to render the boat too stiff, and thereby to destroy its buoyancy. The best material of which the plate can be made under these circumstances would seem to be wood; and to render it heavy it may be weighted at the bottom. There are various forms of centre-board. The most simple is a plain plate, dropped evenly down; but being very apt to jam it is not much used. It is, however, in many respects, the best. But the favourite arrangement is the board which swings on a pivot, and of this there are many patterns, of which some, almost semi-circular in shape, are called *cheesecutters*. In another form one board works inside another, opening like a fan, so that the depth of keel can be better calculated. This, though apparently good in principle, is not much used except for canoes. The exact position of a centre-board is of great moment; it depends upon the shape of the boat, the use to which she is to be put, and the sail area. For sea boats a great depth of centre-keel is not found to answer, while on smooth waters it may be considerable. In all measurements for racing, the board is let down to its fullest extent. For boats intended to be beached, the centre-board is peculiarly well suited; but it is not on this account to be concluded that the invention has its origin in beached boats, since, long before it ever came into general use, it was habitually employed in boats which were never hauled up on land. In one form or another, indeed, whether as lee-board or centre-board, it may be said to date from time immemorial.

Centre-castle.—The raised part of a ship's hull amidships.

Centre of buoyancy.—The centre of gravity of the water displaced by any vessel.

Centre of Effort.—That point in a sail at which all wind force may be said to act. Theoretically, the geometrical centre of the sail area, but in practice, probably not, because the sail is not perfectly flat nor presents a uniform angle to the wind.

Chafe.—To rub or wear away by rubbing.

Chaffer.—Spoken of a head sail, and more particularly of a jib, when it keeps shivering.

Chafing gear.—Bindings, sometimes of leather, attached to the rigging where there is any danger of two parts rubbing together.

Chain.—Chain is becoming more used in shipping every year, and is now, therefore, made in a variety of shapes and sizes. The principle upon which the manufacture is founded may be quoted, thus:—"Much depends upon the shape of the links in order to obtain the greatest resistance of a chain; and as long as the strain is kept in the direction of the axis, the strongest form will be obtained when the sides of the chain are parallel to the line of strain. But as this is often in a direction perpendicular to the axis, it is essential to introduce a stay which should maintain the sides invariably in their position, and to resist any unequal compression of the metal in the sides." The stay here spoken of is often seen in cables, and constitutes that which is known as the "stud link"; it is wrought or cast in various patterns.

The most common chains in use (*see* fig.) are: round or end link; close-link; open-link; stud-link; curb. Round-linked chains are not used for nautical purposes, but a circular link usually occurs in cables, at the end of every chain length, and is therefore called an *end-ring*. *Open-link* is the pattern most frequently employed for all general purposes, both at sea and ashore, being the most generally serviceable and the least expensive: cables of small craft are of this pattern. *Stud-link* is found in the anchor cables of large vessels, for reasons above quoted. *Curb chain* is somewhat rare, being expensive; it is powerful, and when twisted becomes quite rigid.

Chain was made in lengths of $12\frac{1}{2}$ fathoms for the Royal Navy, but since 1949 all studded chain cable is made in 15 fathom lengths, each length being termed a *shackle of cable*. The thickness of a chain is measured by the thickness of the bar of which it is made. "A chain of which the section is one inch in diameter breaks with 16 tons; such a chain is equivalent to a 10 in. hempen cable nearly. And the dimensions of the chain cable corresponding to any hemp cable are therefore easily found by nearly dividing the circumference of the hemp cable by 10." The formula for the safe load of a chain in tons has been thus given:

$$D = \sqrt{9\,W} \quad \text{or} \quad W = \frac{D^2}{9}.$$

Where W = the safe load, and D = the diameter expressed in $\frac{1}{8}$ths of an inch, the weight of chain in lbs. per fathom = $\cdot85D^2$. "In order that the ship may be enabled to let slip her cable in case of necessity, chain cables are furnished with bolts at distances from each other of a fathom or two, which can be readily withdrawn."

Chain-locker.—The hold in the fore part of a boat into which the anchor chain descends.

Chains or *channel plates.*—Iron bars or plates on a vessel's sides, running upwards, and receiving the *deadeyes* by which the shrouds are held down. In large vessels the channel plates are kept down by strong chains, hence the name. Where the vessel has *channels* the chains are kept away from the bulwarks by them, but in smaller craft the channels are dispensed with and the plates simply run up the sides somewhat higher than the gunwales. In such craft these plates are frequently called the channels. (*See* CHANNELS.)

Chain bolts.—"Those bolts which are driven through the upper end of the preventer plates and the toe link of the chains." This has reference to large vessels of the old type, when the chain (or channel) plates were held down by iron chains from beneath.

Chain ferry.—A ferry which proceeds by being hauled along a chain laid across a river or channel.

Chain shot.—Two cannon-balls joined by a short length of chain and fired together. Effective against masts, spars and rigging.

Chain stopper.—A short length of chain with a rope tail used to hold a wire rope while it is being made fast to the bitts, etc.

Chamfer.—To take the edge off or bevel a plank, which is then said to have chamfered edges.

Changing rigging end for end.—This consists in turning any such ropes as may be chafing in one place, end for end, so as to bring all parts into equal wear. Rigging changed thus will naturally last longer than when allowed to wear bare without turning; but the ropes in small boats are so short that the practice is not much followed.

Channels (*chain wales—i.e.,* the *wales* upon which certain *chains* are fixed).—In ships these are wooden platforms projecting from the hull on each side of each mast; their office is to keep the *chains* and *channel plates* away from the sides and to give a wider spread to the

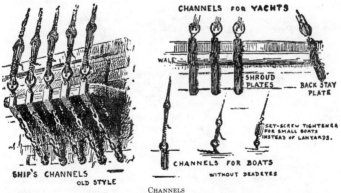

CHANNELS FOR YACHTS

WALE

SHROUD PLATES

BACK STAY PLATE

SET-SCREW TIGHTENER FOR SMALL BOATS INSTEAD OF LANYARDS.

SHIP'S CHANNELS OLD STYLE

CHANNELS FOR BOATS WITHOUT DEADEYES

CHANNELS

rigging. These channel plates or *chain plates* are flat bars of iron running in an upward direction from beneath the channels, and taking the *deadeyes* by which the *shrouds* of the masts are held down. In smaller craft and in many modern vessels the channels proper disappear, the plates remaining in their place; while in sailing boats even these plates are dispensed with, and both channels and plates may become little more than eye-bolts. The name *channels* is still retained, however, so that as far as amateur sailing is concerned, channels may almost be described as *those points on the sides of a boat to which the bases of the shrouds are attached.* When the channels project to any great extent, as is sometimes the case in very narrow boats, they may be called *outrigged channels.* Many barges are without channel plates, because the lee-boards come in the way of them.

2. A narrow arm of the sea between two land areas.

3. The deepest part of shallow water through which the main current flows.

Chanty, or **shanty.**—A chorus song, sung by sailors when working, but now rarely heard. There were two main classes, hauling- and windlass-chanties: the rhythm being determined by the class of work to be done.

Chappelling.—*Chappelling* a ship is "the act of turning her round in a light breeze of wind when she is close-hauled, so that she will lie the same way she did before. This is commonly occasioned by the negligence of the steersman, or by a sudden change of the wind." (Falconer.)

Charring.—Burning the external surface of wood. It is a valuable process for the preservation of piles or any timbers which may be subjected to alternate exposure to the air and submersion in water. The water line of all piles is, as is well known, the part most liable to decay; charring is found to some extent to delay this decay.

Chart.—Roughly speaking, a map of the sea bottom and coast projections, for the use of navigators. Any person intending to cruise round the coast should be provided with charts, and should first learn to read them. The first man to draw charts for seamen was probably Marinus of Tyre in the first century A.D.

Charter-party.—A contract in mercantile law between the owner of a ship and one who hires part or the whole of it under specified conditions.

Chasse-marées.—The coasting and fishing vessels of the French shores of the Channel, once seen in our own ports. They were bluff bowed and lugger rigged, with one, two, or three masts, often carrying topsails.

Cheat the devil.—Using soft expletives where strong ones would most naturally occur.

Check.—To stop or impede motion, as to check the anchor's cable from veering out. But the word is more frequently used to mean to slack away a little and then hold on. When applied to a rope or the sheet of a sail, it will mean to ease it off or let it go a little.

Cheeks.—Generally speaking, brackets or stoppering pieces on a spar or elsewhere. Thus the knee pieces fastened to a ship's stem are sometimes called cheeks. On a mast the cheeks are brackets a short distance below the mast-head, and upon these are placed the *trestle trees,* which support the *cross-trees.* (*See* MAST.) The *cheeks of a block* are the two sides of its shell. (*See* BLOCK.)

Cheese-cutter.—A form of centre-board. (*See* CENTRE-BOARD.)

Cheesing down.—Coiling a rope on the deck ornamentally with each flake flat or almost flat, in a circular or figure-of-eight pattern.

Chess-trees (in a ship).—"Two small pieces of timber on each side of it, a little before the loof, having a hole in them, through which the main tack runs, and to which it is haled down." (Bailey's Dictionary.) Pieces of wood bolted, perpendicularly, one on each side of the deck of a ship and bored with holes on the upper part. They are employed to hold the tack of a square mainsail to windward, and for this purpose are placed as far before the mast as the length of the main beam, the tack line of the sail passing through the holes.

Chimes.—The intersection of the lines forming the sides and the bottom of a flat-bottomed boat.

Chinckle.—A small bend or bight in a line.

Chine.—1. "That part of the waterway which is left above the deck, that the lower seam of *spirketting* may more conveniently be caulked" (Falconer),—the spirketting being the *strakes* on the ends of the beams. 2. The back of a cliff; as the Black Gang Chine (Isle of Wight).

To chine out.—To hollow out slightly.

Chips.—The name by which a ship's carpenter is often spoken of, and hence the popular phrase "a chip of the old block".

Chock.—1. Any nondescript blocks of wood, as wedges used to prevent anything from shifting when a vessel rolls, or as rudder chocks which fix a rudder in case of emergency, etc. 2. The pieces used in *filling* the *timbers* of a vessel to its planks, *i.e.*, filling up the shape where necessary so that the curves of the planking shall be preserved. (*See* diagram under FRAME.)

Chock-a-block.—One block hauled close up to another, so that the power they give is destroyed until they are drawn asunder or *overhauled.*

Choke a luff.—Preventing a tackle from walking back by passing a bight of the fall between a sheave and the rope rove through it, causing it to jam.

Chops of the channel.—The westerly approaches to the English Channel.

Chronometer.—A specially constructed clock or watch from which Greenwich time is obtained. It is of great importance in navigating, as it is from the difference between Greenwich time and ship's time that the vessel's longitude is ascertained.

CHOCK-A-BLOCK

Chow chow.—A popular term for eatables; from the Chinese.

Chuck.—Sometimes called a *fairlead* or *leadfair*. A guide for a rope or chain, over the gunwale of a boat. It is most usually of metal: in yachts sometimes of brass. Fairleads are of different forms; but any ring or eye-bolt which leads a rope is a fairlead (*which see*).

Cinque Ports.—The five English ports of Dover, Hastings, Romney, Hythe and Sandwich, to which were later added "the ancient towns" of Rye and Winchelsea. Until the 16th century they furnished ships and men for the Royal Navy in wartime, in return for certain privileges. The Lord Warden of the Cinque Ports is today some person of distinction.

Cirrus.—The cloud called "mare's-tails". Seen towards evening it often portends wind to follow, especially if giving the appearance of having been torn.

Clamp.—On a boom, the cleat, at the after end, through which the reef-pendants are passed, when reefing the sail. (*See* under BOOM.)

To *clamp,* in carpentering or shipbuilding, is to fix two pieces of wood together by a mortise or a groove and tongue, so that the fibres of each crossing each other may prevent warping.

Clap on.—To put on—as to clap a purchase on to a tackle. Also spoken of men, as to clap several hands on to a purchase.

Clapper.—A fitting between the jaws of a gaff to prevent that from jamming as it descends the mast. Sometimes called a *tumbler.*

Clasp hook.—A hook which clasps a ring, or stay, or rope. It is included in the general term *hank.*

Class.—The class of a boat is the group to which she belongs, as schooner, yawl, etc. In yacht racing it is the group in which she is placed after measurement. A vessel is said to *outclass* others when she is very much superior to those in her own class.

Clawing off.—This generally presupposes a vessel to be close into or being driven on to a *lee shore,* and the act of getting away by sailing her as close to the wind as she can be made to go while still keeping good way on is called clawing off.

Clean.—The sharp part of a ship's hull, under water, both forward and aft.

Clearing.—The passing of a vessel through the Customs after she has visited a foreign port. The Board of Trade directs that any vessel, after visiting a foreign port, shall report herself to the officers of the Customs, at the first British port she enters. As a signal that she has been abroad she must fly the ensign from sunrise to sunset, and expose a light under her bowsprit by night, until she has been cleared.

Clearing hawse.—(*See* under HAWSE.)

Cleat, kevel, or **cavil.**—A species of hook, usually of two arms, fastened to the deck or any other suitable and convenient part of a boat, around which sheets, halyards, springs, etc., may be wound without being knotted. Cleats are of various forms,

VARIOUS CLEATS

as will be seen by the figure. They are required to sustain great strains and sudden jerks, and must, therefore, be securely fixed. Where several are placed close together they are, for additional security, fixed to a strengthening plate, or plank, which is called a *rail*. A *thumb-cleat* or *spur* is a small wedge let into a spar to prevent a rope from slipping; it is also found in various parts of the vessel. (*See* fig. p. 52, also THUMB CLEAT.)

Clench, or **clinch.**—1. To jam down.

With ropes.—To jam down by a half hitch.

2. *Clench building.*—Another term for clincher, or clinker, building. (*See* BUILD.)

Clew.—The clew is the lower corner of a sail, and unless otherwise described is the *after* lower corner; but the *tack,* or *forward* corresponding corner, is sometimes called the *weather clew.* This will apply equally to square or fore-and-aft sails; but in square sails each lower corner is a clew, and each becomes the tack (or weather clew) alternately, as the ship comes about. This, however, cannot be the case in fore-and-aft rig, since the forward part of such sails always remains *in situ*; and therefore in yachts and such like craft the clew will always be the *after* lower corner of the sail, and though the tack may often be spoken of as the "weather clew" it still always remains the tack, *i.e.,* the *forward* lower corner.

To *clew up* is to gather up a sail by its clew-lines.

Clew garnets, clew lines.—On square sails will be lines, or ropes, attached to the clews, *i.e.,* to the *lower corners*; from thence they run to a block fastened to the middle of the yard. On the lower sails, or "courses", as these are termed, these same lines are called the *clew garnets,* the name *lines* being only appropriated to the clew ropes of the topsails. The use of these clew lines, or garnets, is to draw up the clews of the sails to the middle of the yards so that they may be furled. Clew lines in fore-and-aft rigged vessels, sometimes called *tripping lines,* answer much the same purpose, but they will naturally be differently disposed. The clew line of a *gaff topsail,* for instance, is attached to the clew (*i.e.,* the *after* lower corner), passes across to the forward end of the topsail yard, and thence down on deck: by hauling upon it the topsail is then clewed up to its yard. (*See* fig. under TOPSAIL.)

A *great clew.*—When square sails gore outwards towards the clew, that is, are considerably wider at the foot than the head, they are said *to have a great clew.* And when yards are very long so that the sails are more than usually wide, they are described as *spreading a great clew.*

Clew to earing.—An expression which describes the condition of a square sail when the foot has been drawn up to the head, *i.e.,* the clew to the earing.

Click.—A small stopper, or pawl, dropping into the teeth of the rack-wheel of a windlass to prevent the wheel from running backwards.

Clincher, clinker, clench, or **lapstrake.**—A method of building a boat in which the strakes overlap. (*See* BUILD.)

To *clinch.*—To jam down—the same as to clench.

Clinometer.—An instrument consisting of a pendulum and a graduated arc, by which a vessel's list, or heel, is determined.

Clip.—That part of a gaff or boom which is fashioned into horns, or jaws, so as to partly encircle a mast. (*See* under GAFF.)

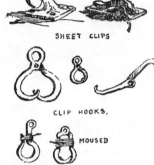

Clip-hooks or *sail-hanks* (sometimes called *sail-hooks*).—A combination of two hooks jointed together to face each other, so as to clip a rope on each side. To keep them from shaking apart they are usually *moused* at the neck. (*See* MOUSE.)

Sheet clips.—Small metal implements fixed to the deck in certain sailing boats or small yachts (more especially those intended for single-handed sailing) to take the place of sheet cleats. A rope being passed into one of these is firmly gripped until, being lifted, it is immediately released.

SHEET CLIPS

CLIP HOOKS.

MOUSED

VARIOUS CLIPS

Clipper.—A name applied to fast sailing ships.

Clipper bow.—A bow whose stem curves forward as it rises above the waterline.

Close-hauled.—The manner in which a vessel's sails are disposed when she is sailing as close to the wind (*i.e.,* as nearly against the wind) as she can go; *e.g.,* in fore-and-aft rig, the sheets hauled close, and in square rig the yards braced up, the sheets well home, and the bowlines hauled taut. So, therefore, to be sailing with *taut bowline* is to be close-hauled. When thus close-hauled to the wind a boat is said to be sailing *on the wind, by the wind,* or *full and by the wind,* and if, when close-hauled, she carries a *lee-helm* she is said to be *hauling on the wind.* (*See* under LEE-HELM.)

CLOSE-HAULED

Close-lined.—(*See* LINE.)

Close quarters.—In close proximity. Yard arm to yard arm.

Close-reefed.—When all the reefs are taken in so that the area of the sails may be as small as possible. (*See* fig., p. 55, also under REEF.)

Close-winded.—A boat is sometimes said to be close-winded when she can sail very close to the wind.

Cloth (of a sail).—One of the strips of canvas which go to compose a sail is so called. (*See* SAIL.)

Clothe.—To put on the sails and furniture to a vessel; that is her masts, rigging, and all accessories. In other words, to fit her out.

CLOSE-REEFED

Clubbing.—Drifting with the tide with an anchor down; a vessel clubbing will therefore be taken stern first. This method of dropping down on a tide is only employed when the tide runs very strong, and it is necessary to keep the boat under command of the rudder. It may be seen daily at Yarmouth; the sailing wherries coming in from the rivers on an ebb tide drop their anchors short, and by this means club down to their quays. Without some such method of opposing the strength of the current, they would be swept past their landing places.

Club-hauling.—"In navigation, a critical mode of tacking, resorted to only in perilous situations, when a ship has no other escape from running ashore. It consists in letting go the lee-anchor as soon as the wind is out of the sails, thereby bringing the ship's head to wind. She will then pay off, when the cable is cut and the sails are trimmed. By this process the tack is accomplished in a far shorter distance than it could otherwise be." (Brande and Cox.) In the last volume of James' Naval History (ed. 1837) will be found an account of the club-hauling of H.M.S. *Magnificent* off the coast of France between the reef of Chasseron and the Isle de Ré, during a south-westerly gale. Captain Marryat, in his "Peter Simple", mentions club-hauling, and Peter in his examination says that one of his former captains performed "the hauling business". The operation, with a sailing yacht, would consist of paying an anchor out astern and then hauling on it by a *spring,* so as to cast off the boat's head.

Clyde lug.—(*See* LUG.)

Coach.—In rowing, one who teaches a crew, or prepares them for a race. 2. The forward cabin space under the poop or quarter-deck (17th and 18th centuries.)

Coak, or **bush.**—The central piece of the sheave of a block. It is usually of gun metal and of curious form—this being to prevent its turning in the sheave. The section is in the form of an equilateral triangle, upon each of the sides of which a semicircle is described; and in the centre it is bored with a hole through which the pin runs.

Coaming.—A raised edge or planking round a hatchway or the well of a yacht. Its use is to prevent any water which may wash over the deck from getting down below, and to effect this properly it should not (except in small boats) form one continuous wall round all hatchways, but should leave the spaces between them open, so that water shipped may run off to leeward instead of being allowed to come aft.

Coast.—That part of the land which is washed by the sea. To coast is to sail along a coast, or to follow the coastline.

Coaster.—A vessel trading along the coast of a country.

Coastguard.—"A semi-naval organisation of seamen, mostly living along the shores of the United Kingdom, intended originally for the prevention of smuggling; but since the removal of prohibitive import duties, and the consequent decrease of smuggling, converted into a force for the defence of the coasts." The men were old men-of-war's men of good character, liable to service at all times. The service was under a controller-general having rank as a commodore. Its principle work today is in initiating and co-ordinating rescue services. It is now under the Department of Trade and Industry.

Coat.—A coat of tar or paint is one application of either.

Cobbing.—"A punishment sometimes inflicted at sea. It is performed by striking the offender a certain number of blows on the breech with a flat piece of wood called the cobbing-board." (Falconer.)

Coble.—An open boat varying in form according to locality. The coble of the Northumbrian coast is a boat of somewhat remarkable appearance, and equally remarkable in its suitability to the work demanded of it; it sails well, rows well and beaches well, and is the safest boat one could well find. The following is the description of it as given by Mr.

NORTHUMBRIAN COBLE

Davies in his "Boat Sailing for Amateurs": "The bows are very sharp, and very high, with a great sheer to throw off the sea, and depth to give lateral resistance. The sharp bows rapidly fall away, until all the after portion of the boat is quite flat and shallow. The keel, which commences with the bow, ends amidships, and from there to the stern are two keels, or draughts, one each side of the flat bottom. The stern is very raking, and the rudder projects a considerable distance below it, as shown in the figure. Thus the entire lateral resistance of the boat is given by the deep bow and the deep rudder. These boats are very sensitive to any touch of the helm; they will go wonderfully close to the wind, and at a perfectly marvellous speed; their sharp, flaring bows throw off any reasonable sea, and altogether they are admirably suited for the work which they have to undergo. Then, when they have to be beached, their bows are turned to the sea, the rudder is unshipped, and the boat backed ashore, where she sits high and dry, as far as her stern is concerned." These boats are usually rigged with a standing or dipping lug. Cobles are also employed on the rivers and lakes of Wales and the borders.

Cock.—In ancient days the general name for a *yawl*.

Cock-a-bill or *a'cock-bill.*—An expression signifying that an anchor hangs over a vessel's sides with its flukes extended. (*See* ANCHOR.) To cockbill a yard is to top up one yardarm so that it is higher than the other.

Cock-boat.—An old name for a small boat only used on rivers or smooth waters.

Cock-pit.—1. In old battle ships, the cockpit was the after portion of the lowest deck, and in frigates was assigned to the use of the midshipmen. 2. In yachts it is the lower part of the well. 3. In sailing boats, the open space in the deck. In the two latter cases, however, the word *well* is more frequently used.

Cockle shell.—A term used to describe a small or very light boat, which is supposed to be no safer on the waters than a cockle shell.

Code signals.—A collection of signs or symbols reduced to an orderly arrangement and made use of by vessels at sea or from stations ashore. There has been since 1857 an international nautical code which made general use of three methods,—viz., flags, long distance signals, and the semaphore, (the present International Code employs flags and morse symbols); and besides this code there are various others less commonly employed, and others, again, used by individuals or by shipping companies, called private codes. For a description of the signals employed in the International Code see under SIGNALS.

Cofferdam.—Space between two bulkheads or walls, that receives and retains any liquid that has leaked through one wall.

Cog.—Prevalent type of vessel between 1200 and 1400 A.D. It had a straight stem, stern rudder, and a single mast and square sail.

Coil.—1. (In commerce.)—A coil of rope is a certain quantity (113 fathoms). 2. (On shipboard.)—A coil is a heap of

Cog, *c.* 1350

rope coiled up. 3. To coil rope is to lay it, or make it up, in a series of coils or rings; and this, with ordinary rope, is done in the direction of the hands of the clock. The hollow space in the middle is called the *tier*. One circle is a *fake*.

Flemish coil.—Successive ovals, or circles, of rope flat on deck, each coil touching the previous coil, the end being in the centre.

Collapsible boat.—A boat which for convenience of taking it on board a small vessel is capable of being folded up into a small space. Several forms of these boats have been invented from time to time, but none have come into general use. The Berthon is, perhaps, most used. Mr. Davies, in his "Boat Sailing for Amateurs", describes one or two of these.

Collar Knot.—(*See* KNOTS.)

Collier.—A vessel employed in the coal trade.

Collision.—When two vessels collide they are said to be *in collision*; and the same term is employed in the past sense, as "they were in collision". The Board of Trade issue instructions for the Prevention of Collisions at Sea; and these constitute that which is popularly called the *Rule of the Road* (*which see*).

Colours.—The ship's national ensign.

Column.—A line of two or more ships sailing in formation. 2. A derrick post.

Comb, or comb-cleat.—A small wooden board through which ropes are passed to be led fair. (*See* CLEAT.)

Come.—A word used at sea under various circumstances, as "The anchor *comes home*", i.e., it drags. A ship is said to *come to* when she luffs right up into the wind or stops in a certain spot. So also, when she *comes round* in tacking, she is said to have *come about*. And the order in sailing to *come no nearer* will mean that she is not to be brought too close to the wind, to impress which meaning upon the mind of the beginner the French equivalent, "*Pas au vent*", is, perhaps, more explicit. To *come up* the fall (rope) of a tackle, is to slacken the rope. To *come up the capstan* is to let it go a contrary way to that in hauling up, and is, therefore, to slacken it. To come up with another vessel, or some landmark, is to overtake or pass it.

Commander.—In the Royal Navy an officer holding a position between the captain and the lieutenant.

Commodore.—The senior captain of a squadron when there is no admiral present. The senior master of a shipping line and the elected head of a yachting club are usually called, by compliment, the commodore of that line or club.

Common bend.—(*See* KNOT.)

Companion.—Properly the *covering* over a ladder or staircase in a ship; but the ladder itself is popularly called the companion.

Compass.—An instrument which, by means of a magnetised bar, indicates the magnetic meridian. The disc or face of the mariner's compass consists of a circular card, sometimes transparent, the circumference of which is divided into 32 parts, called *points*. These points may be again divided into two, each division being a *half-*

point, and these again into *quarter-points.* Thus there are 32 points in the compass, and between each are half and quarter points. Each point is named and marked on the card with the initial letters of its name, as N. for North, N. by E. for North by East, N.N.E. for North North-East, N.E. for North-East, and so on. The *cardinal points* are North, South, East, and West: these cut the card into four quarters, and each quarter is divided into 8 points, the whole 32 being as follow:—

North	opposite to		South
North by East	,,	,,	South by West
North North-east	,,	,,	South South-west
North-east by North	,,	,,	South-west by South
North-East	,,	,,	South-west
North-east by East	,,	,,	South-west by West
East North-east	,,	,,	West South-west
East by North	,,	,,	West by South
East	,,	,,	West
East by South	,,	,,	West by North
East South-east	,,	,,	West North-west
South-east by East	,,	,,	North-west by West
South-east	,,	,,	North-west
South-east by South	,,	,,	North-west by North
South South-east	,,	,,	North North-west
South by East	,,	,,	North by West
South	,,	,,	North

Repeating these points, with their opposite equivalents, in the order above given, is called *boxing the compass,* and is required in some examinations. Then, however, the *half-points* are often asked, rendering the repetition somewhat more tedious. But the student will be astonished to find how quickly he will master this task when once taken in hand. The manner of pronouncing the names of the points is as follows:—

Nor'east (or west)	...	Sow-west (or east)
Nor' Nor'-east (or west)	...	Sow Sow-west (or east)
Nor'-east b' east (or west)	...	Sow-west b' west (or east)

In boxing the compass with the half-points:—

North ½ East	is opposite	South ½ West
North by East ½ East	,, ,,	South by West ½ West
West ½ North	,, ,,	East ½ South
North-west ½ North	,, ,,	South-east ½ South

and so on from North to East and thence to South.

Compass card.—A ship's compass card is usually graduated in degrees as well as in points. The graduations, if *quadrantal,* begin at north and are numbered up to 90° east and west, and at south numbering up to 90° east and west; or else they may begin at north and increase in a clockwise direction to 359°. For instance, N.E. becomes N.45°E., or 045°; and N.W. is N.45°W. or 315°.

It has been stated that the dial of the compass is a card upon which the points are marked. The north point is always to be distinguished at a glance by a large arrow head. This card is fixed to an iron bar or needle laid exactly in the line marking north and south, one end of it having been previously magnetized. It is then either balanced on a pin or floated in spirit in a semi-globular basin; this basin, by an arrangement of two rings, called *gimbals,* set at right angles, and one working within the other—being so contrived that whatever position the ship may assume it always keeps the horizontal. But it does not revolve: the card revolves, but the case, though always *horizontal,* retains the same position with respect to the keel line of the vessel. Upon the inside of the basin, and in a line with the keel (or, in other words, directly in a line with the head and stern of the vessel), is made a distinct line or mark, called the *lubber's line (see* diagram under LUBBER): and

it is by this mark that the vessel is steered. For if the ship be moving due north the lubber's line will exactly meet the arrow head on the dial of the compass. But if her head be turned easterly, the lubber's line will travel round the dial until it meets the letter E. So also, if she be turned south-east, the lubber's line will reach the S.E., and finally, if she be steered due south, the lubber's line will have moved half round the compass, stopping at the S. or southern point on the disc. The lubber's line represents, therefore, the ship's head; and at whatever point

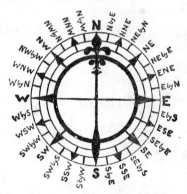

MARINER'S COMPASS

it stops on the compass card, in that direction will the ship be moving.

It is necessary to state, however, though without entering into any discussion on the theory of magnetic attraction, that the needle does not actually point due north. Not only may it be attracted by any mass of iron brought close to it, but in different latitudes its direction varies. In iron ships there is always a counter attraction to be overcome, the amount of which varies according to their *position* (N. and S. and E. and W.) when building, and indeed in every ship the compass has always to be tested and corrected before starting on a voyage. This difference of a ship's compass from the true magnetic meridian is called the *deviation of the compass,* and the methods of dealing with this form almost a science in itself. Those who would know more of the subject may be referred to J. Klinkert's "Compass-

Wise", or to C. A. Lund's "Compasses in Small Craft". The case in which a deck compass is set, with its box and pedestal, constitute that which is known as a *binnacle*. A binnacle does not affect the compass because the same attraction is exerted all round, and, moreover, because it is surrounded by bars of iron which counteract each other's influence; but small compasses, as used in boats or yachts, are very liable to be deviated by any iron or steel which may be brought too near them, and they should be kept as free as possible from all such influences.

It may be well, in conclusion, to remind the novice that whenever a compass is placed on board a boat, its lubber's line, or whatever may take the place of a lubber's line (such as the handle of the compass), should be set exactly fore-and-aft, that is in the same line as the keel.

A small compass hanging or fixed to the ceiling of a cabin on shipboard is called a *tell-tale*. By it the captain can see the course of the ship without going on deck.

Gyro compass.—Large modern ships carry a *gyro compass* in addition to a magnetic one. The *gyro compass* consists fundamentally of a rapidly rotating wheel connected to a compass card, and derives its directive power from the fact that a rapidly revolving wheel, free to move in any direction, can be induced to align its axis with the earth's axis. Gyro compasses therefore point to the true, or geographical north. *Repeater compasses* can be driven by the *master gyro* and placed at any convenient position for steering, etc.

Composite.—A system of building large ships with an iron framing and wood skin. It was brought in soon after the construction of ships with iron was begun, and admitted of great strength being attained, and the possibility of copper sheathing, which on an iron hull is impossible. It was hoped by this means to obtain a vessel with the strength of an iron ship and the freedom from fouling of a wooden ship; but experience has shown that the wasting of the iron from the effects of galvanic action between the copper and the iron fastenings renders the system almost impracticable. Large yachts are still, however, built in this manner.

Con, conning (sometimes pronounced "cun").—To direct a steersman. A person who directs the helmsman of a ship how to keep her head is said to be *conning* the ship. Thus on men-of-war we find a *conning tower,* which is a sort of elevated armoured deck house, containing the compass, and from which a good look-out may be obtained, or the tower on the upper deck of a submarine from which she is conned when on the surface.

Conservators of the Thames.—"A body of modern creation representing the Imperial Government, the City of London, and the commercial interests of the river, and exercising the general powers of harbour and conservancy board over the lower river and estuary, as well as those of conservancy on the upper river as far as Cricklade."

Contraband.—Prohibited, illegal. Applied to goods forbidden to be imported or exported.

C

Convoy.—A number of merchant ships in company and under the orders of a senior officer.

Copper.—This is the best material wherewith to preserve the bottom of a boat from the attacks of barnacles, etc., as well as from the action of the water; and a boat covered or "sheathed" with it is called *copper bottomed*. It is customary in the case of yachts to wait, before doing this, until the vessel is a year or two old, as copper is found to rot the skin of a new boat, besides which the timber has a tendency for the first few months to swell or "grow", while the copper remains the same. The principal action of the water being at the water line, some boats are coppered only round that part, at a considerable saving of expense. Intending purchasers of boats should remember this, and make careful examination before buying, for it is occasionally the practice of dishonest people to describe a boat thus sheathed as *copper bottomed*. As a substitute for copper, Muntz metal (*which see*) answers well, and there are various paints sold which also profess to preserve ship's bottoms. Nothing, however, is so useful for wooden vessels as copper.

Coracle.—A small boat originally used in fresh water fishing. Its origin dates back probably to pre-historic times. In Wales and the West of England it is still used, being made of wicker, covered with leather, and carried by the fishermen upon their backs.

Corinthian.—This word has come to mean *amateur*. The Corinthian Yacht Club was originally founded as a down-river branch of the London Rowing Club; its object being the same as that of other clubs, viz., the encouragement of yacht and boat sailing by amateurs. Its headquarters were at Erith, but it has also a very flourishing branch at Burnham-on-Crouch and is known as the *Royal* Corinthian Yacht Club.

WELSH CORACLE

Cordage.—Collective name for all fibre ropes and lines.

Cork jacket.—A waistcoat or jacket made of a number of corks or pieces of cork, completely encircling the body, as a preservation against drowning. No boat should be without some sort of life preserving belt. (*See* LIFE BELT.)

Corposant.—(*See* CASTOR AND POLLUX.)

Corsair.—A name given in certain parts of Europe to a pirate, or his vessel. Corsairs, for centuries the dread of the Mediterranean coast, have existed there almost to the present century, as the attack upon the racing yacht *Ailsa,* on her homeward passage from the south of France in 1895, may serve to show.

Corvette.—One of the smaller vessels of war: the name is a relic of the days of wooden ships, when a corvette was a flush-decked vessel carrying between 18 and 30 guns.

Counter.—An extension of a vessel's body beyond her stern-post, or, in other words, that part of her which projects beyond the stern-post. In many instances the counter is purely ornamental, having no actual use, while some go so far as to say that it is materially detrimental to buoyancy. In some vessels, however, it becomes almost a necessity, as, for instance, in cutters; for without it there would be no means of getting at the reef pendant, while it is also useful in a yawl for manipulating the mizzen.

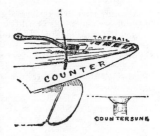

Counter-stay.—One or more small timbers or stays projecting aft of the stern-post of a vessel to take the weight of the counter. They are, of course, within the counter and unseen.

Countersunk.—Bolt heads are often countersunk in the same way as the head of an ordinary screw (*see* fig.) so that they may not protrude beyond the surfaces they hold down. The shackle pins of anchor cables are also countersunk. (*See* CABLE.)

Course.—The course of a vessel at sea has been thus described: "The angle which the ship's track makes with all the meridians between the place left and the place arrived at." In a more homely meaning it is the direction in which a ship travels; thus her course is N.E. when she is moving in a north-easterly direction.

The *courses,* in a square rigged vessel, are those square sails which hang from the lower masts. Thus in a full rigged ship the main, fore, and mizzen sails will be the courses; the bark is without the mizzen course; the barkentine has but the fore course.

COURSES

Cove.—A small creek, inlet, or bay.

Covering board.—The outer deck plank which covers the timber heads.

Cowl.—A metal fitting for collecting and directing an air-stream to a particular place.

Coxswain (pronounced "cox'un").—The steersman of a boat. In rowing language he is usually spoken of as the "cox". His position is one of responsibility, for during his office he has command of the boat; and that his orders should be implicitly obeyed stands to reason, for the backs of all the rowers are turned in the direction in which they are moving. It is not safe, therefore, except on open and uncrowded waters, to put the tiller or rudder lines into the hands of any but an experienced person, and once there it is equally unsafe and foolish for any among the crew to interfere with him. The neglect of these simple though essential precautions has led to the unnecessary loss of more than one life.

Crab.—1. A small capstan. It consists often of little more than a pillar with two or three small whelps (upright pieces) about it to prevent the rope from slipping. The small windlasses by which bathing machines are drawn up on a beach are sometimes called crabs. Falconer describes a crab as a sort of capstan, worked by bars like a large capstan, but with the bars passing through the head instead of being merely inserted as with the larger machines. 2. Another engine called a crab is a lever of wood, having claws at the working end, and used in the launching of vessels.

CROMER CRAB-BOAT

Crab-boat.—1. A boat used in crab fishing. 2. An open sailing boat at one time common on the coast of Norfolk—hence called the *Cromer crab-boat.* A description of it is given by Mr. Christopher Davies in his "Boat Sailing for Amateurs".

To *catch a crab.*—An accident which may occur in rowing. It consists in failing to catch the water with the oar, and, by the violence of the effort, falling backwards. The "art" is naturally more practised by beginners, but is not confined to them, for the catching of a crab has lost many a trained crew a race.

CATCHING A CRAB

Crackerhash, Crackerjack.—A savoury dish made from ship's biscuits.

Crack on.—A man who causes a ship to carry more sail than conditions warrant is said to crack on (or carry on). The term may also be applied to the ship.

Cradle.—1. Blocks or beams of wood placed so that a boat may stand on shore. 2. A frame used in the launching of a vessel for sending her gently down into the water.

Craft.—A general term applied by sea-faring men to any collection of small decked vessels. Though the term is, properly speaking, one of multitude, it is often used in the singular number. Thus "river craft" means those vessels, generally, which navigate a river; while the phrase "a nice little craft" is spoken in admiration of a single boat.

Crank, or **cranky.**—A vessel is said to be crank when she fails in the quality called *stiffness* (*which see*), or, in other words, when she careens over to a large extent in a light breeze, and therefore, cannot carry much sail; or when, from want of ballast, she is in danger of overturning.

Cranse-iron.—A cap or ring at the end of a bowsprit, usually made with several eyes round it. The ring prevents the spar from splitting and the eyes take the blocks through which pass the *bob-stay* and *topmast-forestay* and *bowsprit-shrouds.*(*See* under BOWSPRIT.)

Crawl.—A place in which to confine fish, etc. (French, *bordigue.*)

Creasote, or **kreasote.**—A heavy oil, apparently closely related to carbolic acid; it possesses peculiar antiseptic and preservative qualities, and is made use of in various ways. Wood steeped in it is preserved both by the exclusion of air and by the destruction of organic impurities. It is a poison when undiluted, but when largely diluted it is occasionally used in medicine.

Creek.—An inlet on the coast or in a river up which the tide runs. In some cases, estuaries or small rivers, when resorted to as havens by small craft, are called creeks.

Creel.—(*See* KREEL.)

Creeper.—A term sometimes given to a sort of grapnel (*which see*).

Crew.—The crew of a vessel consists of all those who are on board, except the master, for the purpose of navigating her. (*See* also ALL-TOLD.)

CLEW CRINGLE

REEF CRINGLE AND PENDANT

CRINGLES

Crimp.—One of those agents who, before the establishment of Sailors' Homes, used to take seamen in, board them, find them ships, and finally rob them of their all.

Cringles.—Loops or eyes, formed in the bolt ropes of sails. Through them ropes are passed so as to gather up the margins of the sail; and to them *pendants* are hung for tying down the sail in reefing. In fore-and-aft rigged craft they are found in the lower portion of the leech of a main or mizzen sail for passing short lanyards in reefing, and are then called *reef cringles.* If the ropes are left permanently in these cringles, as is sometimes the case, they are called *reef pendants*; while ropes hanging from the head of a sail (more particularly of a square sail) are called *earings.* Iron cringles are sometimes called *hanks.*

Cross-jack *yard* (pronounced "crojek" or "crotched").—In full rigged ships, the lowest yard on the mizzen mast. (*See* under JACK and YARD.)

Cross-jack sail.—The sail bent (attached) to the cross-jack; being of little service it is not much used.

Cross-pawls (in shipbuilding).—Pieces of timber which keep the sides of a vessel together whilst in her frames.

Cross-piece.—A piece of wood or iron crossing another. Thus the piece which crosses the bitts of a bowsprit is called the crosspiece or *crossbitt.* (*See* BOWSPRIT.)

Cross seas.—This term is applied when the surface waves are moving in a direction different to the ground swell; or, as happens during a revolving storm, when the surface waves are travelling in two or more directions simultaneously.

Cross staff.—A navigating instrument, preceding the sextant, for ascertaining the altitude of a celestial body. It consisted of a graduated staff upon which a crosspiece could be moved. The observer adjusted the crosspiece so that the upper end was in line with the celestial body and the lower end with the horizon.

Crossing the line.—Crossing the Equator.

Cross-trees.—The arms extending, near the head of a mast, at right angles to the length of the vessel, and to the extremities of which the topmast-shrouds are stretched for the purpose of giving support to the topmast. Cross-trees may be of iron or wood, and in one piece or two. Many topsail-barges have them folding upwards, for convenience in lowering the mast for up-river work. They are then sometimes called *jack* cross-trees. For the manner of fixing cross-trees to the mast *see* under MAST and TRESTLE TREES.

Crotches (in shipbuilding).—1. Timbers placed upon the keel in the forward and after parts of a vessel, where her form grows narrower. 2. Supports for a boom. (*See* CRUTCH.)

Crow.—An iron lever.

Crowfoot.—A radiation of many small ropes from one, used in securing awnings, etc. (*see* fig.).

Crow's nest.—A lookout position near the masthead protected from the weather.

Crowd.—To set an extraordinary force of sail is said to be *crowding on sail.* A colloquial substitute for the word "crew".

Crown.—Of an anchor. (*See* ANCHOR.)

Cruise.—A voyage within moderate limits, either of pleasure, as in a yacht, or of business, as with a fleet, when it goes out for some special purpose.

CROWFOOT

Cruiser.—A warship of medium power, often faster but less heavily armed and armoured than a battleship. 2. A boat which is intended for cruising; with yachts the word is used in contradistinction to racers.

Crutch.—A trestle supporting the boom of a fore-and-aft sail when at rest (*see* fig.). Its use is to take the weight of the boom off the halyards. Its place is sometimes taken by a prop called the *mitchboard* (*which see*). Metal rowlocks are occasionally called *crutches*.

Cuddy.—1. On shipboard, a small cabin; sometimes the cook-house on deck. 2. In a half-decked boat the space enclosed is occasionally called the cuddy.

Cunningham's topsails.—A modified form of *double topsails*, employed in square rigged ships since their introduction by Cunningham, the topsail rolling up when the yard was rotated. (*See* DOUBLE TOPSAILS.)

Curragh.—A boat with a wooden frame covered with hide or canvas.

Currents.—Running movements in the waters, often partially independent of the tides. There are currents along every coast and in every river. Those of his own locality should be, to some extent, known by anyone who would become a good sailsman.

Customs regulations.—(*See* CLEARING.)

Cut.—To *cut a sail.*—To unfurl and let it fall down.

To *cut a feather.*—To make the foam fly as when, with the speed of the ship, it curls itself into something like the form of a feather.

Cutting down line.—"A curve line used by shipwrights in the delineation of ships; it determines the thickness of all the floor-timbers, and likewise the height of the deadwood afore and abaft. It is limited in the middle of the ship by the thickness of the floor timber, and abaft by the breadth of the kelson; and must be carried up so high upon the stern as to leave sufficient substance for the breeches of the rising timbers." (Falconer's Dictionary.)

Cut and run.—To cut a hemp anchor cable and sail from an anchorage as quickly as possible.

Cutlass.—A short sword used by men-of-war's men.

Cutter.—"Sooner or later," says Mr. Christopher Davies, in his work on "Boat Sailing for Amateurs", "everyone in whom the love of sailing remains, will, if his means and opportunities permit, go in for cutter-sailing on the deep blue sea. The cutter is the national rig, and it

CRUTCH

MITCH BOARD

CRUTCHES

CUTTER

SLOOP

FIG. 1

is in an all-round way the best, as it is certainly the prettiest." 1. The cutter has but one mast (the main), and under ordinary circumstances spreads but four sails, main and top-sails, foresail and jib; and occasionally she adds another, the jib topsail. But when racing her spread of canvas is much increased; an enormous balloon jib

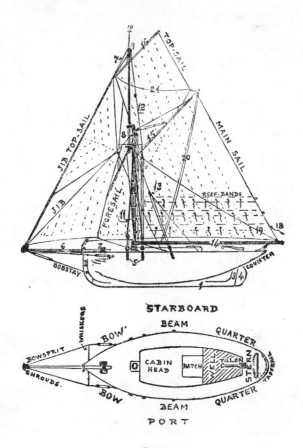

Fig. 2

takes the place of the everyday headsails for *reaching,* while for running she may carry no less than four sails on her mast alone; though it must be noted that this full complement of *press-canvas,* as it is called, is very seldom seen. (*See* diagram under BALLOON CANVAS.) The cutter differs from the sloop in the rigging of the bowsprit and fore-stays. In the cutter the fore-stay comes down to the stem-head of the vessel, and the bowsprit is *reeving* (moveable). In the sloop the fore-stay runs to the end of the bowsprit, which is *fixed*: the fore-stay then changes its name, and becomes known as the *jib-stay* (*see* fig. 1, p. 62). This difference is further commented upon under the heading SLOOP. The principal parts of a cutter-yacht are as follow (fig. 2): (1.) Keel. (2.) Stem-post. (3.) Stern-post. (4.) Rudder. (5.) Channels. (6.) Bowsprit. (7.) Bowsprit bitts. (8.) Masthead with cap and yoke, *trestle-tree,* and *cross-tree.* (9.) Topmast hounds. (10.) Truck. (11.) Shrouds. (12.) Topmast shrouds, terminating in the legs. (13.) Backstays. (14.) Boom. (15.) Gaff, the upper end of which is the *peak.* (16.) Topsail yard. (17.) Topmast fore-stay. On the main sail are the *reef bands,* upon which hang the *reef points,* and at their extremities the *reef cringles,* through which *pendants* are rove as at 18. (19.) Topping lift. (20.) Peak lines or flag halyards. (21.) Topsail clew line.

2. *Cutter.*—A row boat attached to a man-of-war.

3. *Cutter* (in rowing matches).—A boat which follows the competitors. They often follow important sculling matches, carrying the trainers or coaches of the competitors, each of whom is allowed, under certain restrictions, to direct the progress of his man. In such a case the boat used as cutter is usually an eight-oar.

Cutter stay fashion.—The method of turning in a *deadeye* with the end of the shroud down. (*See* diagram under DEADEYES.)

Cutting his painter.—Making off hurriedly—a slang term.

Cut-water.—That portion of the stem of a vessel which cleaves the water as she moves. (*See* fig. under ENTRANCE.)

D

Dabchick.—A sporting term for a modern racing sail-boat of the smallest class.

Dandy.—A small mizzen sail is often thus called: it is usually triangular (*see* fig.). A boat setting this or any such small mizzen is sometimes called "dandy-rigged".

Dandyfunk.—A dish resembling cake, and made from ship's biscuits which have been pounded into fragments.

Davit.—A light crane on a ship's sides for lowering and lifting boats. The projecting beam over which the anchor is hoisted is also sometimes called a *davit*. (*See* fig.; also under FISH.)

DANDY

Davy Jones.—The spirit of the sea. Said to derive from "Duffy", a negro term for "ghost", and "Jonah": or, a pirate of that name who made his prisoners walk the plank.

Davy Jones' locker.—The bottom of the sea, because that is the receptacle of all things thrown overboard. And those who have been buried at sea are said to have gone to Davy Jones' locker.

Day mark.—A beacon visible only in daylight.

Day's Work.—The calculation of a ship's position and of her progress during 24 hours.

Dead.—A term variously used at sea and in shipbuilding. Thus in sailing:

Dead beat.—Said of a sailing vessel's required course when it lies directly to windward.

Dead calm.—A calm in which the surface of the sea is perfectly smooth.

Dead beat compass.—A magnetic compass which, when disturbed, returns to the magnetic meridian without much oscillation.

Dead head.—Any large block used as an anchor buoy.

Dead horse.—The completion of labour which had been paid

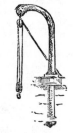

DAVIT

EAST INDIAMEN IN A DEAD CALM, 1826

for in advance used sometimes to be hailed by seamen, by dragging a dead horse, or something made to resemble it, round the ship and then swinging it out on the yard arm.

Dead lights.—Plates fitted over portholes to protect them or to prevent lights inside the ship showing outboard.

Dead peg.—A dead peg to windward is making progress dead in the teeth of the wind. (*See* BEAT.)

Dead reckoning.—The reckoning of a vessel's situation based on the course steered and the distance run; but without minute observation as with the sextant.

Dead water.—The water which closes in astern of a ship as she moves forward.

Dead wind.—A wind directly opposed to the course of a ship, which may be spoken of as sailing *dead against* the wind, or making a *dead peg* to windward.

Dead slow.—The slowest speed which will give steerage way.

To *deaden way.*—To check a ship's progress.

In shipbuilding:

Dead flat, otherwise called the *mid-ship bend.*—It is the lowest member of the largest timber (rib) in a vessel (each rib being composed of several pieces).

Dead rising, or *rising line of floor.*—The line along the bottom of the interior of a vessel where the *floor-timbers* join the lower futtocks.

Dead woods.—Strong wooden members connecting the foot of the head post and that of the stern post with the keel, and also taking the ends of the lower strakes of a vessel. That one holding the head post is called the *fore deadwood,* that one on the stern post the *after deadwood.* (*See* diagram under FRAME.)

Dead weight.—The total weight, in tons, of the cargo, stores and fuel carried by a vessel at her maximum permitted draught.

Dead works.—A name at one time given to that part of a vessel which is above the water when she is laden. The name is now called the *freeboard.*

In the rigging of a ship:

Deadeyes.—Stout discs of wood through which holes (usually three in number) are pierced for the reception of thin ropes called *lanyards*: they are employed as blocks connecting the shrouds with the channel plates. The holes are the eyes, and because they are not fitted with pulleys they are called "dead", hence: "*deadeye*". Deadeyes are of various shapes, though the disc form is far the most usual. The *heart* has but one eye, the lower edge of which is serrated or "scored", so as to grip the lanyard. The *collar-heart* is open at the lower ends (*see* fig. p. 72).

Dead-ropes.—Those ropes which do not run in any blocks.

Decca Navigator.—A type of ship-borne radio aid which fixes the ship's position if within about 300 miles distance from the shore transmitters.

Deck.—Generally speaking the covering of the interior of a ship, either carried completely over her or only over a portion. Large ships and steam vessels may have various decks, as in the following list:—

Main deck.—The principal and often the only deck in a vessel.

Anchor deck.—A small elevation in the bows.

Awning deck.—One completely covering over a main deck.

Bridge deck or *bridge house.*—A deck amidships upon which the bridge is placed.

Fore-castle deck.—One covering a deck fore-castle.

Hurricane deck.—An upper-deck extending across a vessel amidships, usually for the officers in command.

Lower deck.—One below the main deck.

Monkey deck.—Another name for the anchor deck.

Orlop deck.—The lowest in the ship. In old battle ships this deck was below the water line; the cock-pit and certain of the store rooms were upon it.

Poop deck.—One covering the after part of a vessel and forming a poop.

Promenade deck (on passenger ships).—A deck covering the saloon, usually reserved to the use of first-class passengers.

Quarter deck.—That part of the decking which covers the quarters; or it may be a separate deck raised over that portion, when it is called a *raised quarter deck.*

Shade deck.—Much like an awning deck, but less enclosed.

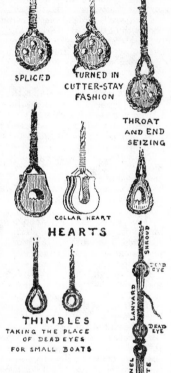

SPLICED　TURNED IN CUTTER-STAY FASHION

THROAT AND END SEIZING

COLLAR HEART

HEARTS

THIMBLES
TAKING THE PLACE OF DEAD EYES FOR SMALL BOATS

VARIOUS DEADEYES

Spar deck.—A deck above the main deck.

Top-gallant-forecastle deck.—A large anchor deck.

Well deck.—That part of the main deck which constitutes the well.

Working deck.—A spar deck.

The different types of vessels classed in Lloyd's register are decked as follows (*see* fig. p. 73).

1. *Flush deck,* that is having nothing raised above the deck beyond the head of the engine and boiler casings. 2. Vessel having *monkey forecastle, bridge house* and *hood* for the protection of steering gear. 3. Vessel having *top-gallant-forecastle,* bridge house, and *poop.* 4. Vessel having top-gallant-fore-castle, bridge house, and short raised *quarter-deck.* 5. *Well-decked vessel,* having top-gallant-forecastle, with a long poop and bridge-house combined. 6. Also known as *well decked vessel,* having top-gallant-fore-castle, with a long raised quarter-deck and bridge-house combined. 7. *Shade decked vessel,* having continuous up-

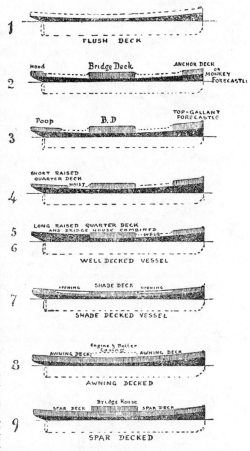

per deck of light construction with openings in the sides. 8. *Awning decked vessel,* with continuous upper deck of light construction, and the sides completely enclosed above the main deck. 9. *Spar-decked vessel,* with the scantlings above the main deck heavier than that in the awning decked vessel, but not so heavy as in a "three decked vessel".

Deck head.—The underside of a deck.

Deep.—A gulf or channel in the sea, as the "Barrow Deep" in the estuary of the Thames.

Deep.—A leadsman's call before naming a sounding in fathoms that are not marked on a leadline, *e.g.,* "Deep nine." (*See* LEAD.)

Degaussing.—Neutralising a ship's magnetic effect to protect her from magnetic mines.

Demurrage.—Money forfeited by the charterer for delaying a vessel beyond the time specified.

Departure.—The distance made good due east or west when sailing on any course.

Depth.—*Depth measure.*—In ships this is taken inside, from the underside of the beams to the kelson; in open boats it is taken outside, from the top of the gunwale to the underside of the true keel.

Depth of a flag.—The perpendicular height, the length being called *the fly.*

Depth of a sail.—The longest cloth (or strip of canvas.)

Derelict.—Forsaken. The term applies to ships from which the crews have been withdrawn and in which no domestic animal is left. Sometimes also it means the ebb-dry foreshore.

Derrick.—Generally speaking, a crane consisting mainly of one large beam, the foot of which rests either upon the ground or on deck, or on a *table* at the base of a mast. (*See also* FLOATING DERRICK.)

Destroyer.—Originally, Torpedoboat Destroyer, it took over the function of the torpedoboat. A fast, unarmoured vessel, armed with guns, torpedoes and depth-charges.

Deviation of the compass.—The difference in direction of a ship's compass from the true magnetic meridian, caused by the near presence of iron. (*See* COMPASS.)

Devil.—A word with various meanings.

Devil bolts.—A name given to bolts with false clenches, or to those which may be otherwise faulty, in the building of a vessel by contract.

Devil's claw.—A strong split hook grasping the link of a chain, and sometimes used on cranes for gripping a weight.

Devilfish.—The fearful octopus "Lophius Piscatorius". (*See* Victor Hugo's "Travailleurs de la Mer".)

Devil seam.—That seam in a vessel which is about on the water line.

Devil's smiles.—Gleams of sunshine in stormy weather, which come, alas, only to deceive.

Devil's table cloth.—A name for the fleecy white clouds often seen in windy weather.

The devil to pay.—An expression, referring to the *devil seam,* implying an unpleasant situation, or that something will have to be paid without the wherewithal to do so. The full term (as employed by the ancients) is more self-explanatory, *The devil to pay and no tar, or pitch, hot*: a difficult job to be done and no preparation made. (*See* PAY.)

Dghaisa, or **Dysa.**—A Maltese boat with tall stem and stern posts, and pushed by oars.

Dhobi.—(Hindustani)—The customary name for clothes which are to be washed.

Dhow.—The general name for an Arab vessel rigged with a lateen sail or sails, indigenous to the Persian Gulf, Red Sea and Indian Ocean. The *baghla,* two masted, has a high poop like a 17th century European ship; The *boom,* also two masted, is double-ended with a long straight bow and bowsprit. The master of a dhow is called a *nakhoda.*

Diagonal build.—A method of boat building in which the planks run diagonally across the heads. (*See* BUILD.)

Dinghy.—A small open boat usually attached to a yacht, and useful for all general purposes. Of late years, some dinghies, of more than ordinary size, have been fitted with engines. A dinghy, though of course a necessity to a yacht, is often somewhat of a burthen on a cruise, in consequence of which several inventions have from time to time been brought in for rendering it collapsible. Many are now inflatable. The dinghy is by some people called the *"punt".*

BAGHLAS, 1928

Dip.—To dip is to lower and then raise again. Thus to dip a flag is a salute, and it may be dipped a varied number of times according to the personage saluted. (*See* SALUTE, and at THE DIP.)

DINGHY

Dipping lug.—A lug sail which must be lowered and set again every time a boat carrying it changes her tack. (*See* LUG.)

Displacement.—The weight of water displaced by any vessel, and therefore the weight of the vessel herself. (*See* RATING.)

Distress.—In want of assistance. In small craft a signal of distress is made by hoisting a ball, or anything like a ball, above or below a flag, or by flying the ensign upside down. At night signal must be made by rockets, preferably red, or fires. (*See* SIGNALS.)

Ditch.—The sea. *To ditch* is to throw overboard.

Ditty box, ditty bag.—A small box or bag in which a seaman kept his personal belongings.

Dividers.—An instrument for measuring distance on a chart, consisting of two pointed legs joined by a hinge.

Divisions.—The daily morning muster and prayers of the ship's company aboard one of H.M. ships. Instituted by Admiral Kempenfelt in 1780.

Dock.—An artificially constructed basin for the reception of vessels. It may be either a wet dock, in which ships are unloaded, or a dry dock, in which they are either built or repaired.

Dockyard.—An enclosed area in which the work connected with the building or fitting out of ships is carried on.

Docking bridge.—A small athwartship bridge on the poop, to give a clear view to the officer in charge aft when docking the ship.

Doctor.—Nickname for a ship's cook.

Dodger.—A piece of canvas spread as a wind screen for a man on watch.

Dog.—*Dog-stopper.*—A stopper on a cable to enable it to be *bitted*.

Dog-house.—A short deckhouse or hatchway raised above the level of the cabin top.

Dog-watch.—The short watches, or spaces of time, into which the 24 hours of the day are divided on sailing ships. They are only of two hours' duration each, the ordinary watches being of four hours', and their use is to shift the watches each night, so that the same watch (gang of men) need not be on deck at the same hours. They are from 4 to 6 p.m. and from 6 to 8 a.m. (*See* WATCHES.)

Dog vane.—A small strip of bunting put in the rigging to show the wind direction to the helmsman.)

Dogger (old term).—"A Dutch fishing-vessel navigated in the German Ocean; it is equipped with two masts, a main mast and a mizzen mast, and somewhat resembles a *ketch*. It is principally used for fishing on the Dogger Bank." (Falconer's Dictionary.) This vessel in the Dutch and Scandinavian languages was known as a *pink*.

Dogger-men.—Men engaged in the Dogger Bank fisheries.

Doggett's coat and badge.—A celebrated race for Thames watermen's apprentices. Its origin is thus given in Faulkner's "History of Chelsea". "Mr. Thomas Doggett, a native of Ireland, was an actor on the stage and made his first appearance at Dublin; but his efforts not meeting with sufficient encouragement, he removed to London, where he performed with great reputation, and by his talents, industry, and economy, acquired a competent fortune and quitted the stage some years before he died. In his political principles, he was, in the words of Sir Richard Steele, 'A Whig up to head and ears'; and he took every occasion of demonstrating his loyalty to the house of Hanover. One instance, among others, is well known; which is, that in the year after King George the First came to the throne, in 1715, Doggett gave a waterman's orange-coloured coat and silver badge to be rowed for; on the latter is represented the Hanoverian horse; but the newspapers of the day will have it to represent the wild unbridled horse of liberty. This contest takes place on the first day of August, being the anniversary of that King's accession to the throne, between six young watermen, who have just completed their apprenticeship; the claimants starting off on a signal being given at the time of the tide when the current is strongest against them, and rowing from the Old Swan, near London Bridge, to the White Swan at Chelsea."

Dogging.—Passing a line or smaller rope around a larger rope.

Doldrums.—The frequently windless zone along the equator which lies between the prevailing winds of north and south latitudes.

Dolphin.—An iron or wooden structure in a harbour for mooring ships. The name sometimes given to those posts, more usually called bollards, on a quay or pier to which *hawsers* or *springs* may be fastened.

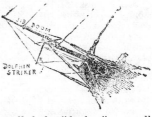

Dolphin striker.—A small spar rigged at right angles beneath the bow-sprit in large vessels for the extra staying of the jib boom.

Donkey.—*Donkey engine.*—Often called the "donkey", a small engine on ship-board (or ashore) to do light work such as hauling in the cable, working the derrick, etc.

Donkeyman.—An engineroom petty officer in a merchant ship, whose duties once included tending the donkey engine and boiler.

Donkey topsail.—The jack-top-sail (*which see*) is sometimes thus called.

Donkey's breakfast.—A seaman's straw mattress.

Dory.—A flat-bottomed, hard-chined boat, first used by Grand Banks fishermen, a number stowing neatly inside one another on board the parent vessel.

Double.—In ship-building, *doubling* is, generally, a method of restoring old clincher-built hulls. It consists in covering each *strake* (line of planking) with a new planking cut so as to be flush with the

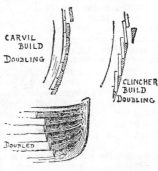

DOUBLING

lands (overlapping edges). Thus a doubled boat may appear to be carvil built, while she is really no such thing. Doubling certainly renders old boats fit for further service, but it is often practised for the sake of deceiving buyers, and must, therefore, be looked upon with caution. People who invest in old boats should survey them very carefully beforehand, and if they are found to be doubled, the reason should be known.

Doubling a cape, in sailing, is going round a cape or headland.

Double sculling (in rowing).—The propulsion of a boat by two persons, each using sculls. It is much practised on the Upper Thames; and (for pleasure purposes) mostly with a coxswain. In racing, however, a rudder is often dispensed with, and the steering performed by the bow sculler.

Double banked (also in rowing).—A system at one time in vogue for ships' long-boats of placing two rowers on each thwart, or *bank* (French *banc*—bench). (*See* BANK.)

Double topsails.—In square rigged ships—a pair of topsails, the result of dividing one big topsail into two small ones, called respectively the *upper topsail* and the *lower topsail*. This method was introduced to meet the difficulties of working so large a sail as the old style of topsail; instead of reefing a single topsail, the upper topsail was furled. It was found to answer so satisfactorily that it has since been employed in all modern ships.

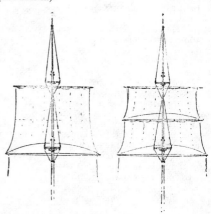

SINGLE AND DOUBLE TOPSAILS

Double up.—To duplicate mooring ropes.

Dowel.—A small cylindrical piece of wood let into a deck plank to cover the head of a fastening bolt.

Down.—To "down" a sail, mast, etc., is to lower it.

Downs, or *dunes* (from the ancient dunes).—Banks of sand thrown up by the sea and carried forward by the wind.

The Downs.—A famous shipping road along the eastern coast of Kent from Dover to the North Foreland, and where excellent anchorage is to be obtained and shelter during westerly gales. It is here that the British Fleet used to meet.

Downhaul.—A rope by which a sail or spar is hauled down or in. Thus the *jib downhaul* hauls the jib in, along the bowsprit, while the *peak downhaul* brings the peak down. The downhauls in small craft are very often, in fact most often, only halyards or sheets turned to the use. Such are the *throat, peak, jib,* and *topsail* downhauls; the throat-downhaul being merely the *tack tricing line* made fast for the time to the *boom stays* or elsewhere; the *peak lines* or *flag halyard* doing service as the peak downhaul; the *jib outhaul* as the jib downhaul; and the topsail downhaul, which is more truly a downhaul than any, serving also as a *tack line.* A large foresail (or in a square rigged vessel, a staysail) is sometimes furnished with a downhaul which leads from the tack of the sail to its head, and thence to the deck. The sail can thus be hauled down and into the vessel.

Down-helm.—To put the helm to leeward. (*See* HELM.)

Sailing *down* the wind is "running".

Dowse or **Douse.**—To lower or slacken suddenly; expressed of a sail or rope. To extinguish a light.

Drabler (only of old ships).—"An additional part of a sail, sometimes laced to the bottom of the *bonnet* on a square sail." It appears that the square sails in small craft were at one period increased in size by the addition of a lower strip of canvas called the bonnet (*which see*), and to this again was added another strip called the drabler. These strips were sometimes buttoned and sometimes laced to the sail, the latter through small loops sewed to the bonnet or drabler and called *laskets.* The drabler is now extinct, though the bonnet remains in certain fore-and-aft rigged vessels. (*See* NORFOLK WHERRY.)

Drag.—To drag is to draw a frame of iron or wood, sometimes furnished with a net, and called the *drag* or *dredge,* along the bottom of any water, either for something lost or for taking fish. (*See* DREDGE.)

To drag for an anchor is to draw the bight of a chain or rope along the bottom, each end being in a boat.

An anchor is said to *drag,* or *come home,* when it loses its hold.

Draught, or **Draft.**—The draught of a vessel, or, in other words, the depth of water she *draws,* is the vertical depth of the immersed part of her; that is, the distance of the lowest point of her keel (or any other specified point) from the surface of the water.

Draught marks.—Figures on the stem and sternpost to show the ship's present draught and for finding her trim. The lower edge of the figure marks the draught.

Draw.—*Drawing.*—The state of a sail when inflated and the lee sheets taut, and therefore carrying the vessel on her course.

Let draw.—To draw over the sheets of foresail or jib when coming about.

To *draw upon* any object or moving vessel is to gain upon it.

A draw.—A short rope for drawing down part of a sail, as the tack of a lug sail.

Dredge (often pronounced "drudge").—A *dredge* or *dredger* is a machine for clearing or deepening rivers, canals, etc. There are also *dredges,* sometimes called *drags,* drawn along the bottom by boats for the purpose either of disturbing the mud or of fetching up any object, such as oyster dredges.

Dredgerman (drudgerman).—One who works a dredge.

Dress (a ship).—To deck her out with colours (flags).

Drift.—To drift is to be carried with a stream or current, and with a vessel it implies that she is not under control.

Drifter.—A fishing vessel which streams very long buoyed nets.

Drive.—To drive or to be driven is (of a ship) to drift; it is thus described by Falconer:—"To carry at random along the surface of the water as impelled by a storm or impetuous current. Driving is generally expressed of a ship, when accidentally broke loose from her anchors or moorings."

Driver, or **spanker.**—The *fore-and-aft* or *gaff sail* on the mizzen mast of a ship or bark.

Drogue.—(*See* SEA ANCHOR.)

Drop.—*To drop.* This term is often used with reference to moving a vessel a short distance, or to letting her drift with the tide. Thus she may *drop up* or *drop down,* according to the direction in which she is carried.

Drop anchor.—To let go the anchor.

Drop astern.—To go, to remain, or to be left astern of a vessel.

Drop keel.—Another name for the centre-board (*which see*).

Drop pawl.—A pawl which drops upon each tooth of a rack wheel. (*See* PAWL.)

The *drop of a sail.*—The depth of a sail, expressed more generally of a square sail, as "the main-sail drops 30 ft".

Drowned.—The method most recently devised for restoring the apparently drowned is the *Mouth to Mouth method. Immediately* (1) clear the patient's mouth, take a deep breath, and blow into his mouth. Repeat half a dozen times. (2) Apply *cardiac massage.* Lift the patient's legs to run blood back to his heart. Strike the breastbone sharply with the fist. Press the lower half of the breastbone (not the ribs), fairly forcibly about once every second. After 15 seconds return to mouth respiration and alternate these actions.

Dub (in shipbuilding).—To work with the adze on a spar and the like.

Duck.—1. To dive, dip, or lower.

2. *Duck.*—Fine canvas used for the sails of light boats, and also for the trousers of seamen.

Ducking at the yard arm.—An old punishment (now extinct), consisting of swinging a man up to the yard arm and then dropping him into the water.

Dumb barge.—A barge or lighter which has no means of propulsion.

Dunnage (at sea).—"The name applied to loose wood or rubbish placed at the bottom of the hold to raise the cargo either for purposes of ballast, or to keep it dry, or to prevent it shifting."

Dutchman.—A name given to any Dutch craft, of which there are many classes; but the one or two-masted vessels, with overhanging bows and very curved sheers, common on the east coast, are often classed as Dutchmen.

Dutchman's log.—A chip of wood thrown overboard forward. The time of its passage between two marks on the gunwale enabled the speed of the vessel to be calculated.

Dyke.—A large ditch or fissure in marsh or low lying lands such as saltings. In the east of England the word is pronounced "deek".

DUTCHMAN

E

Eagre, or **eagor** (also *acker*).—An eddying (or eager) ripple on the surface of flooded waters. A tide swelling over another tide, as in the Severn. (*See* BORE.)—(Smyth.)

Earings, or **reef earings.**—Small ropes attached to cringles (loops or eyes) in the bolt ropes *at the head* of sails. The following has reference to square rig:—

Earings.—"Small ropes fastened to cringles (loops) in the upper corners, and also to the *leeches* of sails, for the purpose of fixing the leeches of the sail to the yard. The first or head earings fix the corners of the sail permanently, the second being used only in reefing." (Brande and Cox.) There is a difference between *earings* and *reef earings,* as follows:—The former are spliced to the cringle; the latter are rove through a cringle having an eye spliced in it, so that it may the more easily be renewed. (Falconer.)

Ease.—*Ease away.*—In sailing, to slacken away gradually; as of a rope.

Ease the helm.—The order to a helmsman to reduce the amount of helm when hard over.

Ease the ship.—To put the helm hard a'lee when she is expected to plunge. This may well be done in small craft, and is also done in large vessels, notwithstanding much opposition to the practice on the part of writers on the art of sailing, who hold it to be impossible to influence the motion of the vessel in so short a time as would be necessary to put her into a coming wave.

Easy.—To pull, or go, less vigorously.

Easting.—Distance eastward; just as northing is distance northward.

Ebb.—The reflux of the tide.

Ebb dry.—That portion of a solid or hard foreshore which is daily covered at high tide and left dry at low.

Eddy.—A circular motion in water, caused either by its meeting with some obstacle and circling round it, or by the meeting of opposite currents. Eddies are frequent round the piers of bridges when the tide runs swiftly, and may often be dangerous to small boats. This is particularly the case under the bridges of the Thames. In such cases, therefore, it is wise to be cool and careful, and to keep strict attention to the boat's course, that she be not swung round.

Eight-oar.—A boat rowed by eight oars. On the Upper Thames it is usually understood to mean a racing outrigger.

Elbows (in shipbuilding).—(*See* KNEES.)

End (of a rope).—The *end* of a rope is spoken of in contradistinction to the *bight*, which is that part between the ends; but a bight is also more generally looked upon as a bent part of the rope (*see* BIGHT). The *standing end,* otherwise called the *standing part* of a rope, is that end which is fixed or made fast, the part hauled upon being called the *running end* or *part.*

End for end.—To reverse a rope so that one end occupies the position previously held by the other, and thus a different part of the rope is subject to wear.

End on.—The situation of a vessel when pointing directly at any object; thus if, at night, we see both the red and green lights of a ship we know her to be end on. This term is employed in the "Regulations for Prevention of Collisions at Sea".

END ON

End ring.—1. Of a chain, a round ring generally terminating the chain. (*See* figure under CHAIN.) 2. A ring or cap fitted over the end of a spar. It prevents the spar from splitting, and is generally made with eyes or hooks round it to carry small blocks. It is found on gaffs, bowsprits, etc., that on the bowsprit being generally called the *cranse-iron.* (*See* figure under BOWSPRIT.)

Ensign (usually pronounced "ens'n").—The flag carried by a ship as the insignia of her nationality. The ensign of Great Britain consists of a red, white or blue field (or ground), with the device of the Union (*see* UNION JACK) in the first canton (*i.e.,* the upper quarter nearest the mast). The white ensign displays the cross of Saint George, *i.e.,* a red cross on a white field, with the Union in the first quarter; the red and blue ensigns are without a cross. Ships of war fly the ensign of St. George, *i.e.,* the white ensign; the Naval Reserve the blue; and the Mercantile Navy the red. All three were once used in the Royal Navy, there being an Admiral of the White, of the Blue, and of the Red. The distinctions have, however, been discontinued: by a rule of 1864 all men-of-war carry the St. George's ensign. Certain yacht clubs have also the privilege of flying particular ensigns, as in the case of the Royal Yacht Squadron, which flies the white. The ensign is hoisted in a steam vessel, or large ship, on a pole over the taffrail; on a schooner, brig, etc., at the peak of the main gaff; on a cutter or sloop, at the peak; on a yawl, at the mizzen peak, unless the mizzen be a lug-sail, when it is

R NAVY

NAVAL RESERVE

MERCANTILE

BLUE   RED

ENSIGNS

sent up at the main peak; and on a row boat over the stern. In port it flies between 8 a.m. and sunset; at sea only when meeting strangers. Turned upside down it is a signal of distress. Displayed under any than ordinary circumstances it becomes a signal. (For further reference to its use by yacht clubs *see* BURGEE.)

Entrance.—That part of the hull of a vessel (aft of the cut-water) which throws off the water as she moves. (*See* fig.)

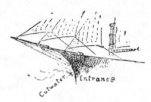

Equinox.—(Lat., aequus, *equal,* and nox, *night.*) "In astronomy, the time at which the sun passes through the equator in one of the equinoctial points. When the sun is in the equator, the days and nights are of equal length all over the world, whence the derivation of the term. This happens twice every year, namely, about the 21st of March and the 22nd of September; the former is called the *vernal* and the latter the *autumnal* equinox." (Brande and Cox.) Storms at this time of year are called the "equinoctial gales".

Escutcheon.—The plate upon which a ship's name is written is sometimes thus called.

Euphroe.—A piece of wood in which holes are bored to take the separate parts of a crow's foot. (*See* CROW.)

Europe (rope).—A dark brown tarred rope, now almost superseded by manilla. Bits of old Europe used to be sent to prisons with which to make oakum.

Even keel.—A boat is said to be on an even keel when she lies evenly in a fore-and-aft direction (*i.e.,* in the direction of the keel). (*See* diagram under KEEL.) She is also sometimes erroneously so described, especially with rowers, when she is upright in the water, canting neither to right nor to left.

Every.—*Every inch of that.*—An exclamation. To belay a rope without letting an inch go.

Every rope an end.—Every rope running freely.

Every stitch of canvas.—All sail set and no possibility of adding more.

Eye.—Generally speaking a small hole or loop, as:—

EYES

Eye of a block strop.—That cringle or hole in any rope or sail from which a block is suspended.

Eye of an anchor.—The hole in the head of the shank in which is the ring.

Eye bolts, screw eyes, bolt eyes.—Screws or bolts, the heads of which form rings. When they are employed for guiding the sheets of sails they are sometimes called *fair leads* (see FAIR.)

Eye splice.—An eye made in the end of a rope, either wire or hempen, by turning over the end and splicing it into itself. (*See* Knots.)

Eyelet hole.—An eye in a sail, either to take rope or lacing. It is usually strengthened with a small metal ring.

Flemish eye.—An eye at the end of a rope, not spliced, but bound with yarn (*see* fig. p. 84).

Eyes (on a sail).—Rings sewn into the luff and leech of a sail to take the ties or lashings when reefing. Also holes in the sail to admit of short ropes (reef points) being passed through them.

The eye of the wind.—The exact direction from which the wind is blowing. Dead to windward.

In the eyes of her.—The most forward part of a vessel.

Eyebrow, or **Wriggle.**—A semicircular guttering above a port hole or scuttle.

Eyot (pronounced "eight").—Any small island in the Upper Thames, as "Chiswick Eyot", one of the points often mentioned in the records of rowing or sculling matches over the *championship course.*

F

Fag.—*Fag end* of a rope; the end which is apt to become untwisted, or *fagged out,* and is therefore *whipped,* or bound, with yarn to prevent this.

Fair.—*Fair weather.*—In the north the simple word "fair" often means this.

Fair wind.—A wind which takes a ship on her course without the necessity of tacking.

Fair way.—A navigable tract or channel of water, either at sea, in a harbour, or up a river.

Fairlead (on the deck of a vessel).— Any ring, bolt, eye, or loop which guides a rope in the direction required (*see* fig.). It is sometimes called a "chuck".

Fair curves (in shipbuilding).—"The lines of a boat taken indiscriminately either vertically, horizontally, transversely, or sectionally, should all result

FAIRLEADS

in regular even curves without any severe or sharp angular bends. The curves fulfilling this test are termed *fair curves.* In a boat properly designed the curves in all directions should be fair." (Winn, "Boating Man's Vade Mecum.")

Fake.—A slang term used under almost any circumstances and signifying almost anything. Thus to *fake* sometimes means to make a thing look right when it is not so, or to get a job over, no matter how.

To *fake a rope.*—(*See* CHEESING DOWN.)

Fall.—Roughly speaking, a rope to be hauled upon (fig. 1). Thus the fall of a tackle is the rope upon which men pull, as the *bobstay fall,* the rope which taughtens the bobstay; the *cat fall,* the rope hauled upon when the cat-block is secured to the anchor in bringing it into the ship, etc.

Fall aboard.—To run foul of another vessel.

Fall astern.—To drop astern of (*i.e.,* behind) another vessel.

Fall calm.—To become calm; a sudden drop of the wind.

Fall down to.—To drift on an ebbing tide from some place or mooring to another.

FIG. 1

Fall home.—(*See* TUMBLE HOME.)

Fall off (from the wind).—In sailing, a boat is said to fall off when her tendency is to run away from the wind, and therefore to make considerable leeway. Occasionally a boat may be in the habit of doing this when put up into the wind, in consequence of her not having sufficient gripe of the water forward. It is a bad and dangerous fault. In centre-board boats it may sometimes be counter-acted, at great trouble, by shifting the board forward. (*See* LEE HELM.)

Fall not off.—A command to the steersman to keep the vessel's head close to the wind.

False keel.—An addition to the main keel. It not only acts as a protection to the main keel, but enables the vessel to take a better hold of the water. (*See* FRAME.)

Fanal.—A lighthouse. (French.)

Fancy line.—A line running through a block beneath the jaws of a gaff and used as a down haul. When it is attached to the *tack* of the sail so as to be able to trice that up it becomes a *tricing line*.

Fang.—*Fangs* are the valves of pump boxes. Hence, to pour water into the pumps of a vessel to enable them to start working, or to *fetch*, is to *fang the pumps*.

Fantod.—One of many opprobrious names given by seamen to an officer who is somewhat fidgety.

Fardage.—*Dunnage* (when a ship is laden in bulk).

Fashion pieces (in shipbuilding).—The aftermost timbers of a vessel which form or "fashion" the shape of her stern.

Fast.—*To make fast.*—To fasten—spoken of a rope when lashing anything with it, but not when *belaying*.

Fathom.—The unit of measurement for depths of water and lengths of rope used in most maritime countries. It was the measurement across the outstretched arms of a man, standardized as 6 feet, which is 1·8256 metres. Charts, which used to show soundings in fathoms, now generally show them in metres.

Fay.—To join two pieces of timber by thinning down the ends and fitting them to each other.

Feather (in rowing).—The act of turning the oar as it leaves the water at the finish of a stroke, so that, in the recovery of the stroke, the blade passes over the surface of the water horizontally, thereby presenting the least resistance to the wind as well as to the water should the blade accidentally touch it. No one should learn to row without feathering; in fact, it should come naturally, as the arms are thrust forward; and as the recovery finishes the oars should be in position to take the stroke. Feathering at sea in this manner is impossible, for the waves might catch the oar at every stroke; but here the act has a different intent, the blade of the oar being kept pretty much at the same angle throughout both stroke and recovery; not at right angles to the water, but at an angle of something like 45 degrees. This constitutes the great difference between sea and river rowing; a difference so great that many well-trained river boatmen require some little practice before they are able to pick up the knack of the sea style. In smooth waters the blade of the oar is put in at right angles to the surface, and a steady even pull is taken with it until the stroke is complete, when, as it comes out, it is quickly turned flat. At sea, on the contrary, the oar goes into the water at an obtuse angle, which, directly pressure is put on it, causes it to dip itself somewhat deep; the rower then puts his weight upon it and pulls down (not along), thus lifting the oar instead of actually pulling it. This, indeed, is the only way in which the long, heavy oars used by fishermen can be handled.

A *feathering paddlewheel.*—The paddles were mechanically adjusted to enter the water vertically and remain vertically while submerged.

A *feathering propeller,* or *screw.*—The blades are turned fore and aft to reduce resistance when the vessel is under sail alone.

Feather edge.—A sharp edge of a plank sawn diagonally across its section. Planks thus sawn are said to be feather edged. In *doubling* a clincher-built boat the planks of the outer covering or doubling will have to be feathered. (*See* DOUBLING.)

FEATHER EDGE

Feel (the helm).—When the helm of a vessel requires something of a pull to bring her up into the wind the steersman may say that he feels the helm.

Felucca.—A small vessel or boat of the Mediterranean, propelled by oars or lateen sails.

Fend, fenders.—To *fend off* is to push off any heavy body from another so as to avoid contact. So a *fender* or *fend off* is a cushion, usually of rope or yarn, inserted between two boats or between a boat and any other object for the purpose of *fending it off* from the other. Fenders are of various forms. The *pudding fender* is made of old rope worked up into a large round pad, not altogether unlike a pudding of handsome dimensions: it is always to be seen on large vessels, steam-boats, etc. The plain *fender rope* is made of one or more short pieces of rope folded so that the ends meet and are served or bound together with yarn. Some fenders are of sawdust, contained in a bag of painted canvas: these, however, are apt to swell and become hard, and are unsuitable, therefore, for anything but show purposes. Cork, on

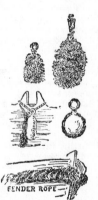

FENDER ROPE

FENDERS

FENDER ROPE ROUND SKIFF

the other hand, or oakum covered in leather, are useful. India rubber, too, in the form of rings, is very good. For a boat which is subject to a good deal of knocking about, such as a yacht's dinghy, no better form of fender can be employed than a thick rope running all round the sheerstrake, and this is now being adopted even in pleasure boats. In many Thames skiffs small fenders (often of sawdust, and painted white) appear to exist as much for ornament as for use; being slung permanently round the rowlocks, to which, it must be admitted, they give a neat and finished appearance. Yachtsmen, however, have an objection to this, and never allow fenders to remain out board while under way.

Ferry.—A boat or vessel plying across a narrow piece of water.

Ferry boats are of various kinds, from the mere open boat to the chain worked pontoons or steam passenger boats crossing wide rivers.

Fetch.—To attain. "We shall fetch to windward of the lighthouse, this tack."

To *fetch way.*—To make way; but Falconer gives it as follows:— "To be shaken or agitated from side to side." Modern usage "to break adrift".

The pumps fetch.—They begin to work.

Of waves: the distance of open water traversed before they reach the ship, or the coast. The longer the fetch the higher, generally, the waves.

Fid.—A bolt of wood or iron which fixes the heel of a topmast or bowsprit. The fid of a mast rests, when the topmast is lifted, in the *fid holes* upon the *trestle-trees,* thereby preventing the topmast from coming down. (*See* diagrams under MAST.)

Splicing-fid.—A spike for opening the strands of a rope.

Fiddles.—The rails fitted around tables during rough weather, to prevent articles from sliding over the edge.

Fiddle block.—A block with one sheave larger than another, and which, therefore, can take two sizes of rope; from which circumstance it is also often called a *thick-and-thin block.*

Fiddlehead bow.—The stemhead of a vessel finished off with a scroll like that at the head of a violin, but sometimes referring to a clipperbow.

Fiddley.—The casing round a funnel and stokehold.

Fiddler's Green.—An imaginary sailor's paradise.

Fiferail.—A plank or rail upon which a group of belaying-pins are fixed. They are often seen on the shrouds of large yachts, where they take some of the halyards; and in ships, where all halyards belay by the shrouds, the fiferail may be fitted with powerful *cleats.*

Figurehead.—The figure or other carving which used to, and occasionally still does, adorn the prow of wooden ships. Properly

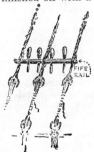

FIFERAIL

applied they should represent the subject of the ship's name.

Figure-of-eight-knot.—(*See* KNOTS.)

Fill.—To fill the sails is so to trim them that the wind may act upon them.

Fillets.—Small projecting bands, of square section, on any spars or mouldings.

Finishing.—The final work on and ornamenting of the hull of a ship.

Fish.—The name of an apparatus for hauling in the *flukes* of an anchor in a ship. It consists of the *fish davit,* a timber or iron bracket projecting from the bows of the ship, and to this is attached the *fish tackle,* which consists of the *fish block,* the principal block of the tackle, and the purchase on which is obtained by hauling upon the *fish fall*—*i.e.,* the rope leading from the fish-blocks. (*See* figs. under DAVIT.)

To fish a broken spar is to bind stiffening planks around it.

Fisherman.—One who lives by fishing, whether on salt water or fresh. But one who loafs about the shore, or who lets out boats, is not a fisherman.

Fisherman's bend.—A knot used in securing an anchor to a rope, and sometimes for bending sails to halyards. (*See* KNOTS.)

Fisherman's walk.—An extremely confined space on the deck of a vessel, "three steps and overboard," or, in other words, no larger an area than the deck of a fishing boat. The term is sometimes used in derision of what yachtsmen call their "quarter deck." (Smyth.)

Fishgig, or **Fisgig.**—A four-pronged harpoon for spearing fish by hand.

Fitting out.—"Getting in the masts, putting the rigging overhead, stowing the hold, and so on." (Capt. Basil Hall.)

Flag.—A flag has been defined as a banner indicating nationality, occupation, or intelligence. The flags of nationality are *standards, ensigns, jacks.* Those of occupation are such as indicate the service or occupation of those who fly them, as *war, trading, pilotage, yachting,* etc. Those of intelligence are called signals, and are of various forms and colours. They are of three shapes, the *square,* the *pointed,* and the *double-pointed* or *swallow tail.* (*See* under SIGNALS.)

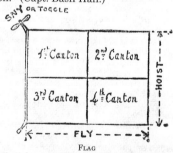

FLAG

The *standard* is the flag, bearing the sovereign's arms or those of a nation. (*See* STANDARD.)

The *ensign* is the signal of nationality. (*See* ENSIGN.)

The *jack* is a flag of smaller size. (*See* JACK.)

A *pennant,* or *pendant,* is a long pointed flag generally used in conjunction with signals. (*See* PENDANT.)

A *burgee* is a pointed or swallow tail flag mostly used by yacht clubs. (*See* BURGEE.)

A *wheft,* or *whiff,* is a flag with a stop passed round it half way along the fly. It then has some special significance.

A *house flag* is a square flag distinguishing a particular shipping company. (*See* HOUSE FLAG.)

A *member's flag* is a small flag belonging to a private member of a yacht club. (*See* MEMBER'S FLAG and BURGEE.)

A plain white flag in war is the flag of truce. A yellow flag is the mark of quarantine. A red flag or burgee alone signifies that the vessel or barge upon which it is displayed carries an explosive cargo. A black flag is the old flag of piracy. An ensign hoisted upside down is a signal of distress. Half mast high, it means mourning; when dipped it is a mark of salutation or respect, the number of dips being according to the person or object saluted.

The parts of a flag are the same as the parts of an escutcheon in heraldry. The perpendicular depth of a flag is called its *hoist, height,* or *depth.* Its length is called the *fly.*

Flag lieutenant.—An officer appointed to attend a flag officer as his personal assistant.

Flag officer.—An officer entitled to bear his own distinguishing flag at his mast head: Admirals, Vice Admirals, Rear Admirals. Commodores and Vice Commodores of yacht clubs are also so styled.

Flag of Convenience.—A foreign flag under which a ship is registered to avoid taxation, etc.

Flag ship.—That ship of a fleet which flies the admiral's flag.

Flake.—To coil a rope so that each coil, on two opposite sides, lies flat on deck alongside the previous coil, so that the rope will run freely.

Flare, or **flam** (a flying out).—The peculiar outward and upward curve in the form of a vessel's bow. When it hangs over she is sometimes said to have a "flaring bow". (*See* FALL and FRAME.)

Flare up lights.—Lights used on the deck of a vessel as signals. They burn only a few seconds. (*See* LIGHTS and SIGNALS.)

Flash.—*Flashing Light.*—A light that suddenly appears, the interval between flashes being longer than the flash. (*See* LIGHTS.)

Flash vessel.—A vessel all paint outside but without much order within.

Flat.—Level ground under the sea and generally near the shore; as the Kentish Flats, in the estuary of the Thames. Otherwise a shoal or shallow place.

Flats (in shipbuilding).—The futtocks amidships.

Flat-floors, also called *bearers,* because they bear the floor boards, are small beams across the lowest part of a vessel. They are made flat above, so as to bear the flooring, and hollow underneath (somewhat in the form of arches); or if of solid pieces, are pierced underneath with arched apertures, called *limbers,* these limbers, or passages through them, being necessary to allow any bilge water to run fore and aft. (*See* LIMBERS.) In open boats they are often dispensed with, their place being taken by the *footwaling*. (*See* diagram under FRAME.)

To *flat in a sail.*—To haul it in flat.

"Flat as a board."—An expression used in admiration of a sail which sets very free of creases, as it is the pride of yachtsmen to see them.

"Flat aback."—Said of a ship or sail when the wind is on the fore side of a sail and pressing it back.

Flaw.—A sudden breeze or gust of wind. A sudden change in the direction of the wind. Fickle winds.

Fleet.—A fleet is a number of vessels under one ownership or command. Thus we may have "ships of the Blue Funnel fleet" or a fishing fleet. *The fleet* is the name generally given to the ships of the Royal Navy or a detachment of it.

Fleet train.—An assembly of auxiliary vessels, such as oilers and store ships which accompany and serve a fighting fleet.

Fleet water, a fleet.—Shallow tidal water; a shallow place. Hence the names Benfleet, Northfleet, Purfleet, etc., and also Fleet Street.

To *fleet blocks.*—To free or loosen the blocks of a tackle, when drawn close together. Falconer gives the following definition of the term: *"To fleet* is to change the situation of a tackle, when the blocks are drawn together, or what is called *block and block* by sailors; also to change the position of the deadeyes, when the shrouds are becoming too long, which is done by shortening the shroud and turning in the deadeye again, higher up. The use of fleeting is, accordingly, to replace the mechanical powers into a state of action, the force by which they operated before being destroyed by the meeting of the blocks or deadeyes. Fleeting, therefore, is nearly similar to the winding up of a watch or clock."

To *fleet a cable, or hawser,* is to allow it "to slip on the whelps (upright pieces) of the capstan or windlass, from the larger to a part of the smaller diameter". ("Dictionary of Mechanics.")

Flemish.—*Flemish coil.*—To coil a rope in fanciful patterns, as in the figure of 8. A *French fake* is a modification of this.

Flemish eye.—An eye at the end of a rope not spliced but sewn with yarn. (*See* diagram under EYE.)

Flemish horse (in square rig).—The outer portion of a *horse,* the horse being a rope hanging below a yard upon which a man may stand while reefing; and the horse is hung upon short ropes called stirrups.

Flense.—To strip the blubber from a whale.

Flinders Bar.—A bar of "soft" iron fixed vertically to a binnacle to equalize the magnetic attraction of the forward and after portions of the vessel.

Flying Dutchman.—A mythical ship whose captain Vander-elcken was supposedly condemned to sail for ever round the Cape of Good Hope. Sight of it is said to portend disaster.

Foam.—The fallen or flying spray of the sea.

Float.—Abbreviation of "paddle float" or "float board".

Floating anchor.—(*See* SEA ANCHOR.)

Floating bridge.—A form of ferry, hauled by chains across a stream.

Floating dock.—A huge iron vessel, having a double case with large intervening space between, into which ships can be floated for repair.

Floating harbour.—A breakwater of spars, etc., fastened together and moored, as a protection for a vessel lying at anchor; its object being to keep off the violence of the sea.

Floatsam.—(*See* FLOTSAM.)

Flood.—*Flood tide.*—The flowing or rising tide. The tide is said to be at its flood when it is at its highest, and therefore slack. But the turn from ebb to flow is also the flood, and it is just before this flood that vessels which are waiting for the turn get under weigh; thus we come to appreciate the meaning of the well-known lines "There is a tide in the affairs of men which, taken at the flood, leads on to fortune."

Flood gate.—A tidal gate or sluice gate.

Floor.—That portion of the inside of a vessel which is below the water line.

Floors.—The vertical transverse plates between the inner and outer bottoms of a steel ship.

Floor boards, foot boards, or *bilge boards.*—The loose planking lying over the floor timbers and flat floors; they cover the ballast and keep the bilgewater out of sight.

Flat-floors or *bearers.*—Small beams supporting the floor-boards. (*See* FLAT-FLOORS.)

Floor plan.—A longitudinal section of a vessel, showing her plan at the water line, or any other line parallel to it.

Floor timbers.—The lower members, or "timbers", of a vessel's ribs (for the ribs of ships are composed of several pieces, called futtocks). The upper ends are called the *floor heads.* (These parts are illustrated in the diagrams under the heading FRAME.)

Flotilla.—A fleet of small vessels.

Flotsam.—Goods and fittings which remain floating after a ship has foundered. The term flotsam is also applied by fishermen to the floating spawn of certain fishes, or shellfish, as the spat of the oyster in its swimming state.

Flow.—*Flowing tide.*—The tide rising. When the ebb ceases, the tide is said to flow: thus, "The tide flows at 5 o'clock" will mean "the tide will cease running down and begin to run up at 5 o'clock."

Flowing sheet.—The sheets loosened or "eased off", and the ship, therefore, running before the wind, or nearly so.

Fluke.—The *palm* or hook of an anchor. (*See* ANCHOR.)

Fluky.—Said of a light breeze which varies in strength and direction.

D

Flush.—Smooth, or of an even surface—spoken often of the joints of planks when placed together.

Flush-deck.—A deck running from stem to stern without the interruption of forecastle, booby hatch, or other cabin head. (*See* diagram under DECK.)

Flute.—A small vessel with a broad beam and rounded stern. 2. A war vessel who had some of her guns removed to allow troops or stores to be carried.

Fly.—1. Of a flag, its length, the perpendicular height being called the *hoist, height,* or *depth.* That part of a flag which flutters in the air, in contradistinction to that part near the mast, is also called the fly.—2. The card upon which are marked the points of the compass.

Flying block.—A large flat block used in hoisting tackle of yards.

Flying jib.—A triangular sail set out beyond a jib or middle-jib. (*See* JIB.)

Flying jib-boom.—An extension of the jib-boom: only seen on large vessels. (*See* under JIB.)

"*Flying kites.*"—This popular expression has its origin at sea. The smallest and highest sails are made of the lightest material, for which reason they are called kites. Such are the smaller studding sails and sky sails (sometimes spoken of as sky-scrapers). When set they constitute the last stitch of canvas a ship can carry, and she is then said to be "flying her kites". Hence, when a person makes much show with little substance he may be said to be "flying kites"; and, in commerce, one who makes much exposition of paper money without the wherewithal to meet it, is worthy to be placed in the same category.

Flying start.—A start for a sailing match by boats which are already under weigh, but which are required to be behind an imaginary line when the signal to start is given.

Fly-to.—To luff up suddenly—*i.e.,* to run head to wind suddenly. *Set flying.* (*See* under that head.)

Fly-boat.—A 16th to 19th century Dutch coasting vessel, flat-bottomed and broad-beamed with a high stern, rigged with one or two masts either carrying square or sprit sails.

Flying light.—Said of a vessel in ballast whose loadline is well above the waterline.

Fog.—When the horizontal visibility is less than half a mile *fog* is present; when the visibility is between one half and one mile *mist* or *haze* is the term used.

Fog bell.—A bell rung at intervals of not more than one minute by a vessel at anchor. Sometimes refers to a bell rung in fog by a lighthouse, or at a pier head, or to a bell on a navigational buoy.

Fog signals.—Made by vessels under way and made upon the steam whistle or equivalent instrument, and such signals are laid down in the International Regulations for Preventing Collisions at Sea. (*Which see.*)

Foot.—Generally speaking the lowest part of any object. 1. Of a spar, the lowest end; 2. Of a sail, the lower edge. The lower weather corner of the foot (*i.e.*, the end nearest the mast on a gaff sail, or nearest the foremost point on a head sail) is called the *tack,* the other corner being the *clew.*

Foot-boards.—The same as *floor-boards* (*which see*).

Foot-rope.—A rope stretched below a yard or jibboom for men to stand on when handling sail. Once called a *horse.* The *bolt rope* along the foot of a sail.

Footwalings.—Narrow planks or battens laid along the timbers (ribs) in the lowest part of a boat. They answer to the burdens in large vessels and protect the skin from the weight of the ballast. In open boats the footwaling often takes the place of the flat-floors.

Fore-foot.—The fore end of a ship's keel, upon which the *stem-post* is *stepped.*

Fore.—*Fore part* (of a vessel).—Forward.

Fore-and-aft.—A term much used throughout this work, for it describes one of the only two manners in which sails can be applied to a vessel. The meaning of the term "fore-and-aft" is, *in the direction of a line drawn from stem to stern of a vessel*; that is, from the forward or *fore* to the after or *aft* part; and such sails, yards, and spars as are set in this direction constitute that which, among sea-faring men, is known as *fore-and-aft rig.* Such sails as yachts and sailing boats carry are fore-and-aft sails; and such as are set in a direction *across* the ship are called *square sails,* constituting the *square rig* of most merchantmen. (*See* RIG.)

Forebitter.—A song sung by seamen off duty, on the forecastle (by the fore bitts). It was not a chanty, which was sung while at work.

Forecastle (pronounced *fokes'l*).—Properly speaking, the forward deck, which is often raised above the main deck; hence its name. The space beneath it is the cabin of the crew; and this is popularly called the forecastle. *Forecastle head,* or *Monkey forecastle* is another name for a smaller forecastle or anchor deck. (*See* diagram under DECK.)

Forecourse.—In square rig, the lowest sail on the fore-mast. It is sometimes called the fore-sail. (*See* COURSES.)

In shipbuilding and seamanship the following, among other terms, are used:—

Fore-foot.—The fore end of a ship's keel, on which the *stem-post* is *stepped.*

Fore-halyard, or *foresail halyard.*—The rope or halyard which elevates the foresail. In fore-and-aft rig it has its origin at a point near the mast head, from which it runs downwards towards the *stem-head* of the boat, and passing through a movable block, returns through a fixed block on the mast, to the deck, where it belays, in small craft, usually on the *starboard* side of the mast. When the foresail is to be set, its head is attached to the lower block, which is furnished with a hook or clip-hooks, and the halyard is hauled up taut. When it is to be taken in, this lower block is brought down to the stem-head, where it is hooked, and the halyards are then taughtened just enough to prevent the *pendants,* or out-hanging portion, from swinging about.

Fore-hooks.—Strengthening timbers in the bow of a vessel, binding the other timbers together. (*See* BREAST-HOOK.)

Foreland.—A high piece of land jutting out into the sea, as the North and South Forelands.

Fore-lock.—A sort of linch-pin or split-pin through the end of a bolt to prevent it from getting out of position. Also the braces of the rudder (*which see*).

Fore-lock hook.—In rope-making, a winch on a block by which yarns are twisted into strands.

Foremast.—Generally the mast nearest the bow of a vessel. In all three and four-masted ships the most forward is the foremast, as is also in such two-masted ones as the schooner, brigantine, etc. But there are several rigs peculiar to smaller craft (such as the *ketch, yawl,* etc.), in which the forward mast is vastly taller than the sternmost, and in such cases the forward one becomes the main mast, the after one being called the mizzen, while the *foremast* is absent.

Fore-peak.—A space in the bows of a vessel forward of, or below the forecastle. The name is also sometimes applied to the forecastle itself, when raised above the deck of a sailing ship.

Fore-rake.—So much of the forward inclination, or run, of the stem of a vessel as overhangs the keel.

Fore-reach.—The distance a sailing vessel will shoot up to windward when brought head to wind when tacking, or the progress a vessel may make to windward when hove to. To overtake another vessel and reach ahead of her.

Fore-runner.—Usually a piece of bunting attached to a log-line at a certain distance (measured in fathoms) from the log. It takes the place of a knot. (*See* LOG.) A length of chain shackled on to an anchor to which the rope cable is attached. This takes much of the chafe of the sea bed from the rope, and increases the holding power of the anchor.

Foresail.—1. In square rig usually the *forecourse,* though in vessels which carry no forecourse it is the fore *stay* sail, and even in ships, from the fact that the forecourse is not always set, the fore stay sail is often called the foresail. 2. In fore-and-aft rig:—In the *schooner* it is a gaff sail on the fore mast. In the *cutter* and *yawl* it is a triangular sail extending from the lower mast head to the stem head, running by means of *hanks,* or a *lacing,* on the *forestay,* and corresponding, therefore, with the forestay sail of square or schooner rig. In the *sloop* it is often absent, the fore stay being run out to the end of a fixed bowsprit, and carrying a large jib which extends aft almost to the mast. The value of a foresail lies in the fact that its effort is within the boat. This gives it a power which, sometimes, in a fresh breeze, will bury a boat's head, and in such a case it is as well to take it in, leaving the jib as the only head sail. But it is in consequence of this power that we are able to deduce the following:

Rule for working jibs and foresail.—When a vessel is going about, the jib acts before the foresail, but its power is soon expended. It is, therefore, brought over first (as soon as its effort is seen to be finished) and sheeted home, while the foresail (by laying aback) completes the work of bringing the vessel's head round. This is an operation requiring nice judgment and some little experience. The mistake of bringing the head sails over too soon is particularly to be avoided: it may almost be said, indeed, that it is better to be too slow than too quick; though much, of course, must depend upon the general behaviour of the craft.

Balloon foresail.—A large foresail used in racing and extending aft, sometimes beyond the shrouds. (*See* BALLOON CANVAS.)

Fore-sheets.—The ropes which work the foresail. In square rigged ships it is the aftermost of the ropes attached to the clews of the *fore course,* the weathermost being the *tack.* But the foresail, in fore-and-aft rigged vessels, being a head sail, running on a *fore stay,* and therefore corresponding to the forestay sail in a ship, is worked by two sheets, or perhaps more correctly by a doubled sheet looped at the bight (or bend) to the clew of the sail, and each half of which is brought aft through *fairleads* on either side of the bows to be belayed either amidships, or, in small boats, within reach of the helmsman. In small craft the fore-sheets are usually distinguished from the jib sheets by being *thinner,* running inside of and being belayed *forward of* the jib sheets. In fishing craft fore-sheets are sometimes dispensed with, their place being taken by *pendants* on the leech of the sail; the clew travelling on a *horse,* and the pendants being made fast to the shrouds. This constitutes what is called a "working foresail". A stopper knot should be made at the end of each fore-sheet when it is rove through its fairleads, to prevent them from being jerked away. A figure-of-eight knot answers this purpose well, and is easily made. (*See* KNOT.)

Fore sheets.—The forward part of a boat, right in the bow.

Fore-shore.—That portion of a coast which lies beyond the boundary of the land territory. It is usually covered at high water. The foreshore in estuaries and rivers is often the property of the lords of the manors adjoining it, otherwise it belongs to the Crown.

Fore-stay.—The fore-stay is a rope, now almost always of wire, running from the lower masthead to the stem of the vessel or to the bowsprit end: its office being to prevent the mast from falling backward under the weight of the sails. It is usually *eye-spliced* and passed over the head of the mast and down to the shrouds.

The following relates to full-rigged ships:—

Fore top-mast.—The first top-mast on the fore-mast. (*See* MAST.)

Fore-top-sail and yard.—The sail set on the fore top-mast and suspended on the fore top-sail-yard.

Fore top-mast-stay.—A rope, or stay, running from the fore-top mast head down to the bowsprit end, and supporting the mast from being drawn backward.

Fore top-mast-stay-sail.—A jib-shaped sail set on the fore top-mast-stay. It is sometimes called the *middle-jib.*

Fore-top-gallant-mast (pronounced "forty garn must").—The second top-mast on the fore-mast. (*See* MAST.)

Fore-top-gallant-sail and yard.—The sail set on the fore-top-gallant-mast, and suspended on the fore-top-gallant-yard.

Fore-top-gallant-stay.—A stay running down from the fore-top-gallant-mast head to the jib-boom-end, and supporting the mast from being drawn backward.

Fore-top-gallant-stay-sail.—The sail set on the fore-top-gallant-stay, but it is usually called a *flying jib*.

Fore-royal-mast.—The extension of the top gallant mast. (*See* MAST.)

Fore-royal-sail and yard.—The sail set on the fore-royal-mast, and suspended on the fore-royal-yard, which yard lowers, or is "sent down" until it reaches the fore-top-gallant-yard, when the sails are furled.

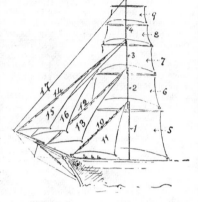

1. Fore-mast
2. Fore-top-mast
3. Fore-top-gallant-mast
4. Fore-royal-mast
5. Fore-course
6. Fore-top-sail
7. Fore-top-gallant-sail
8. Fore-royal-sail
9. Fore-sky-sail
10. Fore-stay
11. Fore-stay-sail
12. Fore-top-mast-stay
13. Fore-top-mast-stay-sail or inner jib
14. Fore-top-gallant-stay
15. Fore-top-gallant-stay-sail or flying-jib
16. Middle-jib
17. Fore-royal-stay

Fore-royal-stay.—A stay reaching from the fore-royal-mast head to the end of the jib-boom, and supporting the mast from being drawn backwards.

Fore-sky sail.—A sail sometimes set above the fore-royal. (*See* LIGHT SAILS.)

Forge.—To force violently, as a ship over a shoal by a great press of sail.

To forge ahead.—To go on ahead of or gain upon another: or simply to make good way.

Fork-beam.—In ship-building, a small forked beam introduced for the support of a deck where a hatchway occurs.

Forming.—In shipbuilding, shaping partially converted timbers so as to give them the desired form for building.

Forward.—In front of (pronounced forrard.)

Forward part.—The fore-part, in the vicinity of the bows of a vessel.

"Forward all!" (in rowing).—An order to rowers to stretch forward, ready to take a stroke. The order is usually given preparatory either to "go" or to "paddle".

Fother, or **fodder.**—A method of stopping a leak in a vessel at sea: it may be done in various ways, but the principle of the practice is to allow the current of water into the leak to carry so great a quantity of small stuff (such as the threads of yarn or oakum) with it as eventually to stop the leak. To effect this the loose stuff must be lowered to the leak in a piece of sail cloth or some other useful material and be allowed to remain there. There is no doubt that vessels have been saved by this means; but for small craft there is a quicker method of stopping a leak, viz., by passing down a piece of sailcloth, packed with old yarn or any other substance at hand, and drawing it, if the hole be large enough, into the hole, or if it be too small, by fixing the cloth with ropes round the boat.

Foul.—Unpleasant, as bilge water may be, or as the interior of a fishing boat may become when she becomes infested with lice or sea slugs. When any tackle or rope becomes entangled it is said to be foul, as a *foul hawse,* which is an entanglement of the cable of a vessel.

Foul ground is dangerous ground for a vessel to run upon, or which affords bad anchorage.

Foul water.—When a ship comes into water so shallow that, though she does not ground, she stirs up the mud beneath her, she is said to make foul water.

Foul wind.—Contrary wind, preventing a vessel from making way.

To *foul.*—To run into anything, such as a pier, a buoy, or another boat, is to foul or "run foul of it".

A *foul.*—In yacht and boat racing, to obstruct the progress of any other competitor by unfair means or in any way to break the rules under which the race is being contested, constitutes what is called *a foul.*

Found.—A vessel or boat is said to be "all found" when she has masts, rigging, and gear, and all other necessaries for going out, and "well found" when all these are good.

Founder.—To fill with water and sink.

Four.—*Fourcant* (of a rope).— A rope of four strands.

Four-masted barques.—These were once not uncommon. They were square-rigged on three masts, and the fourth mast, called the *jigger* mast, was fore-and-aft rigged. The last sailing vessels built were generally of large size when compared with those built twenty years before. The *Somale,* was in 1897 a four-masted steel barque, 3537 gross tons and 330 feet long.

FOUR-MASTED BARQUE *Hougomont,* 1912

She was the largest owned in the United Kingdom. Many of the large ocean-going steam ships had four masts. There is also a class of vessels called four-masted schooners, which are fore-and-aft rigged on all masts. These ships sail mostly from America: they were fast and close-winded.

Fox.—A sort of strand formed by twisting up several rope-yarns and using them as *seizings,* etc.

Spanish fox.—A seizing made up of a single rope yarn untwisted and retwisted the reverse way.

Frame.—The frame of a vessel is its skeleton. The principal parts will best be understood by reference to the accompanying diagrams.

Frames.—"The bends of timber constituting the shape of the ship's body. When completed a ship is said to be in frame."

Frame reel.—A frame upon which a fishing line is wound.

Frame timbers.—The parts of a futtock (*which see*), as the floor timber, middle timber, top timber, etc.

In the accompanying diagrams the following constructive members (parts of various types of vessels), described each under its own heading, are illustrated. The Roman numbers refer to the figures; the italics to the situation of the members in the figures.

A.

Apron, IV. *g*; VII.

B.

Beams (deck) I. *w*; II. *s*; IV. *l*; V. *h*; VII.
  ,,   (hold), I. *y*.
Bent timbers, heads, or bent heads, III. *e*; VI. *e*.
Bilge, I.
  ,,   Bilge keel, III. *f*; VI. *l*.
Bowsprit bitts, IV. *r*.
Breasthook, IV. *h*; V. *g*; VI. *f*. VII.
Bulwarks (quick work) I. *t*; II. *p*; V. *l*.

C.

Carlines, IV. *z*; V. *j*.
Case, II. *j*.
Chocks, I. *g*.
Clamps, or sea-scarfs, I. *h*.
Coaming, III. *l*.
Counter stay, IV. *y*.

D.

Deadwoods, IV. *d*; V. *c*.
Deck, I. *v*; II. *r*. IV.
Deack-beams, I. *w*. (*See* also BEAMS.)

F.

Fall home, I.
False Keel. (*See* KEEL.)
Fillets, II. *e*.
Flare, I.
Flat-floors, III. *d*; IV. *u*; V. *t*; VI. *p*.
Floor-boards, IV. *v*.
Floor-timbers, I. 2; V. *s*; VI. *n*.
Foot walings, VI. *m*.
Freeboard, I.
Futtocks, I. 1, 2, 3, 4; II. 1, 2, 3; V. *n*. (*See* also GROUND FUTTOCK, MIDDLE FUTTOCK, TOP FUTTOCK.)

G.

Garboard strakes, I. *m*, 2; II. *g*; III.; V. *p* 2.
Ground futtock, otherwise called ground timber or first futtock; and, in the middle of a vessel the navel futtock, I. 1; II. 1; V. 1.
Gunwale, II. *m*; VI. *j*.
  ,,   Gunwale strake, III. *h*.

H.

Heads, otherwise called bent-heads, or bent-timbers, III. *e*; VI. *e*.
Head-sheets, VII. *q*.
Hold-beams, I. *y*.

I.

Inside planking. (*See* LINING.)
Inwale, VI. *k*.

K.

Keel, I. *a*; II. *a*; III. *a*; IV. *a*; V. *a*; VI. *a*.
  ,,   False keel, I. *c*; IV. *c*; V. *a* 2.
  ,,   Rebated keel, II.
  ,,   Keel and garboard united, III.
Keelson, I. *b*; II. *b*; III. *b*; IV. *b*; V. *b*; VI. *b*.
  ,,   Keelson rider, I. *d*.
  ,,   Side or sister keelsons, I. *e*.
Knees, II. *d*; V. *k*.
  ,,   Standard knees, I. *k*.
  ,,   Hanging knees, II. *t*.
Knighthead, IV. *k*; V. *f*.

L.

Limber Boards, I. *f*. Sometimes the same as the *flat-floors* (*which see*).
  ,,   Limber spaces, II. *f*; III. *c*; V.
Lining, I. *l*.; VII.

M.

Mast, IV. *m*.
,, Mast-case, II. *c*; IV. *p*.
,, Mast-step, II. *c*; IV. *n*.
Middle futtock, I. 2, 3; II. 2.

N.

Navel futtock. (*See* GROUND FUTTOCK.)
Nose, VI. *d*.

O.

Outside planking. (*See* SKIN.)

P.

Pad piece, I. *x*.
Partners, IV. *q*.
Planking, inside (*See* LINING and CASE.)
,, Outside. (SKIN.)
Planksheer, I. *r*.

Q.

Quickwork. (*See* BULWARKS.)

R.

Rail, or rough-tree rail, I. *u*; II. *q*; V. *m*.
Rebated keel, II.
Ribs, III. *e*; IV. *s*; V. *n*; VII. (*See* also
FUTTOCKS and BENT TIMBERS.)
Riders, I. 5, 6.
Rough-tree rail. (*See* RAIL.)
,, timber, (*See* STANCHION.)
Rubbing piece, III. *j*. (*See* WALE.)

S.

Saxboard, or gunwale strake, III. *h*; VI. *g*.
Sea scarfs. (*See* CLAMPS.)
Seat. (*See* THWART.)
Sheer strakes, I. *p*.

Shelf. (*See* STRINGER.)
Skin, I. *m*; II. *h*; VII.
Stanchion (Rough-tree timber, or timber-head), I. *s*; II. *n*; V. *n* 2.
Standard knees, I. *k*.
Stem, or stem-post, IV. *e*; V. *d*; VI. *c*; VII.
,, Stem-head, IV. *j*; V. *e*.
,, Stemson, IV. *f*; VII.
,, Stem hand, IV. *e* 2.
Stern, or stern-post, IV. *w*.
,, Sternson, IV. *w* 2.
,, Stern seat, IV.
Strakes, I. *m*; V. *p*.
,, Garboard strakes, I. *m* 2; V. *p* 2;
,, Garboard and keel united, III.
,, Gunwale strake or saxboard, III. *h*.
,, Sheer strakes, I. *p*.
,, Thick strakes, I. *m* 3; *m* 4.
Topmost strake, VI. *g*.
Stringers (or shelf), I. *j*; II. *k*; III. *m*. IV. *t*; V.
r; VI. *r*.
,, Carrying thwarts. (*See* WIRING.)

T.

Thick strakes, I. *m* 3; *m* 4.
Thwart, III. *p*; IV.
Timber head. (*See* STANCHION.)
Top futtock or top-timber, I.4; II. 3.
Transom, IV. *x*.

U.

Upper deck beams, I. *w*.

W.

Wale, I. *m* 4; II. *l*; V. *q*; VI. *h*; VII.
Water line, I.
Water-ways, I. *q*; III. *k*.
Weather-board, IV.
Wiring, III. *n*; IV. *t* 2.

EXPLANATION OF THE FIGURES.

FIG. I.—HALF MIDSHIP SECTION OF A WOODEN SHIP.

a. Keel; *b*. Keelson; *c*. False Keel; *d*. Keelson rider; *e*. Side or sister keelsons; *f*. Limber-boards; *g*. Chocks for filling up to planking; *h*. Clamps, or sea scarfs; *j*. Shelf, or *stringer*; *k*. Standard knees; *l*. Inside planking, or *lining*; *m*. Outside planking, or *skin*, made up of *strakes*; *m* 2. Garboard strakes; *m* 3. Thick strakes at bilge; *m* 4. Thick strakes above water line, called *wales*; *p*. Sheer strake; *q*. Water ways; *r*. Planksheer; *s*. Stanchion, or rough tree timber; *t*. Outside planking above deck, called *bulwarks* or *quickwork*; *u*. Rail, or rough-tree rail; *v*. Deck; *w*. Upper deck beams; *x*. Pad-piece; *y*. Hold beams (*i.e.*, the beams in the hold.)

Timbers.

1. Floor timber, ground futtock or navel futtock (1st futtock); 2. 2nd Futtock; 3. 3rd Futtock (middle futtocks); 4. Top timber (4th futtock); 5, 6. Riders.

FIG. II.—HALF MIDSHIP SECTION OF A STRONG CRUISING YACHT, DOUBLE PLANKED.

a. Keel; *b*. Keelson; *c*. Mast-step; *d*. Knee; *e*. Fillets; *f*. Limber spaces; *g*. Garboard strakes; *h*. Skin; *j*. Case; *k*. Stringers; *l*. Wale; *m*. Gunwale; *n*. Stanchion, or timber-head; *p*. Bulwark planking; *q*. Rail; *r*. Deck;

s. Beam; *t*. Hanging knee.

Timbers.

1. Ground futtock; 2. Middle futtock; 3. Top-timber.

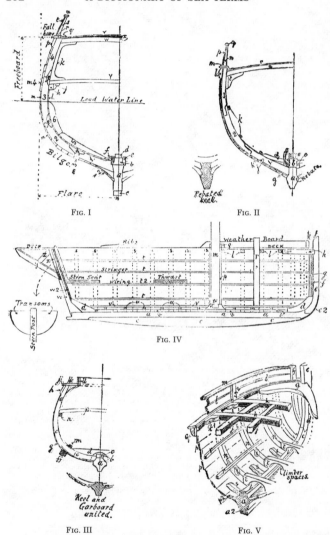

FIG. I

FIG. II

Rebated keel.

FIG. IV

Transoms

Stern Post

FIG. III

Keel and Garboard united.

FIG. V

Limber spaces.

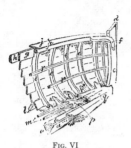

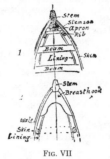

FIG. VI

FIG. VII

FIG. III.—HALF MIDSHIP SECTION OF AN OPEN SAILING-BOAT.

a. Keel; *b.* Keelson; *c.* Limber spaces; *d.* Flat floor; *e.* Bent timber, head, or bent head (*rib*); *f.* Bilge keel; *g.* Planking; *h.* Saxboard, or gunwale strake; *j.* Rubbing piece (the edge of the gunwale); *k.* Waterway (side deck); *l.* Coaming; *m.* Stringer; *n.* Wiring (stringers carrying thwarts); *p.* Thwart (seat).

FIG. IV.—LONGITUDINAL SECTION OF A HALF-DECKED SAILING-BOAT.

a. Keel; *b.* Keelson; *c.* False keel; *d.* Deadwoods (stem and stern); *e.* Stem-post; *e* 2. Stem-band; *f.* Stemson; *g.* Apron; *h.* Breasthook; *j.* Stem-head; *k.* Knighthead; *l.* Beams; *m.* Mast; *n.* Mast-step; *p.* Mast-case; *q.* Partners; *r.* Bowsprit bitts; *s.* Ribs, or *timbers*; *t.* Stringers; *t* 2. Wiring (stringers carrying thwarts); *u.* Flat floors; *v.* Floor boards; *w.* Stern-post; *w* 2. Sternson; *x.* Transom; *y.* Counter stay; *z.* Carline.

FIG. V.—PART FRAME OF A FISHING VESSEL.

a. Keel; *a* 2. False keel; *b.* Keelson; *c.* Deadwood; *d.* Stem-post; *e.* Stem-head; *f.* Knighthead; *g.* Breasthook; *h.* Beams; *j.* Carlines; *k.* Knees; *l.* Bulwark planking; *m.* Rough-tree rail; *n.* Futtocks (ribs); *n* 2. Stanchion, or timber head; *p.* Strakes; *p* 2. Garboard strakes; *q.* Wale; *r.* Stringers; *s.* Foot-timbers; *t.* Flat floors. 1, Ground futtock.

FIG. VI.—PART FRAME OF AN OPEN BOAT.

a. Keel; *b.* Keelson; *c.* Stem; *d.* Nose; *e.* Bent heads, heads, or bent timbers; *f.* Breasthook; *g.* Saxboard (the topmost strake); *h.* Wale, or rubbing piece; *j.* Gunwale; *k.* Inwale; *l.* Bilge Keel; *m.* Foot walings; *n.* Floor timbers; *p.* Flat floors; *q.* Head sheets; *r.* Stringers.

FIG. VII.—(1) SECTION OF STEM-POST AND APRON.
(2) STEM AND BREASTHOOK.

Frapping.—In emergency, the bracing together of ropes so as to increase their tension. The term also sometimes signifies the binding up of anything with ropes to prevent its bursting, a practice which, as applied to ships, appears to be very ancient, for St. Luke mentions, in his description of St. Paul's voyage (Acts xxvii., 17), that "they used helps, undergirding the ship". But the practice is extinct: Falconer, writing more than a century since, describes it even then as a remnant of the floating coffins. The word *frap* still exists, however, meaning "to bind" or "draw together". At sea the *frappings* of the shrouds (to the masts) are called *cat-harpings*.

Fray.—To become torn at the edge, as of a sail; or untwisted, as of a rope.

Free.—*Sailing free.*—Sailing with the wind abaft the beam.

Freeboard.—That portion of the vessel's side which is "free" of the water; that is, which is not submerged. Statutory freeboard is measured from the load water line to the deck where the distance is shortest. (*See* diagrams under FRAME.)

Freight.—The sum of money paid for the hire of a vessel or part of her is her *freightage.* Hence that which she carries has come to be regarded as her freight.

French fake.—A species of *Flemish coil* (*which see*).

Fresh.—*Fresh breeze* or *fresh gale.*—That which on shore might be called a high wind. Thus the wind may be said to be *blowing fresh.*

Freshen, Freshen the nip.—To veer or haul a rope slightly, so that a part subject to chafe or nip is moved away and a fresh part takes its place.

Freshen hawse.—To let the cable veer out a little. The term is a relic of the days of rope cables, which, being always liable to chafe and wear bare at the hawse holes, were constantly being freshened. They were *served* with canvas or leather; but this serving being quickly worn through required constant fresh application of the *service* (binding material); and this was called freshening.

Fresh way.—When a vessel increases her speed she is said to get fresh way.

Fret.—To chafe.

Frigate.—In the days of sailing navies a frigate was a full-rigged ship with from 24 to 38 guns carried on a single gun-deck. Faster and more lightly built than two- or three-decked vessels they did not lie in the line of battle, but were used for scouting and for commerce protection and raiding. The old East Indiamen were often *frigate-built.* This, according to Falconer, "implies the disposition of the decks of such merchant-ships as have a descent of four or five steps from the *quarter-deck* and *forecastle* into the *waist,* in contradistinction to those whose decks are on a continued line for the whole length of the ship, which are called *galley built.*"

During the Second World War they were medium-speed vessels used for escort, anti-submarine and other duties. They rank between *Destroyers* and *Corvettes.*

Frigatoon.—The original frigate is said to have been a Mediterranean vessel, propelled by both oars and sails. At a later time a frigatoon is described as "a Venetian vessel built with a square stern; without any foremast; having only a main mast, a mizzen mast, and bolt-sprit, used in the Adriatick Sea" (Bailey's Dictionary). Smyth describes this vessel as having main and jigger masts and bowsprit, with square stern.

Frost lamp.—A lamp at one time used in light-houses; its advantage being that the oil was kept running in cold weather.

Full.—A sail is said to be full when every inch of it is drawing.

Hence, *keep her full* will mean keep her drawing; or, in other words, do not go too close to the wind.

Full and by the wind.—Sailing as close to the wind as possible with all sails full and not shivering. (*See under* CLOSE-HAULED.)

Full-rigged ship; ship: or frigate.—A ship having three or more masts with their full complement of square sails. Until the introduction of four-masted sailing ships, the "ship" had all the masts, sails, spars, etc., that it was possible to carry. In modern times the name "Frigate" has been given to these ships.

BLACKWALL FRIGATE *Lincolnshire*, 1860

Four-masted vessels were usually barque-rigged, but one five-masted full-rigged ship was built in 1902. She was the *Preussen,* and was 408 ft. long with a beam of 53 ft. She set 47 sails with a total area of 50 000 sq. ft.

Fumigate.—It is the practice to fumigate certain craft, such as fishing vessels, from time to time, when they become infested with vermin. Enormous lice often swarm in these boats, and must be smoked out by lighting a fire over which sulphur and tar or sulphur alone is thrown, and shutting down the hatches for a considerable length of time.

Funnel (of a steam boat).—The chimney for carrying off the smoke, often called the *smoke stack.* But it also plays an important part in creating a draught for the furnaces, and in later times has sometimes been made telescopic, so as to regulate this draught.

Funny.—A narrow sculling boat, pointed bow and stern, and open throughout, accommodating only one person, and at one time employed in sculling matches: it was

FUNNY

usually clincher-built. The funny was never a successful type of boat, being very difficult to keep steady, and was quickly superseded by the *whiff,* and that again by the *wager* or *best* boat.

Furl.—To roll a sail and confine it to its yard or boom.

Furling lines.—Short ropes which are used to secure a sail to the yard or boom, when furled. They are also called *gaskets* and *ties.*

"Furling in a body is a particular method of rolling up a topsail, only practised in harbours, and is performed by gathering all the loose part of the sail into the bunt, about the top-mast, whereby the yard appears much thinner and lighter than when the sail is furled over all at sea." (Falconer.)

Furniture.—The masts and rigging of a vessel with all accessories constitute that which is sometimes called its furniture.

Futtock.—This term is evidently derived from the lowest part, or *foot,* of a timber, and from the *hooked* shape of the piece; hence, *foot-hook* (a hook, in shipbuilding, being anything bent or incurvated). In shipbuilding, a futtock is one of the members composing the ribs of a vessel. The ribs of large ships cannot be made of one piece, as can those of open boats; they consist, therefore, of several pieces or members, scarfed together, each one being called a "futtock". The lowest of these is the *floor timber,* also called the *ground futtock* or (amidships) the *navel futtock*; the one above it is the *second futtock*; above that, if there be one, the *third futtock*; and the top-futtock is the *top-timber.* Thus the floor timber, the middle timbers, and the top timber are all, properly speaking, *futtocks.*

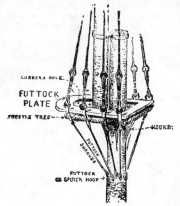

Top, Futtock-plate, Topmast and Futtock Shrouds

Futtock-plank.—The ground futtock, or floor timber, lies above the keel, and upon it rests the *keelson,* which is bolted through to the keel. On each side are the *bilge planks* (both inside and out), that one nearest the keel on each side being called the "futtock-plank." (*See* diagram under FRAME.)

Futtock-plate (in rigging).—Apart from any connection with the futtocks forming the ribs of a ship, the masts of vessels were sometimes furnished with an apparatus called the *futtock-plate and shrouds.* The *futtock plate* was the iron plate at the edge of the top to which the dead eyes of the topmast rigging were attached. The *futtock shrouds* were ropes, or iron bars, connecting the futtock plate with the *futtock* or *spider band* (*see* fig.), to which ratlines were secured by which men could ascend from the lower shrouds to the topmast rigging.

Futtock stave.—A short piece of rop by which the shrouds are confined at the cat harpings.

G

Gaff (sometimes pronounced *garf* or *garft*).—The spar which extends the *head* (or upper portion) of a fore-and-aft-sail, such as the mainsail of a cutter. A sail suspended by a gaff is called a *gaff sail,* in contradistinction to a sail suspended by a yard, which is a *square*

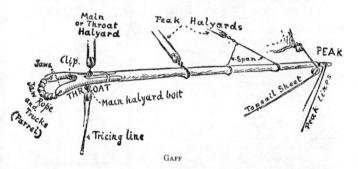

GAFF

sail. The form and gear of a gaff are as follows (*see* fig.):—The lower end is furnished with *jaws* made of hard wood, sometimes metal; and in large yachts a *clapper,* or *tumbler,* is fitted between them to prevent chafing; this portion of the spar being called the *clip.* The jaws partially encircle the mast, the circle being completed by a rope on which several round beads of hard wood, called trucks, have been threaded; this is the *parrel,* which allows the gaff to be raised and lowered without jamming. The upper end of the gaff is called the *peak*; the lower the *throat.* It is hauled up by two *halyards,* the one being fixed to the throat, and therefore called the *throat halyard* (or, in single masted boats, simple the *main halyard*); the other usually at two points further up the spar for elevating the peak, and for that reason designated the *peak-halyard.* In raising the sail these two halyards are hauled on together, so that the gaff may go up in a position almost horizontal; and when the clip is well up the peak is *set up,* and *swigged* upon to make the sail hang flat: in large vessels, a tackle is employed for this latter purpose. In each case these halyards pass through blocks, the number of sheaves in which varies according to the power necessary for lifting the sail. The block through which runs the throat halyard is often attached to the gaff by a double-eyed bolt called the *main-halyard bolt,* the lower eye being underneath, and carrying on it another smaller block, through which another rope is rove communicating with the *tack* of the sail; this is the *tricing-line,* and its object is to pull or *trice* up the luff of the sail, so as quickly to reduce the area it presents to the wind. The peak-halyard blocks are carried in large vessels by *spans,* which are kept from slipping by small excrescences called *spurs* or *thumb cleats.* Over the *guy*-end (after-end) of the gaff is fitted a cap, or *end-ring,* with eyes. The ring prevents the spar from splitting, while the eyes serve to carry small blocks, one for the topsail sheet, another for the *peak-line,* a thin rope used sometimes for hauling down the peak, but mostly as a flag halyard, the ensign or some other flag being often hoisted at the peak as a signal. In small craft and yachts, the gaff is always lowered and stowed away with the boom, the peak-halyards being unshackled when the sail cover is put on, and then replaced by hooking the blocks to *slings* which pass under the boom and round the cover. But in vessels of larger class it is often set without the sail. And as, in such a case, it will naturally sway backwards and forwards, ropes are stretched from the guy end of the peak to the sides of the vessel; these ropes being called *vanes* or *vangs:* The sprit of a barge is always steadied by vangs.

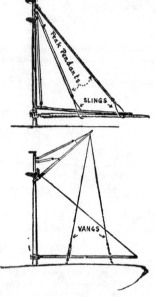

The mainsail of a cutter, sloop, yawl, etc., being set up, it may be desirable to add another sail above it, which is known as a *gaff-topsail,* and is elevated by means of a halyard passing through a sheave or block, attached near the head of the topmast, and the foot of which is stretched along the *gaff,* whence the name. (*See* under TOPSAILS.)

Gain the wind (of another ship).—To get to windward of her.

Gale.—The term as used at sea has a different meaning from that usually understood by it ashore. Formerly applied to any fresh wind it now denotes a wind of over 34 knots (force 8 of the Beaufort Scale (*see* WIND) and above. 1. a *near gale* has a wind speed between 28 and 33 knots. 2. a *strong gale* has a wind speed between 41 and 47 knots. 3. A wind of more than 47 knots is classified as a *storm.* "Half a gale" is a popular term among seamen, who mean by it as strong a wind as can blow.

Gallant.—From "Garland" (*which see*), hence the usual pronunciation of the word, "Garn," as *t'garn* for top-gallant. The word has considerable use at sea. (*See* MAST, SAIL, STAYS, TOP, DECK, etc.)

Galleas.—A compromise type of vessel between the *galley* which was designed to be rowed, and the *galleon* which was sailed. The galleas was provided with oars and had two or three masts with lateen sails. In the 16th to 17th centuries they were used in the summer months in extensive trading voyages as well as in warfare.

Galleon.—A name usually confined to Spanish and Portuguese ships in the 16th century, but the type was also common to North European countries. Sir John Hawkins, in 1570, found that the "high charged" *carracks* (*which see*), were improved by the removal of the very high forecastles, and the galleon, as these more manoeuvrable and weatherly ships were called, became the principal type of large ship. They were usually three-masted; square-rigged on fore and mainmast, lateen-rigged on mizzen mast.

GALLEON, 16th CENTURY

Galley.—An oared fighting vessel of the Mediterranean from about 3000 B.C. to the 18th century A.D. Originally propelled by one bank of oars they subsequently had two banks, when they were called *Biremes,* and then *Triremes* with three banks. *Quadreremes* and *Quinqueremes* were also used, but their names can hardly have referred to the number of levels at which the oars were arranged. The rowers on the upper bank of a trireme were termed *thranites,* of the middle bank *zygites,* and of the lower bank *thalamites,* perhaps 170 oars in all. Mediaeval galleys had but one bank of heavier oars each pulled by several men. Galleys might also have one or two masts and sails. Their principal weapon was the *ram,* but in the 16th century guns were mounted forward, fixed to fire directly ahead. 2. A captain's gig (*which see*). 3. The cookhouse of a ship.

Galliot (pronounced by the fishermen *"galley-yacht"*).—A Dutch vessel of remarkable type. She is very long and narrow, and may reach to 100 tons burden. She is fore-and-aft rigged with two masts, main and mizzen, the latter being little more than a jigger, and answering the same purpose as the same sail does in our own

GALLIOT

sailing barges; that is to assist the rudder in getting the vessel round; and for this purpose it works with the rudder. But the galliot was principally peculiar in the form of her mainsail, the foot of which was enormously long, while the head was extremely short. The vessel is now rare.

Gallow-bitts.—On ships, a frame for the support of spars, boats, etc.: the form is supposed to have resembled a gallows.

Galvanizing.—Nearly all iron fittings to sailing craft are now galvanized, the process being very cheap, and its effect as a preservative against rust lasting a long time. Articles to be galvanized are first pickled, that is immersed in weak sulphuric acid and water (about 1 per cent. of acid); they are then washed in lime water, and afterwards placed in a bath of chloride of zinc for a few minutes. When dry they are continually dipped in melted zinc (which should not be at too great a heat) until a sufficient coating has adhered, any excess being removed by hammering or wire-brushing while still hot.

Gammoning.—In ships the fastening and lashing down of the bowsprit. (*See* fig.)

Gammoning holes.—The holes through which the ropes used in lashing the bowsprit pass (*See* fig.).

Gammoning-iron.—A ring, bolted to the stem head of a sailing boat, and through which the bowsprit passes. It does away with the necessity of gammoning. (*See* under BOWSPRIT.)

Gang.—A number of men employed on any particular service.

Gang board.—A board used for getting on board a vessel from a quay or pier.

Gangway.—1. A narrow platform or bridge passing over from one deck of a vessel to another. 2. That part of a ship's bulwarks which are removable so that persons can walk on board by a gang board. 3. A narrow passage left between the stowage of cargo in a ship to allow of a man going down to make examinations. 4. An order to make way.

Gantline.—A line rove through a block near the masthead used to hoist anything aloft.

Garboard.—The lowest part of a vessel.

Garboard strakes (sometimes called *garboards* in shipbuilding).— The lowest strakes in a vessel, which abut upon the keel. They are also called the *ground* or *sand* strakes. (*See* diagrams under FRAME.)

Garland.—A ring of rope placed round a spar for the purpose of moving it, as, for instance, when swaying a heavy mast. Otherwise a collar of rope wound about the head of a mast to keep the shrouds from galling. A garland in ancient days was a rope used in swaying the topmasts. Hence, when a mast was added to ships above the topmasts, it was called a garland mast; and the word becoming corrupted, eventually resolved itself into "gallant", in writing, though the original pronunciation "garn" has been preserved amongst seamen in speaking to this day.

Garnet.—A tackle rigged from the mainstay or masthead used for hoisting in stores, etc. Also the tackle attached to the clew of a *course.* (*See* CLEW-GARNETS, under CLEW.)

Gaskets.—Small cords by which a sail when furled is kept bound up to a yard, boom, or gaff; there are several, as the bunt-gasket, the quarter-gasket, the yard-arm-gasket. They are also called *ties* and *furling lines.* The gasket, in a steam engine, is the hempen plait used for packing pump pistons, etc.

Gather.—To draw in, as of a sheet.

To *gather way.*—To begin to make headway.

Gatt.—A channel in an open piece of water, as the "Fishermen's Gatt" in the estuary of the Thames. The word is Low German. A gatt must not be confounded with a *gut,* which is only a small waterway, whereas a gatt may be a sheet of water many miles in length.

Gauntlet (properly *gant-lope*).—*Running the gauntlet.*—A form of punishment for an offence revolting to the feelings of the whole crew of a vessel, and therefore giving to every member an opportunity of visiting his own peculiar displeasure upon the offender. It consisted in making a man pass down between the whole crew formed up in two lines facing each other, each man being furnished with a rope-end with which he slashed at the offender as he passed. The punishment is long since extinct, if indeed it ever existed as a recognised practice; but it is from this origin that we have the popular expression "running the gauntlet".

Gear.—A general term which may mean rigging, tackle, ropes, belonging to a spar or sail, or indeed any part of the working apparatus of a vessel, as the gear of the helm, which consists of the wheel, the tiller, the chains, the blocks, and all other necessary parts.

Gearing in machinery is the method of transmitting, increasing, or altering the direction of power, as by cog or gearing-wheels.

Out of gear.—Out of order, or if with reference to gearing in machinery, the act of stopping power in some part while another part is still working is to throw that part which is stopped "out of gear".

Genoa jib.—A large jib, sheeting well aft, its clew overlapping the luff of the mainsail.

Ghosting, or **Ghosting along.**—Sailing well in a very light breeze.

Gib.—Another word for a pin or forelock (a pin through a bolt).

Gift rope.—(*See* GUEST ROPE.)

Gig.—An open boat, usually clincher-built, with a straight sheer and upright stem and gunwale. It is one of the boats belonging to a ship, as the *captain's gig*. At one time the gig was very popular

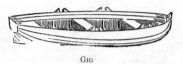

GIG

on the Upper Thames, but has now been almost entirely superseded by the *skiff*.

Gin.—(*See* GYN.)

Gingerbread.—The decorative scroll work carved on large ships from the 15th to the 18th century.

Gimbals.—The brass rings which suspend a compass so as to keep it horizontal. (*See* COMPASS.)

Gipsy/gypsy.—The sprocketed cable-holder of a windlass.

Girdle.—A rope round anything, as a *frapping*. Also an extra planking occasionally placed over the wales in old wooden ships.

Girt.—Bound. A vessel riding under taughtened cables, which hold her by the sides, is said to be girt. 2. The state of a tug when her towrope leads nearly abeam and she may be in danger of capsizing.

Give.—The elasticity which every boat should possess, under strain and shrinkage, is called the *give*. Every member in the building of a vessel is allowed a certain play, or in other words is allowed to "*work*". This adds not only to the strength and endurance of a vessel, but also to her speed; and it is said that so well was this recognised of old that pirates have been known, when hard pressed in chase, to saw through the beams of their boats for the sake of the extra speed to be gained. If a boat have no give, the strain upon her will be much increased, and she will the sooner become leaky.

Give her sheet.—Ease off the sheet.

Give way (in rowing).—Begin pulling.

Give over.—To stop or cease doing anything.

Glass.—A common name for an aneroid barometer.

A long glass.—A common name for a marine telescope.

Glasses.—Binoculars.

Glass re-enforced plastic ("GRP"), or **Glass fibre.**—The material manufactured from finely spun glass threads and resin laminate with which small vessels are now generally constructed.

Glory hole.—Any small space where gear is stowed. The stewards' sleeping quarters.

Glut.—"A patch at the centre of the head of the sail, having an eyelet for the becket rope." ("Dictionary of Mechanics.")

G.M.T.—Greenwich Mean Time. The time kept in longitude 0° at the prime meridian passing through the Observatory at Greenwich.

Go.—*Go!*—The order to start, in racing: it is generally preceded by the question, "Are you ready?" and if no answer is given, the word "Go" follows almost immediately.

Go adrift.—To become loose.

Go about (in sailing).—To come round *head to wind,* so as to come on the other tack. (*See* TACK.)

Go by.—To give a person the go by is to pass, overtake or escape from him.

Go ahead!—Go on! order on steamers to start the engine forward.

Go astern.—To reverse the engine. To move through the water stern first. To take station astern of another vessel.

Going free.—In sailing, the same as sailing free or large. (*See* SAILING FREE.)

Gondola.—A Venetian boat.

> 'Tis a long covered boat that's common here,
>   Carved at the prow, built lightly but compactly,
> Rowed by two rowers, each called "Gondolier",
>   It glides along the water looking blackly,
> Just like a coffin clapt in a canoe,
>   Where none can make out what you say or do.—
>   (Byron—"Beppo.")

Gone.—Broken away; spoken of any sail or spar on a vessel.

Gone.—A common way of expressing that some person has sunk, if drowning, or under any other circumstances to give notice of death without the necessity of using the word. In this sense the term is much used amongst seafaring folk.

Goose (*Gooseneck and shaffle*).—The fitting of a boom to a mast by means of a kind of pin or hook at the heel of a boom which fits into a ring or short cylinder on the mast. The pin is called the *gooseneck,* probably because it is—(in its simplest, hook form) so curved as somewhat to re-

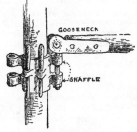

GOOSENECK

semble the neck of a goose or swan. The ring which receives it is the *shaffle.* But a boom is also frequently fitted with jaws (as in a gaff) which partly encircle the mast, and in this case there is usually a ring or shoulder called a *saddle* on the mast which prevents the boom from sliding down. In either case the complete fitting may be called the *boom-stays.*

Goosewing.—The shape of a square sail, when the bunt (middle part) is hauled up while the clews (lower corners) hang. This is supposed to resemble the wings of a goose, and hence a sail so disposed is called a goosewing. This may be done when it is re-

GOOSEWING

quired to reduce sail without reefing, as in heavy weather or for scudding. Studding sails are also occasionally called goosewings. In fore and aft rig means that the foresail is guyed out on the opposite to the mainsail.

Gore.—A small piece sometimes introduced at the corner of a sail, or an increase in the depth or width of any of the cloths.

Gore strake.—In shipbuilding an angular piece of planking or a strake terminating short of the stem or stern posts.

Gorge (of a block).—The groove or *score* in the sheave (wheel) of the block.

Grab.—A coasting vessel employed on the Indian coasts in the 18th and 19th centuries. It was rigged with one or two masts and lateen sails.

Graft.—A decorative finish to an eye splice. After the first tuck had been made the yarns are woven together.

Grain.—A four or five pronged harpoon for spearing fish.

Granny knot.—A knot improperly tied, *i.e.*, one which will slip or come undone when hauled upon. The term may be applied to any knot, but is generally understood to refer to the reef knot. The tying a granny is regarded, among yachting or boating amateurs, as an unforgivable sin. It will be well, therefore, for the beginner to become familiar with a few of the knots in most frequent use before venturing aboard a sailing boat. (*See* KNOTS.)

Grapnel.—A small anchor of several arms or claws arranged in a circular manner at the end of the shank. It is mostly used by small craft, though sometimes as a *kedge* (*which see*). Very small ones are called *hand grapnels*. In old times the grapnel, or, as it was then called, the *grapple* or *grappling iron,* was used by ships in close action for seizing the rigging of an enemy's vessel and dragging the two together preparatory to boarding. Grappling irons are of various forms, and are still used for various purposes, as for holding vessels together when unloading, etc. (*See* fig. under ANCHOR.)

GRAPNEL

Grass line.—A rope made of coir, not particularly strong, but sufficiently light to float upon the water.

Gratings.—1. (At sea).—Open-work or trellised frames placed over hatchways or lights in rough weather. 2. (In boats).—Open work coverings to any part, such as stern or head sheets, etc. They are ornamental as well as useful in allowing a free circulation of air to reach all parts of a boat.

Grave.—To clean a ship's bottom, as by *breaming,* which is burning the accumulation off her.

Graving dock.—A dock in which graving may be done. A dry dock.

Graveyard watch.—The Middle Watch; midnight to four a.m.

Greaser.—An engineroom rating whose duties include lubrication. 2. At one time a fo'c'sle nickname for the Mate.

Great out.—An expression made use of by fishermen when the sea recedes to a more than usual extent during spring-tides.

Green (*Green hand* or *green horn*).—A new hand, or a lubberly fellow.

Green heart.—A wood imported from the West Indies and much used in the making of piers, etc., for fender piles. It was also originally employed for the pins of blocks.

Green sea.—An unbroken wave. A term describing solid water coming aboard.

Grid-iron.—A skeleton framework of wood upon which a vessel may be supported when it is necessary to have the bottom of her inspected, as after she has taken the ground.

Grip (of an oar).—The part gripped by the hand. (*See* OAR.)

Gripe (in sailing).—The hold a vessel takes of the water when under sail, or, in other words, her tendency to run up into the wind. If she carries considerable *weather helm* she is said to gripe well; this, however, may be carried to excess. (*See* WEATHER HELM.)

Gripe (in shipbuilding).—The fore foot or fore end of the keel of a ship on which the stem is set; or, in other words, the sharpness of her stem under water; which is made thus in order to gripe the water.

Gripes (on shipboard) are the ropes and gear by which boats are made secure on deck.

Grog.—A mixture of rum and water. Until 1970 a daily issue of grog was made to ratings in the Royal Navy, a practice instituted by Admiral Vernon in 1740.

Grommet (pronounced "grummet").—A ring of rope which may be made to fit over a spar and to carry a block It is made of a single strand of rope laid up around its own part. Where only small grommets are required, metal rings or eyelets called *thimbles* are usually inserted into the loop.

Ground.—To ground is to run aground, or ashore. If this takes place with a yacht or big boat when the tide is rising, the consequences will not be very serious. With the aid of her sails and sweeps she will soon float. But should the tide be falling, not a moment is to be lost. Her sails are so to be set that she may be backed off as the wind fills them. The best way to effect this when the wind blows off the shore, is to haul one or both of the head sails (jib and foresail) over to windward, and to hold the main sail out in the same direction. The sweeps or a pole may be used to help her off at the same time, but nothing is so efficacious as the sails, until she moves, when sweeps may be of the utmost service. If she does not move within a very few minutes, there is little chance of her coming off until the tide flows again.

Ground swell.—At sea, an undulation of the waters caused by a continuance of heavy gales. Such ground swells are transmitted with great rapidity, even against the wind, and sometimes to great distances; they indicate, by their direction, the quarter in which a gale has taken place, and have been known to come from various directions at the same time. The swell or *wash* (*see* WASH) caused by a passing steam or other large boat is sometimes called a ground swell. This is not, strictly speaking, correct, although it is certainly the case that a steamboat occasionally does, in certain states of the tide, create in narrow channels (such as a river) a true ground swell, which may often be seen coming up some considerable distance behind her, even against a strong run of tide. This is not her wash, and it may even be doubted whether it is in any way caused by her wash; it is more probably the result of her *draught,* considered in connection with the depth (or rather, want of depth) of water in which she is travelling, and the speed at which she goes. Her wash may be followed all along the shore, subsiding as she disappears; some minutes after which the ground swell will be seen coming up, wave after wave, not drawing the water up to it and breaking upon the shore as does the wash, but continuing its uninterrupted course, often gathering strength as it goes. These swells in rivers are sometimes very dangerous to small boats, and care should therefore be taken not to meet them broad-side. Care should, indeed, always be taken in meeting a steam-boat, as at all other critical moments.

Ground tackle.—The name sometimes applied to the gear belonging to moorings, anchors, and such like ground implements.

Ground futtock.—(*See* FUTTOCK.)

Grow.—An expression made use of to describe the position of some of the rigging of a ship, as "the cable grows on the starboard side," *i.e.,* runs out on that side.

Growing.—New boats are said to grow, *i.e.,* to become larger when placed in the water; so that after a year or two there is a measurable difference in their form; and for this reason they are seldom copper sheathed until they have been in the water a year or two.

Grown spar, or *ricker.*—A spar made out of an entire small tree, not cut out of a large one. These are always much to be desired for small craft, being superior to the *made* spars.

Groyne.—A timber construction (sometimes strengthened with stone) on a beach, running out into the sea or from a river bank, and sometimes set in the direction of the main current. It is often called a breakwater (*which see*), though improperly, for its object is not so much to break the force of the waves as to create a natural breakwater by

GROYNE

accumulating a quantity of shingle or sand, thereby elevating the level of the beach and preventing the encroachment of the sea. "A groyne is, in fact, a projection that is carried out from the banks of the sea, or of a river, in a direction perpendicular to, or occasionally inclined to the set of, the current; and it is supposed to act in the first case by retaining the shingle, which has a tendency to move in the direction of the prevailing wind; and in the latter, by diverting the channel in the direction required." (Brande and Cox.) Some engineers are of opinion that these constructions, unless placed so close together as to throw up almost a continuous wall, do more harm than good by creating a back current on the down side which carries with it the shingle or earth they are intended to accumulate.

Gudgeons.—The fittings of a rudder to its stern post. The gudgeons, (occasionally *goodgeons*), are bands of iron terminating in eyes into which the pintles are inserted. (*See* PINTLE and RUDDER.)

Guest rope, guess rope, or **guest warp.**—A rope used to steady a boat in tow. It is an addition to the tow rope. 2. A rope led from forward to the foot of the gangway to help boats coming alongside.

Gunroom.—Originally a compartment of the lower gundeck of a sailing warship used as a mess for (principally) midshipmen, later situated in a more habitable part of the ship.

Gun-tackle.—Originally the tackle applied to a gun. It is a tackle composed of two single blocks, one movable, the other fixed, the standing end of the fall (rope) being fast to the movable block. It increases the power three-fold.

Gun tackle purchase.—In sailing yachts the tackle applied in drawing down the tack of the mainsail is sometimes thus called.

Gunter.—*Gunter's scale.*—"A large plain scale having various lines of numbers engraved on it, by means of which questions in navigation are resolved with the aid of a pair of compasses. It is usually called the *gunter* by seamen." (Brande and Cox.) Used in 17th and 18th centuries.

Sliding gunter.—A peculiar sail adapted to boats. In place of a gaff it has a yard sliding up and down the mast.

Gunwale (pronounced "gunnel").—  It would appear from the name (gun wale) that this portion of a boat must have originally served to support small guns. The gunwale in vessels rests upon the *wale* (*which see*). In an open boat it is the top of, or a piece running round above, the saxboard. In it, at correct intervals, are holes for the rowlocks or tholes. The *inwale* (where it exists) is beneath the gunwale, supporting it, within-board, on the bent-heads (ribs); and on the outside is sometimes fixed another strengthening plank, then called the *rubbing piece* or *wale*. In such boats as the Thames skiffs, where the sides rise up, like wings, to each rowlock, there is, properly speaking, no gunwale.

The *gunwale strake* (in open boats the *sheerstrake* or *saxboard*) is the uppermost strake of a boat. To it the gunwale is fixed.

Gunwale down or *gunwale to.*—When a boat casts over so that her gunwale touches the surface of the water.

Gut.—A small channel, such as may be left by the tide on an ebb-dry foreshore. (*See* also GATT.)

Gutter-ledge.—A fore and aft beam placed along the middle of a large hatchway to support the covers and give them strength to carry any weight. (*See* diagram under HATCH.)

Guy.—A steadying or stay-rope, as the guy of a derrick which steadies its arm as it swings a weight. In sailing boats, it is a rope which serves to keep a sail or spar in *trim*—*i.e.,* in the desired position—as the guy of a spinnaker, which keeps that sail forward. A slack rope extending between two masts, and carrying a block or tackle, is also called a guy.

Guy end.—That end of a spar to which a guy is or may be fixed. The spar is then said to be "guyed."

Spinnaker, fore or *after guy,* are the names sometimes given to the ropes or tackles which haul the spinnaker boom forward or back; but they should more properly be called the spinnaker boom braces. (*See* under SPINNAKER.)

A *guy pennant,* sometimes termed a *lazy guy,* is a rope occasionally used to keep a boom from jerking up and down, in a rolling sea; it must be so fastened round the boom that it can be let go at a moment's notice.

In ships there are various guys.

Gybe.—The swinging over of a fore-and-aft sail when running before the wind. This may be done purposely when slightly altering the boat's course, in which case care should be taken that the jerk of the boom and sail is not too severe; or it may happen by accident and almost instantaneously, in which case there is danger of carrying something away. Gybing may take place with the slightest variation of the wind or of the boat's course, and should, therefore, be constantly looked out for. When it happens unexpectedly, the helmsman who may be fortunate enough to see it coming, should rapidly gather in his main sheet, putting his helm hard down at the same time: the jerk may by this means be, to a certain extent, taken off the mast and stays, and the sheet can then be let out again as required. Beginners are often too apt to let their sail gybe: it is, in yachts, a very dangerous practice.

In large racing yachts, however, gybing is often accomplished in that which would appear to be a most reckless manner. The boom is allowed to fly round amain, and without any check, its weight as it swings over so bending down the boat that the boom strikes the water and thus saves itself.

Gyn, or **Gin.**—A hoisting machine on three tall legs, and fitted with a sort of windlass, and one block, called the gyn block. (*See* BLOCK.)

Gyn tackle.—A system consisting of a movable double and a triple block, the standing end of the fall (*i.e.,* the fixed end of the rope) being fast to the double block. It increases the power fivefold.

Gyro.—A gyro compass. (*See* COMPASS.)

H

Hail.—To salute, accost, call out to, or make a sign to any person.

Hake's teeth, or **hag's teeth.**—"A phrase applied to some part of the deep soundings in the British Channel. But it is a distinct shell-fish, being the *dentalium*, the presence of which is a valuable guide to the Channel pilot in foggy weather." (Smyth.)

Hale.—To *hale*, in old nautical phraseology, is to pull: hence the word became confounded with and eventually corrupted into *haul* (*which see*).

Half.—*Half beams.*—In a ship, short beams extending from the sides only to the hatchways.

Half-breadth plan.—In shipbuilding, the plan of one half of a vessel divided by a centre line drawn through stem and stern posts. It shows *water, bow, buttock,* and *diagonal* lines. (*See* LINES.)

Half-breadth, staff, or *rod.*—In shipbuilding, a rod having marked upon it the half-lengths of the beams of a vessel. It is very precisely measured from the half-breadth plan.

Half crown.—A small circular bight in a rope.

Half davit.—The fish davit (*which see*) is sometimes thus called because it is only a short davit.

Half deck.—In ships, a space in the fore part of a vessel. In some of the old Northumbrian colliers the steerage or fore-castle deck was called the half deck. The apprentices' or cadets' accommodation in a merchant ship, irrespective of where this may be. In sailing boats a half deck is one extending over only a portion of a boat, the rest being open. For racing purposes

HALF DECK

it has been found necessary to define a half decked boat; it must be open aft of the mast, and forward of the transom, this open space not exceeding one half of the internal area of the boat; and the waterways on each side must not exceed (measured from the outside of the boat to the inside of the coaming) one tenth of the beam of the boat. A boat that fails to comply with these conditions must be classed as a *decked boat*.

Half ebb, half flood.—(*See* next page, HALF TIDE.)

Half floor.—In shipbuilding, one of the timbers in the frame of a ship. Its heel is set over the keel, and upon its head rests the second futtock.

Half hitch.—One bend in a rope; part of the process of making a knot. (*See* KNOTS.)

Half laughs and *purser's grins.*—"Hypocritical and satirical sneer." (Smyth.)

Half man.—A name sometimes given, in coasting vessels, to a *landsman* (*which see*) or boy.

Half mast (of a flag).—A flag half mast high is a sign of mourning; on an owner's vessel it is generally kept thus until after the burial. (*See* fig.).

Half-minute glass.—At sea, a sand glass used in running out the old form of log.

Half points (of the compass.)—The mariner's compass is divided into 32 *points*. (*See* COMPASS.) Half one of these divisions is half a point. A half point is therefore 5° 37′ 30″ of the circle.

Half port (in the Navy).—In old ships, a porthole shutter perforated with a hole, through which the muzzle of a gun could be thrust.

Half sea.—An old term for *mid-channel.* (Smyth.)

Half seas over.—Half drunk. The term was used by Swift.

FLAG HALF MAST HIGH

Half speed (with steam vessels). Reduced speed, ahead or astern.

Half tide.—The condition of the tide when half way between its highest and lowest; with a rising tide it is called *half-flood,* with a falling tide *half ebb.*

Half tide rocks are those which show themselves at half-tide.

Half-timber.—In ship-building, a short *futtock.*

Halyard, or **Halliard.**—A rope, sometimes a chain, by which a sail, flag, or yard is hoisted—hence the name—"haul yard." A halyard often consists of two parts: viz., the *pendant,* and a *tackle* or *purchase* hauled upon, which is often called the *fall* (*see* diagrams under that head). Halyards take their names from the spars or sails upon which they act, as *throat-halyards* (those which elevate the throat of a gaff), etc. For reference to any particular halyard, see under the name of its sail.

Hambro, or **Hambrough,** or **hamber line.**—Small line used for seizings, lashings, and a variety of other purposes on shipboard.

Hammock.—A swinging canvas bed much used at sea. "In the language of some tribes in the West Indian islands, the word *hamac* denoted nets of cotton extended from two posts, and used as beds. From them the word was borrowed by the companions of Columbus, who transferred it to us through the Spanish word *hamaca.*" (Brande and Cox.)

Hammock nettings.—In old sailing war ships, a net-work rack in which hammocks were stowed. They were often under the bulwarks.

Hamper.—(*See also* TOP HAMPER.) Height aloft, as the yards, topmasts, etc., of a ship. Smyth describes it thus:—"Things which, though necessary, are in the way in times of gale or service."

Hand.—A term often used for the word "man", as "all hands on deck", "another hand wanted", etc.

Handlass—An old name for a windlass, because worked by hand.

Hand lead.—A sounding lead, weighing between 10 and 14 lbs., is for finding the depth of water beneath a vessel. (*See* LEAD.)

Hand mast.—A pole mast. Otherwise a mast made out of a hand spar. (*See* below, HAND SPAR.)

Hand over hand.—Hauling rapidly, and passing one hand alternately over the other.

Hand rail.—A rail running along any portion of a vessel's deck.

Hand spar.—A round mast of one piece. "Those from Riga are commonly over 70 ft. long by 20 in. in diameter." (Smyth.)

Hand spike.—A bar employed as a lever for lifting heavy objects, or for working a windlass.

To *hand a sail* is to furl it.

To *hand the log* is to haul inboard the log line and rotator.

Handle.—To handle a boat well is to sail, and generally to work, her in seamanlike fashion.

Handsomely.—A term which sounds somewhat contradictory. It means the opposite to hasty, and is used occasionally with reference to ropes or halyards, as "Lower away handsomely", which would mean "lower away gradually, and carefully". Sometimes, too, it is understood to mean "bit by bit", as "Let out the cable handsomely!"—*i.e.*, a little at the time.

Handy.—To be handy is to be capable of turning a hand to anything one may be called upon to do; and especially to be able to do it quickly, and without bungling. A boat is said to be handy when she answers her helm well and is generally well-behaved under all circumstances.

Handy billy.—A small *purchase* or tackle, sometimes called a jigger purchase.

Hang.—Spoken of anything leaning out of the upright, as a mast which may *hang back* if too taut in the backstays, or forward if too loose.

To *hang on* to any rope is to hold it tightly without belaying it. "Hang on", as an expression, often means simply "Hold on".

To *hang the rudder* is to fix it in its *braces* ready for use.

Hanging Judas.—A rope of any kind hanging loose aloft or not properly secured. (*See* IRISH PENDANT.)

HANKS

Hanging knees.—In shipbuilding, knees or supports fastened under deck beams.

Hanging standard knees are others used in somewhat the same manner.

Hang, or *sny.*—Among shipwrights a slight upward curve in a timber is called a *sny:* if its tendency is downwards, it is said to *hang.*

Hanks.—Rings, of wood or iron, or catch-hooks, by which sails may be made to run on stays, or purchase ropes be hooked on to tackles. (*See* fig. p. 121). Thus a foresail runs on to the forestay by hanks. The mast rings are also sometimes called the hanks.

Hank for hank.—An expression signifying that two vessels work to windward together, tack for tack.

Harbour.—A piece of navigable water communicating with a sea or river, having a roadstead, and protected from storms. There are permanent harbours, tidal harbours, and harbours of refuge, often called *havens.*

Harbour gaskets.—With sailing ships, the gaskets with which sails are furled in harbour, or when it is desired to appear smart. They used to be well blacked in the Royal Navy, so as to contrast well with the whiteness of the sails.

Hard.—1. "Hard", in nautical language, is often joined to words of command to the helmsman, signifying that the order should be carried out with the utmost energy, *e.g.:*

Hard up (of the helm), or *hard aweather*—to put the tiller of a vessel quickly over to the windward to its fullest extent.

Hard down, hard alee—to put the tiller quickly over to the lee side to its fullest extent.

Hard over.—To put the helm *over* is to shift it: that is to bear the tiller over to the corresponding position on the opposite side of the vessel: *hard over* is to do this as far as it will go. These terms are more fully explained under the heading HELM.

2. *Hard.*—A solid path or way artificially (occasionally naturally) formed on a soft mud flat or foreshore, its use being that a boat may land its occupants there at any state of the tide.

3. *Hard and fast.*—Fixed or immovable.

4. *"Hard up in a clinch and no knife to cut the seizings."*—An expression sometimes used in a dilemma out of which it is difficult to see the way.

Hardchine.—When the sides of a vessel meet her bottom at an angle, instead of being rounded, she is said to be hard-chined.

Hard Iron.—Iron which is slow to receive magnetism, but retains it when received.

Hardtack.—Ship's biscuits.

Harl, or **harr.**—On the east coasts of Scotland and England, a wet sea fog and easterly wind.

Harness.—A belt and straps fitted with a clip-hook, by which the wearer can secure himself to guard-rail or rigging.)

Harness cask (at sea).—A cask holding food for immediate use.

Harness hitch.—A knot employed in harnessing men to a tow-line. (*See* KNOTS.)

Harpings.—In shipbuilding certain of the *wales* (planks) at the forward part of a hull are thicker than elsewhere: these stronger wales are called harpings.

Cat harpings.—Ropes for *frapping* (girting in) a ship's standing rigging so that the lower yards may be braced up sharp.

Harpoon.—A barbed javelin used in spearing whales.

Hasp.—Generally speaking a fastening, such as a clamp; a bar dropping into a staple.

Hatch, hatchway.—A *hatchway* is an opening in the deck of a vessel through which persons or cargo may descend: it is covered by a movable frame or roof, called a *hatch*; or in large craft by several hatches which are kept down by small beams or rods called *battens.* (*See* BATTEN DOWN.) A small hatchway is sometimes called a "scuttle", as the *forescuttle,* which is the hatchway to a forecastle. (*See* SCUTTLE.)

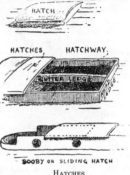

Hatches

Hatch money.—An allowance at one time given to captains for care of cargo.

Haul (*see* HALE).—To pull upon a rope. But Falconer defines the term as pulling upon "a single rope without assistance of blocks or other mechanical powers upon it". Thus to pull upon a *warp hawser* or *spring* by hand is to haul; but if a turn be taken with the rope round a capstan or windlass it ceases to be hauling.

A *haul,* in rope-making, is a large bundle of parallel yarns ready for tarring. In trawling it is the quantity of fish brought in in one lifting of the net. Hence the origin of the term in general conversation.

To *haul the wind,* in sailing, is to get close and keep close to the wind. (*See* CLOSE-HAULED.)

To *haul off.*—To get closer to the wind so as to avoid some object.

Haul forward.—The wind is said to haul forward when it lies before the beam.

To *haul sharp.*—To keep men on half food allowance (old term).

Haul under the chains.—When a ship's masts so strain on the shrouds that the pressure on the chains (or channels) causes her seams to open, she was said to haul under the chains.

Haunch.—A sudden decrease in the size of a piece of timber.

Haven.—A harbour of refuge. Smyth described it as a good anchorage rather than a place of perfect safety. Many of the smaller rivers of our coasts are called havens.

Hawse.—The hawse, with regard to a ship's position at anchor, is, technically, that portion of the water in front of her which extends from the ship herself to the point on the surface of the water directly above her anchor:—*i.e.,* the horizontal distance of her cable; and a vessel is said to *cross* the *hawse* of another when she passes athwart the latter's hawse, *i.e.* that space in the water ahead of her called the hawse. From this we have various names, as for instance, the *hawse of the ship*—that part of her bows in which are the *hawse-holes*; through these the *hawser,* or cable, runs, and they are cut out in large timbers called *hawse-pieces.*

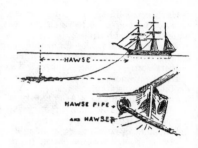

Hawse-pipes are the short iron tubes lining these hawse-holes.

Hawse-blocks, hawse plugs or *bucklers* are plugs for stopping the hawse-holes when the cable is unbent and the ship at sea; or in heavy weather: when in the form of stuffing they are called *hawse-bags.*

Hawse-clamp is an old-fashioned engine in the form of a heavy iron gripper or clamp, through which the hawser is passed, and which prevents it from veering out.

A *hawser,* in the modern meaning, is a small cable, or in other words a thick rope used for holding a vessel to a quay or mooring, or for warping her along: it is, in fact, practically the same as a warp. The origin of the term has possibly some reference to the word "haul", for in old works we find it written *haulter.*

Hawser-laid (in ropemaking) is the designation of a rope laid (or wound up) in the same manner as in a hawser, *i.e.,* in three or four strands. (*See* ROPE.)

Hawse fallen or *hawse fall.*—A ship is described thus when the seas break into her hawse.

Burning in the hawse.—An old sea term, used when the cable endures an extraordinary stress.

When a ship using hawsers to her anchors has two anchors *out,* and the cables are clear, it is said to be a *clear hawse*; when they become entangled in any way, it is a *foul-hawse.* The twists which may occur in cables by the swinging of a ship at anchor have been described as follow:—If the cables are once crossed, it is a *cross hawse.* When another cross occurs, it forms an *elbow.* If a third should come about it is called a *Round-turn.* The act of disengaging this foul (which, should it come on to blow, may prevent cables from being veered by their friction against each other) is called *clearing hawse,* while the veering out, or slackening of the cable, whether to expose new surface to the friction in the hawse-hole, or to allow the vessel to ride more free, is described as *freshening hawse.* Vessels which need to put out two anchors ahead for any length of time may employ the system applied to the Lightships, the chains from all anchors of which meet at one point, where they are attached to a swivel, and joined by only one from the ship. By the working of this swivel the vessel may then swing with every tide, and freshen or shorten, without fear of *"fouling-hawse"*.

Haze.—A thin mist such as that which often overspreads the face of the ocean in summer and clears off as the sun mounts. Meteorologists restrict the term to the obscurity caused by dust or smoke particles in the air.

To haze.—Bullying a man by giving him extra work, and petty oppression generally.

Head.—Generally speaking, the upper or larger end of any object; but under the term are included a great number of meanings.

Ahead means forward or in front, in contradistinction to *astern* which is behind or backward.

The *head of a ship.*—The fore end of her.

By the head, or *down by the head,* implies that the head is depressed, just as *down by the stern* or *heel* signifies that her stern is down.

"How's her head?" is a question often asked with regard to her course.

To *box off her head* is to force her head off from the wind. (*See* BOXING OFF.)

To *head a stream* is to lie with the ship's head pointing against the stream as when she is tide-rode.

A *headland* is a cape or promontory.

A *head-tide* is sometimes spoken of when the tide is against the ship.

Headway.—Progress forward or *ahead*. A vessel when she cannot make progress is said to be unable to make headway.

Head wind, or the *wind ahead,* is a wind contrary to the desired course of the ship. She is *head to wind* when her head is up in the wind.

In shipbuilding—

Heads are the timbers (ribs) of a vessel, or the upper parts of them. They are either *head timbers,* that is, the uppermost *futtocks,* when the ribs are composed of several pieces, or

Bent heads or *bent timbers,* in an open boat, in which each rib is fashioned out of only one piece of timber, this being bent to its required form by steaming.

Head of the keel.—The *forefoot*; the other extremity being the *heel.*

Head knee or *cheek knee.*—The principal knee, or strengthening piece, fayed to the stem.

Head ledges.—The thwartship (running across the ship) ledges, or planks on edge, which form the coaming of a hatchway.

Head sheets (in an open boat).—The flooring boards in the bows, those covering the after floor being the *stern sheets.* (*See* diagram under SHEET.) 2. The sheets of the head sails.

E

Stem-head.—The upper portion of the stempost of a vessel. (For illustrations of these members *see* diagrams under FRAME.)

In the rigging and fittings of a vessel—

Head of the bowsprit is its forward end.

Head of a dead-eye is the outer side of the flat surface, through which the holes are bored.

Head or *drum of a capstan* is the flat upper portion which revolves.

Headfast.—A rope fastened to the stem of a boat or ship. In an open boat it is called a *painter* (*which see*).

Head line is sometimes a rope from the head of a sail.

2. *Head line,* or *rope.*—A mooring rope leading ahead of the ship.

Head of the mast, or *mast head,* is, roughly speaking, the top of a mast, but technically it means that part of a mast from the hounds upwards. (*See* fig. p. 125).

Head rope is the head portion of the *bolt rope* of a sail (*which see*). More often, a hawser leading forward from the bows to a point ahead.

Head of a sail is its upper edge; the lower being the foot. (*See* SAIL.)

Head sails are the forward sails, as the jib and foresail.

Head-stick.—A short stick fitted in the head of some jib-shaped sails to prevent the sail from twisting and the bolt-rope from kinking. It is very useful in boats. (*See* fig., p. 125.)

Heads.—Latrines in a ship. These were once situated right forward in the head of the ship, in sailing men-of-war platforms on each side of the stem.

Heart.—A peculiar type of *dead-eye* (*which see*).

Heart or *heart-yarn.*—The inner yarn in a strand of rope.

Heave.—To pull on a rope or cable with mechanical aid, and therefore to be distinguished from "hauling". (*See* HAUL). To draw anything up. To throw anything. To come within view or sound.

Heave ahead, or *astern.*—To draw a ship ahead or astern by an anchor, a warp, or otherwise.

"Heave and away!" "Heave and rally!"—Encouraging terms to men at a capstan or windlass.

HEAVING SHORT

Heave and pawl.—To turn the cap-stan until the *pawl* may be dropped.

Heave and set.—To ride heavily while at anchor.

"Heave Oh!"—An exclamation used by men all pulling together on a rope or anything else. Also a cry in certain fishing towns, signifying that a shoal of fish has appeared.

Heave short.—To bring a vessel directly above her anchor prep-aratory to weighing. (*See* fig.).

Heave in sight.—To come within sight of another.

Heave in stays.—To bring a vessel head to wind in tacking. The meaning of the term is explained under the heading TACK.

Heave taut.—To pull or haul anything tight up.

Heave the lead.—To throw the lead-line, when sounding. (*See* LEAD.)

Heave the log.—To throw the log chip over the stern in order to measure the speed of the vessel.

Heave to.—To bring a vessel up head to wind, and so to dispose the sails that she makes no progress, when she is said to be "hove to", or "lying to". (*See* TRY.)

Heave up.—To draw or pull up, as to heave up the anchor or a fishing net.

Heaving line.—A light line thrown to connect with a heavier one.

Hebbing (very possibly the more correct term should be *ebbing*).—An old method of taking fish as they come down a river on the ebb tide. The apparatus employed was called a *hebbing weir,* and was extended across, or partly across, the stream. There was at one time a considerable fishery in the Upper Thames, both above and below bridge, for smelt and other salt and fresh water fish, the men employing themselves in this industry being called hebbermen (ebbmen?); and their boats, called *peter boats,* were once seen between Hammersmith and Richmond. But when the drainage of London was emptied into the Thames, the industry gradually declined, and eventually no fish could come into the upper reaches. Hebbing has therefore become obsolete; but since the system of drainage has been improved, and the sewage no longer pollutes the water, the fish have gradually penetrated further up; and it is not impossible that they may, in years to come, once more pass through the city, and again give occasional employment to the hebberman.

Heel.—Generally, the opposite to the *head,* as the after end of a ship's keel; the lower end of any spar or timber. Thus the lower end of a topmast is its heel; and the rope by which the mast is hauled up is the *heel rope.* A vessel is *down by the heel* when her heel or stern is depressed in the water (compare with "Down by the head", under HEAD).

To *heel* is to *careen* or lay her over.

"They made the vessel *heel,*
And lay upon her side";

the *heel,* in such a case is her inclination laterally. She also *heels* over, or "bends", under press of canvas.

HEEL

Heel-post, in some steamships, is a post which supports the end of the propeller shaft.

Height (of a flag).—The perpendicular height, the length being called the *fly.*

Height-staff or *rod* (in shipbuilding), a measuring staff for heights, as the half-breadth staff is for widths.

Helm. — The helm is the steering apparatus of the ship, particularly the *tiller* (*which see*) or handle, (*sometimes called the helmstock.*) To this, many vessels have a wheel added, and large ships a steering engine, while in small open boats the place of the tiller is taken by a *yoke* and *yoke lines,* (*which see*). When a vessel has headway, and the tiller is moved to port, or the wheel moved to starboard, or the starboard yoke line is pulled, the rudder moves to starboard and so does the ship's head.

Steering orders given on shipboard used to refer (with very few exceptions) to the direction in which the *tiller* was to be thrust. Therefore the order "PORT" meant, "put the tiller over to port," the result of which was to send the vessel's head to starboard. In the mid 1930s this was changed, and *steering* orders are now always given in the direct sense; so that *the order "PORT" means that the wheel and the ship's head are to turn to port,* but the tiller moves to starboard.

The following terms have reference to the working of helm when sailing.

Helm up, helm down. — If a beginner receive the order "Helm up!" the first question which will naturally present itself to his mind is, — "Up to what?" a very reasonable question to ask; for if it is to go *up* it certainly must go up to something. And such reasoning will undoubtedly solve the difficulty, for nothing at sea is done without a reason. Now, there is in a boat propelled by the wind but one thing up to which the tiller could be put, viz.: the wind, the very *raison d'être* of such a boat's existence. Helm up, then, must of necessity mean *up to the wind*; and so, in fact, it does, for no matter what position a boat may be in, no matter what turns or twists from that position she may make, no matter whether it be light or dark, foggy or clear; whether the wind be ever so steady or shift from north to south and all round the compass again; whatever the time or whatever the circumstances, a beginner need never be at a loss for the meaning of "helm up": he has but to determine the direction of the wind (and if there be a doubt in his mind over that, the sail, which naturally stands away from it, will quickly dispel it) and up against it goes the tiller without a further thought. Yet, simple as it seems, it is astonishing how many mistakes are made by beginners over this important point; and it must be confessed that to determine at a moment's notice the direction of the wind, when quite fresh to the practice of sailing, is not altogether an easy thing. Moreover, there are times when it appears difficult to determine at all which way "helm up" would mean; as, for instance, when the tiller lies directly in the line of the wind, as it might if the boat be running sheer before it, or when lying head to wind. Here again then a little reasoning is useful. If a boat be sailing with a side wind and the sail stand over on the starboard side, from which side is the wind blowing? Naturally, from the port side, and the boat is therefore on the port tack. For the same reason, then, if the boat be running before the wind with her sail still standing over on the starboard side, the wind must be or must have been blowing, however little, from the port side, and to thrust the tiller over to port is to put it up. Since the helmsman usually sits or stands on the windward side of the tiller he will, literally pull it up towards him, if the vessel is heeling, or pull up the near side of the steering wheel; and he will push them *down* at the order "Down helm."

The meaning of "helm up" having been mastered, that of "helm down", being precisely the opposite in all cases, is already understood, and we come to another phrase made occasional use of with reference to the tiller, viz., *over* or *hard over*. This command is most frequently heard in cases of emergency: it requires, therefore, to be promptly answered: and, fortunately, is not difficult to understand. To put the *helm over* is to shift it, that is, to bear the tiller over the corresponding position on the opposite side of the vessel. *Hard over* is to do this with the utmost energy to its full extent. (*See* under HARD.)

The following are the various expressions having direct reference to the side to which the tiller must be put: —

UP.—Keep her away, pay her off, no higher, no nearer, give her weather helm, are terms equivalent to *bear away*; and all have the same meaning with regard to the tiller, viz.: *helm up*.

*DOWN.—Helm alee.—*Put the helm to the lee side of the vessel, that is, away from the wind, and, therefore, *down*.

*Luff.—*Put the vessel's head up towards the wind; to do which the tiller must be put away from the wind, and therefore *down*.

*Nothing off.—*To keep a boat "nothing off" is to keep her head "right on", or up to, the wind. If she falls away the tiller must be put *down*, which will bring her head once more up.

'Midships, Helm amidships, or *right the helm.—*Put the tiller or let it fall back in the same line as the keel.

*Weather helm and lee helm.—*A vessel is said to carry weather helm when her tendency in sailing is to run up into the wind, and therefore her helm must be kept constantly over to the weather side, or up. She carries lee helm when she tends to fall away from the wind, and so her helm must be kept to leeward, or down. Though some vessels have one tendency and some another, there may also be causes to aggravate these. For instance, if a vessel have too much weight forward, or if the after sails are too much for the head sails, she will have to be sailed with weather helm, for her tendency will be to run up into the wind; while if she has too much weight in her stern), or if the head sails more than counterbalance the after ones, they will carry her head away from the wind, and she will constantly require a lee-helm to keep her up. This is very well understood with respect to large vessels, and taken into due account in the stowing of cargo. For a sailing ship will be very narrowly watched throughout her first voyage, and if it be found that she carries too much weather helm, the greater weight of cargo will, for her next trip, be stowed aft; whereas if she requires a lee helm it will find its way forward. Sea-faring men approve of weather helm; they like to feel that their vessel is *ardent,* to ensure that she will come up into the wind when required to. *Lee* helm is not only objectionable, but in certain cases it becomes positively dangerous; for if, in a sudden squall, a boat cannot quickly be brought up head to wind, the consequences may be serious.

Helmport.—A port is a hole; and the *helm* port is the hole through which the head and stock of a rudder (or helm) passes when the vessel has a counter.

Helmsman.—The man at the helm, that is, who steers the vessel.

Helmstock.—Another word for the *tiller* (*which see*).

Hermaphrodite brig.—The old name for the vessel we now call a brigantine. Being brig-rigged on the foremast and schooner-rigged on the main mast, it was also sometimes called a *brig schooner*. (*See* under BRIG.)

Heron, (*hern, hernshaw*).—A well-known water bird. The commonest of the family *Ardeidœ*. On the East Coast the name *hernshaw* is always used. But it is pronounced "*hand-sor*". Hence, without room for doubt, the explication of the much quoted Shakesperean line ("Hamlet") relating to the differences between "a hawk and a handsaw".

High (*high and dry*).—The situation of a vessel when, being aground, she is left there by the receding tide.

High-charged.—A vessel built with high bow and stern castles.

The *high seas.*—The open sea; that is beyond the limit within which nations claim the rights of jurisdiction.

High water.—The top of the tide; the point of its highest rise; the point of its lowest fall being called *low water.*

High water mark.—The mark left by the tide along the coast when it recedes. It usually means the height to which the highest spring tides rise, and in England it is often marked in certain places by the Trinity House Corporation, this being called the *Trinity high water mark.* (*See* also SPRING TIDES.)

Hike.—A slang expression—to move quickly; as, "hike off," be off quickly. It may also mean to hand or swing something over; as, "hike it over," *i.e.,* "swing or hand it over."

Hitch.—The name given to certain twists made with rope to form knots which may be very easily loosened. The principal hitches are the *half-hitch, two-half hitches, clove-hitch, timber-hitch,* and *blackwall-hitch* (for the method of making all of which see under the heading KNOTS).

The Hitch

To *take a hitch* is simply to take one turn in a rope, or, when applied to the belaying of a rope, to make a bight (bend) in the last turn, keeping the running end under so that it will not unwind (*see* fig.). This is the neatest manner of finishing a belaying.

Hitcher.—Another word for a barge-pole, punting-pole, quanting pole, or boat-hook, called variously according to locality. (*See* under POLE.)

Hobbler.—A coastman of Kent; an unlicensed pilot; one towing a vessel; a watchman.

Hog.—A stout broom, or brush, for scraping a boat's bottom.

Hogging (at sea).—A dangerous thing with a ship, sometimes the result of her taking, or remaining too long on, the ground. It is a falling of her head and stern, the consequence of some accidental weakness in her keel. A vessel which has hogged is either strengthened by a *hog frame,* a sort of huge truss, running fore and aft, or by a *hog-chain,* a chain acting as a tension rod, passing from stem to stern. It may be generally concluded, however, that a hogged vessel is a wreck.

HOGGING

Hog piece.—The fore-and-aft timber joined to the top of a wooden keel, to resist hogging stresses.

Hoist.—To elevate, to haul aloft, with or without the assistance of tackles.

Hoist.—The perpendicular measurement of a sail or flag. Thus the height of a flag is its "hoist", the length being its *fly*; and in like manner the length of a sail, measured up along the foremost leech, is its hoist. So a flag may have a two-foot hoist, a fore-and-aft mainsail a hoist of 10 or 15 feet; a fore-sail or a jib a six or eight foot hoist.

Hold.—The inner space of a vessel in which the cargo is stowed.

Hold beams.—In shipbuilding, beams traversing the hold of a vessel and supporting a lower deck, or hold-floor. (*See* FRAME.)

"Hold hard!"—Stop; desist: something equivalent to *avast* (*which see*).

Hold a luff.—In sailing, to keep close to the wind; to *luff* meaning to go close up to the wind.

Hold a topmast.—A gaff topsail, unless kept close to its topmast by a lacing or jack stay, will be liable, except in a very light breeze, to blow from the mast, or in the language of fishermen it will not "hold the topmast". This is the case with big yard-topsails, which are unsuited, therefore, for working to windward in a breeze.

Hold a wind, hold a good wind.—A vessel is said to hold a good wind when she has no tendency to fall off from the wind; and one boat is said to "hold a better wind" than another when she sails closer to the wind than the other.

"Hold water!" In rowing, to check the boat's headway by placing the blades of the oars vertically in the water and keeping them there.

Holding ground.—The quality of the sea-bed, good or bad, to retain the grip of an anchor.

Holding on the slack.—Lazy. Doing little or nothing.

Holiday.—In painting, or holystoning, a place where the work has been scamped, or overlooked.

Holy-stone.—A soft porous stone used in most ships for the purpose of rubbing or scouring the decks with sand every morning soon after daylight. A large flat piece is called a "bible", possibly because it is used by men kneeling; and a small piece for getting into corners is a "prayer-book".

Home.—The term is applied to anything close up, or in its place. It also implies the situation of a ship. When blocks are drawn together they are said to be "brought home". A square sail, when its clews are brought close down to the yard-arms of its lower yard, is said to be "hauled home". A bolt may be "driven home". A bale or cask in the cargo of a vessel, when stowed close up against another so that neither will shift, is described as "stowed home".

Come home (of an anchor).—The anchor is said to "come home" when it drags—the ship being "home".

Fall home or *tumble home.*—In shipbuilding, the inward inclination of the sides of a bulging ship after they leave the water line. (*See* diagrams under FALL and FRAME.)

Sheeted home.—A sail hauled in as close as necessary is said to be "sheeted home".

Homeward bound stitches.—Widely-spaced stitches made in canvas to hurry completion.

Home Trade.—Seaborne trade between ports in the British Isles and ports between the Elbe and Brest, both inclusive.

Hood.—A covering to a scuttle, companion, or the steering gear of a vessel. (*See* diagram under DECK.) In shipbuilding, the final plank of a complete strake is called a hood, and the end of this plank a *hooding end*. Hence in shipbuilding those ends of the planks which abut on the stem and stern posts are the *hoods,* or *hooding ends.*

Hook.—The epithet *hooked* is frequently applied in shipbuilding to anything bent or incurvated, as the *breast-hooks, fore-hooks, after-hooks,* etc. A *hook* is, in fact, a strengthening knee supporting various members in a ship.

Hook-block.—A block having a hook upon it. (*See* BLOCK.)

Hook-rope.—A rope used for such purposes as dragging a cable ashore when hauling a vessel up to a quay, etc. It is usually whipped at one end and furnished with a *hook* at the other (whence its name).

Hook and butt.—The scarfing or laying of the two ends of timbers over each other.

Hooker.—An old name for a Dutch trading vessel. Also applied to an Irish fishing smack, and to a small Brixham fishing-boat. (*See* HOWKER.) A colloquial name for any vessel.

Hoop.—Usually a band round something. The rings on a mast to which the weather leech of a fore-and-aft sail are bent—sometimes called hanks. (*See* MAST HOOPS.)

Hope.—"A small bay; it was an early term for a valley and is still used in Kent for a brook, and gives name to the adjacent anchorages." Hence we have the "Upper and Lower Hope", the last reaches before the estuary of the River Thames.

Hopper barge.—A barge having doors in her bottom and buoyancy spaces at her ends. Her cargo, usually dredged material, is dumped when the doors are opened.

Horn.—The arm of a cleat or kevel. The jaws of a gaff or boom.

Horns of the rudder.—In certain ships, irons to which the rudder chains are attached.

Horns of the tiller.—Also in ships, the bolts by which the chains are fixed to the rudder.

Horn fisted.—Horny handed—*i.e.,* having rough hands.

Horn timbers.—Bracket or knee-shaped timbers affixed to the sternpost of a boat for the support of the counter.

Hornpipe.—The dance once popular among the sailors of the British navy, and still, to a small extent, performed at festive times. Barrington ("Archæologia," Vol. III.) considered the name of this dance to be derived from a musical instrument of wood, with horn at each end, and formerly used in Wales, called pib-corn (Angl., *horn pipe*).

Horse.—1. In square rigged vessels, a rope for the support of a man. (A)—The rope running beneath a yard upon which the men stand while furling is a horse, also called a *footrope,* and is attached to the yard by short ropes called *stirrups.* (*See* fig. 1.) The outer portion of the horse is called the *flemish-horse.* (B)—A rope stretched from the cap of a bowsprit or jib-boom to the *knight-heads* for the safety of men working on the bowsprit. (C)—A breast-rope over which a man may lean, while heaving the lead.

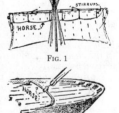

FIG. 1

FIG. 2

2. In fore-and-aft rig, an iron bar or rail, running athwart a deck, or the stern of a boat, upon which a sheet-tackle travels. (*See* fig. 2.) Many yachts, and even open boats, are fitted with a horse for the main sheet block; and in fishing craft we often find one forward of the mast upon which the foresail travels, obviating the necessity for fore-sheets. In this latter case the leech of the foresail carries a pendant (hanging rope) by means of which the sail, when it has travelled over the horse, is held fast to the shrouds. A foresail thus manipulated is called a "working foresail".

Horse-shoe clamp.—In ship-building, an iron strop or clamp gripping the forefoot of the keel.

Horse-shoe rack.—In ships, a curved rack carrying small blocks used in connection with the running gear.

Horsing iron.—In ship-building, a caulker's chisel used for caulking a ship's seams with oakum.

To *horse up.*—To "harden in" the oakum caulking in a vessel's seams.

Irish horse.—Salt beef; and presupposed to be of a certain good age. There is an old verse in connection with the term, as follows:—

"Salt horse, salt horse, what brought you here?
　You've carried turf for many a year.
　From Dublin quay to Ballyack
　You've carried turf upon your back."

This has been called "the sailor's address to his salt beef".

Horse Latitudes.—The area of little wind between, approximately, 30° and 35°N in the North Atlantic, between the "Westerlies" and the North East Trade wind.

Host men.—"An ancient guild or fraternity at Newcastle, to whom we are indebted for the valuable sea-coal trade." (Smyth.)

Hot coppers.—A parched mouth the morning after drinking heavily, especially of bad spirit.

Hounds.—1. Those projections at the lower part of a mast-head which carry the trestle-trees, shrouds, stays, etc. (*See* fig.) They are often confounded with the cheeks. The difference is arbitrary. On large masts such as those of sailing ships, they are usually called the hounds; in small vessels the cheeks. Hence either term may be equally properly used. The hounds are also sometimes called the *bibbs.* In old works they are described as the *holes in the cheeks* of the mast. The jaws of a gaff or boom are occasionally called its *hounds.*

Hounds band.—An iron band near a masthead to which rigging is attached.

Hounding.—That portion of a mast below the hounds; or, in other words, between the deck and the hounds. (*See* fig.)

House flag.—A square flag displaying the device and colours adopted by any mercantile shipping company. Fig. 1 shows its position when flying, and fig. 2 indicates the colours adopted by the P. and O. and Orient lines.

FIG. 1.—POSITION OF FLAG WHEN FLYING

Housing.—1. The *housing of a mast* is that portion below the deck; it is usually square so as to fit inside the mast-case. (*See* diagram under HOUNDS.) 2. The *housing of a bowsprit* is that part of it which lies inboard (within the knight-heads).

A *housing* (*house-line*) is also a small rope used for seizings (*i.e.,* binding-up).

To put a vessel under cover, for laying up, is sometimes called *housing* her.

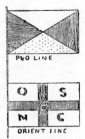

To *house a mast* or *spar* is to take it down, or *strike* it. Thus a topmast lowered and secured to the lower mast, as so often seen in small craft during winter—is said to be housed. The housing of spars in a gale is a very important piece of seamanship, for every sailor knows how much wind they may hold. Indeed so much is this the case that the act of *scudding* under bare poles—*i.e.,* running before the wind without a single sail set, is by no means an un-

FIG. 2.—HOUSE FLAGS
(page 134)

common practice, and may even be done when a gale is no more than moderate. In such vessels as yachts the housing of spars is sometimes, though, of course, on a lesser scale, equally necessary; and even in open boats it may occasionally be well to take down the mast and any other spars which may project outboard, in order that the boat may be buried as little as possible in a heavy rolling sea.

Hove.—"Heave" in the past tense. Thus we may say "we hove to during the squall". But the word is as frequently used in the present tense, as "she is hove to"; "she is hove in stays," etc.

Hovellers.—1. At the Cinque Ports, a name for pilots. 2. As an old term it means those who range the seas around the coast in the chance of falling in with ships in distress.

Hovercraft, or cushioncraft.—A vessel which can support herself a short distance above the surface of the water or land by exerting a downward pressure of air.

Howker, or hooker.—"A Dutch vessel commonly navigated with two masts—viz., a main and a mizzen mast, and being from sixty to two hundred tons burden. It is also the name of a fishing boat used on the southern coast of Ireland and carrying only one mast." (Falconer.) On our coasts the howkers go by the more familiar name of "Dutchmen".

Hoy.—A hoy, before the era of steam vessels, was a vessel acting somewhat in the same manner as do tenders to-day; they carried goods and passengers to and from the larger vessels; but they also coasted.

Hug.—To keep close to in sailing, as to hug the shore, to hug the wind, etc.

Hulk.—A vessel not fit to be sent to sea, or a sailing vessel without masts. The better ones were, and still are, made use of in various ways:—floating storehouses, temporary accommodation, quarantine, and *c.* 1800, prisons. At Leigh, on the Thames, the hull of an old vessel has been turned into a yacht club house; while in a village on the Suffolk coast half the cottages are formed of the inverted hulks of old fishing craft, precisely like that one in which

David Copperfield made his first acquaintance with the domestic arrangements of the Peggotty family. Certain hulls are fitted with sheers for dockyard or other engineering work, and are called *sheer hulks*. But this latter term is often understood to mean nothing more than the mere remnant of a ship, as in Dibdin's song:—

> "Here a sheer hulk lies poor Tom Bowling,
> The darling of our crew."

In the 13th to 15th centuries the hulk was a large merchant ship, especially so-called in the Mediterranean.

Hull.—The hull is the body of a vessel, exclusive of her masts, etc. To hull, or to lie a-hull, is to take in all sail in a storm and to lash the helm.

Hull down.—A distant vessel is hull down when her hull is below the horizon, but her masts and upper works are still visible.

Humber keel.—A clincher built trading vessel, with a single mast and square sail, usually bluff bow and stern, sailing out of the River Humber.

Hung up.—Sometimes to be "hung up" means to be left ashore or without occupation.

Hung up in the wind.—When a vessel has been brought head to wind, in sailing, but refuses to go about, she is said to become "hung up in the wind", or to be "in irons". (*See* In Irons and Tack.)

Hurricane.—A violent storm, distinguished by the vehemence and sudden changes of the wind. Force 12, wind speed 64–71 knots.

Hurricane deck.—In large steam boats, a light upper deck extending across the vessel amidships, usually for the officer in command. (*See* Deck.)

Hurry.—Another word for *staith* (*which see*).

Hurtle.—To send bodily along on a heavy sea or swell.

Husband.—*Ship's husband.*—Of the man called ship's husband in old days Falconer gives the following: "*Ship's husband* (among merchants), the person who takes the direction and management of a ship's concerns upon himself, the owners paying him a commission for his trouble." In 13th and 14th centuries he might have been the sailing master. In the 19th century a marine superintendent.

Hydrofoil.—A fast vessel which, when at speed, lifts her hull clear of the water, supporting herself upon foils, or wings, which project beneath her bottom.

Hydrographer.—One who surveys the seas and coasts, and produces charts and sailing directions.

Hydrometer.—An instrument for finding the density of liquids, and used to find to what draught a vessel should be loaded in fresh water to have a given draught at sea.

I

Idlers.—On shipboard, those who, being liable to constant duty by day, are not subjected to keep the night watches; such are the carpenter, sail maker, etc. But they have to come up with the rest of the crew when "all hands" are called.

In.—*Inboard.*—*Within* the ship, in contradistinction to *outboard,* which is *without* her; the *board* being the side of a vessel. Thus a bowsprit which projects outboard may be reeved (drawn) *inboard.* So also, that portion of an oar or skull which is within the boat when used in the act of rowing lies inboard.

In-haul.—A rope or purchase for *rigging-in,* that is for drawing in a spar or sail, just as an *outhaul* is for rigging it *out.* Thus, in a cutter yacht, the jib, which is set flying (that is, not on a stay), is hauled out along the bowsprit by an outhaul, and brought in by an *inhaul.* (*See* diagram under Jib.)

Inner post.—In shipbuilding, a timber upon which one of the *transoms* is usually fixed.

Inner turns.—(*See* Outer Turns.)

Inshore.—By the shore, towards the shore, as "Let us get inshore," that is "Let us get nearer to the shore."

Inrigged.—Rigged or fitted within or on the side of a boat. The row-locks of row-boats are either *inrigged* or *outrigged,* the former when on the gunwale, as in the ordinary way, the latter when extended on light iron brackets as for racing purposes. (*See* diagram under Rig.)

In the eye of the wind.—In sailing, a vessel making progress at an acute angle with, or, in other words, very close to, the wind is said to be "in the eye of the wind".

In stays.—The position of a sailing vessel when head to wind while going about from one tack to another.

International Code of Signals.—A system of signalling by flags and the morse code, particularly for ships of different nationalities, published in 7 languages. The first edition was issued in 1857 and the last revision made in 1969. (*See* Signals.)

Inwale.—(*See* Wale.)

Irish pennants.—Rope yarns or any fagged old rope ends hanging about the rigging of a vessel which give the ship a bedraggled appearance. The term is used as one of opprobrium.

Iron.—Anything made of iron may be called "an iron", as boom iron, end irons, etc.

In irons. 1. A punishment on shipboard; the old term for handcuffed or chained up. 2. (In sailing).—If a vessel *miss-stays* in *tacking* and cannot be *cast* one way or the other, she is said to be "in irons", or "hung up in the wind". (*See* TACK.)

Iron-bound shore.—A dangerous and rocky part of the coast.

Ironclad.—The name once given to a vessel of war, because she was clad in iron or steel.

Iron-sick.—A term signifying the state of an old vessel when her iron work becomes loose in her timbers; and it may also be applied to the condition of a "composite vessel when her iron fastenings become rotten through the galvanic action which arises between them and the copper sheathing". (*See* COMPOSITE.)

Preservation of iron.—Iron is found to be so liable to rust on exposure to the salt air of the sea that various plans have to be employed in preserving it. The most effective of these methods is *galvanising*. Immersion while hot in boiling oil also preserves the surface, while the simplest method is to paint it. In yachts, in the fitting out of which expense is not considered, brass or gun-metal takes the place of iron wherever possible.

J

Jack.—The term "jack" is applied somewhat indiscriminately by sea-faring men to various spars, sails, ropes, etc. It would appear, speaking generally, to mean something small.

Jack (in flags).—"Something shown, a signal." (Brande and Cox.) The (small) national flag flown from the jackstaff of a warship when at anchor. The *Pilot Jack* of Britain is the *Union* (*which see*), enclosed in a border of white, one-fifth the width of the flag. It is sometimes flown at the jackstaff in British merchant ships. When flown from the foremast it was a signal for a pilot.

PILOT JACK

Jack-block.—A block sometimes used in sending up a top mast.

Jack cross-trees.—1. In a ship, single iron cross-trees at the head of long top-gallant masts, for the support of royal or sky sail masts. 2. In fore-and-aft rigged craft, iron cross-trees which fold up, so as to admit of a mast being lowered. They are often seen in topsail barges, the masts of which have to be lowered in passing under bridges. (*See* fig.)

Jack in the basket.—A name given by fishermen to a basket placed on a beacon for marking a shoal or channel.

Jack-ladder.—A ladder with wooden rungs and rope sides.

Jack-pin.—A *belaying pin* in a *fiferail*.

Jack-staff.—A flag pole erected at the stem head, or bowsprit cap, for flying a jack.

Jack stay.—An iron rod, wooden batten, or taut wire on the upper side of a yard, to which the head of

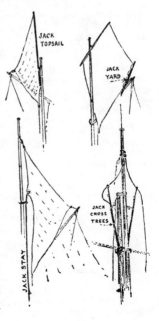

a square sail is bent. It also serves as a hand-grip for men on the footrope. 2. A stay acting also as a traveller. 3. A thin rope used to hold the *luff* of a gaff top-sail to its mast: it is rove through a cringle about midway down the luff of the sail, and passing through a sheave or grommet on the mast, is then brought down on deck and belayed. The jack stay may, therefore, take the place of the lacing of a jib-headed topsail to its mast. (*See* fig.)

Jack topsail (sometimes called a *jacket* or *donkey topsail*).—A fore-and-aft topsail bent (*i.e.*, attached) to a *jack yard,* which carries the sail up above the head of the mast. This sail is a little awkward to manipulate, but it has a certain advantage in light winds, in that it reaches higher than do most other topsails; and as it may be set on a pole mast, it is frequently applied to small boats, and hoisted above a balance lug sail. (*See* fig., also under TOPSAILS.)

Jack yard.—Generally speaking, a yard or pole which extends either the head or the foot of a topsail beyond some other spar. Applied to the head of a jack topsail, it stands, when set, in a vertical position, carrying the head of the sail up byond the head of the mast, and is kept in this situation by hauling down the foot of the yard, which, in this case, secures the tack of the sail. Applied to the foot of a topsail the jack yard carries it out beyond the peak. (*See* fig., p. 139.) In ships we find a *cross-jack yard* (pronounced "crojeck" or "crutched" yard), which is the lowest yard on the mizzen mast. It is always hung; not hoisted with halyards.

Jack-ass rig.—A three-masted topsail schooner. The name sometimes given to the ordinary form of three-masted schooner which sets square topsails on the foremast. It is possible that this name has been given to distinguish the rig from that which may, in this instance, be called the true three-masted schooner; the latter sets no square sails. (*See* SCHOONER.) 2. A four-masted sailing vessel that is

JACK-ASS RIG

square-rigged on the fore and main masts, and fore and aft rigged on the two after masts.

Jacket.—1. A double or outer coat, in the planking of a vessel. 2. The *jack topsail* of a fore-and-aft rigged boat is sometimes called the jacket.

Jacketting.—A scolding. Sometimes an infliction of the rope end.

Life jacket.—(*See* under LIFE.)

Jacob's ladder.—A rope ladder having wooden rounds. A jack ladder.

Jaws.—The horns at the end of a boom or gaff. (*See* GAFF.)

Jaw-rope.—A rope passed through and across the jaws of a gaff, to hold the spar to the mast. It is generally threaded through wooden beads or trucks to prevent jamming, and thus becomes a *parrel* (*which see*).

Jears, or **Jeers.**—Tackles by which the lower yards of a ship are swayed or struck (*i.e.,* hoisted or lowered).

Jetsam (in law).—Goods cast from a ship and sunk, in contradistinction to *flotsam* and *lagan* (both of which *see*).

Jettison (in law) (evidently from the French *jettez-en*).—To jettison is to cast goods overboard, whether to lighten or get a vessel upon an even keel when aground, and thus aid in floating her again, or—on the high seas—that she may ride more easily when in distress.

Jetty.—A small pier or landing place. (*See* fig.)

Jewel block.—In square rig, a block at a yard arm for the halyard of a studding sail. (*See* diagram under BLOCK.)

JETTY

Jib.—One of the head sails in a sailing vessel—triangular in shape. In large vessels it was split into an *Outer jib* and *Inner jib* for ease of handling. It is bent to a stay, called the *jib-stay,* which extends from the fore-top-mast head to the end of the *jib-boom*; but in small craft generally it is set, either standing or flying (according to the rig of the boat), between the lower mast head and the end of the bowsprit. In the *cutter* and *yawl,* both of which have reeving bowsprits, the jib is set flying; in the *sloop,* which has a fixed bowsprit, it is set standing, on the jib-stay, and usually extends aft almost to the mast, thereby doing away with the fore-sail. In either case it is the most forward of all the sails. The jib, not withstanding the fact that it is small and stands *out-board,* is a very important agent in sailing. It *steadies* the boat in her course, helps her round when she is put about, prevents her running suddenly up into the wind, and acts as a good guide to the helmsman, when sailing *in the eye of the wind,* for by its tendency to *chaffer* (or shiver) it tells him when he is sailing too close. Its virtue lies in its position as the foremost of all the sails, and on this account we have the following *rule for working jib and foresail*: When a vessel is going about, the jib acts before the foresail, but its power is soon expended. It is, therefore, brought over first (as soon as its effort is seen to be finished) and sheeted home, while the foresail, by laying aback, completes the work of bringing the vessel's head round. This is an operation which requires nice judgment and some little experience. The mistake of bringing the head sails over too soon is particularly to be avoided: it may almost be said, indeed, that it is better to be too slow than too quick, though much, of course, must depend upon the general behaviour of the craft.

Jibs, in seagoing craft, are of various sizes, to suit all weathers. A large jib will tend in a breeze to bury a boat's head; and some boats are incapable of standing a large one at any time. In the latter case the sail is sometimes cut obliquely at the foot, so as to run upwards from the bowsprit, and this has been found to lift the boat better. Occasionally the head is cut square and fitted with a small batten called a *head-stick*; this acts well where the bolt rope of the sail tends to kink.

Besides the jib in common use, we have the following:

Balloon jib.—A racing sail of enormous size, extending from the topmast head to the bowsprit head. Sometimes the *spinnaker* is carried forward as a balloon jib in racing. (*See* BALLOON CANVAS.)

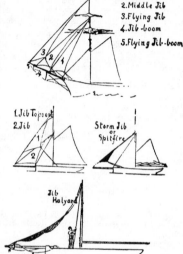

1. Jib
2. Middle Jib
3. Flying Jib
4. Jib-boom
5. Flying Jib-boom

1. Jib Topsail
2. Jib

Storm Jib
or
Spitfire

Jib Halyard

Jib Inhaul
Jib Outhaul

Flying jib.—A jib set out on a jib-boom ahead of the jib. It is used on schooner yachts and trading vessels. (*See* fig.)

Genoa jib, or *Yankee jib.*—A large jib whose clew extends well abaft the mast.

Inner jib.—In ships, the jib next the fore-stay sail.

Jib of jibs (only in large ships).—"A sixth jib," only known to flying-kite men.

Jib topsail.—A jib running on the topmast stay in a cutter or yawl, and set above the other head sails. In these boats it has sometimes been called the flying jib, though this is hardly a correct name, as that sail belongs to schooners and other large vessels.

Middle jib.—A jib belonging to schooners and large trading vessels. It is set flying from the foretop mast or the fore top-gallant mast to the end of the jib-boom. (*See* fig.)

Spitfire.—A name given to a very small jib used in boats; really a sort of trysail, answering the same purpose as the storm jib—*i.e.*, for use only in dirty weather, or to keep steerage way on a boat. (*See* fig.)

Standing jib.—A jib set *standing* (*which see*).

Storm jib.—One for bad weather or winter use; it is made of stout canvas, and often, even for yachts, tanned. (*See* fig.)

Jib-headed sail.—A sail the shape of a jib—*i.e.*, one pointed at the head. Such is the *jib-headed topsail*. (*See* TOPSAIL.)

The following spars and ropes refer also to jibs:

Jib-boom.—A spar running out beyond the bowsprit to carry a flying jib. (*See* fig.)

Flying jib-boom.—A boom run out beyond the jib-boom for the flying jibs. (*See* fig., p. 142.)

Jib down-haul, or *in-haul*; *Jib out-haul.*—The ropes by which the jib is hauled out or in along the bowsprit. Both are attached to the traveller: the *out-haul* runs through a sheave at the bowsprit head and then inboard; the *down-haul,* or *in-haul,* comes from the traveller directly inboard. (*See* fig., p. 142.)

Jib guys.—(Only in large vessels.) Stays supporting a foremast against the pressure of jibs.

Jib halyard.—The halyard which elevates the jib. In large vessels it is often of chain, and is provided with a rope purchase on one side, the chain belaying on the other. In fore-and-aft rigged craft, such as yachts, smacks, etc., this rope takes its origin near the mast head: it runs downwards and through a movable block after which it goes upward again through a fixed block on the mast, and thence down to the deck, where, in small craft, it belays, usually *on the port side of the mast.* When the jib is to be set, its *tack* is shackled to a *traveller* (an iron ring) which runs it out on the bowsprit; and its head to the lower block of the halyard, after which it is hauled up taut. In a sloop, the bowsprit being a fixture, and the forestay made fast to its end, the jib runs up the forestay on *hanks*; but in a cutter or a yawl, the forestay being carried only to the stem-head, the jib is set flying, and the jib halyards then act as a great stay to the bowsprit—more so, indeed, than does the topmast forestay. They must, therefore, be *swigged* up very taut when sail is made, as this helps to strengthen the bowsprit.

Jib-iron.—Commonly called the *traveller.* An iron ring running on the bowsprit, for setting the jib.

Jib sheets.—The ropes which work the jib. They are usually composed of one rope doubled half-way, and fastened at the bight (or bend) to the clew of the sail; and each part is brought down on either side of the forestay, and through *fairleads,* to be belayed, either amidships, or (in boats) within reach of the helmsman. In small craft the jib sheets are usually distinguished from the fore-sheets by being *thicker,* and by being belayed *aft* of the fore-sheets. A stopper knot should be made at the end of each jib sheet when it is rove through its fairleads, to prevent their being jerked away. A figure-of-eight knot answers this purpose well, and is easily made. (*See* KNOTS.)

Jib-stay.—A stay upon which a jib is set. In fore-and-aft rig it is peculiar to the sloop, being run out to the head of the fixed bowsprit, and taking the place of the forestay of a cutter in supporting the mast. This arrangement constitutes the difference between cutter and sloop rig (both of which *see*). In the cutter, however, we also find that which is sometimes called the jib-stay, though, so far as the staying of any spars is concerned, it is no stay at all, and is more correctly called the *jib out-haul,* its office being to haul out the jib along the bowsprit; and to effect this it is usually connected with a *traveller,* or ring on the bowsprit. Being attached to this traveller, it is passed through a sheave at the bowsprit end and then brought in and belayed either by the bowsprit bitts or by the mast. When the jib is to be set it is shackled on to the traveller, and, being hauled about half-way up the mast, is then run out by the *jib-stay,* which is then belayed, while the jib-halyard is *set up* and *swigged* upon.

Jigger.—Usually a small spar, or an extra mast. A bumpkin is often spoken of as a jigger or *jigger-boom.* (*See* diagram under BOOM.) The small mast in certain barges, fitted to, and the sail of which works with, the rudder is sometimes called the jigger. So also any very small mast and sail (though usually one working with the rudder) may be called by the same name: for which latter reason we occasionally hear a fishing boat, carrying such a mast and sail, but otherwise sloop-rigged, called a jigger, or jigger-rigged. The fourth mast in a four-masted ship is the jigger-mast. (*See* under MAST.)

Jigger block.—A *tail* block (*See* BLOCK) or a block to clap on to a rope.

Jigger tackle.—A small tackle on a halyard or some other rope, to increase the purchase. Also, a tackle holding a cable taut as it leaves a capstan. It consists usually of no more than a single and a double block.

Joggled timbers, joggle frame.—When the heads, or timbers (ribs), of a boat are shaped, in the manner shown in the figure under BUILD, so as to receive the strakes of a clincher built boat, they are said to be *joggled,* and to form a *joggle frame.*

John Dory *Jaune Doré,* Fr.).—A well-known fish. John Doré was a notorious French pirate.

Johnnie.—The old naval term for a "bluejacket". The seamen were called the johnnies or jacks, and the marines jollies; and both these names have come into general use in familiar conversation.

Join.—To join a ship is to go to and enter upon one's duty in her.

Jolly.—The name given to a marine, just as bluejacket is called a johnnie or jack. The marines were called the "jolly marines", and hence, the "jollies".

Jolly boat.—1. In the Royal and Mercantile Navies, a small boat used for marketing, landing inferior persons, etc. Some have in recent years been fitted with engines. 2. In yachting, a boat, corresponding to a *dinghy,* but larger.

Jolly jumper.—In old full rigged ships, sails set above the moonrakers, thus making *seven* square sails on a mast—viz., (1) main; (2) maintop; (3) top-gallant; (4) royal; (5) sky rail; (6) moonraker; (7) jumper. But they were always very rare, and only set by the most inveterate of flying kite men. (*See* also LIGHT SAILS.)

Jolly Roger.—The skull and crossed bones black flag of a pirate.

Jonah. A person whose presence on board is supposed to incur misfortune.

Jump.—To make a jump joint with two planks or plates of iron is to put them together (end to end or side to side) in such a manner that they will present a smooth surface. Hence in shipbuilding it is equivalent to *carvel* building (*see* BUILD); and when an iron vessel is so built she is said to be *jump jointed* or *jump pointed.*

Jumper.—A square sail set, on very rare occasions, on certain of the old full-rigged ships: it formed a seventh square sail on each mast (*see* LIGHT SAILS.)

Jumper stay.—A familiar name for the stay called *triatic* (*which see*), and often seen in schooners. It runs from the mast head of the main to the fore, and, therefore, takes the place of the main stay. 2. The stays which run over the jumper struts.

Jumper struts.—Spreaders on a mast that are angled forward to give support fore and aft as well as athwartships.

Junk.—1. A ship common in China and Japan, with battened, balance-lug sails. 2. On ship-board junks are old ropes which by long usage and saturation in salt water have become hard and stiff. 3. Salt meat which has become hard from long keeping is also called junk, because it is said to resemble the old pieces of rope in its texture.

CHINESE JUNK

Jury.—The word, as used at sea, implies a *substitute*. Hence, *jury mast,* a temporary mast, either erected in a new vessel to take her where she is to be masted, or one taking the place of a permanent mast carried away, or one employed where it is impossible to elevate the permanent mast. Barges navigating rivers over which bridges are numerous and low, use jury masts habitually; they were once seen daily on the London river, between bridges. (*See* fig.)

Jury rudder.—A temporary or substitute rudder, or any apparatus enabling a vessel to be steered when her rudder may have been carried away.

K

Kamal.—An Arabian navigational instrument of great antiquity, consisting of a wooden tablet and knotted string (held in the teeth), and used for measuring the altitude of a star and thus ascertaining the latitude.

Kayak.—An Eskimo canoe made of sealskin stretched over a wooden framework. (*See* CANOE.)

Keckling, or **cackling.**—In the days of hempen cables, winding old rope about a cable—or the winding of iron chain round it to prevent chafing. It was done "spirally (in opposition to *rounding* which is close) with three inch old rope, to protect it from chafing in the hawse holes." (Smyth.)

Kedge (Old English, *brisk*).—A small anchor carried by large vessels for use in shallow water, or for keeping the main anchor clear. (*See* ANCHOR.) The small anchors carried by yachts may also be called kedges.

Kedging, or *kedge hauling.*—Working a vessel against tide, or in a narrow channel by means of kedges. The anchor is laid out ahead and the vessel is then hove up to it, the procedure is then repeated. (*See* WARPING.)

Keel.—The word keel "seems originally to have signified an entire ship; for we read that the Saxons invaded England in *caels,* ceols, or cynlis (*i.e.,* keels), and in early times a fleet was described as so many keels. This signification partly lives in *keelage,* which is a duty levied on vessels entering certain ports." The coal-carrying barges of the Tyne and Humber are also still called keels. The keel is the principal timber in any vessel, resembling the backbone of the human frame, while the side timbers constitute her ribs. It is the foundation of the entire structure, and must be of the best material. In small centre-board craft the keel must be sufficiently stout to allow of a slit being cut through it to admit the board. In boats the keel and garboards are sometimes of one piece. (*See* FRAME.)

False keel.—This is a lower piece added to the main keel, usually for the purpose of giving greater depth and weight. It may be of iron or lead; and is either bolted through the keel or, where this cannot be done, secured by plates to the garboard strakes. In large vessels it is composed of two pieces called "upper" and "lower"; it is a great protection to the keel, and is occasionally attached to it in such a manner that, in serious cases of grounding, it may come off, leaving the main keel uninjured; such cases are said to have actually occurred.

Keelson (pronounced, and sometimes written, *kelson*).—An addition to the keel inside the boat. It rests upon the keel and is an indispensable member, taking the stepping of the mast. It also serves to secure the feet of the timbers (ribs) on each side of it. In large vessels we find, in addition to this:

Sister keelsons, or *side keelsons,* which keep the feet of the timbers in their places; also a *keelson rider*—an additional timber laid along and above the keelson in large vessels to take the weight of the masts and distribute it along the keelson, as that does along the keel: it is sometimes called the *false keelson.*

The *keel band,* usually called the *stem band,* is a band of iron helping to bind the head of the keel and the stempost together. In doing this it assists the deadwood; and it further acts as a stout protection to the head of the keel. For illustrations of these parts *see* diagrams under **FRAME**.)

Keel hauling.—An obsolete punishment once apparently practised in the Dutch navy. The culprit was hauled up to the yard arm, weights being attached to his feet, and being suddenly let fall, was dragged by ropes under the keel of the vessel and up to the opposite yard arm. This was repeated a certain number of times according to orders.

Keel rope, or *Limber rope* (in ships).—"A rope running between the keelson and the keel of a ship, to clear the limber holes when they are choked up with ballast, etc."

Even keel and *uneven keel.*—Terms used in expressing the manner in which a boat floats. If she balances evenly in a *fore-and-aft direction* she is on an even keel. If she is depressed either by the head or by the stern she is on an uneven keel (*see* fig.). But the same terms are often, though not correctly, used (especially among rowing men) in reference to her trim generally; so that if she lies over on one side they still say she is on an uneven keel. And of a sculler who keeps his boat very level, laterally, they are apt to say that he keeps it on an even keel.

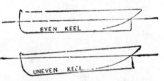

Keel-deeters.—Women who clean out the Northumbrian keels for the sake of the sweepings of small coal.

Keeler.—A small tub.

Keeling.—A name in the North Sea Fisheries for the common cod.

Keep.—"*Keep her away!*"—An order to a helmsman to keep a vessel's head more *off,* that is to keep her more before the wind.

"*Keep your luff!*"—Keep the vessel close to the wind (*see* **LUFF**).

"*Keep full for stays!*"—Keep the sails full preparatory to putting the vessel about (*see* **TACKING**).

"*Keep the land aboard!*"—Keep as near the land as may be safe.

Keg.—A small cask.

Kelds.—The still parts of a river which have an oily smoothness while the rest of the water is ruffled.

Kelp.—A large kind of seaweed. 2. The ash of sea weed, used in the manufacture of iodine.

Kelpie.—A sea bogey or spirit, which haunts the fiords of Northern Britain.

Kelter.—This word has a meaning somewhat akin to the term "fettle", as used by horsemen. A vessel is said to be in fine kelter when she is well ordered and well found, and ready for sea; or when, in fact, she is in "good fettle".

Kempstock.—An old name for a capstan.

Kennets.—Large *cleats* or *kevels* (*which see*).

Kentledge.—A term signifying "pigs", or shaped pieces of iron, as ballast, laid fore-and-aft near the keelson or in the limbers of a vessel, and therefore sometimes called *limber-kentledge*. The term may also mean goods used in lieu of ballast, these being called kentledge goods.

Kerf.—The sawn away slit in any piece of timber.

Kersey.—"A coarse stuff used on many occasions in a ship, such as in *boxing of the stem,* and lining the ports, for the purpose of excluding the water, also to cover the main ropes, etc." (Falconer.)

Ketch.—A sailing vessel with two masts, main and mizzen. Both these masts are fore-and-aft rigged, the mizzen with or without a topsail; and there is, in addition, often a large lower square sail set on the main mast. The ketch was, in fact, of all our coasting traders, perhaps the most capable of variety in its rig. It may set one, two, or even three square sails on the mainmast; as many as four head sails; and one, or even two staysails between masts. These features distinguish it from the yawl (*which see*.)

The ketch was once a common rig for yachts: Lord Dunraven, a contender for the America's Cup in 1893 and 1895, owned one which was occasionally raced.

Kettle.—*Kettle bottomed vessel.*—One with flat floor and bulging sides; resembling, in fact, the form of a kettle.

"A fine kettle of fish!"—"Here's a nice mess to be in!"

Kevel.—A *cleat* (*which see*).

Kevel heads.—The ends of the top timbers (ribs) of a vessel which, rising above the gunwale, serve to belay ropes, or take a round turn so as to hold on by a warp, etc.

Key, or **Cay.**—A low island, or reef. (Spanish *cayo*.)

Key model.—A model sometimes made by yacht builders of a boat they are to build, on the lines laid down.

Key of a rudder.—The fastenings, *i.e.*, the forelocks, pins, etc. Otherwise the *goodgeons and pintles* (*which see*.)

Kid, otherwise *kit* (*which see*). 1. A small wooden tub for grog or rations. It often has two ears by which to hold it. 2. A compartment in a fishing vessel for the storing of fish; but when the "fleeting" system came in (*i.e.*, the system under which vessels fish together in fleets, their catches being taken from them daily by steam boats) the storing of fish on board vessels went out.

Various Ketches

Killick, killock, or **killagh.**—A small anchor; or, along some parts of the coast, a *grapnel,* when it is also called a *creeper.* It once meant a wooden anchor weighted with a stone.

King.—*King Arthur.*—A game at one time played on board vessels. A certain person represented the king, in which enviable position he was subjected to as much sousing as his subjects chose to give him; and this went on until he was able to make one of the party laugh, when it became that one's turn to assume royalty and receive his share of drenching.

King's bargain.—An old naval term. A strange man pressed on board a king's ship might turn out a good or bad bargain to the king.

King's benchers.—Another naval term applied to those galley orators who loved to hear the sound of their own voices, or to make long speeches.

King's own.—Still another relic of old days. It was ·one of many names given to the salt beef supplied to the people. (*See* also JUNK, "Irish Horse," under HORSE, etc.)

King plank.—The centre-line plank of a planked deck.

King post.—A strong post or bollard. A samson post.

King's parade.—The quarter deck of a man of war, which is saluted when stepping on it, in honour of the king.* In medieval times a crucifix or other religious emblem was placed at the break of the quarter deck which was saluted by all who passed it.

King spoke.—The spoke of a steering wheel which is uppermost when the helm is amidships. It is marked, often by a turk's head knot made round it.

Kink (in a rope).—A sharp bend (drawn almost to a loop); always dangerous, but more especially so in wire roping. "Rope used in the artillery service is coiled *with the sun, i.e., from* left to right, in which direction the yarns are also twisted, so as to avoid *kinking.*"

Kippage (old term).—A ship's company and equipment, (from "equipage").

Kit.—Any small vessel or tub capable of containing provisions or liquids, such as the soup sometimes given at sea. Sometimes, too, the term would appear to signify a ration, as a "kit of beef". A boat's *baler,* or any old can or pot employed in that capacity, is also occasionally dignified by the name of kit. (*See* also KID.)

A *kit* also means a person's clothing, such as may be put in a kit bag.

Kites.—A general name for additional light sails set in a following breeze.

Knees.—"Crooked pieces of timber, having two branches or arms, and generally used to connect the beams of a ship with her sides or timbers." They may be of wood or iron; elm or ash are the best woods, and the knees are of one piece naturally grown to the shape,

---

* These terms should perhaps find their place under the heading *Queen.* As ancient terms they are, however, placed as in old works.

which renders them very costly, and for which reason they are now often replaced by iron brackets. A wooden vessel contains a vast number of knees. Knees are also called *elbows,* and sometimes *chocks.* They are variously named, according to their position and use: as *dagger knees,* those placed obliquely; *diagonal knees, hanging knees, helm-post knees, lodging knees,* those placed horizontally in the ship's body; *standard* or *standing knees,* with one arm vertical; *transom knees, wing-transom knees,* etc.; *knee of the head,* usually called the *cutwater* (*which see*), etc.

Knightheads (in shipbuilding).—The heads (or small posts) at the stem of a vessel, between which the bowsprit runs. In small craft the stem-head forms one of these posts, and another smaller one is set up, usually on the port side of it; in this case the smaller head is called the knighthead. It will be seen that since the bowsprit in such craft as yachts, sailing boats, fishing smacks, etc., usually runs out on the deck, the bulwarks cannot be carried right up to the stemhead. One of the offices of the knightheads, therefore, is to take the

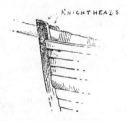

forward end of the bulwarks, leaving an aperture for the bowsprit to pass through. The case is different in large vessels, where the knightheads are carried up on each side of the stemhead, being, in fact, prolongations of the foremost cant-timbers of the ship. Here they are sometimes also called *bollard-heads.*

Knot.—*A knot,* a nautical mile per hour, is a measure of speed, but sometimes, though erroneously, used as synonymous with a nautical mile. (*See* MILE.) The name is derived from the knots formerly tied in the log line to determine a ship's speed. (*See* LOG.)

Knots (the fastening of ropes).—The art of knot-tying at sea must necessarily be perfect; for the whole safety of a vessel under sail depends upon it. There are a vast number of knots if all those which have been invented for various purposes be counted; but a few only need occupy the attention of the amateur sailor. These, however, are absolutely essential to his safety, and with them he should become completely familiar. The knots in general use at sea may be classed (for present purposes) as follow:—*splicings, whippings, lashings, hitches, bends, bowlines,* and *stopperings.*

N.B. It is important in making knots to take plenty of rope in hand, and not to make them too near the end. The tech-

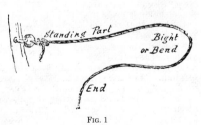

FIG. 1

nical names for the various parts of a rope are (*see* fig. 1, p. 151)—1. The *standing part*; 2. The *bight* or bend; 3. The *end*.

SPLICING.—The object of this is to join two ends of rope permanently together. There are three forms of splicing in general use: 1. The *long splice*; 2. The *short splice*; 3. The *eye-splice*.

1. "*The long splice* is used to unite two ends which have to pass through a block. It is formed by untwisting the two ends, and interweaving the strands of one in the alternate strands of the other: they must be hauled well through and beaten with a marline spike." Beyond this, it is impossible to teach on paper the method of making this splice; but it is easily to be learned from some fisherman, and is a very useful art to be master of.

2. *The short splice* is for joining two ends of rope together for ordinary use. This, too, though easily learned, is difficult to teach on paper. The accompanying diagrams (fig. 2) will, however, explain the principle of the method. 1*st motion*: Unlay the strands of each rope and *marry* them, that is, place the ends close together, so that the unlaid strands fit into each other as in the fig. 2*nd motion*: Take the left-

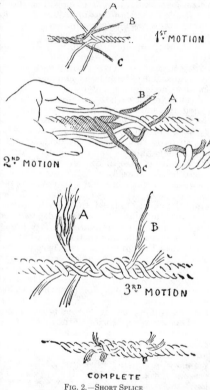

COMPLETE

FIG. 2.—SHORT SPLICE

hand rope and the three strands of the right-hand one firmly in the left hand. Take the strand A, pass it *over* the strand nearest to it and *under* the next (as in the small figure): this is the middle strand; see that this is right and the others should follow. Do the same with the other two strands B and C. Turn the ropes and do the same with the opposite three strands. The first portion of the splicing is now accomplished. Repeat it a second time. *3rd motion:* Unlay each of the six projecting strands (as at A), and cut half the yarns away (as at B), the object of this being that the splice may be finished off neatly. Pass all these reduced strands once more (or if necessary twice) under the main strands and cut off the ends, not too close. The splice is complete.

3. *The eye-splice* (fig. 3) forms an eye or circle at the end of a rope. The end of the rope is unlaid, and a portion of the standing part, sufficiently far down, is laid open to receive the loose strands, which are spliced in just the same way as in splicing two ropes together.

WHIPPING.—To whip a rope is to bind the end of it with twine or spun yarn, so that the end may not unravel. The simplest method of whipping known as a *Common Whipping,* is as follows (fig. 4): *1st motion:* Lay the yarn on the rope an inch or more from the end and begin binding. *2nd motion:* Continue binding until within three or four laps of the finish. Then make a large bend with the yarn, holding the

FIG. 3.—EYE SPLICE

end firmly down with the thumb. Continue binding with the yarn at A, taking it over B. *3rd motion:* Having taken three or four laps over the yarn B, pull the end C tightly down. Cut it off, and the whipping is complete.

LASHING.—The commonest lashing is the *reef* or right knot. It has a multitude of uses, but it derives its name (reef) from the fact that reef points are always tied with this knot. It is with the reef knot that the mistake so often occurs which results in an unsafe fastening called the "*granny*". The diagram (fig. 5, p. 154) will show the difference between these. The invariable rule for tying the reef knot is—whichever end is uppermost after the first motion, must be

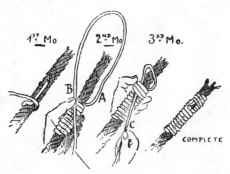

FIG. 4.—WHIPPING

uppermost in beginning the second. The reef knot, when so tied that it may be more easily undone, is called a *draw knot,* and may be either single or double. In the *single draw knot,* the first motion of the reef knot having been made, a bend is made in one of the projecting ends, and that bend or double-end is used to finish the knot with the other single end. In the *double draw knot* both projecting ends are doubled and the knot is finished with them, making, in fact, a bow.

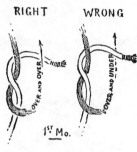

Besides the reef knot, ropes may also be lashed together with the common bend, the carrick bend, and others, while the lashing of spars is accomplished by the use of the various hitches, bends, etc.

HITCHES.—Of the hitches there are various sorts, the most useful being as follow:—

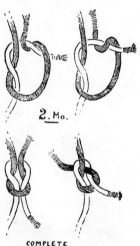

Fig. 5.—Reef or Right Knot and "Granny"

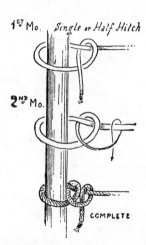

Fig. 6.—Two Half-hitches

1. *"Taking the hitch."*—This is merely the turning-under of a halyard or sheet end, to complete the belaying of it round a belaying pin or a cleat. (*See* fig. under HITCH.)

2. A *half-hitch* is merely a turning-in of the end of a rope.

3. *Two half-hitches.*—Another turn or hitch taken in the rope. This knot is useful for quickly bending a rope round a post; making fast the painter of a boat to a rail; bending a rope to a ring; tying clew lines of hammocks, etc. (*See* fig. 6, p. 154.)

4. *Clove hitch.*—One of the simplest and yet most useful knots ever invented. It is one by which a weight can be hung to a smooth mast, and is generally used where a rope is passed round any spar to be hauled on. It may be employed, however, in place of the half-hitch and often in place of a bend, as for fastening a jib to its stay, etc. The clove hitch may be made in two ways, that is, either round a spar, or in the hand and then slipped over the spar. (*See* fig. 7.)

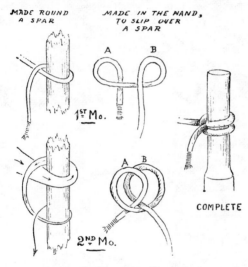

FIG. 7.—CLOVE HITCH

5. *Timber hitch.*—For taking a rope quickly round a bollard or a spar, or for moving a weight. The end of the rope is taken round the object and simply turned over twice as in the diagram (fig. 8, p. 156).

6. *Blackwall hitch.*—To make fast a rope to a hook for a temporary pull: it is not unlike "taking the hitch". The knot is very simple, as will be seen from the diagram (fig. 9, p. 156).

7. *Harness hitch.*—This knot derives its name from the fact that it is often used to harness men to a tow-line. It has various other uses, however, inasmuch as it enables a loop to be quickly made in a rope the ends of which are already engaged. Its one disadvantage is that

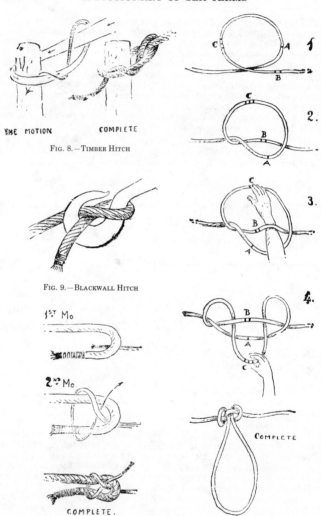

THE MOTION   COMPLETE

FIG. 8.—TIMBER HITCH

FIG. 9.—BLACKWALL HITCH

1ˢᵀ Mo

2ᴺᴰ Mo

COMPLETE.

FIG. 11.—COMMON BEND

1.

2.

3.

4.

COMPLETE

FIG. 10.—HARNESS HITCH

when being drawn tight it is apt to turn itself in such a manner as to slip, even though it may be quite correctly made. Extreme care must, therefore, be taken in drawing it close; but when once tight it is safe. For practice this knot may be made on the ground, or on a table; but for use it is generally made in the hand, when it is best to place the right foot on the right hand part of the rope, or a foot on each side. (Reference must be made to fig. 10, p. 156.) *1st motion*: Make a large loop, laying right over left. *2nd motion*: Pick up A and bring it over B. *3rd motion*: Place the hand under B and grasp the rope at C. *4th motion*: Draw C right through, as in the diagram, and tighten.

FIG. 12.—DOUBLE SHEET BEND

BENDS.—The bends also are numerous and varied. They derive the name from the word *"bend"*, which means to "fasten on", as bending a sail to the spars, one rope to another, a rope to an anchor or ring, etc.

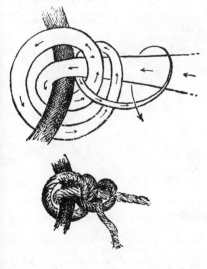

FIG. 13.—
FISHERMAN'S BEND

FIG. 14.—
HALYARD BEND

1. *Single Sheet Bend,* or *Common bend* (fig. 11, p. 156).—Almost the only knot by which two ropes of greatly differing sizes can be joined together. To make the knot let one rope be regarded as stationary, the other as working. Bend the left hand, or stationary rope, into the form of a simple hook, and then pass the working rope as shown. When this knot is used to bend a rope to a cringle, or a sheet to its sail, it is called the

2. *Double Sheet bend* (fig. 12, p. 157), which is formed by passing the end of the rope through the cringle and taking two turns round that, *under the bight.*

3. *Fisherman's bend* (fig. 13, p. 157), for bending a rope to a ring or to the shackle of an anchor. 1*st motion*: Two turns round the ring, going *over* the standing part each time. 2*nd motion*: Two half hitches, the first enclosing both turns.

4. *Halyard bends.*—Top-sail or lug-sail halyards may be bent to their yards in several ways, the most usual being the Clove hitch, the Fisherman's bend, or that which is sometimes called the *top-sail halyard bend,* in which three turns are taken round the spar, beginning the knot by passing the rope underneath, and then finishing as in the diagram (fig. 14, p. 157).

BOWLINE.—This knot is extremely useful. It serves to make a large loop at the end of a hawser or any other rope, which may be thrown over a bollard for hauling on to. A running knot may also be made by passing the main part of the rope through this loop. The bowline may be left permanently on the rope, for

Fig. 15.—Bowline   Fig. 16.—Collar Knots

use at any moment. The diagram (fig. 15) will explain the method of making it.

COLLAR KNOT (fig. 16), for fitting shrouds to a small mast. Two ropes being taken (or one long one doubled into two legs), a simple overhand loop (*see* fig.) is made in the middle of one, and the other rope passed through this, the loop being then passed over the head of the mast. Thus there will be four shrouds, two on either side. The fishermen occasionally use this in case of their shrouds breaking.

STOPPER KNOTS.—These are for preventing the end of a rope from flying loose or slipping through some ring or fairlead, and may be therefore of various sorts. The simplest is the common *overhand* or *thumb* knot, which is no more than a turning-in of the end of the rope. An equally simple and very elegant one, and one less likely to jam, is the *figure of eight,* with which the ends of jib or foresail sheets are often stoppered. Both will be understood by the diagram (fig. 17). Another is the *Matthew Walker.*—"A knot so termed from the originator. It is formed by a half-hitch on each strand in the direction of the lay, so that the rope can be continued after the knot is formed, which shows as a traverse collar of three strands. It is the knot often used on the end of the lanyards of rigging, where dead-eyes are employed."

SLIP KNOT or *running knot.*—A very simple knot (*see* diagram, fig. 18), which draws anything very close and slips easily.

FIGURE OF   OVERHEAD
EIGHT   KNOT
FIG. 17

Among other knots the *sheepshank* (fig. 19) will be found useful, its object being to shorten a cable or warp both ends of which are engaged. A study of the diagram will make the method plain.

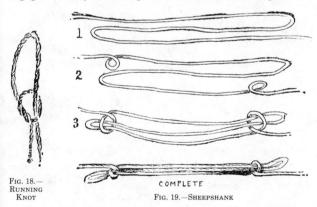

FIG. 18.—
RUNNING
KNOT

COMPLETE

FIG. 19.—SHEEPSHANK

Koff.—"A small two-masted vessel formerly employed in the Dutch fisheries. It had two masts, main and fore, with a large sprit sail abaft each. This arrangement enabled her to sail very close to the wind, and she could set square sails if the wind happened to be astern." (Brande and Cox.)

Kraken.—A fabulous sea monster, sometimes depicted as an enormous octopus, inhabiting Norwegian coastal waters.

Kreel, or **creel.**—A framework of timber for taking fish, or for preserving them in the water. An osier basket or pot. A crab pot. A fishing basket.

Krennels.—The smaller cringles on a square sail for bowline bridles, etc.

L

L.L.L.—The three L's,—Lead, Latitude, Look-out. The motto to which the old seamen pinned their faith, in preference to putting any trust in modern appliances.

Labour.—When a vessel pitches and strains in a heavy sea she is said to labour.

Lacing.—A thin rope for lacing a sail to a boom or yard, or to a stay. A foresail may be made to run on the fore-stay either by shackles or by a lacing. In racing yachts the mainsail is usually laced to the boom; but in cruisers this plan is seldom followed. A jib-headed top-sail is occasionally laced to the topmast of a yacht; and a jack-topsail to its yard.

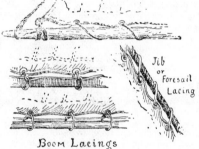

Boom Lacings

LACINGS

Laden in bulk.—Carrying loose cargo, such as grain, coal or ore.

Ladies' ladder (in ships).—Shrouds rattled too closely, *i.e.,* shrouds in which the ratlines (*which see*) are so close together that a lady might walk up them without difficulty.

Lagan, or **Ligan,** or **ligsam.**—In law, a term applied to goods jettisoned, but secured by a buoy for future recovery. (*See* FLOTSAM and JETSAM.)

Laggers.—A name at one time given to men who were employed in taking canal barges through tunnels, which they did by lying on their backs and working with their feet along the head of the archways. This was once seen on the inland canals, and was as often as not assisted in by the women who lived on board the canal boats.

Lagging and priming of the tides.—A phenomenon of the tides, in consequence of which the intervals between high water at any particular place are irregular. The cause is the combined action of the sun and moon. Lagging is an increase in the time interval between successive high waters, priming is a decrease in the time interval. (*See* MAKING OF THE TIDES.)

Lagoon.—A sheet of water connected to the sea but nearly surrounded by a reef or land.

Laid up.—A vessel unrigged or dismantled during winter; or lacking employment.

Laid up in ordinary.—A naval term signifying that a ship is laid up in a state of total inaction.

Lamb's-wool sky.—White masses of fleecy cloud, often portending rain.

Land.—*Lands.*—In boat-building, the overlapping part of the planks in a clincher-built boat. (*See* "Clincher-building", under BUILD.)

Land breeze.—A wind blowing seaward from the land, usually in the evening.

Landfall.—The first land seen after a voyage.

Land-locked.—A bay or haven almost surrounded by land, and, therefore, a safe haven.

Landmark.—Any conspicuous object on land, serving as a guide or warning to ships at sea.

Landsman.—At sea, the rating of a sailor; the second-class ordinary seaman. Formerly it meant one who had not before been to sea.

Lanby.—Large Automated Navigation Buoy.—Increasingly used in place of a lightvessel.

Lanyards.—Short pieces of rope having various uses at sea, the most important of which is the taughtening down of the shrouds of a mast by the deadeyes (*which see*). One end of the lanyard being passed through one of the holes in the upper dead-eye, is stop-knotted to prevent its drawing out; the other end is then rove up and down through all the holes in the deadeyes, hauled taut, and, to keep it taut, is lashed round the lanyard itself in a system of clove hitches.

Lapstrake.—The method of boat-building called *clincher-building.* (*See* BUILD.)

Larboard.—The old term for "port", or the left-hand side of a vessel. The word being too much like "starboard" in sound, was officially abolished.

Large.—"A phrase applied to the wind when it crosses the line of a ship's course in a favourable direction, particularly on the *beam* or *quarter.*"

To *sail large* is, therefore, to go forward with a wind large. It is the same as *sailing free,* or *off the wind*; and the opposite to sailing *close-hauled* or *on the wind.*

Lash.—To bind or make fast by ropes. (*See* KNOTS.)

A *lashing* is a rope securing any movable object.

Lash the tiller.—To tie the tiller down on one side or the other, as is sometimes done in ships when *trying,* or in fishing boats when trawling or dredging. With the tiller lashed a vessel is confined on a certain tack and unable to run away from the wind. Hence, in general conversation, when a person makes a determination from which he will not be moved, he is sometimes said to "Lash the tiller".

Lascar.—An Indian seaman. The head lascar is the *serang,* who may have beneath him a *tindal.* A lascar quartermaster is a *sekunni.*

Lasher.—On the Upper Thames, the body of water just about the fall of a weir and usually marked by a system of white posts set up on the stonework. The lasher is often marked "Danger": in any case it is well to keep away from it.

Laskets, or **latchets** (occasionally called *keys*).—Small lines sewed to the *bonnet* or to the *drabler* of a sail to lash, or lace, one to the other.

Latching eye, or *latchet eye.*—The loops in the head of a *bonnet* through which the *laskets* are passed.

Lasking (old term).—*To go alasking* is much the same as sailing *large* (*which see*).

Lastage.—The ballast or lading of a ship.

Latch.—A "dropping to leeward". (Winn).

Latchet.—*See* LASKETS.

Lateen.—A rig peculiar to vessels navigating the Mediterranean and other eastern seas. It consists of a triangular sail of large size bent to a very long yard. This rig was at one time very much employed on the rivers of Norfolk and Suffolk, but has now become entirely obsolete. The mast was stepped well forward, was without shrouds or stay, and raked forward. The sail was bent to a yard above and a short boom below, the yard being of immense length, sometimes twice that of the boat itself. (*See* DHOW and FELUCCA.)

LATEEN SAIL

Latitude.—Distance north or south of the Equator, expressed in degrees and minutes of arc.

Launch.—1. In the Royal Navy, the largest boat belonging to a ship.

2. To *launch.*—To put a new vessel into the water. The act is always attended with a certain amount of ceremony.

3. A *launch,* in the popular meaning of the word, is a small vessel propelled by some motor, and generally used in harbour or river service, or for pleasure. Such launches at first were propelled by either steam engines or electric motors, but coal being dirty and electricity both expensive and inconvenient, they have been superseded by internal combustion engines, at their first appearance unpopular because of their smell.

Lay.—1. This word at sea often means to "go", as *Lay forward or aft,* Go forward or aft.

To *lay out upon a yard* is to go out towards the yard arms.

To *lay in off a yard.*—To return towards the mast.

To *lay aboard.*—To go alongside.

To *lay a course.*—To keep the ship's head on a required course.

2. In another sense the term means to rest quiet, as *to lay to*, to *heave to.*

To *lay on one's oars,* in other words to *rest on the oars,* is to leave the oars horizontal above the water, blades flat.

To *lay in the oars.*—To boat the oars; to unship and lay them down in the boat.

3. But in another sense, again, it may imply precisely the opposite, as "*Lay to*" (in rowing), an encouragement to row hard, or, in any work, to go to work with a will.

To *lay up.*—To take a vessel out of service.

4. In shipbuilding, to *lay down* the lines of a vessel, is to delineate her form according to rule (*See* LINES), and when it is thus shown her lines are said to be "laid down".

Laying off.—The modelling in thin wood of any section of a vessel under construction.

5. In ropemaking, the *lay of a rope* is the direction in which the *strands* are twisted. Thus if they turn in a *right hand* direction, as is the general case, they constitute that which is called *hawser-laid,* while *left-handed* rope is called *cable-laid, cablet,* or *water-laid.* (*See* ROPE.)

6. *Lay-day.*—The day by which a cargo must be shipped or discharged, "and if not done within the term, fair weather permitting, the vessel comes out on demurrage,"—*i.e.,* compensation may be claimed by the shipper, for delay. Thus we have the description of Captain Cuttle:

> "A rough hardy seaman,
> Unused to shore's-ways,
> Knew little of ladies,
> But much of *lay-days.*"

Lazarette, or **Lazaretto.**—A small compartment, usually aft, where stores are kept. 2. A vessel or building used as a quarantine hospital.

Lazy.—An extra. *Lazy guy.*—A rope or tackle by which a boom is held down so that it may not swing about in rough weather.

Lazy painter.—An additional and smaller rope than the proper painter. Used as a temporary mooring.

Lead.—1. (For sounding).—A leaden weight attached to the end of a line and used to ascertain the depth of water beneath a vessel and the nature of the soil. There are two lead lines, the *deep sea lead* carried only by large vessels, and the *hand lead* with which every form of sailing craft should be furnished. The hand lead is 20 fathoms in length, and has a distinguishing mark at every fathom; these divisions are called *marks* and *deeps,* or *dips.* In a regulation lead line there are nine marks placed at the intervals 2, 3, 5, 7, 10, 13, 15, 17, 20: the rest are the deeps. The marks 2, 3, and 10 may be known by small pieces of leather, the 2 having two ends, and the 3 three ends, while the 10 has a hole through it. The fathoms 5 and 15 are marked by white bunting; 7 and 17, red; 13, blue; and 20 by two knots. The weight may be of any shape, but it should have a hollow bottom which may be filled with tallow, so that a portion of soil is brought up, thereby enabling an experienced person to judge his position by reference to his notes, or chart. As the depth of water on charts is increasingly shown in metres, it may be convenient to mark the leadline in metres as follows: 1 and 11 metres—1 strip of leather; 2 and 12 m.—2 strips of leather; 3 and 13 m.—blue bunting; 4 and 14 m.—green and white bunting; 5 and 15 m.—white bunting; 6 and 16 m.—green bunting; 7 and 17 m.—red bunting; 8 and 18 m.—

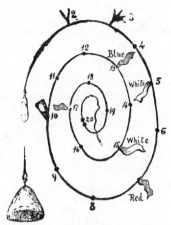

HAND LEAD.

yellow bunting; 9 and 19 m.—red and white bunting; 10 m.—leather with a hole in it; 20 m.—leather with a hole in it and 2 strips of leather. In heaving the lead it should be swung well out forward and stopped running the moment it jerks. To know when it does this it must be allowed to run through the hands. It is interesting to notice that the sounding lead is mentioned by Lucilius (*c.* 120 B.C.). It was also the *sund-gyrd* of the Anglo-Saxons. (*See* SOUNDING.)

2. *Lead* (for ballast).—The best but at the same time the most expensive ballast for small boats. (*See* BALLAST.)

Leading.—1. (Of a tackle).—The *leading part* of a tackle is that part of the rope which leads towards the standing (or fixed) end, and is, therefore, the moving part of the rope. (*See* TACKLE.) Smyth describes it as the rope of a tackle which runs between the fall and the *standing part,* and generally confounded with the fall.

2. (Of the wind).—A *leading wind* is a free or fair wind, in contradistinction to the term a *scant wind* (*which see*).

Leading block.—A block used to change the direction of the rope led through it.

Leading edge.—The forward edge of a moving object such as a rudder, or the luff of a sail.

Leading line.—A line passing through two clearly charted objects, along which a vessel can proceed with safety.

Leading lights.—Lights which, when in transit, identify a leading line. *Leading marks* perform a similar function.

3. *Leading strings.*—Another name for yoke lines. (*See* YOKE.)

Leak.—Any split, hole, or fissure in the hull of a vessel which allows water to enter. When a vessel suddenly develops a leakage she is said to have *sprung a leak.* Small leaks may sometimes be stopped by *fothering* (*see* FOTHER): in boats it is customary to apply *tingles.* (*See* TINGLE.)

When a boat lets in the water between her planks she is described as *leaky*: this may be the result either of laying up ashore, or of age and strain. In the latter case, and if the boat be *clincher-built,* it is sometimes remedied, for a time, by *doubling* (*which see*).

Lean bow.—A sharp *entrance* (*which see*).

Leather (of an oar).—That part of the oar which works in the rowlocks. It is so called because it is bound with leather. (*See* OAR.)

Lee and **Leeward** (pronounced *loo*-ard or *lew*-ard).—The lee side of a vessel is the side *opposite* to that upon which the wind blows; the other side being called the *windward* or *weather* side. *Leeward* means "on the lee-side"; thus a vessel *to lee-ward* would be seen over the lee side. To be *under the lee* of

FIG. 1

any vessel, object, or shore, is to be under its shelter; that is, on the lee side of it. So that if we pass close under shelter of a large ship which may take all the wind out of our sails, we come *under its lee*; or if we lie at anchor close under a shore *off* which the wind is blowing, and receive, therefore, the shelter of its cliffs, we lie *under the lee* of that shore.

A *lee shore,* on the other hand, is a shore upon which the wind blows; so that if we are driven by the force of the wind to-wards such a shore we are said to be driven *upon a lee shore.* (*See* fig. 1.)

A *lee tide* is a tide running in the same direction as the wind blows. A *tide under the lee* is a tide in a direction *opposite* to that of the wind.

In explanation of this let us suppose ourselves sailing with the wind *abeam.* (*See* fig. 2.) If the tide is in the same direction as the wind (or, in other words, if it runs towards the *leeward*), carrying us away with it, we have a *lee tide.* But if the tide runs to *windward,* that is, up against the wind, it is a *weather* tide; and because it presses against the lee side of the boat, it is, therefore, said to be *under its* (the boat's) *lee.* (fig. 2.)

Lee-way is the difference (or distance) between the course *steered* by a vessel and that actually run, when the wind is on any part of her side. In fig. 3, p. 167 A is the position of the ship. If the wind be coming from the direction marked and the point B is to be made, the helmsman will take into account the action of wind, and will steer his boat towards another point C, some distance to windward of B. AC is, therefore, the course to be steered, or steered, AB the course actually run or made good. The angle between AB and AC is the leeway. Lee way must always be calculated upon when sailing with a side wind. Naturally with a lee-tide there will be very much more lee-way made than if the tide be under the lee; and this will become very apparent to the beginner as soon as he takes the tiller in hand. Very much more lee-way will also be made by flat-bottomed vessels such as barges, than by those having deep keels or centreboards which present a wide surface to oppose a current. To counteract this tendency to lee-way, therefore, such flat-bottomed vessels are furnished with:—

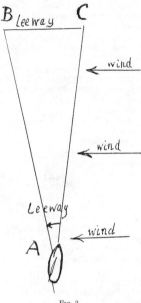

Fig. 3

Lee-boards (fig. 4), which are flat boards let down on either side of a wall-sided vessel, such as the *Stumpy*, a barge with no topmast, here shown, and serving in the place of a keel. There is one on each side of the vessel, and that one on the *lee* side is lowered when sailing, the pressure of the water keeping it in place.

Lee-bowing.—Sailing a vessel against an adverse tide so that the tide is on the lee bow instead of the weather bow, and thereby pushing the vessel to windward.

Lee-helm.—Keeping the tiller to leeward in order to keep the vessel on course. (*See* HELM.)

All these terms are in daily use among seafaring and yachting men, and should be thoroughly understood by the beginner.

Lee-gage.—The distance to leeward of any given object, in contradistinction to *weather-gage* (which see).

Fig. 4

Lee-fanges.—"Ropes reeved into cringles of sails to haul down those parts of such sails," necessary before lacing or unlacing a bonnet.

Lee-hatch.—A cant phrase, as "Keep off the lee hatch," which means, "Do not let the vessel make more lee-way than can be helped."

"Lee ho!"—Equivalent to "'*Bout ho!*" A shout of warning given by a helmsman to those in his boat, that he is going to put about. Upon hearing this warning, all those on board will do well to lower their heads, or by some other means to get out of the way of the boom as it swings over.

Lee runners.—Another name for those *backstays* which are slackened as sails go over. They are called *lee* runners because it is those on the *lee*-side which have to *run* or be loosed.

Leech (meaning "lee-edge").—The aftermost (back-most) or *lee* margin of a sail. This definition will apply equally to all sails; but there is this difference to be noted between those of the square rig and those of the fore-and-aft, viz., as square sails change their positions constantly, there can be no such thing as a permanent after edge, while, if they are set with the wind directly aft, the edges of each side are, theoretically, in the same position. But in fore-and-aft rig such is not the case: the edge of the mainsail nearest the mast, for instance, is always the foremost edge of the sail, and is permanently, therefore, the *luff*; and for the same reason the edge of the sail away from the mast is always the *leech*. Either side of a square sail, on the other hand, is the luff when it is the weather edge, and the leech when it is the lee edge.

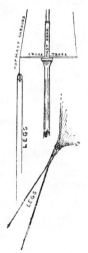

Leech lines.—In square rig, lines from the leeches, or edges of a square sail, on either side, to blocks hung on the yard. Leech lines brail up the sails.

Leech rope.—The *bolt-rope* running along the leech of a sail.

Left-handed.—The description of a rope whose strands trend to the left as they go away from the observer.

Leg.—1. Roughly speaking, when a rope resolves itself into two or more parts it is said to have legs. Thus, the topmast shrouds in a yacht continue only a little below the cross-trees. The reason for this is that when the top-mast is *housed* (lowered for a time) its shrouds may be of only such a length as to be conveniently secured close to the main shrouds. For were they so long as to reach the deck when the mast was elevated there would be difficulty in stowing away so much wire-roping when the mast was down. It is evident, however, that when the topmast is raised, its shrouds must be set up (tightened) by some means or other; and the most convenient method of accomplishing this is to fix a block at the end of the shrouds, through which block a line, or hempen rope, is rove, so that when it is hauled upon, the shrouds are tightened, and when the mast is struck, this tackle may be unshackled and stowed away in a convenient place. This rope, then, is called the legs. (*See* fig., p. 168.)

At sea, almost any rope which branches out in more than one direction is said, as above mentioned, to have legs.

2. *Legs* are also wooden beams which support a boat in an upright position when she lies high and dry.

"To have her legs on."—An expression often used of a boat when she sails fast.

Long-legged.—Said of a vessel when she draws a great depth of water, and would, therefore, require very long legs to support her high and dry.

3. *Leg-of-mutton sail* (sometimes called shoulder-of-mutton sail).—A triangular main sail sometimes used in small boats; and occasionally as a *trysail* in small yachts. It is an adaptation from the *Mudian* rig (*which see*), and derives its name from its shape, which is supposed to resemble a leg or shoulder of mutton.

Length.—There are two measures of length to a boat; 1st. Length on the water line; 2nd. Length over all, which is her entire length from stem to stern.

Let.—*Let draw* (spoken of sails).—To let the jib or foresail go over, as a boat goes about. (*See* under JIB and FORESAIL.)

Let fall.—An order given when setting a square sail after the gaskets have been released, to let go the clew lines, bunt lines and leech-lines so that the sail can be sheeted home.

Let fly.—To let go the sheets fully.

Let go.—To slacken away a rope and let it go altogether.

Let out a reef.—To increase the area of a sail which has been reefed by loosening the reef points, and letting the confined (or reefed) part of the sail go.

Let run.—To let go a rope or chain so that it runs out of its own accord.

Letter of Marque, or **Mart.**—Authorization to attack enemy ships as reprisal for loss suffered, or as an act of war.

Levanter.—A strong easterly wind in the Mediterranean.

Liabilities.—It is with a boat as with a house; and, indeed, the liabilities are greater on the boat. All money owing on a boat, all dues or claims upon her, pass over, when she changes hands, to the new owner. Purchasers of second-hand craft will be wise, therefore, to satisfy themselves before completing a contract that the property is free: and it is always well to have a written guarantee to this effect.

Liberty.—Leave to go ashore.

Liberty-men.—Those belonging to a ship's company who are ashore on leave.

Lie.—*Lie by.*—To lie close to another vessel.

Lie over.—To be heeled or careened over, as a boat, when sailing under press of canvas, lies over.

Lie within 4 points, 6 points, etc.—(*See* under SAILING.)

Lie on the oars.—To pause in rowing: the same as *lay* on one's oars (*which see*).

Lie to (in sailing).—To remain without motion. (*See* LAY TO.)

Life.—*Lifeboat.*—The lifeboats of the Royal National Lifeboat

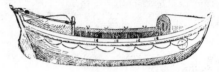

LIFEBOAT

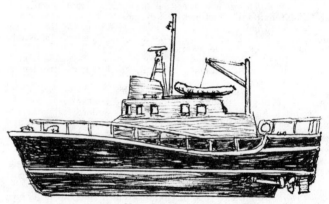

MOTOR LIFEBOAT *c.* 1983

Institution (founded in 1824) were about 30 ft. long with 8 ft. beam, nearly flat bottomed and weighted with a heavy keel. They were propelled by eight or twelve oars, rowed double-banked; and also rigged with two masts carrying working-lug and mizzen and fore-sails. Some were later furnished with a steam engine and propeller, and now all are fitted with powerful internal combustion engines. The bow and stern rose about 2 ft. above the main portion, forming air-tight chambers: compartments also ran all round just below the gunwales. The boat had a false bottom raised above the water line, the space between this and the bottom being packed with cork; and through this space ran several valves, being open tubes through which, should a sea fill the boat, her false bottom being above water line, the water was immediately discharged. Thus the boat was unsinkable and almost uncapsizable; and should she capsize must quickly right herself. An efficient lifeboat is held capable of carrying one adult person to every 10 cubic feet of capacity; to which capacity she must also have 1½ ft. of air-tight compartments. Lifeboats are kept up entirely by voluntary contributions, and the Institution is, consequently, always in want of funds and support. The number of lives it saves annually may be counted in hundreds. Lifeboats have always been manned by volunteers.

LIFE-BUOY

Lifebuoy.—The ordinary ring-shaped Kisbie Lifebuoy is of canvas-covered cork, others are horseshoe-shaped. It cannot be too strongly urged that they be always kept handy, ready to be thrown to anyone who has fallen overboard. A lifebuoy must be capable of supporting 32 lbs. of iron for 24 hours in fresh water.

To use a life-buoy.—Keep as low as possible in it: a person endeavouring to raise the body out of the water by the life-buoy is in danger of being turned over.

To throw a life-buoy.—It should be thrown flat, as a quoit is pitched. This must be done with judgment and coolness; and if a person fall overboard from the fore end of a vessel, the life-buoy must be carried aft before being thrown.

AN EARLY TYPE OF CORK LIFE-JACKET

Lifejacket, or *Lifebelt.*—A buoyant jacket or belt worn to support a person when in the water. It may be of solid type with cork or kapok enclosed in canvas and secured with

INFLATED LIFE-BELT

tapes tied round the body, or of an inflatable type, sometimes automatically inflated by a cylinder of carbon dioxide. It must be capable of supporting 16½ lbs. for 24 hours in fresh water. Everyone learning to sail should wear one type or another.

Life-line.—1. Any rope stretched along part of a vessel to prevent a person from falling overboard. 2. Any rope for throwing to a drowning person. Such ropes are always kept in readiness at the various stations of the Royal Humane Society. 3. The rope looped around the outside of a lifeboat, or *grabline.*

Life-saving rocket.—A rocket designed to be fired from the shore to pass over a stranded vessel and carrying a light line. (*See* ROCKET and BREECHES BUOY.)

Liferaft.—A raft shaped like a very large Kisbie lifebuoy with a grating in the middle, (*Carley Float*), or one which may be inflated and which is usually fitted with a protective canopy.

Lifts.—In square rigged ships, ropes passing through blocks at the mastheads, taking the weight of the yards, and enabling them to be canted or squared. "The yards are said to be squared by the lifts when they hang at right angles with the mast, *i.e.,* parallel with the horizon when the vessel is upright in the water."

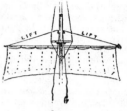

LIFTS

Topping lift.—A rope passing through a block at the mast-head and down to the guy end of a boom, to enable it to be *topped* (lifted) when reefing, tricing, etc. (*See* TOP.)

Light.—A vessel is said to be "light" when she is without cargo, and consequently high out of water.

To light is a term sometimes used by sailors instead of to help; as "Light to", that is "Light along that rope" or carry it along in the required direction.

Light sails.—In square rigged ships, the *flying kites*; *i.e.*, as a rule, the sky sails and their accompanying studding sails. But there were extraordinary occasions when some of the old line-ships and East Indiamen could set no less than three sets of square sails above the royals; viz.—the *sky sails,* the *moon rakers,* and the *jumpers* (or jolly jumpers). A ship thus equipped and with her six jibs was literally under every stitch of canvas, even to the last pocket-handkerchief.

Lights.—Rules concerning the lights which are to be carried and shown by vessels at sea are contained in full detail in the International Regulations for Preventing Collisions at Sea, (Rules 20 to 30).

In brief: *Vessels underway,* (except vessels under oars who may just show a white light), in order to indicate the direction in which they are moving, carry on the port side a red light, on the starboard side a green light, and at the stern a white light.

In addition to the side and stern lights:

A *vessel being driven by an engine* carries a white light on her foremast and, if of 50 m. or more in length, a second masthead light abaft and higher than the foremast light.

A *vessel towing another* carries *two* foremast lights, one over the other, or *three* if the tow exceeds 200 m. in length.

A vessel *trawling* carries a green light over a white light, if engaged in fishing by other means than trawling, a red light over a white light.

A *pilot vessel* on duty carries a white light over a red light.

A *vessel not under command* and therefore unable to get out of the way of another vessel, carries two red lights, one over the other. A vessel constrained by her deep draught to keep to a channel *may* carry *three* red lights.

A *sailing vessel may* also carry a red light over a green light.

Every vessel at anchor shall carry a white light forward and, if of

50 m. or more in length, at the stern and lower than the forward light, a second white light.

Lighthouse.—A tower exhibiting a powerful light at its head—a landmark by day and by night, for which reason they are of various forms. (*See* figs.) In ancient times a lighthouse (that of Pharos, at Alexandria, in *c.* 250 B.C.) became one of the wonders of the world. The appearances of lights differ so that navigators can identify the lighthouse. This is done by varying the characteristics of the light and the interval between its appearances. The light may be *fixed,* that is showing continuously; but more often *flashing* in which the period of light is shorter than the period of darkness separating the flashes; or *occulting* in which the period of light is longer than the period of darkness; and flashes may be single or arranged in groups.

ROCK LIGHTHOUSE

PILE LIGHTHOUSE

Light ship.—A light ship may be called a floating lighthouse securely moored on the margin of some dangerous rock or sand. These ships are of peculiar form, and easily recognized. Those stationed round the British coasts, and often elsewhere, are painted red with their name in large white letters.

Lighter.—A powerful hull or barge, flat bottomed, for transporting heavy goods ashore or up rivers. They are extremely com-

THAMES LIGHTERS

mon on the London river, and elsewhere where they could be seen dropping either up or down with the tide, being steered through the bridges by long sweeps (or oars.) (*See* fig.)

Ligsam.—Another name for *lagan* (*which see*).

Limbers.—Apertures between the frames, floors and the skin of a ship through which water may run away to the pump well in the lowest part of the hull. The limbers of a ship may therefore be called her main drains. They are gutters along her keelson, and receive her bilge-water. (*See* diagram under FRAME.)

Limber boards.—Short pieces of planking forming part of a vessel's lining, and usually capable of removal, so that the *limbers* may be cleared. (*See* FRAME.)

Limber kentledge. (*See* KENTLEDGE.)

Limber passage.—The passage on each side of the keelson.

Limber strakes (in shipbuilding) are the planks running along the lowest part of a vessel.

Limejuicer.—A British ship or seaman (hence "Limey"). A term deriving from the official issue of limejuice in British ships as an antidote to scurvy.

Linch-pin.—A small iron pin passing through some shaft axle or bar. In an anchor or in a shackle it is usually called a forelock.

Line.—A small rope: as *bunt lines, clew lines, tricing lines,* the *lead line,* etc.

The *line.*—At sea the Equator is called the line. In the old days of sailing ships great festivities took place on crossing the line, and a man was not considered a sailor until he had, so to speak, received the freedom of the sea by an initiation, at this time, which, from all accounts, appears to have been more enjoyable for the onlooker than for the principal performer. The practice is still kept up to a minor extent.

A *line of ships.*—Originally a fleet entered into battle in lines: either in *line ahead* (one behind the other), *line abreast,* or *quarter line,* (on the port or starboard quarter) or in a *windward* or *leeward* line. Hence a company of ships came to be known as a line. This then is the origin of the word as used by a firm which owns a "company" of ships, and therefore calls itself a *line.* Hence, also we have the name *liner,* originally a battleship of the line; to-day one of the ships belonging to a line and sailing regularly between specified ports.

To *line.*—To lay one piece of anything over or inside another. Hence *lining* in ship-building—the inside planking of a vessel within her ribs, or ceiling. But in those boats which are built with a double planking, one immediately over the other, both outside the ribs, the usual lining is often absent; and here the inner planking is called the lining or *case,* the outer one being the skin. (*See* diagrams under FRAME.) In the lining of a vessel the planks usually have a space between them to allow a free circulation of air: when, however, they are fitted close up it is called *close-lining.* Old yachts, and especially those for sale, may sometimes be found "close-lined": this may very possibly have been done to hide defective ribs, a fact which should be borne in mind by purchasers. In sailing boats of the better class, lining is often dispensed with altogether, as it is in almost every case with row boats.

Lines (in marine architecture).—The drawings of the *form* or shape of an intended vessel. These drawings are three in number: 1. The *sheer plan*; 2. the *half-breadth plan*; 3. the *body-plan.* The sheer plan is the side view on which are laid off the length, heights of all parts from the keel, etc. The half-breadth plan shows the horizontal or floor plan on any water line. The body plan is the end view showing the curves of the sides at any point in her length; "and since the two sides are exactly alike, the left half represents the vertical sections in the after part of the body, and the right half those in the fore part." Thus, lines running parallel to the surface of the water (such as the water lines) appear as straight lines parallel to the keel in the sheer plan; as straight lines at right angles to the keel in the body-plan, and as curved lines on the half-breadth plan. The delineation of vessels intended for speed, as racing yachts and boats, is one of the most occult branches of marine architecture; for it rests neither altogether upon mathematical rules, nor upon the rule-of-thumb, and is always subservient to the method of *rating* which may, at the time, be in vogue.

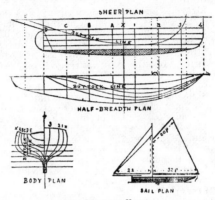

THE LINES OF A YACHT

Lines of flotation.—*Water lines*; horizontal in the sheer-plan, etc.

Load water line.—The line of deepest immersion of a ship.—*i.e.,* when she is loaded.

Buttock line.—A vertical section taken longitudinally along the boat. (*See* diagrams). It gives the form of the *buttock,* and of the *run* (both of which *see*).

Concluding line.—A line rove through holes in the wooden treads of a rope ladder to contract them into a small space.

Deep-sea line.—The sounding line for use in great depth.

Hand line.—The line for shallow sounding (*see* LEAD).

Life line.—A rope extended in various positions about a ship for people to lay hold of. Also a rope thrown to any person who may fall overboard. (*See* under LIFE.)

Tarred line.—A rope painted with or dipped in tar, in contradistinction to a *white line*—one not tarred.

Line-throwing apparatus.—*See* ROCKET.

Link.—One of the component members of a chain, of which there are various patterns, as *stud link, close-link, open-link,* etc. (*See* CHAIN.)

Link-worming.—In the days of hempen cables, a method of worming cables with chain so that they should not chafe in the hawse pipes.

Lipper (leaper?).—A sea which just rises above the bows or gunwale. Also the spray from a small sea.

List (sometimes pronounced by the fishermen "lust").—An inclination. Thus a vessel may be said to take "a list over to starboard" or to port.

Listing (in shipbuilding and repairing).—The cutting out of the edge of a plank in a ship's side, so as to expose the timber (rib) beneath it.

Lizard.—A short length of rope with a thimble spliced into one end and used as a fairlead, or for the attachment of a boat's painter.

Lloyd's.—The well-known institution called Lloyd's has been in existence since the year 1716. Its name is derived from a coffee house kept by Edward Lloyd, to which all interested in shipping matters resorted. From thence it was removed, and eventually located in the new Royal Exchange. Besides undertaking all matters of insurance through its members, it publishes, annually, a voluminous inventory of shipping intelligence, known as *Lloyd's Register of Shipping,* the importance of which, in the mercantile world, cannot be over-rated and a daily *Lloyd's List* of shipping movements.

Lloyd's Register of Shipping.—Established in 1760, publishes technical rules for the building and maintenance of ships. *Lloyd's Agents* can be found in very many ports and have a wealth of technical and local knowledge.

Load line.—A mark cut into a merchant ship's side and painted to show the greatest draught to which she may be loaded.

Loafer.—A name given to a man who hangs about by the waterside, either to pick up a job, or, if occasion prompt, to pick up anything else. They are sometimes called *"shore rakers"*; possibly from "raking the shore". It is not advisable to employ such men where watermen or fishermen can possibly be obtained.

A *'long-shore loafer* is one who loafs along the shore, though the name is sometimes given to those who fish or find other honest employment along shore; these are not to be included in the same category as the loafers above mentioned.

Lobscouse.—A stew of meat and vegetables.

Loch.—A word of Gaelic origin. A lake or an arm of the sea in North Britain or Ireland.

Lock.—"In internal navigation, the part of a canal included between two floodgates, by means of which a vessel is transferred from a higher to a lower level, or from a lower to a higher. It is also applied to the contrivance by which vessels are maintained at the level of high tides in harbours exposed to variations of level." (Brande and Cox.)

Locker.—A compartment on board a boat, for the stowage of anything. Small cupboards are called lockers, as well as the compartments into which the chain drops, and that in which ropes, small sails, and such like necessities are stored.

Davy Jones' locker.—The bottom of the sea.

Lodestone.—"The name given to magnetic iron ore when endowed with magnetic polarity; in which case it constitutes the native magnet or lodestone." It is this with which the needle of the mariners' compass is rubbed to enable it always to point towards the north.

Lodging knees.—In ship-building, deck-beam knees. (*See* KNEE.)

Log.—The instrument used to measure the speed of a vessel or the distance run through the water. The most primitive manner of calculating this velocity appears to have been for a person to heave a "log" or a chip of wood over the bow of the vessel, and to run with it until he reached the poop, the speed at which he ran forming the basis upon which the ship's speed was reckoned; and it is said that wonderfully accurate results were obtained by this rough method. This method of determining the speed by timing the passage of the log chip between two marks is known as the *Dutchman's log*. About 1570 the *English* or *Common Log* was introduced and was used until this century. It consisted of a piece of wood in the form usually of the quadrant of a circle about 5 in. or 6 in. in radius, and a quarter of an inch thick, and so balanced, by a leaden weight, as to float perpendicularly almost immersed in the water. This was called the "ship", or "chip" and was fastened to one end of a long line called the *log line* by a bridle, the other end being wound on a reel, placed in the stern part of the vessel. The "ship" being *heaved,* or thrown into the water, theoretically kept its place while the line ran off the reel as the ship moved, the length unwinding in a given time giving the rate of

A "HARPOON" LOG

sailing. This was calculated by knots made on the line at regular intervals and a sand glass which ran a certain number of seconds. "In order to avoid calculation, the length between these knots was so proportioned to the time of the glass that the number of knots unwound while the glass ran down should be the number of miles the vessel was sailing per hour." This, then, is the origin of the *knot*—the nautical mile. The log being heaved at certain times in each watch, the particulars were entered in the vessel's book, which was therefore called the *log book* or *log,* and which contained, besides, all details relating to whatever transpired during a voyage. The log-book is still used. But the system just noticed is difficult to use at high speeds and was superseded by various forms of self-registering rotators, which give the distance run of the vessel. These are towed astern, and, revolve with a speed proportionate to that of the ship, and may be read at any time. They are still often referred to as a "patent log". The most modern type are *bottom logs*. At some inches from the ship's bottom a small propeller is rotated by the ship's movement through the water. At each revolution an electric contact is made, and the ship's speed and the distance run through the water are both shown on dials on board.

Log boards.—Boards placed together, and opening like the leaves of a book, used in old ships upon which to enter the records of the ship each day; from whence it was copied into the log book. *Log slates* were similarly used.

Log book.—The ship's journal. Everything, including the courses and distance the ship has made, her position, and anything which may have happened on board, is entered therein. For a person to be entered in the log book is called being *logged,* and, if for offence, is a serious matter.

Log wood.—A dye-wood from America.

Long.—*Long boat.*—A strong row-boat propelled by eight or ten oars, usually *double banked.* The largest row-boat carried by a ship.

LONG BOAT

Long gaskets.—Gaskets used at sea, in contradistinction to those used in harbour. (*See* GASKETS and HARBOUR GASKETS.)

Long-jawed.—Rope which has, by much wear and strain, become such that the strands are straightened out, enabling it to coil both ways.

Long timbers.—In ship-building, timbers rising from the *dead woods* and running upwards in one piece, instead of being made up of several *futtocks.* (*See* FRAME.)

Long-legged.—Said of a vessel when she draws a great depth of water.

Longship.—A Norse warship of *c.* 900 A.D. It was rowed by 40 to 50 oars and had one mast and square sail

Long shore (along shore).—A 'long shore man is one who pursues his vocation along the shore, in contradistinction to those whose business takes them some distance from the shore; such are watermen or boatmen and the like, as opposed to seamen or fishermen. 'Long shore men are, however, often very good sailors.

Longitude.—Distance east or west of a *first meridian,* expressed in degrees and minutes. The first meridian is that which passes through Greenwich.

Loo.—A pronunciation of the word lee (*which see*), as in "loo-ard" for "leeward".

Loof.—1. The old name for *luff* (*which see*).

2. (Of a ship.) That portion under the bows of a vessel which curves inwards towards the stem.

3. To *loof.*—To be in a certain direction, as a plank "loofs fore-and-aft," etc.

Look-out.—The person posted to keep a continuous look out, and to report anything sighted. The attention of a steersman, in whatsoever craft, should never, under any circumstances, be taken off his work; and at the same time it is always well for all on board to keep a good look out.

Loom.—1. (Of an oar.) That part from the *leather,* or fulcrum, to the grip, or handle. (*See* OAR.)

2. An object is said to loom or loom up, when, under certain states of the atmosphere, as in fogs and occasionally towards evening, it appears larger than we suppose it to be. Probably the absence of the detail with which we are familiar gives a breadth to the object to which we are not accustomed; it must be remembered, too, that we see objects under such circumstances from a much shorter distance than usual. The reflection of a light in the sky when the light itself is hidden below the horizon.

3. *Loom gale.*—An easy gale, in which topsails may be carried.

Loose.—To *loose a rope.*—To let it go.

To *loose a sail.*—To unfurl or set it.

To *loose for sea.*—To unfurl and make sail for going out.

Lop.—To lop over is to lay over suddenly.

Lose way, or **lose ground.**—To reduce speed, fail to keep position, recede.

Loss.—In insurance "total loss is the insurance recovered under peril, according to the invoice price of the goods when embarked, together with the premium of insurance. Partial loss upon either ship or goods, is that proportion of the prime cost which is equal to the diminution in value occasioned by the damage." (Smyth.)

Lost (of a ship).—Wrecked, foundered or cast away.

Lost day.—The day which is lost in circumnavigating the globe to westward.

Low.—"*Under low sails.*"—A ship is sometimes spoken of as such when sailing under her *courses* and close-reefed topsails only.

Lower.—To let down.

Lower cheerily.—To lower expeditiously.

Lower Deck.—A term used in the Royal Navy to denote all ratings, as differentiated from officers.

Lower handsomely.—To lower gradually.

Lower topsail.—In square rigged ships, a topsail which is the result of cutting a heavy square topsail in half, thus making two (an upper and a lower) where only one used to be. As these two halves are more readily worked than the original whole, the system is now commonly followed on all modern ships. It is more fully described under the heading *double topsails.*

Lubber.—A term, not altogether of endearment, used among sailors. A contemptuous name given by seamen to those who are not versed in their own art.

Land-lubber is the title appropriated to a landsman.

Lubber's hole is a name given to the space through which access may be obtained to the top (at a lower masthead) by a slower but less dangerous means than that ordinarily taken by active seamen over the futtock shrouds; for which reason it is considered only worthy of a lubber, or land-lubber. (*See* diagram to FUTTOCK PLATE.)

Lubber's line.—The mark in the mariner's compass case which shows the exact fore-and-aft direction of the ship. Thus, whatever point comes under the lubber's line tells the direction in which the ship's head lies. The origin of the name is not altogether plain, unless we suppose that seamen have the faculty of calculating the exact position of such a line without its presence.

LUBBER'S LINE

Lubberland.—"A kind of El Dorado in sea story."

Luff.—The *luff* of a sail is its weather edge. (*See* SAIL.)

To *luff* in sailing, is to bring a vessel's head closer to the wind.

To *luff up* or *luff round* is to throw her head right up to the wind.

To *luff into a harbour* or bay, is to sail into it close-hauled to the wind.

To *spring a luff.*—To yield to the helm and allow the vessel to go nearer the wind.

Luff hooks.—"Tackle with two hooks, one of which is to hitch into the cringles of the main and fore-sail, and the other into a strap or pulley rope let into the chess-tree, etc., its use being to succour the tackles in a large sail." (Bailey's Dictionary.)

Luff tackle.—A tackle consisting of one double and one single block. A *double luff tackle* is a tackle consisting of two double blocks.

The word "luff" was anciently expressed "loof", in explanation of which we have the following: "The loof is that part of a ship aloft which lies just before the timbers called chess-trees, as far as the bulk-head of the forecastle.

"*Loof pieces* are those guns that lie in the loof of a ship." (Bailey.)

Lug.—*Lug sail.*—A four-sided sail, bent to a yard, and slung to the mast in a fore-and-aft position. There are three kinds of lug sails in general use, the *standing* or *working,* the *dipping,* and the *balance*; to these may be added the *Clyde* lug, which is less common, though still often seen, and is, in fact, only an enlarged standing lug.

WORKING LUG

1. *Standing* or *working lug.*—This sail is bent to a yard, and may be with or without a boom: if without, it has one particular advantage to beginners; for when the sheet is let go the sail holds no wind, or, in popular language, becomes little more than a flag. Yet the use of it will not teach the art of sailing, because there is danger that the tyro, getting accustomed to letting go his sheet in heavy puffs of wind, will do likewise when he comes to handle a boat rigged with a boom sail; the consequences of which may often be serious, for a boom sail holds the wind, and by letting it go the boat may be capsized.

2. *Dipping lug.*—Much used at sea at one time, but inconvenient

except in making long reaches, for the tack being carried to the stem post of the boat, it is necessary to drop, or "dip" the sail (hence the name) each time the boat goes about, and reset it on the other side of the mast. It is nevertheless a very powerful sail, and in skilful hands the dipping is quickly accomplished; and by the tack being carried forward it becomes both lug and foresail in one.

DIPPING LUG

3. *Balance lug.*—Once the favourite sail for pleasure boats and small yachts rigged with lug sails. It has a lower spar, called the boom, which may be extended beyond the stern, and sometimes even beyond the stem of the boat; and which allows, therefore, of a very large sail, well suited to quiet waters, though somewhat dangerous at sea, especially when *running,* for the boom, if very long, is liable to catch the waves.

4. *Clyde lug.*—This is a standing lug carried to a great height on a mast stepped well in the bows; the yard is long and heavy; and the sheet of the sail travels on a horse on the transom of the boat.

BALANCE LUG

It need hardly be said that all sails must be kept close in to their masts, for otherwise great loss of power will result. This has always presented more or less difficulty with lug sails. The simplest and commonest method of overcoming it is by an iron ring travelling on the mast and also hooked to the yard. All those, however, who have had experience of this method, agree that it is imperfect; the ring being liable to jam. A number of schemes have been recommended in its place; each person is inclined to regard his own invention as the best, and some go as far as to tell us so. It is found, however, that a system invented by and

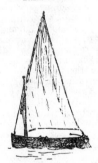

CLYDE LUG

working admirably with one person, often fails altogether to satisfy another. The diagram (p. 182) illustrates one or two of the schemes generally found useful. A shows a device recommended by Mr. Davies ("Boat Sailing for Amateurs"), B is the plain ring, and C a plan often employed with success. In the last the line D, after passing round the mast, hangs loosely until the sail is set up, when it is tightened, thus bringing the yard close to the mast, and in lowering there is little fear of jamming. But the beginner with lug-sails will do well to obtain information as to the various methods of forming a *parrel,* and having done so, he is at liberty to make use of the one he finds most convenient.

Lugger.—A boat rigged with lug sails. They were of various types and common to most of the northern countries, being mostly employed by fishermen on account of their extreme handiness. They may be single-masted, two-masted or three-masted, and often set top-sails. The sails employed in these vessels, which often reach a considerable size, are either standing or dipping lugs. Of all luggers in the world, those of the town of Deal are thought to hold the highest reputation; but all along the coasts they were worked in a manner often wonderful to see, and go out to sea when no other boat could live.

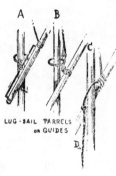

LUG-SAIL PARRELS or GUIDES

Lumper.—One employed in the loading or unloading of a vessel.

Lunar.—Pertaining to the moon. "Lunars," or Lunar Observations, were those taken with a sextant of the moon for the purpose of ascertaining the longitude, before chronometers were in use.

LUGGERS

Lurch.—A heavy roll or jerk to one side.

Lutine bell.—The bell of H.M.S. *Lutine,* which foundered in 1799 while carrying £1 400 000 in gold. The bell was recovered in 1859 and now hangs at Lloyd's, London, and is struck before the announcement of important news to members.

M

Mackerel sky.—High clouds arranged in bands across a blue sky.

Made.—*Made block.*—A block the shell of which is composed of several parts. (*See* BLOCK.)

Made eye.—A Flemish eye (*which see,* under EYE).

Made mast.—A mast made of several parts, as the lower mast of a large vessel. (*See* MAST.)

Magazine.—A compartment or building in which explosives are kept.

Maiden voyage.—The first voyage that a vessel makes after all trials have been carried out.

Mail.—*Mail boat.*—A boat carrying letters, etc. From the following it will be seen how the term came into use: "Mail (French, *malle*).—A word which signified originally the bag containing letters forwarded by Government for the public convenience, but it was soon afterwards extended to the letters themselves, and it is now used also for the conveyance in which they are forwarded."

Main.—In all rigs of vessels the word main applies alike to the principal mast and the principal sail it carries. In a ship we find the *main mast* rigged with the *main shrouds, main stays, main halyards,* etc., and carrying the *main sail* (called the *main course* if a square sail), which is bent to the *main yard.* Above this rises the main-top-mast with the main-top-sail, the main-top-gallant mast with the main-top-gallant sail, and, sometimes separate, the main-royal mast with the main-royal and sky sails. The position of the main-mast varies in different rigs, as given under the heading MAST.

Main halyards.—The halyards (ropes) which elevate the main sail. In fore-and-aft or gaff main sails (those stretched on a gaff) the throat halyards—those attached to the throat of the gaff—are usually called the main halyards, to distinguish them from the peak halyards, which elevate the peak of the gaff. But both these may be included under the one term "main halyards". (*See* diagram.)

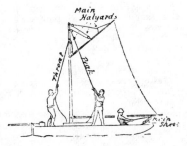

Main sheet.—The rope controlling the main sail. In square-rigged ships it is the aftermost (for the time being) of the ropes attached to the clews of the *main course,* the weathermost being the *tack.* And when the ship goes about these two change their names. The main sheet of a fore-and-aft rigged vessel runs through a block attached to the after end of the boom, if there be one, or otherwise to the clew of the main sail; and through another block on deck, which may be fixed or travel on a *horse,* the number of times it passes through these blocks depending upon the power required to work the sail. In large racing yachts the purchase is enormous; and a system of tackle upon tackle being employed, the main sheet assumes the form of almost a network of ropes.

Main stays.—The stays which support the main mast. Thus we find in a ship the main stay, running from the main-mast head forward to the base of the fore-mast. Upon the mainstay may be set the main-staysail. There are also the *main-top-mast stay* and stay-sail, etc.

Main and foresail rig.—This term is employed for want of a better. Its meaning will be obvious; a boat is rigged with a large main sail and foresail, or possible with a jib. The rig is frequently applied to the racing boats known as *half-raters.*

Main and mizzen rig.—This is a rig frequently seen in small boats, on account of its general handiness for all seasons, and it is peculiarly adapted to very long boats. The rig consists of a mainsail, which may be a balance lug and a mizzen with or without the addition of a fore-sail. Mr. Christopher Davies in his "Boat Sailing for Amateurs" makes various remarks upon the utility of this rig and of a variety of it in which the mizzen works with the tiller, much in the same way as the jigger of a barge.

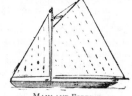

MAIN AND FORESAIL

Main deck.—The principal deck on a vessel having several decks. (*See* DECK.)

"*Mainsail Haul*".—An order given when tacking a square-rigged vessel, to brace the main and after yards to the new tack, leaving the fore mast yards aback to help the ship's head to pay off.

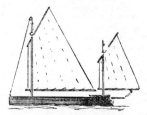

MAIN AND MIZZEN

Main yard men (old term).—Men on the sick list.

Make.—An expression signifying "to reach" or "attain to". Thus, to make a harbour is to reach it; to try and make any object, to try and reach it.

Make eight bells.—To strike four double strokes at the turn of a watch, *i.e.,* at 4, 8 a.m. and p.m. and at noon and midnight.

Make fast.—To secure.

Make headway.—To move forward, generally, expressed as against some difficulty, as against a head-wind or tide.

Make sail.—To set sail.

Make water.—To leak.

Making her number.—Said of a vessel indicating her name by signal flags.

Making of the tides.—The tides are highest and lowest about new and full moon, when they are called *spring tides,* and smallest at the intermediate times (first and last quarters of the moon), when they are known as *neap tides.* From the period of neap to that of spring tide, therefore, the tides must be increasing in strength and volume, and are then said to be *making.* (See LAGGING OF THE TIDES.)

Making way.—Moving ahead, or astern, through the water.

Mal-de-mer.—A malady which often overtakes those unused to the motion of the sea. Sea sickness.

Man.—To place the right complement of hands upon a ship or any part of it.

To man a boat.—To place in her her full number of rowers.

To man the yards.—To range the people on the yards, rigging, etc., of a vessel, either in honour of some person or in commemoration of some event, as a salute.

Man-hole.—A hole in an engine's boiler, or elsewhere, through which a man can crawl when necessary to examine the inside.

Man-ropes.—A general name for protecting guard ropes used in ascending a ship's sides, hatchways, etc.

Manly.—A term sometimes used by the fishermen to describe the seaworthiness of a vessel. If she is handy and a good weather boat she is said to behave herself "like a man", or in "manly" fashion.

Manifest.—A document carried by a merchant ship showing details of the ship, her cargo and master's name.

Manilla.—"A valuable cordage made in the Philippines, which not being subject to rot does not require to be tarred." (Smyth.) Manilla hemp is the best hemp for rope-making that there is.

Mare's tails.—Long wisps of high cirrus cloud.

Marina.—A yacht harbour which usually provides fuel, fresh water and other facilities besides moorings.

Mariner.—Anciently, a first-class, or able-bodied seaman, in general someone employed on a sea-going vessel.

Marines.—A corps of soldiers, trained in warfare ashore and afloat and often serving on board warships. The Royal Marines are sometimes called the "jollies", in contradistinction to the name "johnnies", given to the seamen, or bluejackets.

Marks.—*Marks and dips,* or *deeps.*—Certain divisions on the hand lead-line to show depth at a glance or by feeling. (See LEAD.)

Marline.—Small line, composed of two strands very little twisted. It may be either white or tarred. Marline is commonly used to secure the parcelling of a rope—that is binding canvas round it, to prevent its galling. It is also the material employed in securing the bolt ropes to large sails by marling hitches, instead of sewing.

Marling.—A series of spaced overhand knots made along a lowered sail, hammock, parcelling of a rope, etc., to secure it. (*See* SERVE.)

Marling spike.—A pointed instrument of iron used to open the strands of rope when splicing, marling, etc.

Maroon.—"To put one or more sailors on shore upon a desolate island, under pretence of their having committed some great crime. This detestable expedient has been too often practised by some inhuman commanders of merchant ships, particularly in the West Indies." (Falconer.)

Marry.—To join ropes together, as it were in the bond of matrimony. Thus:—1. (In splicing rope.) To place the strands of one rope between those of another preparatory to splicing them. 2. (In working ships.) *To marry ropes, braces,* or *falls.*—To hold two such ropes together, and, by pressure, to haul in on both equally.

Marryat's code.—"Code of signals for the Merchant Service," compiled by Captain Frederick Marryat, R.N. in 1817, the forerunner of the International Code of Signals introduced in 1887.

Martello towers.—The name given to the small circular forts, or towers, met with along the East and South-East coasts, and placed there in view of the meditated and boasted invasion of England by Bonaparte. "The name is usually supposed to be derived from a fort in Mortella (Myrtle) Bay, Corsica, which, after a determined resistance, was at last captured by the British in 1794."

MARTELLO TOWER

Martingale.—The rope extending from a jib boom end downwards to a dolphin striker; its office being to stay the jib boom in the same manner as the bobstays stay the bowsprit. (*See* diagram under DOLPHIN STRIKER.)

Martnets.—An obsolete name for the leech lines of a square sail, their use being to bring the leech of a sail to its yard to be furled. This is called *topping up on the martnets.*

Mast.—"A long piece, or system of pieces, of timber, placed nearly perpendicularly to the keelson of a vessel to support the yards, or gaffs, on which the sails are extended. When a mast is one entire piece, it is called a *pole-mast*; but in all large vessels it is composed of several lengths, called *lower, top,* and *top-gallant* masts—sometimes a fourth, called a *royal* mast, which, however, is usually in one piece with the top-gallant mast." (Brande and Cox.) Under this heading it may be most generally useful to describe the gear employed to support the mast and top-mast of a cutter or yawl yacht, referring the reader to the figures (opposite), and where technical terms are made use of, to the definitions under their respective headings. A mast is said, when set up, to be *stepped,* because its foot is fitted into a *step,* or *chock,* the office of which is to distribute the weight of the mast over as great a part of the keelson as may be possible. It is held upright to the level of the deck by a framework called the *mast-case*; and is further strengthened, on the deck itself, by a frame called the *partners*. The lower portion of the mast is usually square, this part being called the *housing*, because it is housed, or enclosed in the

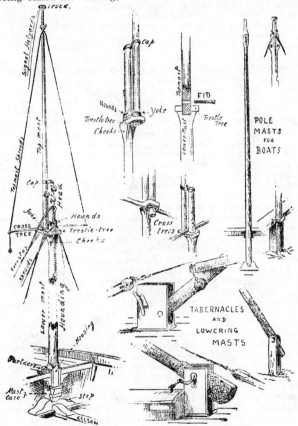

THE PARTS OF A MAST   VARIOUS MASTS

mast case. The mast is not, however, fitted very closely in its mast-case, but, on the contrary, is allowed a little play in these parts, in case they, or the deck, should swell or become strained, and press upon it, a possibility which might be attended by serious consequences; it depends, largely, for its support upon its shrouds and stays. In such craft as certain barges, or the Norfolk wherries, not only is the stowage room usually occupied by the mast housing required for cargo, but beyond this there is the constant necessity to lower the mast in passing under bridges. The mast is, therefore, set up on deck, its housing working in a casing called the *tabernacle*. The mast being stepped, is now to be rigged. At a short distance from the mast head are the *hounds,* otherwise called the *cheeks,* on which the *shrouds* rest (supporting the mast laterally), together with the *back-stays,* which prevent it from falling forward, and the *fore-stay,* which keeps it from falling backward; all of these serving to hold it securely up. That part of the mast from the deck upwards to the hounds is called the *hounding*: the part above this is the head. The shrouds communicate with the *shroud plates,* often called the *channels,* on the vessel's sides, by bottle-screws or by means of *lanyards,* rove through the *dead eyes,* which enable them to be made taut. The back stays with their tackles run further aft; while the fore-stay runs down to the stem-head. Just above the hounds, and supported by them, are the *trestle-trees,* which, in their turn, are short pieces of wood running fore and aft and bearing the *cross trees.* The cross trees give lateral support to the topmast. At the mast head projects an iron ring, called the *cap*: through it the topmast runs; and between the trestle trees is usually another ring, called the lower cap, or *yoke,* answering a like purpose. The topmast is placed forward of the lower mast, and thus runs up between the trestle trees and in the caps. When raised so that its heel is just above the level of the cross tree, a bolt of iron, the *fid,* is passed through a hole at its heel called the *fid-hole*: the fid rests upon the trestle-trees, and on it the whole weight of the topmast is carried. The topmast is then said to be *fidded.* The topmast fidded, requires *staying.* A short distance below the *truck* are small cheeks, placed there, as on the lower mast, for the reception of the topmast shrouds and stays. The shrouds are stretched over the extremities of the cross-trees and brought down only a little below them, their ends being usually attached to ropes, called *legs,* which, by means of a *purchase,* serve to haul them taut. The reason why these shrouds are not brought down to the deck when the topmast is set (as are the main shrouds) is this:—if they came down to the deck when the topmast was up, they would be so long when it came down that it would be difficult to coil them out of the way; whereas, by keeping them short they only just reach the deck when the topmast is struck, and (the legs being detached) they can be comfortably stowed away. The *topmast forestay* prevents the topmast from falling backward; it runs down from the mast head to the bowsprit head. The *topmast backstays* keep it back and belay, therefore, some distance aft of the mast; they can be slackened out as the sail swings over. Upon the lower mast, between the trestle-trees and the cap, are hung the various blocks through which pass the halyards; and, on the topmast, those for the topsail and jib topsail halyards. Such is the mast of a large yacht; but many boats are without a topmast, as are the mizzen masts of yawls, and generally of ketches, these being, in fact, nothing more than poles; and hence they are called, as above mentioned, *pole-masts*.

Masts are variously named, according to the rig of the vessel:—In a full-rigged ship the masts are three in number, viz., the *main,* the *fore,* and the *mizzen,* the main being in the centre and the mizzen aft; and as the *ship* appears to be the standard by which other vessels are compared, it would seem to follow that all vessels are, more or less, but modifications of it. Thus in *four-masted ships* there is one mast added, viz., the *jigger,* and they carry, therefore, *fore, main, mizzen,* and *jigger* masts; a fifth mast is named *spanker.* The *bark* and the *barkentine,* like the ship, carry the three masts, the difference between these and the ship being in the modification of the rigs. In *schooners, brigs,* and *brigantines,* the mizzen has been cut off, leaving the two masts *fore* and *main.* The main is, in these, therefore, the after one. In *ketches, yawls,* and some *barges,* there are also two masts, but the fore has been cut off, leaving the *main* and *mizzen,* and here, therefore, the main becomes the forward mast. In *cutters, sloops,* and in many fishing craft, both fore and mizzen have been cut off, leaving only one mast, the *main. Luggers* have sometimes three masts and sometimes two, in the latter case, generally, the *main* and *mizzen.*

There are also masts which constitute no general part of a vessel's rig; as *jury masts,* which are temporary masts, set up before the permanent masts are stepped, to take the vessel only a short distance, or in place of one accidentally carried away. Barges are usually fitted with "juries" for getting up and down rivers when the bridges are so numerous that the main mast cannot be elevated between them: they were very often to be seen on the London river, between bridges. (*See* fig. under JURY.) A *tow mast* is one used in river and canal towing. (*See* under TOW.) A *jigger* is a small mast or an extra mast. The small mast fitted to, and working with, the rudder of a barge, is sometimes called the jigger.

The following terms are used with reference to masts:—

Spent mast.—A mast is said to be spent when it is broken in rough weather and rendered useless.

Spring the mast.—A mast is sprung when it is cracked or badly strained, though it need not necessarily be spent.

Raking masts.—A mast set out of the upright is said to *rake.* Schooners, yachts, and steamboats have often raking masts; with other vessels it is not so usual. The rake is generally understood to mean an inclination backward; but on some occasions the inclination is forward, when it is described as *raking forward,* or *stayed forward.* (*See* fig. under RAKE.)

In the manufacture of masts the following terms are often employed:—

Armed mast.—A mast made of more than one tree.

Bipod mast.—A mast consisting of two legs, joined at the top and separated athwartships at their base, so that no shrouds are needed.

Cage mast.—A lattice mast of steel, fitted principally in U.S. battleships of the early twentieth century.

Made mast.—A mast made up of several united pieces, in contra-distinction to one consisting of a single piece or tree. Large made masts are stronger made than of one pole, and less liable to *spring,* but for small vessels the pole is the more elastic. Some yachts have hollow wooden masts, usually of spruce, scarfed and glued. Modern yacht masts are more often metal tubes, of stream-lined section, with halyards contained within their length. Ship's masts, which support derricks, radar scanners, etc., and the lower masts of more recent sailing vessels (as well as their lower yards) are built of steel plate.

Rough mast.—A spar fit to make a mast out of, or before the mast is made of it.

Tripod mast.—A mast consisting of three legs, their heels sep-arated in a triangle. Used in battleships they often supported fire-control tops, etc.

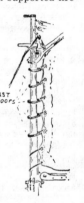

Wooden masts and other spars are sometimes seen to be apparently cracked along (or between) the fibres; but this, though defective, does not materially affect their elasticity. Large knots, on the other hand, are sometimes dangerous; and all holes, bolts, or screws, piercing the fibre, tend to weaken the spar. There is an old saying having reference to the masts of fore-and-aft rigged boats, viz., "Mainmast strong and topmast long." Old sayings are often true sayings.

MAST HOOPS

Mast hoops, or *rings,* sometimes called *hanks.* The rings, either of ash, cane, or metal, en-circling a mast, and to which a lower fore-and-aft sail (such as the mainsail) is fastened. To these rings the sail is said to be *bent on,* down that portion of it called the *luff,* or *weather leech.*

Mast-rope.—Another name for the *heel-rope* (*which see*).

Master.—The captain of a merchant vessel, who holds a master's or extra-master's certificate. Once, in the Royal Navy, the officer responsible for the navigation of the ship.

Master-at-Arms.—The chief petty officer responsible for main-taining discipline on board.

Mate (in a ship).—Literally, the master's assistant. There may be in a merchant vessel as many as four or five mates; they are officers under the captain. In the Royal Navy a Master's Mate was a petty officer appointed to assist the Master.

Matthew Walker.—A stopper knot which takes its name from the originator. (*See* KNOTS.)

Maul.—A large iron hammer.

Top maul.—A hammer with an iron handle used in large vessels to drive the fid in or out of a top mast, and for this purpose it is often attached to the mast head.

"Mayday".—(The pronunciation of the French "*m'aidez*," "help me!") The international spoken radio signal of distress.

Measurement of vessels.—The calculation of their capacities upon certain data. (*See* TONNAGE, DISPLACEMENT, RATING.)

"Meet her".—The order given to a helmsman to check the swing of the vessel's head.

Member's flag.—A small flag displayed by a yacht belonging to any particular club, and the device on which is registered and numbered in the yacht club's books. Each member may have his own flag. (For its use *see* under BURGEE.)

Mend.—*To mend sails.*—To loose and bend them afresh on their spars.

Mercator's projection.—A system of representing the curved surface of the earth on a flat plane, in which the meridians are parallel straight lines, and the vertical latitude scale increases to the poles. Most charts are drawn on this projection.

Meridian.—An imaginary line on the earth joining the poles and passing through the equator at right angles. The First, or Prime Meridian, passes through Greenwich.

Mesh.—The space between the lines of a netting.

Mess (at sea).—A company of officers or men who eat or live together.

Mess kid.—A wooden vessel for holding food. (*See* KID and KIT.)

Messenger.—A light rope used to haul in a heavier one. 2. A rope which, being attached to a heavy cable, is hauled in by a capstan, the cable itself being too large to grip the barrel. The messenger is often attached to the cable by smaller ropes called *nippers,* and is then said to be *nipped on.*

Metacentre (in hydrostatics and naval architecture).—That point in a floating body upon the position of which the stability of the body depends.

Mete stick (on ship board).—A measure used in stowing the cargo in order to preserve proper levels.

Middle ground.—A shoal in the middle of a navigable channel.

Middle topsail.—Smyth gives the following definition of a middle topsail:—"A deep roached sail set in some schooners and sloops on the heel of their topmasts, between the top and the cap." This is a remnant of the old rig of cutters, sloops, etc., which once carried square sails.

Midships.—The same as amidships—*i.e.,* in the middle portion of a vessel.

"Midships".—The order to put the helm or steering wheel to its central position.

Midship beam.—The beam upon which the extreme breadth of the ship is formed.

Midship bend.—The broadest frame in a ship, called the *dead flat.*

Midshipman.—The rank in the Royal Navy above the cadet, and below Sub-Lieutenant. Gentlemen's sons apprenticed to the sea in the merchant navy are also called, by courtesy, midshipmen. "Middy" was the popular abbreviation of this word.

Midshipmen's nuts.—Biscuits all broken into pieces.

Mile.—The sea or Nautical Mile = one sixtieth of a degree of latitude, and varies from 6,046 ft. on the Equator to 6,092 ft. in lat. 60°.

Nautical Mile for speed trials, generally called the Admiralty Measured Mile ....
$$\begin{cases} 6,080 \text{ feet} \\ 1\cdot151 \text{ statute miles} \\ 1,853 \text{ metres.} \end{cases}$$

Miller.—*To drown the miller.*—To put too much water into grog.

Mine.—An explosive charge, either moored below the surface or lying on the sea bed, exploded by contact with the hull of a passing ship, or by the noise of her passage (an acoustic mine), or her magnetic field, or other means.

Miss stays.—A vessel is said to miss stays when, in tacking, she fails to come about, and gets hung up in the wind. (For a fuller meaning of the term *see* under TACK.)

Mitchboard.—A prop or stanchion with a semicircular groove cut into its upper end for the support of a boom when at rest. It is sometimes employed instead of a *crutch* to take the weight of the boom off the halyards. (*See* CRUTCH.)

Mizzen.—(Fr., *artimeno*; Ital., *mezzana*).—The word applies to both mast and sails.

Mizzen mast.—The after-most mast in vessels of 3 masts, as described under the heading MAST.

Mizzen sails.—Those bent to a mizzen mast. The following may be interesting as relating to the origin of the name "mizzen". "The word occurs in Italian as mezzana, a lateen sail, and in French as *mizaine,* a fore-sail, and must be traced to the Latin *medius,* and the Greek *mésos,* its application arising from the mizzen yard in a galley being in the middle line of the ship, while the other yards were carried *across* the deck." (Brande

and Cox.) Our business here is with the mizzen as applied to yachts and sailing boats. In yachts its presence constitutes a *yawl,* and though apparently one of the most insignificant of the sails, it is yet one of the most useful; for by its aid a vessel will stand up to the wind in a gale, though the mainsail be altogether lowered; she can also get under weigh with it and a foresail; and in large boats it saves the necessity of taking several hands. At the same time, however, the space occupied by the mizzen, where, in a cutter, the boom would extend some distance over the taffrail, precludes the possibility of the yawl rig being so fast as that of the cutter. In sailing boats of any great length the mizzen is found to be of the utmost value, though not suited to those which are short. It also forms part of the *main and mizzen* and of the *canoe* rig. In barges and ketches it is always found; the barge carrying one so small in comparison to the mainsail that one might well wonder that it can be of any service. Here, however, it is often set up on and works with the rudder, giving that member a double power over the long and often deeply laden hull. In the ketch it is a larger sail, sometimes without a boom, and frequently surmounted by a topsail; and in many fishing boats it is also found. The mizzen is, in a word, a useful sail, depriving the vessel of some speed, but rendering her infinitely more handier than those in which it is dispensed with; and one of its great advantages is that, to a great extent, it does its own work.

Moderate. —*Moderate breeze.* —A breeze in which all sail can be comfortably set. Force 4, wind speed 11–16 knots.

Moderate gale. —A wind necessitating that all reefs be taken in to make all snug. The term *"moderate gale"* is no longer used: *"Near Gale"* is the equivalent: Force 7, wind speed 28–33 knots.

Mole. —A huge stone breakwater or sea wall.

Monitor. —A low freeboard, shallow draught warship, mounting one or two heavy guns for coastal bombardment.

Monk's seam. —In sails, a seam sewn down the centre of the two seams by which the cloths of large sails are united.

Monkey. —A prefix meaning small or short. 2. A weight, as that of a pile-driver.

Monkey block. —A small single block have a swivel strop. "Also those *nailed* to the topsail yards in some ships, to lead the bunt lines."

Monkey fist. —A knot, resembling a Turk's Head knot, sometimes put in the end of a heaving line to increase its carrying power.

Monkey forecastle. —A small elevated forecastle or anchor deck. (*See* diagram under Deck.)

Monkey gaff. —A gaff hoisted above a spanker gaff.

Monkey island. —The navigating and compass position on top of the wheelhouse or chart house.

Monkey jacket. —A uniform jacket as distinguished from a frock coat.

Monkey spars. —Reduced spars.

Monsoon. —The seasonal winds of certain latitudes in the Indian Ocean, China Sea, and West African coast.

Moon-rakers, or **moon sails.** —In ships, square sails set above the sky sails. They are very rarely seen, and then only in the lightest winds. They come under the head of *light sails* (*which see*).

Moor, mooring. — To moor is to take up a mooring, but sometimes the same term is used to signify bringing a vessel to two anchors: and a vessel with an anchor out both ahead and astern is said to be moored; as she may also be when both anchors are brought to one cable (as described under SWIVEL). A permanent mooring is an arrangement of weights sunk below the ground under water. To these a chain is made fast and attached at the other end to a rope, and that rope to a buoy. Boats lying habitually in one harbour have moorings in it.

When a sailing boat desires to take up her mooring, she comes up to it, if possible, head to wind and tide; but as neither winds nor tides accommodate themselves to the convenience of individuals there are various methods of doing this which only experience can teach. This is, indeed, one of the nicest and most difficult feats presented to the amateur in everyday work. Presuming, however, that the bow of the boat has been brought to a standstill just over the mooring (which, after all, is the whole end of the matter), the buoy is picked up and taken aboard, and the chain also brought aboard and shackled, or belayed, round the bowsprit bitts, when the boat is secure. It is important to remember, in taking in the buoy-rope, to bring as much in as possible before belaying, as if there be any way on the boat and not sufficient rope inboard, that already secured may be torn out of the hands.

To *slip the mooring* is merely to let it go, the buoy always showing where it may be found again.

To *moor by the head.* — To ride with two or more anchors down by the head.

Mooring for a fair berth. — Mooring in a place of safety; spoken of ships coming to an anchorage.

Mooring for east and west. — Anchoring according to the run of a tide or high wind, so as to keep out of danger.

Mooring block. — An object to take the place of an anchor. The sunken stone or wooden baulks which form a permanent mooring are sometimes thus called.

Running moor. — The first anchor is let go while the ship still has headway and the second after she has gone further ahead.

Mop. — A broom with a cloth head, always useful on board.

To *mop along* is a slang term often used of a sailing boat, to express the fact that she moves quickly.

Morse. — The Morse Code, consisting of groups of dots and dashes, or "shorts" and "longs", each representing a letter of the alphabet or a numeral, was invented by Samuel Morse, an American, in 1844. The symbols can be transmitted by sound, light, radio, or by the waving of a flag.

The words placed alongside each letter and figure are used to prevent mistakes arising from the similar sound of some letters. For example: "n d" may be mistaken for "m b," but "november delta" is unmistakable.

A	Alpha · —	N	November — ·
B	Bravo — · · ·	O	Oscar — — —
C	Charlie — · — ·	P	Papa · — — ·
D	Delta — · ·	Q	Quebec (Kibbeck) — — · —
E	Echo ·	R	Romeo · — ·
F	Foxtrot · · — ·	S	Sierra · · ·
G	Golf — — ·	T	Tango —
H	Hotel · · · ·	U	Uniform · — —
I	India · ·	V	Victor · · · —
J	Juliet · — — —	W	Whisky · — —
K	Kilo — · —	X	X-ray — · · —
L	Lima · — · ·	Y	Yankee — · — —
M	Mike — —	Z	Zulu — — · ·

Figures

1	Unaone · — — — —	6	Soxisix — · · · ·
2	Bissotwo · · — — —	7	Setteseven — — · · ·
3	Terrathree · · · — —	8	Oktoeight — — — · ·
4	Kartefour · · · · —	9	Novenine — — — — ·
5	Pantafive · · · · ·	0	Nadazero — — — — —

Mortar vessel.—Under the old system of naval warfare, a vessel carrying a heavy mortar, a powerful, but short-range gun with a fixed elevation.

Mortar and Rocket Apparatus.—(*See* ROCKET.)

Mother Cary's chickens.—A name given by seamen to the birds known as *stormy petrels*, or *storm birds* (*Procellaria pelagica*). These are able by the help of their wings to walk, as it were, upon the water.

Mother Cary's goose.—Another of the same family, only considerably larger (*P. gigantea*).

Mould.—In shipbuilding this term has a meaning peculiar to itself.

To *mould* is to draw out in their proper dimensions the several parts of a ship, for the guidance of the builder.

Moulding dimensions, as applied to any piece of timber, are its depth or thickness.

Moulded breadth is the measurement across the *skeleton* of a vessel outside her *timbers* (ribs); not across her planking, for that is not supposed to exist when the moulded breadth is spoken of.

Mount.—Expressed of a battleship—as "she mounts twenty guns".

MOUSING A HOOK

Mouse.—A *mouse.*—A thickening made in part of a rope. "A knot or knob wrought on the outside of a rope by means of spun-yarn, parcelling, etc., as the knot wrought on the stay of a ship which prevents the collar from closing round the mast head." (Falconer.)

To *mouse a hook.*—To pass a *yarn* or *fox* round a

hook to prevent it from clearing itself of whatever it may be fastened to.

The Mouse.—An important bank of sand in the estuary of the Thames.

Mud pattens.—Boards to be fastened to the feet, for walking on very soft mud. They are difficult for beginners to manage; and it is best, therefore, for anyone to take an oar or pole with him when necessity obliges him to put on mud pattens.

Mudian, mugian, or **Bermuda rig.**—A *mudian* is one of a class of boats originating from the Bermudian Islands, and far more important in the history of yacht-building than is often allowed. The following were the main features of the true mudian: it was short, of considerable beam, and of great draught aft; the stern post and keel combining together to form a deep curve. It had one mast, of extraordinary length, usually unsupported except for a jib-stay. The length of this mast is said to have sometimes reached two, or even three, times that of the keel. It set two sails, a main and a jib, the latter running out on a short jib-boom or bumpkin. The main-sail was triangular in shape, its head being

MUDIAN RIG

taken up to the head of the mast, and its foot stretched on a boom extending far out beyond the stern. It is to this vessel that we are indebted for many of the improvements introduced in years past into the designs of our own fastest yachts. The Bermudians, says Smith, "claim to be the fastest craft in the world for working to windward in smooth water, it being recorded of one that she made five miles dead to windward in the hour during a race; and though they may be laid over until they fill with water they will not capsize". We occasionally see rated racing boats rigged Bermuda fashion, though the height of the mast is never such as that spoken of above. At one time the rig was popular in a modified form, the main becoming a sort of *leg-of-mutton* sail (*which see*); and for beginners, who may have the

MUDIAN RIG MODIFIED

opportunity of choosing the class of boat they will take up, probably no safer or more instructive rig could be recommended. Another rig hailing from the same islands, and having two masts, is described under the heading BERMUDA RIG.

"Scud like a mudian."—From the above, the meaning of this expression will explain itself. It implies "be off quickly", or "as quickly as a mudian".

Muffle (oars).—To put soft material round the leathers of oars to prevent noise. (Only done in warfare.) To restrain a sail which is flapping in the wind.

Mugian Rig.—(*See* MUDIAN RIG.)

Multihull.—A vessel with more than one hull, e.g. a catamaran or trimaran.

Mumbleby or **Mumblebee.**—A name applied by Brixham fishermen to a boat midway in size between a *hooker* and a *trawler*.

Muntz metal.—A substitute for copper in the sheathing of the bottoms of vessels. It answers well and is much less expensive than copper, but cannot compare with it as a permanent covering. It is an alloy of copper and zinc.

Muster.—To assemble together for the purpose of resuming or commencing work. The word would properly appear to mean the calling over of names, as from a muster-roll.

Muzzler or **Dead Muzzler.**—A strong head wind. A wind blowing right on the muzzle.

N

Nab.—A reef of rocks below water. The name of such a reef off the east of the Isle of Wight, marked by the Nab lightship.

Nails.—*Clincher nails* have square shanks. They are driven and withdrawn without splitting planks.

Single deck nails.—Nails about 5 in or 6 in in length.

Double deck nails.—About 7 in long. Both these used in fixing large timbers, such as decks, carlines, etc.

Ten-penny nails.—About 2¼ in in length (originally tenpence per pound).

Nail sickness.—Minor leaks caused by erosion of nails in a wooden hull.

Nao (Spanish), Nau, Nef (French).—A general name for a ship from the 13th to 16th centuries. (Latin *navis,* a ship.)

Narrows.—Small passages between lands, submerged or dry, or between sands, as "The Narrows", a name met with in many rivers and estuaries.

Nautical Almanac.—An annual publication containing astronomical and, sometimes, much additional information essential for navigation.

Nautical mile.—(*See* MILE.)

Nautophone.—A fog-signal sounding a high note.

Naval.—Pertaining to ships, or to a navy.

Naval architecture.—"The science of designing the forms for vessels." It is, therefore, distinct from shipbuilding, which is "the application in practice of the theoretical designs of the naval architect".

Naval cadet.—A gentleman's son training for service as a naval combatant officer.

Naval crown (with the Romans).—"A crown of gold or silver, adorned with the figures of beaks of ships, which it was their custom to give as a reward to those who had first boarded an enemy's ship." The naval crown has become a charge in heraldry consisting of alternate ships' sterns and square sails.

Naval reserve.—An auxiliary naval force, originally formed in 1859, for men and officers.

Naval hoods, or *hawse-bolters* (in shipbuilding).—Large pieces of thick timber above and below the hawse holes.

Navel pipe.—A large tube connecting the chain locker to the deck, through which the anchor cable passes.

Navicert.—A certificate issued to a neutral ship to allow her to pass through a blockaded zone.

Navigation.—That branch of science which teaches the sailor to conduct his ship from place to place. "To understand the principles of navigation and their practical application, it is necessary that the mariner should be acquainted with the form and magnitude of the earth, the relative situations of the lines conceived to be drawn on its surface, and that he should have charts of the coasts and maps of the harbours which he may have occasion to visit. He must also understand the use of the instruments for ascertaining the direction in which a ship is steered, and the distance which she sails; and be able to deduce from the data supplied by such instruments the situation of the ship at any time, and to find the direction and distance of any place to which it may be required that the ship should be taken." (Brande and Cox.)

Navy.—The ships and seamen of a country, but often referring only to war vessels.

Naze (Fr., *nez,* a nose, as in Cap Gris Nez, a cape on the north coast of France).—A projecting piece of land, as Walton-on-the-Naze, Essex. (*See also* NESS.)

Neap.—*Neap tides.*—The lowest tides, taking place about five or six days before the new and full moons. Any influence, such as winds, which tends to prevent the tide from reaching its expected height, is said to "neap" or "nip" it.

To be *beneaped* is to be left aground by a receding *spring* tide, in such a position that the next tide does not take the vessel off, and she must, therefore, remain until the following spring tides.

Neck.—1. Of a gaff or boom, that part immediately behind the jaws, commonly called the *throat* (*which see*). 2. Of an oar, that part immediately before the blade. (*See* OAR.)

Ness (Fr. *nez,* a nose).—A projecting piece of land, usually of low level, as Orford Ness, Sheerness, etc. (*See also* NAZE.)

Net.—*Nettings.*—Nets of rope, placed at various parts of a ship, either for stowage or for protection against danger.

Torpedo nets.—Steel nets extended on booms beyond and round a ship of war to prevent the entrance of projectiles under water.

Nettles, or **knittles.**—The small lines which attach the canvas part of a hammock to the ring on the *lanyard.* The loops or buttons of a sail's *bonnet* are also sometimes so called. (*See* BONNET.)

News.—"Do you hear the news?" "a formula used in turning up the relief watch." (Smyth.) That is (in other words), the cry with which those who have completed their watch summon those whose duty is to relieve them.

Night watches.—"Night was originally divided by the Hebrews and other Eastern nations into three watches. The Romans, and after them the Jews, divided it into four, the first of which began at sunset and lasted until about 9 p.m., the second till midnight, the third till 3 a.m., and the last terminated at sunrise. The ancient Gauls and Germans divided their time, not by days, but by nights; and the people of Iceland and the Arabs do the same at this day. The like was observed by our Saxon ancestors." At sea the difference between night and day is not taken into account, and the night watches are the same as the day. (*See* WATCHES.)

Nip (of a cable or hawser).—To secure it with a *seizing* or clamp.

Nippers.—Short lengths of rope temporarily fastening the cable to the *messenger*.

Selvage nippers.—Rope rings used when the common nippers are not strong enough to resist a strain.

To freshen the nip is to move a rope slightly so that a different part bears upon a fairlead or sheave.

Nock.—In sail-making, "the foremost upper corner of gaff-sails and of a jib-shaped sail having a square tack". These jib-shaped sails with square tack, as if a large piece of the foremost point had been cut off, are now rare, though occasionally seen in the stay sails of old vessels. In them the nock runs down the forward mast as shown in the figure.

Nock earing.—The rope fastening the nock of a sail.

Nog.—A treenail driven through the heel of a *shore* (the shore being a timber supporting a vessel on the slips). The shore is then said to be nogged, and the operation is called *nogging*.

Noggin.—A small cup or spirit measure of about a quarter of a pint.

No higher (in steering), no nearer to the wind, *i.e.*, that the boat is getting a little too close to the wind, or, that, therefore, the helm should be put a little up, or towards the wind. (*See* under HELM.)

No man's land.—In ships, a space amidships, but neither on the starboard nor on the port side, from which circumstance the term is supposed to be derived.

No nearer (Fr., *pas au vent*).—The French is more explanatory of this term than the English. It is practically the same as *no higher*; being an order to a steersman not to go so close to the wind as to decrease the speed of the vessel. A boat may be capable of sailing very close to the wind, and on occasions this is a very useful quality, but she will make more speed by being kept a little off. If speed is desired, therefore, and the boat is getting too close to the wind, it will be well to keep her "no nearer", or "no higher".

Noose.—A running knot.

Nore.—An important spit of shifting sand at the mouth of the river Medway, in the Thames estuary, and at the head of which is placed the well known Nore lightship. It is the first passed on leaving the Thames.

Norfolk Broads.—A tract of land on the east side of Norfolk and Suffolk, penetrated by three main rivers—the Yare, the Waveney, and the Bure—of which there are various tributaries. These rivers widen out in parts into large meres or open spaces called broads, whence the name of the district. This is the happy hunting ground of shooting-men and amateur yachtsmen, and of those who love an open space.

Norfolk wherry.—A sailing barge peculiar to the rivers of the "Broads" district of Norfolk and Suffolk. The hull is pointed bow and stern, but the bow is to be distinguished by the *eye,* which is a white patch painted somewhat in the form of a boat's transom. (*See* fig. 1.) The wherry has one mast, and carries only one sail (being, in fact, the parent of the popular una rig), the peak of which is carried up to a

Fig. 1

great height, so that the vessel penetrates into the upper reaches of the rivers where the trees overhang, and the banks are high, this peak may rise above them, and, by thus catching the wind, bring it down into the body of the sail, acting, in fact, in exactly the same manner as the topsail of a cutter. And, indeed, it may be shown (*see* fig. 2) that though the Norfolk wherry actually sets no topsail, its spread of canvas is equivalent to that of craft which do: by hiding (in the fig.) the right-hand or cutter mast we have the wherry sail; by hiding the left-hand or wherry mast, we have the main and topsail of the fishing bawley or yacht. The size of the wherry sail is also capable of increase

Fig. 2.—Norfolk Wherry

by the addition of a *bonnet,* laced or buttoned along its foot, and always used with fair winds. (*See* fig. 1.) Except in this instance, the bonnet is almost obsolete. The mast of the wherry works in a *tabernacle:* it is without shrouds or any support beyond the forestay, which stay also acts as a fall for lowering and elevating it. The wherry is a very close-winded vessel, carrying a powerful weather helm, and is unsurpassed on its own waters, though experiments have shown it to be unsuccessful elsewhere. It did the greater part of the carrying trade of the district; and of late years, steam was applied to it with tolerable success.

Norman.—A short bar thrust into one of the holes in a capstan, so that a turn may be taken.

North.—The principal of the four cardinal points of the compass, and on the mariner's card usually marked by an ornamented arrow head or a fleur de lys, to distinguish it from all the others.

NORWEGIAN SHIP'S BOAT

Northing.—The difference of latitude made by a ship in sailing northward; or, in other words, the distance towards the north made by her in a specified time.

Norwegian.—*Norwegian skiff.*—A boat of peculiar form and wonderful buoyancy. (*See* fig.)

Norwegian yawl.—A Scandinavian sailing boat, yawl rigged, and notable for its buoyancy. It is said to be the parent of the *peter boat* (*which see*). Smyth speaks of it as follows:— "This, of all small boats, is said to be the best calculated for a high sea; it is often met with at a distance from land, when a stout ship can hardly carry any sail."

NOSE

Nose.—The iron piece protecting the stem-head of an open boat. From this, the foremost point of the boat itself is sometimes called the nose. (*See* accompanying figure, also diagrams under FRAME.)

Nothing off.—To keep a boat nothing off, is to keep her head up to the wind and not let it fall off to leeward. (*See also under* HELM.)

Number.—A flag hoist denoting a ship's name.

Nun Buoy.—A buoy in the shape of a double cone, now called a conical buoy.

NUN BUOY

O

Oakum.—The substance to which old ropes are reduced when unpicked. It is used in caulking the seams of boats, and in stopping leaks, etc.

Oar.—By this is understood, to-day, the single oar, handled by one man alone, in contradistinction to *sculls,* which go in pairs, both being handled by the same person. The oar is longer, and, therefore, a more powerful lever than the scull; but it is found in practice that a given number of men propelling a boat by sculls make considerably greater speed than the same crew using oars. The propulsion of a boat by means of oars is called *rowing*: when sculls are used it is no longer rowing, but *sculling.* This distinction is of importance to those who would wish to be correct in their rowing phraseology. *Sweeps* are long oars used by sailing-boats, barges, lighters, etc. (*See* SWEEP.) The oars used by fishermen are very long and heavy, with very long inboard. They are difficult to use, but immense power is to be gained with them.

The parts of an oar, scull, or sweep are as follow (*see* fig.):—A is the *blade,* the curve in which is called the *feather.* At sea oars are usually without the feather; but in smooth waters it is almost invariable. B is the *neck*; C the *loom*; D the *grip.* By some, the whole distance included from blade to grip is called the loom, if not fitted with a leather. E is the *leather.* F the *button.* The loom of an oar or scull may, of course, be shortened, but it may also be lengthened some inches in the following manner. The head of the grip being paired off quite flat, a hole is bored down it into which a piece of hard wood (or in its place a double-threaded bolt) is firmly fitted. A new grip is then made, in which a hole is also bored, and this is fitted or screwed on to the old grip, the joint being further secured by the aid of glue. This is frequently done on the Upper Thames, and is found to answer well if the substance of the oar or scull is stout enough to admit of it.

It may be well to warn purchasers of second-hand oars or sculls to be wary of those with newly painted blades; the paint is occasionally put on to hide flaws or knots.

Back oars.—To press backwards on the oars so as to stop the progress of a boat. It is usually called *backwater* (*which see*).

OAR

"Get your oars to pass."—An old expression signifying that the oars should be got ready for rowing.

Lay on the oars.—To pause in rowing and lay the oars flat just above the water. It is the same as to:

Rest on the oars, or, in other words, to take a rest in rowing.

Out oars.—To get oars out ready for use.

Ship and *unship oars.*—To *ship* oars is to place them in the rowlocks ready for use: to *unship,* to take them out of their rowlocks and replace them in the boat or elsewhere. (*See* SHIP.)

Shove your oar in.—To intermeddle; as, Don't shove in your oar, *i.e.,* Don't meddle.

Toss oars.—To lift the blades vertically up into the air, all together, as is often done in the Royal Navy, either as a salute or preparatory to shipping or unshipping.

Ochre.—A reddish chalk used by shipbuilders in marking timbers when forming them.

Occulting.—A navigation light in which the period of darkness is less than the period of light.

Off.—1. In general nautical conversation this word means "away from the shore", thus: an offshore wind signifies that the wind is blowing from the shore to seaward. "The vessel is standing off" describes her as withdrawing from the land.

2. It may also mean *near to* or *abreast of,* as "we lay off Dover".

Off and on.—Nearing and withdrawing, as with a ship tacking, which stands "off and on the shore" alternately.

Off the reel.—At once, quickly. Just as the log line would run off the reel. (*See* LOG.)

Off the wind.—Sailing with the wind *abaft* the beam (Compare this with *On the wind.*)

Offing.—Those aboard vessels lying in a bay or harbour speak of the *offing,* meaning thereby the outside sea, where the water is deep and the force of a gale is felt. It may, under other circumstances, denote any part of the sea at a distance.

To *keep a good offing* is to keep well off some shore.

Nothing off.—To keep a boat right *on,* that is, as near to the wind as she will bear.

Oil.—*"Oil on troubled waters."*—It is a well-known fact that drops of oil dropping from a bladder placed over a ship's stern, will smooth the surface of the sea, where the waves are breaking, and prevent them from overrunning her, the reason being that the friction of the wind upon the waves is reduced.

Oil-skins, or *oileys.*—"Oileys" is the fisherman's term for oilskin clothes, used in rainy or rough weather. These men sometimes made their own "oileys", and formerly always did so. The manner in which these suits were made was simple: having been cut out of coarse calico, and made up, they were steeped in linseed oil and then hung out on a line, being constantly reversed until quite dry. This was generally done in the spring, to allow the oil ample time to dry before the following winter, it often taking several months. Everyone boating or yachting during the winter should be possessed of a suit of oilskins.

Oil motors or *engines.*—More correctly *Internal Combustion Engines,* either *petrol engines* using petrol or gasoline as fuel or *diesel engines* using a heavier and cheaper oil as fuel, have almost entirely replaced steam engines in small craft and large ships are often propelled by diesel engines. Advantages of oil over steam engines are that, because of an absence of boiler, they occupy less space; they require no time to raise steam; and they are labour-saving.

Old boats.—Beware of them.

Old horse.—Old salt beef. (*See* Horse.)

Old Man.—A colloquial name for the master of a merchant ship.

Oleron.—*Laws of Oleron.*—"Certain laws of the Navy or Marine which were framed and drawn up by Richard I at the island of Oleron, near the coast of Poictou, the inhabitants of which have been deemed able mariners for these seven hundred years past. These sea laws, which have been reckoned the most excellent of the kind, are recorded in the Black Book of the Admiralty."

On.—The opposite to "off". So the wind may be "on the shore"— *i.e.,* blowing towards it. In sailing we may have the wind *on the beam, on the bow,* or *on the quarter,* terms which will explain themselves.

To be *on.*—To be in the act of doing something. Thus we may say, "There is a high sea on."

To be *sailing on the wind* is to be sailing with the wind before the beam, and therefore close-hauled. (Compare this with *Off the wind.*) In square-rigged ships this is called sailing on a *taut bowline.*

End on.—Meeting a vessel on end. (*See* END-ON.)

"One, two, three and belay!"—The song with which the seamen bowse out the bowlines; the last hauling being completed by "Belay oh!" "One for coming up!" A final pull on a rope to gain rather more than is required to allow for the slight loss when turning up.

Ooze.—The thin mud which settles along the banks of certain rivers. It is so light as almost to float, and is sometimes of unfathomable depth.

Open.—*Open boat.*—A boat absolutely without decking.

Open hawse.—A clear cable (when a vessel is riding by two anchors.)

Open roadstead.—A hazardous refuge, offering but poor protection to vessels.

Open sea.—The same as the high sea—*i.e.,* beyond the three mile limit over which a country claims jurisdiction.

Opposite tacks.—Two vessels, one on the port tack, the other on the starboard, are said to be on "opposite tacks". Hence, in general conversation, when two persons are at cross purposes, the same is often said of them.

Ordinary seaman.—"The rating of one who can make himself useful on board, even to going aloft, and taking his part on a topsail or top-gallant yard, but is not a complete sailor, the latter being termed an able seaman." (Smyth.)

Orient.—The East; or the eastern point of the horizon.

Orlop (from "over-lop").—*Orlop beams.*—Beams in a ship, extending across the lower part of the hold, and therefore often called *hold beams.*(*See* diagram under FRAME.) They sometimes support that which is called the *orlop deck,* which may be the lowest deck in a ship, or a temporary platform forming a sort of deck. In the old warships certain of the store rooms were on this deck, and, in frigates, the midshipmen's berth.

Otter.—A board fitted with a bridle and line which tows at an angle under water and is used, for example, to keep open the mouth of a trawl, and in sweeping for mines.

Out.—In the offing: at a distance. Away from the shore. Thus "there is a good breeze out" means that there is a good breeze out in the offing, though it may not be felt on shore. "The vessel is standing out", she is sailing away from the shore.

Outside has something of the same meaning, and implies "out at sea": generally spoken by those in a harbour or river, as "it blows hard outside", which would mean that it was blowing hard at sea, though not, possibly, felt in the haven; or "we are going outside", we are going outside the river into the sea, etc.

Out board.—Board means the *side* of a vessel, therefore "outboard" means *outside her,* or beyond the gunwale. Thus a bowsprit runs outboard, etc.

Outboard engine.—A portable motor attached to the stern of a boat, with a vertical shaft driving an immersed propeller.

Out-class.—One vessel is said to "out-class" another when, as a result of more modern improvements, she is greatly superior to another in her own class.

"Out or down!"—A threat sometimes used at sea by one summoning another to his watch—"Out you get, or down goes your hammock!"

Out-haul.—A rope which hauls out something, as the jib outhaul does the tack of the jib. (*See* JIB.)

Outer jib.—One of the head sails of a ship. (*See* JIB.) Large vessels usually set two standing jibs, the outer and the inner.

Outlicker, or *outlier.*—Corruptions of *outrigger (which see).*

Out port.—A port on the coast of the United Kingdom away from London, or from a ship's headquarters.

Out-regan.—A canal or ditch navigable by boats.

Outside planking.—The outer strakes of a vessel, which are variously named, as the garboard strakes, wales, etc. (*See* diagrams under FRAME.)

Out of trim.—The state of a ship not properly balanced in the water. (*See* TRIM.)

Outer turns and *inner turns.*—Expressions used with regard to square sails. "The *outer turns* of the earing serve to extend the sail outwards along its yard. The *inner turns* are employed to bind the sail close to the yard." (Smyth.)

Out-rig.—To extend anything out from the side of a vessel; hence,

Outrigger.—A projecting piece from any part of a vessel, which serves to give greater leverage or base to oars, ropes, sails, etc. An extension to each side of the crosstrees of a sailing vessel to spread the backstays. (*See also* CHANNELS.) A small boomkin (or bumpkin), such as is often used for the working of a mizzen, is sometimes called an outrigger. The term, however, has a more familiar application in the case of rowing boats, and more especially those used for racing. In these, outriggers are light projecting brackets supporting the rowlocks, and giving a vastly greater length of leverage for the oars or sculls. On rivers they are now always employed, and of late years have often been adopted in pleasure skiffs, when, however, they project in a lesser degree and are known as *half-outriggers*: but these skiffs are less convenient in crowded or narrow waterways than those which are *in-rigged,* that is, which have the rowlocks (or tholes) on the gunwale or saxboard. A boat fitted with outriggers is usually called "an outrigger". (*See* diagram under RIG.)

2. The log, or float, rigged out from the side of a canoe to provide additional stability.

Outward bound.—A ship on its voyage away from home.

Ouvre l'œil.—"A mark on French charts over supposed dangers." A vigia (*which see*).

Over.—*Over-bear.*—One vessel overbears another if she carries more sail in a fresh breeze.

Overboard.—Over the side of the ship. The "board", in nautical phraseology, means the side.

Overblow (of the wind).—To blow so hard that a vessel can carry no topsails.

Overcast.—1. (Of the weather).—Cloudy: the sun not seen. 2. In ship-building, to overcast is to measure up—hence,

Overcasting staff.—A measuring staff used by ship-wrights.

Overfall.—The eastern-county name for certain banks or shoals near the surface of the sea, such as Blakeney Overfall; Sherringham Overfall; Stuky Overfall, near the Norfolk coast. Also another name for a *tide-rip* or *race* (*which see*).

Overhand (in knots).—A simple knot made by passing the end of a rope over its standing part, and then through the bight. It may also be called a thumb-knot. (*See* KNOTS.)

Hand over hand (In hauling on a rope).—Hauling in quickly and with one hand passed alternately over the other.

Overhaul.—1. To examine or inspect.

2. To catch up or overtake.

To *overhaul a rope.*—To slacken it off.

To *overhaul a tackle.*—To open out or extend its parts—that is, its blocks and ropes—so that they may be made use of again, when they have been brought close up, or *fleeted.*

Over-masted.—A boat is thus described when her masts are too long, which in yachts is not of rare occurrence. In such cases masts are cut down, and often with great benefit to the boat.

Over-pressed.—A vessel carrying too much sail.

Over-rake (of the waves of the sea).—When the waves break over a vessel at anchor they are sometimes said to over-rake her.

Over-rate.—A racing yacht or sailing boat is said to be over-rated when she is too much handicapped. Hence, a person of whom too high an opinion is held, is spoken of in the same manner.

Over-rigged.—Spoken of a vessel having more or heavier gear than necessary.

Over-risen.—Too high out of the water.

Over-run.—When the waves overtake a vessel and come in upon her, they are said to over-run her.

Over-sea.—From a foreign port.

Over-shoot.—To give a vessel too much way, so that, in coming up to a mooring or pier, she misses the mark and shoots beyond it.

Overtaking.—In the Regulations for Preventing Collisions at Sea, an overtaking vessel is one that is coming up with another from any direction more than two points abaft her beam. Any vessel overtaking any other shall keep out of the way of the vessel being overtaken.

Owner.—A Royal Naval nickname for the Captain.

Ox.—*Ox bows*—Bends, or reaches, in a river.

Ox-eye.—"A name given by mariners to a small cloud or meteor, seen at the Cape of Good Hope, etc., which presages a dreadful storm. It appears at first in the form or size of an ox's-eye, but descends with such celerity that it seems suddenly to overspread the whole hemisphere, and at the same time forces the air with such violence, that ships are sometimes scattered several ways, some directly contrary, and many sunk downright." (Falconer.)

Oyster.—*Oyster-laying.*—A place, either in the sea or in some river, where oysters are bred or fattened.

Oyster dredge.—The implement with which the "dredger man" drags the bottom of a "laying" for oysters. In old days he often accompanied his labours by a monotonous chant, which also served to charm the oysters into his dredge. Hence the old lines:—

> "The herring loves the moonlight,
>   The mackerel loves the wind;
> The oyster loves the dredgerman's song,
>   For he comes of a gentle kind."

P

Packet.—A small passenger or mail boat. "This word meant originally a vessel appointed by Government to carry the mails between the mother country and foreign countries or her own dependencies." (Brande and Cox.)

Pad, or **pad-piece.**—A piece of timber laid (when required) upon the beams of a vessel to form the lateral curve (or camber) in the form of the deck. (*See* diagrams under FRAME.)

Paddle.—The oar or propeller used by canoeists, and having its origin among savage nations; a *double-paddle* has a blade at both ends. To paddle, therefore, in canoeing, is to propel the boat with the paddle.

Paddle boat-hook.—A boat-hook and paddle combined. It forms part of the inventory of an Upper Thames pleasure skiff, and is a very useful implement. (*See* BOAT-HOOK.)

To *paddle* in rowing with oars or sculls has another meaning, viz.: to row easily, *i.e.*, not at a high speed.

Paddles (on a steam boat).—The flat boards on the propelling wheels; though the wheels are occasionally spoken of as the paddles; and the coverings over the wheels are called the *paddle boxes*.

Paddle boat.—A steam vessel propelled by paddle-wheels.

Paddy's hurricane.—A dead calm; or, at best, a breeze insufficient to float a pennant.

Painter.—A rope attached usually to a ring inside the stempost of an open boat, by which it may be made fast alongside a quay, etc.

"Cut your painter."—A slang expression for "Be off!"

Pair-oar.—A boat rowed by one pair of oars. It was also the name sometimes given to the old London wherry.

Palm.—In sail-making, a contrivance for taking the place of a thimble, and used by seamen and sail-makers. It fits the ball of the thumb and palm of the hand.

Palm of an anchor.—The flattened side of the fluke. (*See* ANCHOR.)

Panting.—The in-and-out movement of a ship's plating, particularly in the bows, caused by variation in the water pressure. Counteracted by *panting-beams*.

Parallel sailing (at sea).—Sailing on a circle parallel to the Equator.

Parallels of latitude.—Lines drawn round the earth parallel to the Equator.

Parbuckle.—A method of lifting a cask or some other heavy object, by doubling a rope into two legs, passing them under the object and hauling on both together.

Paravane.—A device towed from the bows of a ship as a protection against moored mines. The paravane towed like an *otter* (*which see*) and the towing wire cut through the mines' mooring.

Parcel.—To parcel rope. (*See* SERVE.)

Parclose.—The *limber-holes* in a vessel are occasionally called by this name.

Parliament-heel.—"A term used to imply the situation of a ship when she is made to stoop a little to one side, so as to clean the upper part of her bottom on the other side, and cover it with a fresh composition." (Falconer.) But the term often means only a slight heel, as when a vessels lays over under canvas.

Parrel.—Generally speaking, any apparatus which keeps a yard to its mast. Thus the parrel of a *gaff* is a rope upon which is strung a row of hard wooden balls and encircling the mast, the ends being attached to each jaw of the gaff. (*See* fig. 1, also under GAFF.) The parrel of a lug sail may be either an iron ring on the mast or a loop made in the halyard. (*See* LUG.) The *rib-and-truck* parrel was a device often used in old ships, and may still be occasionally seen. It consisted of a number of battens or ribs, between each of which a series of trucks (small wooden balls) were strung (*see* fig. 2). The lines being unreeved, these parts would fall into a number of disjointed pieces. Hence the term "ribs and trucks" is sometimes used to mean mere fragments.

GAFF
PARREL

FIG. 1

FIG. 2

Parrish-rigged.—A vessel, or anything else, with inadequate or worn-out gear.

Part.—*To part.*—To be driven from the anchors; said of a ship when she breaks her cable.

Standing part and *running part.*—Parts of a rope in use. (*See* under each heading and under TACKLE.)

Partners.—The framework which supports the mast by the deck. (*See* MAST.)

Pass.—A term used by seamen to express the accomplishment of something, as to pass the gaskets, to pass a lashing, *i.e.,* to take turns with a rope round a yard, etc.

Pass the word.—To relay an order or a summons.

Passe volant.—"A name applied by the French to a *quaker* or wooden gun on board ship; but it was adopted by our early voyagers as also expressing a movable piece of ordnance." (Smyth.)

Passenger.—A person carried in a ship, but who does no work in her. Persons taken in pleasure boats are sometimes called thus, and if, in the course of a rowing match, any rower becomes disabled he is said to have become a passenger.

Pattens.—(*See* MUD PATTENS.)

Pawl, or **drop pawl.**—A small stop, or catch, which prevents a moving object from going beyond a certain limit, such as the pawl of a rack wheel, which stops the wheel from running backward; the pawl of a capstan, which acts in the same manner; a mast pawl, which confines a lowering mast in its place; a rowlock pawl, which may be a metal catch or merely a piece of rope across a pair of rowlocks preventing an oar from being dislodged, etc.

Pawl bits.—Timber to which the pawls of a large capstan are attached.

Pay.—To give a coating of tar, or any other material to anything requiring it. Thus a ship's bottom may be *payed* with pitch; a rope with tar; a spar with grease, etc. So also to *pay a seam* of the decking of a vessel is to pour melted pitch into the seam.

Pay away.—To slacken off; usually said of a rope, or the sheet of a sail, when it requires to be loosened out.

Pay off.—1. To pay the men's wages and dismiss them. 2. In sailing, to allow a vessel's head to fall alee—*i.e.,* away from the wind. Sometimes, in *tacking,* a boat's head refuses to pay off: at such times she may be assisted by holding the headsails to windward. If she does not then come round she becomes "hung up in the wind". (*See* TACK.)

Paying off pennant.—An extremely long pennant flown by R.N. ships when proceeding home to pay off at the end of a commission.

Pay out (of a cable or any other rope).—To slacken it out. Almost equivalent to *pay away.* Sometimes to pay out means to slacken away gradually, bit by bit, instead of letting the rope or cable go off as it will.

Pay round.—To turn a vessel's head round, away from the wind, as in paying off.

Peak.—1. The upper end of a gaff. But it is also the uppermost corner of a sail carried by a gaff.

Peak halyards are the halyards which elevate the peak. They usually consist of a tackle. The rope being first secured to the gaff at a point not far distant from the peak, passes through a block at the mast head, thence to a block lower down the gaff, back again to another block on the mast, then down to the deck, where it is belayed in small craft, usually to the port (left-hand) side of the mast ("peak to port"). The *pendants* of the peak halyards are those parts of the rope which run between the mast and the gaff. When the mainsail, having been lowered, is to be covered with the sail cloth, these pendants must be detached, and either hooked to slings or strops which pass under the boom, or looped round the boom as it rests on the crutches.

PEAK

Peak line.—A small rope passing through a block at the guy end of the gaff. It is sometimes called the *flag halyard,* because the ensign or some other flag is often hoisted at the peak as a signal. The peak line is also much employed to haul down the peak when the gaff jams.

Peak purchase.—In large vessels, a purchase applied to the peak halyards to swing them up taut.

2. The *peak,* on the fluke of an anchor, is the apex of the fluke. It is often called the *bill.* (*See* ANCHOR.)

The *anchor apeak.*—The anchor brought to such a position that it stands perpendicularly on the ground. (*See* ANCHOR.)

To *stay peak,* or *ride a short peak* or *long peak* (of old ships).—When the cable and forestay were in about the same straight line it was a *short peak.* With the main stay and cable in a line, it was a *long peak.*

To *peak.*—To raise a yard or gaff obliquely to its mast.

Fore peak.—A place in the fore part of some small vessels in which stores may be kept.

Pegging to windward.—Making a *dead peg* to windward. The same as working to windward. (*See* under BEAT.)

Peggy.—That member of the crew whose duty it is to keep the forecastle clean.

Pelorus.—A compass card without needles. It is mounted on a stand and fitted with sight-vanes.

Pencel.—A small streamer, wheft, or pennant.

Pendant, or pennant (pronounced "pennant").—1. A long pointed flag, usually a signal, as the *answering pennant* in the International Signal Code, or the *commodore's broad pennant* in the Royal Navy.

2. (In rigging.)—It must be understood that a halyard is often a tackle, the ropes of which are often distinguished into two parts— (1) the *pendant,* or that part

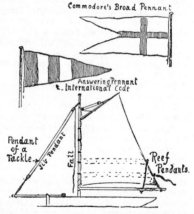

which runs between the blocks, and (2) the *fall,* which is the part hauled upon. Thus the *fore pendant* is that part of the fore halyard which runs out from the mast-head to the stemhead, when the foresail is down. The *jib pendant.*—The same out-running part of the jib-halyard. *Peak pendants.*—Those parts of the peak halyards which run out between the masthead and the gaff. And, since these parts of the halyards are called pendants, so may the *bob-stay* ropes be counted in the list, which includes several—and, in ships, a large number of others.

But there are also other pendants, which are short hanging ropes, unconnected with blocks, used for a variety of purposes, as *reef pendants*—short lines sometimes rove through cringles on the leech of a sail at the time of reefing, or sometimes hanging permanently, their office being to lash down the clew of the sail, prior to reefing. And, in this sense, the *tack,* which is a short rope hanging from the tack of a fore-and-aft sail, for hauling the tack down, is also a pendant.

People.—At sea, a ship's company was always known by this term, more particularly in the Royal Navy; but it did not include the commissioned officers.

Peter boat.—A row and sailing boat, short, pointed bow and stern, almost half-decked, and having a sort of well in which to keep fish. It was used by the fresh-water fishermen of the Thames. Formerly there was a considerable fishery for smelt, lamprey, and various fresh and salt water fish above and below London, and these peter boats were largely employed. (*See* HEB-BING.) The below-bridge peter boats were of larger size than those used higher up, but of the same class. The peter boat is so named after St. Peter, the patron of fishermen. They originate from Norway and the Baltic (*see* NORWEGIAN YAWL), where they are said to have been no more than 25 ft in length, with 6 ft of beam. "Yet," says Smyth, "in such craft, boys were wont to serve out seven years' apprenticeship, scarcely ever going on shore."

*Up-River
Peter Boat*

Peter man.—1. "One who fishes in the river of *Thames* with an unlawful engine." (Bailey, 18th century.) 2. "The Dutch fishing vessels that frequented our eastern coast." (Smyth.)

Petty Officer.—The ranks below commissioned officers. Derived from the French "petit" = little.

Pharos.—In popular language, a lighthouse; but the word has almost gone out of use. It was derived from the great light tower built between 283–247 B.C. on the island of Pharos at the mouth of the harbour of Alexandria, and which came to be looked upon as one of the wonders of the world.

Pick.—*Picking up a wind.*—Going out of one's course to find a wind. The practice is common with sailing ships when passing from one trade wind to the other.

Pickle.—Any artificial preservative or preparation for metal or wood. Iron is pickled, that is, steeped, in sulphuric acid and water before being galvanised. Wood may be payed with a coating of creasote or sulphate of copper, which preserves it against wet or dry, barnacles, etc.; and this also may be called a pickling.

Pier.—Piers may be either of wood, iron or stone, and are erected either to facilitate the landing of passengers and goods from vessels;

as breakwaters; or solely as pleasure promenades. Those made of stone are often called *moles,* more especially when of great width. Of the first sort the pier of Southend, at the mouth of the Thames, may be noted; it is the longest in the kingdom, probably in the world. At Tynemouth is a long stone pier, or narrow mole, which serves as a breakwater at the mouth of the great northern river. Pleasure piers are to be found at Brighton, and other seaside resorts. A small pier, at which goods may be landed from barges and such like craft, is sometimes called a *jetty (which see).* Piles are sometimes called piers because they support a weight, as do the piers, or pillars, of a church.

Pier-head jump. —Joining a ship at the last moment.

Pig (of iron). —Pig iron is very useful as ballast for a sailing boat, and has this advantage, that it is cheap.

Piggin. —A little pail with a long handle. It may be a baler or what not.

Pike. —A bar of iron, or a bar of wood shod with iron; originally used in boarding an enemy's vessel. In military affairs it was used until the introduction of the bayonet.

Pil, or **pyll** (perhaps from the Dutch). —"A creek subject to the tide."

Pile. —A piece of timber or iron, driven, with others, into the ground or into the bed of a river, for the support of a pier, bridge, etc. The following is mainly from Brande and Cox's "Dictionary of Science, Literature, etc.": "They may be round or square, and when of wood must be of a quality which does not rot under water, or which is able to resist the attack of the *Teredo navalis,* and other boring worms or insects. Oak, elm, fir, hacmatac, green-heart, etc., are the woods most generally employed for the purpose. The end of the pile that enters the ground is, in these cases, pointed and shod with iron; and the top of it is bound with a strong iron hoop to prevent the piles being split, or their heads beaten up to a kind of pulp, by the violent strokes of the monkey by which they are driven down. Iron piles are now much used, and they are made large enough to allow the foundation to be carried down to the bottom of their penetration."

1. *Pile-driver.* —"An engine for driving piles. It consists of a large monkey, or block of cast iron, which slides between two guide posts. Being drawn up to the top of its course, and then let fall from a considerable height, it comes down upon the head of the pile with a violent blow, proportioned to the weight of the monkey multiplied by the height, diminished, of course, by the friction that the monkey meets with in its descent." It may be worked by hand or by steam: the monkey is lifted with a catch-hook, which, as it reaches the top of the machine, is caught by a spring and disconnected, thus allowing the weight to drop automatically. In some cases, where the nature of the soil will allow of it, screw piles are employed. These are round iron piles to which are fitted large screw flanges; and the pile being turned by machinery screws itself to the desired depth. Southend pier, at the mouth of the Thames, is

supported entirely upon screw piles, a distance of a mile and a quarter.

2. *Pile-driver* (of ships).—A name given to a vessel which pitches heavily in a sea way.

3. *Pile-up.*—Run ashore.

Pilot.—A man qualified and licensed to take ships in or out of a harbour, or channel, at certain fixed rates, his fees being calculated upon the ship's draught of water. The origin of the pilot's office is to be found, according to Wedgwood, in the word *peilen,* to sound; his duty before the existence of charts being to navigate his vessel by means of the sounding lead. In the 15th and 16th centuries the *pilot* was a ship's navigator, and the term is applied today to a navigating officer. 2. Volumes of the Admiralty Sailing Directions are referred to as "*Pilots*", *e.g.* "The Mediterranean Pilot."

Pilot flag.—A flag, the upper half white and lower red, denoting "I have a pilot on board".

Pillars.—In ship-building, pieces of wood or iron supporting the decks in some vessels, and acting as the columns of a church.

Pillar of the hold.—A main stanchion with notches in it, which may be used as steps in descending to the hold.

Pillow.—A block of timber whereon the inner end of some spar, such as the bowsprit, is rested.

Pin.—Of a block, the axle.

Belaying pin.—A pin, forming a sort of cleat, round which a halyard or any other rope may be belayed. In a yacht or sailing boat several of them will be found around the lower part of the mast, in the *spider-hoop,* for the belaying of the halyards. In larger vessels they are often fitted into a bar or *fife-rail* at the side of the boat, or across the shrouds, when they may also be called *jack-pins.* But they may be placed wherever convenient.

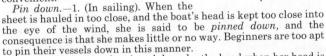

Pin down.—1. (In sailing). When the sheet is hauled in too close, and the boat's head is kept too close into the eye of the wind, she is said to be *pinned down,* and the consequence is that she makes little or no way. Beginners are too apt to pin their vessels down in this manner.

2. A vessel is said to be *pinned down* by the head when her head is low down in the water, either on account of an excess of weight forward, or, if at anchor, when her cable is too short.

Pinch-gut money.—An expression used by merchant seamen for money paid to them, in certain vessels, at the end of a voyage, to the value of such stores as they were entitled to but have not drawn.

Pingle.—An old name for a small north-country coasting vessel.

Pink.—In the Dutch fisheries, a two-masted boat of the ketch type. (*See* Dogger.) "A name given to a ship with a very narrow stern. Those used in the Mediterranean Sea differ from the Xebecs only in being more lofty and not sharp in the bottom; they are vessels of burden, have three masts, and carry lateen sails." (Falconer, 1790.)

Pinnace (in the Royal Navy).—An open boat once propelled by oars, in modern times fitted with engines, working either by steam, or oil. The boat ranges from 30 feet or more in length, and is used for general purposes. A pinnace of the 16th century was a small vessel of about 20 tons generally acting as a tender to a larger ship.

Pinrack (at sea).—A rack or framework on the deck of a vessel, consisting of blocks and cleats for the working of ropes. (*See* RACK.)

Pintles.—The pins on a rudder which fit into the gudgeons, or eyes, on the stern-post of the boat. (*See* RUDDER.)

Pipe.—Summon with a *boatswain's whistle*.

Pipe down.—The call on the boatswain's pipe, made in a warship for the hands to turn in. Hence, in speech, "Shut up. Stop making a nuisance of yourself."

Piping the side.—The ceremonial blowing of a boatswain's pipe on the arrival on board, or departure, of a naval captain or visiting dignitaries.

Piracy.—Felony on the seas or in harbour. Various acts are now enumerated as piracy, such as violence, boarding against the will of the master, etc. Acts of piracy have occurred in the China Sea, on the coast of West Africa and elsewhere during this century (*See* CORSAIR.)

Pitch.—The residuum of boiled tar. It is valuable both for preserving the planks of new vessels and for hiding the defects of old ones.

2. The distance a vessel would advance in one revolution of the propeller if there was no slip.

3. The up-and-down motion of a vessel's bows.

Pitch a yarn.—Tell a story.

Pitch pole.—To be overthrown in a fore-and-aft direction.

Plain sailing.—*Plane sailing.*—(*See* SAILING.)

Plank.—*Planking* (in shipbuilding).—The covering of the ribs of a hull with planks disposed in strakes; in other words, the *skin* of a ship. (*See* FRAME.)

Plank on edge.—A slang or jocular term for a very narrow boat, supposed to resemble a plank on its edge.

Planksheer, or *plankshare* (the sheer plank).—The outermost plank of the deck, or, in other words, the plank in a deck which is nearest the side of the vessel. It usually overlaps the sheerstrake and has apertures cut along its sides to admit of the timber heads (the head of each rib) projecting through it. It is usually of hard wood; sometimes of handsome wood, such as mahogany, and in these cases adds considerably to the appearance of the deck.

Plankton.—The mass of very small animal organisms which drifts in the oceans.

Plate.—In shipbuilding, usually a flat piece of iron. Thus *channel plates* are flat bars fastened to the sides of a vessel, and bent over the channels where those exist, or taking their place where they are dispensed with. (*See* CHANNELS.)

Back-stay plates.—Smaller bars than the channel-plates, and fixed to the vessel's sides further aft than those, to take the tackles of the back-stays. They are usually so set as to follow the line of the stays, so that there may be no lateral strain upon them.

Futtock plate.—A large plate at the heads of the masts in large vessels, to take the shrouds of the top-mast. (*See* under FUTTOCK.)

Play.—The motion of all the members of the frame of a vessel as she sails. (*See* GIVE.)

Pledge.—A string of oakum used in caulking.

Plimsoll Mark or **Line.**—The circular mark with a horizontal line through it on the sides of a merchant ship, which indicates the depth to which the ship may be loaded. Introduced in 1876 by Samuel Plimsoll to prevent the overloading of merchant ships.

Plug.—Ships' boats and boats intended for beaching often have a hole cut through the bottom to let out any water which may accumulate in them. The stopper to this hole is called the plug, or bung: it may be either a cork or a patent screw-plug.

Plumb.—Perpendicular.

To *plumb.*—To test the perpendicularity of anything, just as carpenters do, with the plumb-line and weight; the weight actually being the plumb.

Plummet.—The name sometimes given to the leaden weight attached to the *lead-line* (*which see*).

Ply (from "apply").—To *ply an oar* is to row.

To *ply for hire,* as with watermen, to seek or ask for hire.

Point.—In geography, a projecting cape, as Portland Point.

To *point a rope.*—To untie the ends, take out a portion of them, and weave a sort of mat round the diminished portion so that it may easily go through a hole, etc.

To *point a sail.*—To fix the reef points.

Point the yards to the wind.—With square-rigged vessels, to brace the yards sharp up when the vessel lies at anchor, so that they may not receive the impulse of the wind.

Points of the compass.—The thirty-two parts into which the card of the mariner's compass is divided. (*See* COMPASS.)

Cardinal points.—The four main points of the compass—North, South, East, and West.

Reef points.—Short ropes hanging from small eyes across a sail, to secure part of the sail in *reefing* (*which see*).

Polacre (Fr.).—"A ship with three masts, usually navigated in the Mediterranean: each of the masts is commonly formed of one piece, so that they have neither tops nor cross-trees; neither have they any *horses* to their yards, for the men stand upon the top-sail yards to loose or furl the top gallant sails, the yards being lowered sufficiently down for that purpose. These vessels are generally furnished with square sails upon the main mast, and lateen sails upon the fore and mizzen masts. Some of them, however, carry square sails upon all the three masts, particularly those of Provence, in France." (Falconer.) The class is now extinct.

Pole.—A rod used for pushing a boat along. For large craft, such as barges, it should be a "ricker"; that is, a young tree in itself, not made out of a plank. There are various poles: the *barge-pole,* the *quanting pole,* the *punting pole,* etc. The quanting pole, or quant, as it is generally called, is peculiar to Norfolk. (*See* under QUANT.) The punting pole is much used up river, both on the Thames and elsewhere: it requires some experience to work properly.

The pole of a mast.—The upper end of the highest mast, which rises above the rigging.

Pole mast.—A mast complete in itself; that is without the addition of a topmast: such is the mizzen of a yawl, or the mast of a lug-sail-boat. Many of our river barges have only pole masts. (*See* fig.)

Under bare poles.—Having no sail set (only spoken, in general, of square-rigged ships).

Scudding under bare poles.—Running before the wind without any sail set. (*See* SCUD.)

Pompey.—Sailors' slang for Portsmouth.

Ponente.—(Italian) West.—A westerly wind in the Mediterranean.

POLE
MAST OF
BARGE

Pontoon.—"Anciently, square-built ferry boats for passing rivers, as described by Cæsar and Aulus Gellius." A low, flat vessel, a number of which being placed together may carry a bridge, as some of those over the Rhine, etc. A portable boat.

Poop.—Properly an extra deck on the after part of a vessel. (*See* diagrams under DECK.) When raised over a *spar deck* it is sometimes called a *round house.*

Poop royal.—"A short deck or *platform* over the aftermost part of the poop in the largest of the French and Spanish men of war, and serving as a cabin for their masters and pilots. This is the top gallant poop of our ship-wrights, and the fore-mentioned round house of our merchant vessels." (Smyth.)

Pooping.—To be pooped.—When a sea comes over the stern of a vessel it is said to "poop" her. The effect of being pooped in an open boat will naturally be either to swamp her, or very nearly so. The importance, then, of keeping before the sea, when running, need hardly be enlarged upon. It may be accomplished by crowding on sail, but this can only be done with judgment.

Pooping sea.—A wave which threatens to run over a vessel is thus called.

To *poop another vessel.*—To run the bowsprit of one vessel under the poop of another.

Poppets.—Timbers used in launching a vessel. Also small pieces in the gunwale of a boat filling the rowlocks.

Popple.—A slang term for the roughness of the sea. When it blows there is said to be "a good popple on", or a *poppling sea,* meaning that the sea is quick and short.

Port.—The left hand side of the vessel when facing forward (*see* fig.).

Aport.—Towards the port side, as "put the helm aport"—*i.e.,* put it over to the left-hand side.

Port tack.—A vessel is on the port tack when the wind is blowing on her left-hand side (*see* fig.). In meeting or passing a vessel on the starboard tack that one on the port tack must *give way*—that is, pass astern, or by some other means get out of the way. This is one of the most important rules of the road—the *port tack gives way.* (*See* RULE OF THE ROAD, and STARBOARD TACK.)

ON THE PORT TACK

Ports, port-holes.—Openings in the sides of a vessel, as the round holes or windows so often seen in ships.

Port flange.—A piece of wood placed over a port.

Port sills.—The planks of timber which lie horizontally in the framing of a port-hole, top and bottom; like window sills.

In port.—In harbour—the *port* in this instance being the destination of a vessel.

Portmen.—"A name given in old times to the inhabitants of the Cinque Ports. The burgesses of Ipswich are also so called." (Smyth.)

Port mote.—A mote or court held in port (old term).

Port reeve.—Like shire-reeve (sheriff), a magistrate having certain jurisdiction in a port (old term).

Port fire.—A stick or ribbon of composition for communicating fire from a match to the priming of some weapon, as, in these days, to a rocket.

Port last, or *portoise.*—The same as gunwale (old term).

Wind aport.—With the wind blowing from the left. With the wind aport a vessel is, therefore, on the port tack.

Portolano.—Sailing directions for the Mediterranean in use from the 12th to 15th centuries.

Portuguese man-of-war.—A name given to one of the *acalephæ* of the tropical seas—the *Physalis pelagica.* A stinging jelly fish with a "sail" and long tentacles.

Posted (old Naval term).—Promoted from commander to captain. Hence the term *post captain.*

Pouches.—In vessels which are laden in *bulk,* strong *bulkheads* (called pouches) are placed across the hold to prevent the cargo from shifting.

Poulterer (on shipboard).—He whose business it is to look after such stock as the poultry, in consequence of which he is also known as "Jemmy Ducks". He has other duties besides, however.

Powder Monkey.—A boy in a warship whose duty during action was to carry charges of gunpowder from the magazine to the guns.

Pram.—A dinghy built with a small transom at the bow as well as at the stern.

Pratique.—License granted by the medical authority of a port, without which a vessel may have no dealings with the shore.

Prayer book.—A small flat piece of holystone which may be got into narrow crevices. A large piece of the stone is called the *bible*, because used in a kneeling posture. A smaller piece, the prayer book.

Press.—*To be pressed.*—To be reduced to straits. In old days, to have been taken forcibly for Naval service.

Press canvas.—The fullest amount of canvas a racing yacht can carry when running directly before the wind. (*See* under BALLOON CANVAS.)

Press gang.—In old days, a gang of men sent out from a ship to take men by force into service.

Preventer.—An additional rope supporting another when that one is subject to unusual strain. Such are *preventer braces* on square-rigged ships, which strengthen or take the place of the usual braces.

Preventer bolts, in the preventer plates of large vessels.

Preventer plates, broad plates of iron below the chains in large ships.

Preventer stay, or *preventer back stay.*—In fore-and-aft craft, a topmast back-stay easily slackened when the main-sail swings over, from which cause they are occasionally called *runners*.(*See* diagram under CUTTER.)

Prick.—To *prick out* on the chart (at sea) is to mark the course and situation of a ship on the chart, after making the proper observations.

Pricker, in sail-making, a small instrument with which to make holes in sails.

Pricking sails.—A method once in vogue of strengthening old sails. It consisted in running a middle seam between the two seams which unite each of the *cloths* of it. The term may mean, however, merely the stitching of two cloths of a sail together.

To *prick for a soft plank.*—To look out for an easy berth.

Pride of the morning.—A misty dew at sunrise.

Privateer.—The following is Falconer's account and definition: "Privateers are vessels of war armed and equipped by particular merchants, and furnished with commissions from the State to cruise against and annoy the enemy by taking, sinking, or burning their shipping. These vessels are generally governed on the same plan with His Majesty's ships. The commission obtained by the merchants empowers them to appropriate to their own use whatever prize they make, after legal condemnation; and Government allows them besides £5 (35 Geo. III. c. 66) for every man on board a man-of-war or privateer, taken or destroyed, at the beginning of the engagement; and, in case we are at war with more potentates than one, they must have commissions for acting against each of them; otherwise, if a captain carrying only one against the Danes, should in his course meet with and take a Frenchman, this prize is not good, but would be taken from him by any man-of-war he met, and could not be condemned (*for him*) in the Admiralty, as many have experienced."

Prize.—In war time, any vessel taken at sea from an enemy.

Proa.—A narrow sailing canoe of the Ladrone Islands with an outrigger. It travels so swiftly as to have received the name of "flying proa". The boats of the Malays are also called proas.

Procession of boats.—Boats in procession. The sight is very pretty, and often takes place at night, each boat being illuminated or decorated. In the last years of the 19th century these processions were revived at Richmond, Kingston, Molesey, and elsewhere on the Thames, and should be seen by all who have the opportunity.

Profile draught.—In the lines of a ship. "A name applied to two drawings from the sheer draught; one represents the entire construction and disposition of the ship, the other her whole interior work and fittings." (Smyth.)

Proof timber.—In the lines of a ship. "An imaginary timber expressed by vertical straight lines in the sheer draught to prove the fairness of the body." (Smyth.)

Promenade deck.—(*See* DECK.)

Protest.—A sworn statement concerning possible damage caused during a voyage.

Prow.—The beak or pointed cut-water of a galley or other vessel.

Pucker.—In sail-making, a wrinkled seam.

Puddening, or **Pudding.**—A wreath or circle of cording or oakum fastened round a mast to support the yards. They were employed in old battleships in case the ropes by which the yards were held were shot away. The lump of material was called the *dolphin*. A puddening was also laid round the ring of an anchor to prevent a hempen cable from chafing. And at the present day, a row boat's nose is sometimes puddened to act as a permanent fender, or a thick hempen rope may be carried entirely round the gunwale. This is not uncommon on the best Thames skiffs; while the Gravesend watermen's boats always had the nose puddened.

Pull.—In rowing phraseology the word "pull" is generally used instead of the word "row".

Pulpit.—The guard rail round the bows of a yacht.

Punt.—A flat-bottomed, square-ended boat usually propelled by a pole. The last years of the 19th century, punting has become a very favourite amusement on the Upper Thames; punt racing has been organized, and a champion has sprung up among us. Racing punts are of extremely light build, and, properly punted, may be made to travel at an extraordinary speed. The art of punting is by no means so easy as it looks. The pole is worked on one side only, the punter standing in one place, somewhat forward. The principal fault to guard against, is that of letting the pole get under the boat, the consequences of allowing this to happen in a heavy punt being very unpleasant: care should, therefore, be taken in casting it to keep it

H

well away. Various forms of punts have, of late, come into fashion, some propelled by sail, some by paddles, and others by sculls. Rough punts are also much used, in the upper reaches, for fishing.

Puoys.—Spiked poles propelling barges or keels. (Smyth.)

Purchase.—To *purchase* is to raise or move any heavy body by means of mechanical powers, as a tackle, windlass, etc. Hence the tackle itself has become known as the purchase; and when a person is able, by its means, to get a steady pull upon anything, he is said to get "a good purchase".

Purchase blocks.—Those used in a tackle for moving weights.

Purchase fall.—The rope of a tackle hauled upon. (*See* TACKLE.)

Purser (from *purse*).—"Formerly an officer in the British Navy, whose chief duty consisted in keeping the accounts of the ship to which he belonged; but he also acted as purveyor. The title of this officer has been, since 1844, *paymaster*." (Brande and Cox.) The title is still retained, however, in passenger ships.

Purser's dip.—The smallest dip-candle (old term).

Purser's grins.—Sneers.

Like a purser's shirt on a handspike.—A comparison used in describing clothes fitting very loosely.

Purser's stocking.—A "slop" article, and therefore capable of fitting any man, or, at least, of stretching itself to any man's fit.

Pusher.—The sixth mast, from forward, of a vessel.

Pushpit.—The guardrail round the stern of a yacht. (*See* PULPIT.)

Put.—*Put about.*—To turn a vessel's head about so that the wind takes her on the other side; in nautical language, called putting her on the other tack. (*See* TACK.)

Put back.—To return to port for some reason after having left.

Put into port.—To run into some intermediate port from stress of weather, or for any other cause.

Put off.—To quit or push off from a pier or quay: to start on a voyage.

Put to sea.—To start on a voyage to sea.

Q

"Q" ship.—A merchant ship with concealed armament and naval crew, used to decoy a submarine to within gun range.

Quadrant.—The instrument once used in navigation, but now long since superseded by the sextant (*which see*). 2. A horizontal plate fitted to the head of the rudder stock to take the steering chains, or made with a toothed rack to which the pinion of the steering engine is engaged.

Quant.—Quanting is a method of punting a vessel peculiar to Norfolk. The quanting pole (called the quant) is long and fitted with head and toe pieces, as in the figure. It is used in ferry-boats and in the large sailing wherries belonging to the district, which have a narrow decking left each side of the vessel's hold expressly to enable a man to work the quant, the head of which he places against his shoulder, applying his weight thereto and walking the whole length of this deck.

Quarantine.—The restriction placed on a vessel arriving from a foreign port until granted pratique.

Quarantine flag.—The yellow flag Q of the International code signifies "My vessel is healthy and I request free pratique".

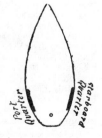

QUANT

Quarter.—Literally, says Smyth, one quarter of the ship: but in common parlance applies to 45 degs. abaft the beam. In other words the quarters are those portions of the sides of a vessel about half way between beam and stern; and, in their position aft of the beam, may be said to correspond with the bows, which lie forward of the beam.

Quarter boats.—The ship's boats carried on her quarters.

Quarter-cloths.—Painted strips of canvas placed along the nettings on the upper deck to protect the hammocks stowed there.

Quarter deck.—That portion of the deck covering the quarters. (*See* DECK.)

Quarter fast.—A rope or hawser holding a vessel by the quarter. It is much the same as a quarter *spring* (*see* next page).

Quartermaster.—A petty officer, or senior rating, whose duties at sea are principally steering, or supervising the steering, of the ship.

Quarter point.—A subdivision of the compass card = 2° 48′ 45″. (*See* HALF POINT.)

Quarter slings.—Supports attached to the quarters of a yard (*see* below).

Quarter spring, or *chain.*—A rope or chain from a vessel's quarter to some other object. It is sometimes used in yacht racing when the boats start from a fixed point: on the firing of the gun the quarter spring is hauled upon, and the yacht's stern being thus canted in the required direction, she is enabled to fill her sails and make way.*

Quarter wind.—Wind blowing on the vessel's quarter.

Quarters.—The position in which men should place themselves when called to their duties. These stations are listed on the *Quarter-bill.*

Quarters of a mast.—A term applied to some of the divisions on a large mast, where the diameters are set off for lining or marking.

Quarters of the yards.—Spaces into which yards are divided; they are termed first, second, and third quarter, and the outer end or *yard arm.*

Quay.—An artificial landing place built along the shore.

Queen (*Queen's ship, Queen's parade,* etc.).—For the sake of preserving the old and more permanent name, where these and like terms are defined, they are placed under the heading KING.

Quick.—*Quicksand.*—Shifting or loose sand: as it were "living" sand. Quicksands may occur in patches on firm sand, without anything to mark their presence, or they may be whole banks of sand. Their depth is often unfathomable, whole ships disappearing into them.

Quick saver (in square-rigged ships).—"A span formerly used to prevent the courses from bellying too much when off the wind." (Smyth.)

Quick work (in shipbuilding).—That part of a vessel's planking which is above the *wale.* It is, in fact, part of her *bulwarks.* It is sometimes of deal, which, as it does not require the fastening nor the time to finish that other parts do, is called *quick work.* (*See* diagram under FRAME.) But Smyth gives the following: *Quick work.*—1. All that part which is under water when she is laden. 2. That part of the inner and upper bulwarks above the covering board. 3. The short planks worked in between the ports. In general parlance quick work is synonymous with *spirketting.*

Quid (of tobacco).—That piece of tobacco which once might often have been discovered within the mouth of a seafaring man. "*Quid est hoc?*" ("What is this?") asked one, tapping the swelled cheek of his messmate. "*Hoc est quid*", promptly replied the other. More probably a variant of "cud".

Quinquereme.—A large Roman vessel, but probably *not* with five banks of oars. The Greek equivalent is *penteres.*

Quoin.—A wedge, used to elevate a gun, or to prevent a cask, for example, from rolling.

---

* The terms *quarter spring* and *quarter chain* are sometimes abbreviated into the mere word *quarter.*

R

Rabbet, or **Rebate.**—In shipbuilding, a groove or channel incised by a peculiar form of plane along a piece of timber to receive the edge of a plank. The word is derived from the French *raboter,* to plane. So in the making of a wooden ship the *rabbet of the keel* is a groove along each side of the keel made to receive the edges of the *garboard* (or lowest) *strakes* (planking). Similar rabbets on the stem and stern posts receive the ends of the ship's planking.

Race.—*Tide race, tide-rip, whorl* or *overfall.*—"A strong rippling tide or current; as Portland Race, which is caused by the projection of the land with the unevenness of the ground over which the tide flows, and which is one mile and three quarters long, in the direction east and west." At Alderney is another important rip. These currents or overfalls appear to be the result of uneven bottoms and cross tides. They are somewhat dangerous to small craft. A short description is given in the "Voyage of the yawl *Rob-Roy.*"

Racing.—The rapid revolution of a ship's propeller and engine when the stern lifts while pitching.

Rack.—1. A frame of timber containing several sheaves or fairleads for ropes. In small craft almost any fairlead may be called a rack. Also a rail for belaying pins.

Rack sheaves.—A range of sheaves on a rack.

2. To *rack.*—To seize two ropes together. Hence:—

To *rack a tackle* (*i.e.,* the ropes of a tackle).—To seize the two running ends together so as to prevent them from running out of the blocks; by which means any object suspended by the tackle is prevented from falling, even if the *fall* be let go.

Racking.—The material (spun yarn or whatever may be used in its place) by which the ropes of a tackle are racked.

3. *Rack.*—The cloud above that which is called the scud.

Racon.—A radar beacon which transmits a signal on receiving a radar signal from a ship and thus shows the range and bearing of the beacon.

Radar.—From "Radio Detection And Range". A system of showing the presence and position of objects by beaming short radio pulses from a rotating aerial and timing the return of echoes from them.

Raddle.—To interlace.

Radio.—The general name for methods of signalling or communicating through space by electro-magnetic waves.

Radio beacon.—A radio station which transmits signals so that a ship may obtain a bearing of the beacon by means of her *direction-finder.*

Radio Direction Finder.—An instrument for detecting radio signals and showing the direction from which they originate.

Raft.—A group of any timbers attached together to form a float.

Raft ports.—Square holes (a *port* being a hole in a ship's side) in the bows or buttocks of timber-carrying vessels to allow of loading and unloading timber without taking it over the deck. They were often seen in Scandinavian vessels.

Rag-bolt.—An iron pin with a number of gashes cut on its shank to keep it from slipping.

Rails.—Narrow planks or bars placed in various parts of a vessel, as the *fiferails,* into which belaying pins may be fitted. (*See* FIFERAIL.)

Taffrail.—The rail over the aftermost part of a vessel. (*See* TAFFRAIL.)

Rough rails, or *rough-tree rails.*—The uppermost rails round a ship; or any timbers placed temporarily on a vessel's sides, or elsewhere. (*See* diagram under FRAME.)

Rails of the dead.—Curved timbers on each side of a ship's stem supporting the headknees, etc.

Raise.—"*Raise tacks and sheets.*"—In square rigged ships, an order given to adjust them as the yards are braced round.

Raise a mouse.—To make a mouse or collar on a stay. (*See* MOUSE.)

Raise the wind.—To procure money (a shoreman's expression).

Rake.—The seaman's name for an inclination or slope: thus the rake of the masts; the rake of the stem or stern, etc., will mean the inclination of any of these from the perpendicular. Sometimes the *run* of a vessel is called the rake. As applied to masts, unless otherwise defined, raking implies a slant *backwards.* (*See* BERMUDA RIG for an example.) When they slant forward they are spoken of as being stayed forward or having a *forward rake.*

To *rake* in old naval warfare was to fire into the head or stern of another vessel.

Rakish (of a ship).—Having a smart appearance. Being a fast vessel.

Rally.—To haul in rapidly. Spoken of a rope or tackle, as "Rally in the main sheet!".

Ram.—A massive projection under water at the bow of a ship of war. The ship herself was also called a ram.

Ram's head.—An old name for a large main-halyard block.

Ran.—In rope-making a reel of twenty yards. "Yarns coiled on a spun-yarn winch" (Smyth).

Randan.—A system of rowing with a pair of oars and a pair of sculls. The stroke and bow hands use the oars, the one in between them the sculls.

RANDAN

A boat thus built is often called a randan; it is a continuation of the style of the old Thames wherries.

Range.—1. At sea, the length of rope or chain required for any particular purpose, and coiled up ready for use. Thus, a sufficient length of chain (and usually a certain allowance over) drawn out on deck to allow an anchor to run out without impediment, so that it may get a good hold of the ground, is the *range of the cable*.

2. On ship board, a large cleat in the waist of a ship is occasionally called a range.

3. In gunnery, the distance any projectile will travel from its gun, within which distance is called "within range". Also any distance decided for gun practice; as a "one mile range".

4. The range of a navigational light is the greatest distance it can be visible to an observer with a given height of eye.

Rap.—*Rap-full.*—An order given to a helmsman in sailing; thus, *Keep her rap-full*—Do not come too close to the wind, or "Lift a wrinkle of sail".

Rasin.—In shipbuilding "a member bolted to the wale and cut in for the deck carlines." (Winn.)

Rasing iron.—Tool used by caulkers for clearing a vessel's seams.

Ratchet, or **ratchet wheel.**—A wheel (usually accompanying a windlass) the rim of which is formed into large teeth and into which teeth a pawl drops so as to prevent the wheel from running backwards.

Rate.—The classification of a vessel for certain purposes. Thus a vessel may be rated A1 at Lloyd's; or a yacht may be rated a 10 tonner, or a 20 rater, etc. Old warships were rated according to the number of guns they carried. The largest ships, First rates, usually carried more than 100 guns; Second rates (84 or more guns), and Third rates (70 or more guns) were termed *line-of-battleships*. Fifth rates and Sixth rates (up to 32 guns) were usually known as *frigates*.

Rating (of yachts for racing purposes).—A manner of so measuring certain areas in yachts that boats of various forms and sizes shall compete on equal terms. The principle and wordwide rating rule today is the International Offshore Rating Rule, Mark III, used in such international events as the Admiral's Cup and the "Ton Cup" classes. The formula employed takes into consideration length, beam, depth; sail-area; draft and freeboard; engine and propeller; stability and movable keel factors. "As a very rough guide, a boat whose rating in feet is more than 10% below her waterline length in feet can be said to 'rate well'. A boat whose rating is more than her waterline length rates badly." (Bruce Fraser.)

Rating.—The status of a seaman. In British ships the (ascending) order is: ordinary seaman; able seaman, leading seaman; petty officer; chief petty officer.

Ration.—A certain allowance of food served out to those on board a ship or elsewhere.

Ratlines (pronounced "ratlins" or "rattlings") **rattling down.**—The name is possibly derived from a supposed resemblance to rats' tails.— Small lines crossing the shrouds of a ship and forming the steps of ladders. Fixing these rat-lines to the shrouds, which is done by a simple seizing and clove hitches, is called *rattling down the rigging*. When they are placed too closely together they constitute that which is called, in derision, a "lady's ladder".

Rat-lines

Reach.—In a river, the distance between two bends; that is, in which the stream makes no decided turn. From this we have

To *reach*.—To sail *on the wind*: as from one point of tacking to another, or with the wind nearly abeam (but always ahead of the beam). While reaching, therefore, a vessel makes no turn *about*. (*See* TACK.)

"Ready about."—An order or command to *stand-by* (be ready) to put a vessel about, *i.e.*, round on another tack. (*See* TACK.)

RATLINES

Rebate (in shipwrighting).—A cutting-in on some timber, so as to allow another to fit into it. Thus a keel is often rebated where the floor timbers abut upon it. (*See* diagrams under FRAME.) (*See* RABBET.)

Rechange.—The tackle and gear kept in readiness for emergency on shipboard.

Reckoning.—(*See* DEAD-RECKONING.)

Recovery (in rowing).—The act of taking the oar out of the water after a stroke, and throwing the arms and body forward in pre-paration for another stroke. The recovery is deemed of the utmost importance in racing: it should be brisk and lively and full of swing; not too quick, for that destroys the swing; not too slow, for that allows the momentum of the boat to be deadened.

Red Ensign.—A red flag with the Union flag in the upper inner canton. The flag proper to the British Merchant Navy, fishing vessels, and yachts which do not have a warrant to fly a Blue Ensign. Before 1864 it was flown by the senior squadron of the British fleet which was divided into red, white and blue squadrons.

Red Duster.—An affectionate name for the Red Ensign.

Reef.—1. (Of rocks.) A low ridge of rocks, usually beneath the surface of the sea. 2. (Of a mast.) To reef a topmast is to reduce its length and make a new fid hole. 3. (Of sails.) To *reef*.—To reduce the area of sail spread to the wind. Sails attached to yards (*i.e.*, square sails) are reefed at the head by men going out on the yards. Gaff sails are reefed at the foot, as are also all staysails, jibs, etc. The method of reefing the sails of small craft is described below.

Reef-bands.—Horizontal bands of canvas running across a sail, and perforated with holes or eyes, at intervals, to receive *reef points*.

The holes are prevented from tearing out by having small brass rings, called *thimbles* or *eyes*, fitted tightly into them. Without these bands the sail would be liable to rend from the strain on the points when reefed, though in very small sails the bands are often dispensed with. (*See* SAIL.)

Reef-cringles.—The eyes or loops in the bolt rope on the leech of a sail through which the *reef-pendants* are rove. (*See* fig.; also under CRINGLES.)

Reef-down.—The operation of reefing, and more particularly of close reefing, is often cal-led *reefing-down,* and a ves-sel sailing close-reefed is said to be "reefed-down".

Reef earings.—The ropes attached to the *cringles* on the upper sides of a square sail, and by which the up-per corners of the sail are secured to the yard prepara-tory to reefing.

Reef knot.—In reefing a sail, its foot is furled up as high as the reef points, and these are lashed under it, the same knot being always used in doing this, from which circumstance it has become known as the *reef knot.* (*See* KNOTS.)

Reef line (in square rig).—A rope acting as an aid to men who are at the earings.

Reef-pendants.—Short ropes rove through the cringles on the lower leech of a gaff-sail, and often through a hole in the boom-cleat, and by which the clew of the sail is secured to the boom (if there be one) pre-paratory to reefing.

Reef points (sometimes called *nettles*).—Short pieces of rope hung, one on each side of a sail, from the eyes in the reef bands, and used to confine the reefed portion of the sail. The simplest method of keeping these

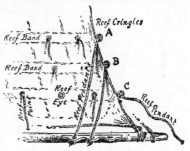

MAINSAIL

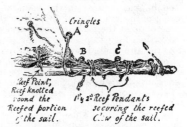

MAINSAIL WITH TWO REEFS

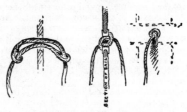

METHOD OF PASSING REEF-POINTS

reef points in the sail is to pass a short rope half through the eye and sew it down. Another method, and one sometimes used, on account of its greater strength, for large sails, is to have each reef point of two ropes, with a small eye spliced on the end of each, just large enough to take the end of the other. Each of these ropes being passed through the eye in the sail, one from each side, the end is rove through the eye of the other and pulled tight (*see* fig.).

Reef tackle.—A purchase or tackle applied to a reef earing, or to a reef-pendant (when reefing) for hauling in the corner of the sail, which is too large to be managed by simple hand power.

Close-reefed.—To be sailing with all reefs taken in. (*See* CLOSE-REEFED.)

Reefing.—Reefing is a difficult operation in a high wind (the only time it is necessary); but it has so often to be done, that a few notes on the subject, as applied to fore-and-aft rigged craft, may be found useful. Sometimes, under stress of circumstances, and especially if short of hands, it may be best to drop the sails altogether, one at a time, take in the necessary reefs, and then set them again. But under more favourable conditions this is hardly needful, and the process is usually conducted as follows:—

To *reef the mainsail,* and, in a yawl, the mizzen, the boat should be put up head to wind; after which, the boom being slightly *topped up,* so as to relieve the sail of its weight, the peak settled (lowered), and the sheets hauled taut—the first, second, or third reef cringle (according to the number of reefs to be taken) is hauled down by its pendant and secured to the boom,—or, if there be no boom, the corner of the sail is tightly bound up by the pendant, the same thing being done at the *tack,* or weather edge of the sail. The foot of the sail is then furled up as far as the necessary reef-points (beginning from the after end), lashed, and the sail set up once more.

To *reef the foresail.*—The boat being put up to the wind, the sheets are shifted to the (first or second) cringle of the leech, and the tack pendant passed through the corresponding cringle in the luff, after which the foot of the sail may be furled and lashed by the reef points, and the tack made fast.

To *reef the jib.*—This necessitates that the sail be hauled in, unbent, reefed as the foresail, and reset. It is an awkward operation, and one taking time, for which reason jibs are seldom reefed, but instead replaced by smaller ones, the sailor being careful to secure each corner of the second sail as the first one is unbent.

To *reef a lugsail.*—If it be a *balance* lug, it is reefed round the boom to which the foot of the sail is laced: if a *dipping* or *standing* lug, the foot is, of course, furled and tied in the usual way.

Reel.—A machine upon which various lines may be wound, such as the *deep-sea reel,* that reel which contains the deep-sea line.

Hand reel, the reel for the hand-line.

Log reel, the same for the log-line.

A *twine reel,* "in rope-making, is formed, generally, of four small oak bars, about eighteen inches in length, one of which is made to slide, for the convenience of taking off the twine."

Yarn reel.—A reel upon which to wind yarn.

Reeve.—1. Generally speaking, to pass something through a hole. To reeve a tackle is to pass a rope through its blocks. To reeve a bowsprit is to draw it inboard (in small craft it runs in a ring at the stem and between bitts, and may therefore be said, in a sort of way, to be passed *through* them); and a bowsprit which can be so passed in and out (as in a cutter) is described as a *reeving* bowsprit. And since to reeve is to pass something through, to draw it out again is properly called *unreeving.*

2. *Reeving,* with caulkers, is opening the seams of a vessel's sides with an instrument called the *reeving iron,* so as to admit oakum.

Reeving beetle.—The largest hammer or mallet used by a caulker.

Reefer.—A short, double-breasted jacket. Hence a nickname for a midshipman. 2. A cargo ship fitted with refrigerating apparatus but capable of carrying other cargo also.

Refit.—Repair of damages, or an alteration to rigging.

Regatta.—A general meeting together of any sorts of boats for racing, promenading, or any description of aquatic sports; it is sometimes called a water frolic. The word is of Venetian origin.

Register.—A ship's Certificate of Registry, containing particulars of her dimensions, rig, machinery and the names of her owner and master.

Regulations for Preventing Collisions at Sea, last revised in 1972, consist of 38 Rules and 4 Annexes. Rules 4 to 19 are Steering and Sailing Rules; rules 20 to 31 describe the lights and shapes required to be shown by night and day; rules 32 to 36, Sound and Light Signals; and Annex IV gives a list of Distress Signals which may be used. The seaman should undoubtedly become quite familiar with these regulations. (*See* RULE OF THE ROAD.)

Reigning winds.—The winds which prevail in any particular district or locality.

Relieving tackles (at sea).—Temporary tackles for the relief of others under great strain. Those that are sometimes attached to the tiller of a vessel consist of two tackles with a continuous rope rove through both. The force of the sea on the rudder causes one tackle to render, but the other one to resist.

Remberge.—"A long narrow rowing vessel of war, formerly used by the English. Its name is derived from *remo* and *barca,* and it seems to have been the precursor of the Deal luggers." (Smyth.)

Render as a sea term has several meanings, as *to render a rope in coiling,*—so to coil it that it will run off without hitch or kink. Hence when a rope runs free it is said to *render.*

To *render a tackle.*—To yield or give way to its resistance, to slacken it off, etc.

Respondentia.—"A loan made upon goods laden in a ship, for which the borrower is personally responsible; differing from bottomry, where the ship and tackle are liable. In bottomry the lender runs no risk though the goods should be lost, and upon respondentia the lender must be paid his principal and interest, though the ship perish, provided the goods are safe." (Smyth.)

Revenue cutter.—A cutter rigged vessel, sharp-built and fast, formerly employed in the prevention of smuggling and enforcing of Customs regulations.

Rhodings (in ships).—Bearings on which the axles of pumps work.

Rhumb.—In navigation "the track of a ship which cuts all the meridians at the same angle. A ship sailing always towards the same point of the compass, or on the same rhumb, describes a loxodromic curve. This being the simplest curve, is the route usually pursued". (Brande and Cox.) If, then, a ship moves in such a direction, her *course* is on a rhumb-line, and the distance she makes is her *nautical distance.* "And hence", says Smyth, "seamen distinguish the rhumb by the same names as the points and winds, as marked on the end of the compass. The rhumb line, therefore, is a line prolonged from any point of the compass in a nautical chart, except the four cardinal points; or it is a line which a ship, keeping in the same collateral point or rhumb, describes throughout its whole course."

Ribs.—The timbers which form the skeleton of a boat. The ribs in a ship are like the ribs in the human frame; they are lateral appendages to her back-bone or keel, encompassing the trunk and preserving the cavity of the hull.—Ribs in large vessels are made up of several pieces called *futtocks, head timbers,* etc. (*see* FUTTOCK); but in small boats they may be of one piece bent to the shape required, and are then known as *heads, bent-heads* or *bent-timbers.* (*See* diagrams under FRAME.) When the "timbers" of a vessel are spoken of without further distinction, the term frequently means her ribs.

Ribs of a parrel.—Small strips of wood which, in combination with wooden beads (called *trucks*), formed the yard guides or parrels of old ships. (*See* PARREL.) Hence because of the number of parts of which this parrel was formed the term *ribs and trucks* has come to mean "fragments".

Ribands, or **ribbons.**—*Riband.*—The moulding round a vessel's side, or the painted decoration. A sail is said to be torn to ribbons when it is so damaged by the wind as to be no longer of any use. Such a thing is by no means so impossible as the term might imply; for sails are frequently torn to mere shreds by the force of a gale.

Ribbands (in shipbuilding).—Planks bolted outside the ribs to give stability to them during the building of the vessel.

Ribband shores.—Shores, or supports, holding up the frame of a ship while building.

Ricker, or **grown-spar.**—A spar made out of a young tree, in contradistinction to one hewn out of a plank. Rickers are stronger, more elastic, and in every way superior to hewn spars. They may generally be recognized by their knots, which will naturally be small and round.

Ricochet.—"Denotes a bound or leap, such as a flat piece of stone makes when thrown obliquely along the surface of the water." Generally spoken with reference to projectiles.

Ride.—1. To lie at anchor.

Ride athwart wind and tide.—A vessel is said to ride thus when, the wind and tide being in opposite directions with about the same force, she lies in a position which is the result of these opposing forces, and that, generally, is sideways to both.

Ride aport-last (old term).—Riding with the lower yards on the gunwales. (*See* PORT-LAST.)

Ride easy.—When the vessel does not labour or strain.

Ride hard.—To pitch violently in the sea so as to strain.

Ride out a gale, to live through it without dragging the anchor.

Riding light.—The light on the forestay carried by a vessel when anchored at night.

2. "A rope is said to ride when one of the turns by which it is wound about the capstan or windlass lies over another so as to interrupt the operation of heaving."

Riding bitts.—Massive frames of wood or iron round which a cable is turned when a ship lies at anchor, or *rides*.

Rider.—A sort of long *rib* fixed occasionally in a ship's hold, when she has been enfeebled by service; though she may be sometimes built with them for extra strength. They are variously named as *kelson rider, lower futtock riders, mid-futtock riders,* etc. (*See* diagrams under FRAME.)

Ridge.—A long group of rocks near the surface of the sea.

Ridge rope.—A rope to which awnings are attached.

Rig.—The rig of a vessel is the manner in which her masts and sails are fitted to her hull. There can be but two rigs, viz., *square* and *fore-and-aft.* The first is that in which the sails are hung *across* the vessel, as in ships; the second, that in which they lie in the direction of her *length,* as in cutters, yawls, etc. These two, in ships, are always more or less combined, but whenever a vessel carries square sails she is said (with very few exceptions) to be *square rigged.* Yet though there are but two rigs, the variety in each is almost infinite. The following list will give some idea of those most commonly seen in British waters; and for the separate description of each, reference must be made under its own heading. It must be noted, however, that there are no hard and fast rules absolutely distinguishing vessels closely allied in the disposition of their gear, as, for instance, are sometimes the schooner and the brigantine. The rig of vessels has, moreover, considerably changed throughout the years. The old brig has long since given way to the brigantine, now rarely seen, and the majority of the small vessels built today are, schooners, ketches, yawls, cutters and sloops.

Rigs on sea-going vessels:—(1) *Four-masted* barque or bark; (2) *Full-rigged ship* or modern *frigate*; (3) *Barque* or *Bark*; (4) *Barquentine* or *Barkentine* ; (5) *Schooner,* with two or more masts, if with square topsails *Topsail Schooner*; (6) *Brig*; (7) *Brigantine*; (8)

Ketch; (9) *Yawl*; (10) *One, Two,* or *Three-masted lugger*; (11) *Cutter, gaff* or *bermuda* rigged; (12) *Sloop*; (13) *Lateen rigged,* one or more masts with lateen sails, as in a felucca or dhow; (14) *Junk rigged,* one or more masts with battened, balance-lug sails, as carried in far eastern vessels.

The following are the usual rigs of boats: Main and mizzen (both masts having lug sails); una rig; cat rig; leg of mutton sail; sprit and foresail; dipping lug; balance lug (with boom); standing lug (without boom); Clyde lug (very high); sliding gunter; canoe rig (battened sails); main and foresail (a rig for small raters).

IN-RIG and OUT-RIG.—Anything which does not extend beyond the side of a boat is said to be *in-rigged,* and in like manner anything projecting may be called *out-rigged.* Thus a rowing skiff in which the rowlocks are on the side of the boat itself is in-rigged, while a racing-shell, in which they are extended far out on iron brackets (out-riggers), may be called out-rigged. So also if the shrouds of a sailing boat are extended beyond the sides they are out-rigged; and a mizzen set so far astern that it must be worked by a bumpkin is out-rigged. (*See also* under IN-RIG and OUT-RIG.)

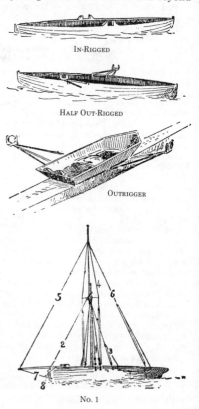

IN-RIGGED

HALF OUT-RIGGED

OUTRIGGER

No. 1

Rigging.—The system of cordage in a vessel by which masts are supported and sails extended and worked. There must be two sorts of rigging, therefore, viz., stationary and movable: the first is called *standing rigging,* and the other *running rigging.*

The standing rigging consists of *shrouds, stays,* and all such ropes or chains as hold spars in their places.

The running rigging comprises *halyards, sheets, clew-*

lines, and *tacks,* and all moving ropes connected with the sails, flags, etc.

The *lower* rigging implies that of the lower masts, the *upper* or topmast rigging that of the topmasts; and these terms apply no matter what the *rig* of the vessel may be.

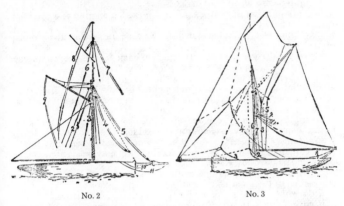

No. 2   No. 3

The accompanying diagrams show the rigging of a small cutter yacht. No. 1 is the standing rigging; Nos. 2 and 3 show the running rigging, the first being devoted to the halyards, the second and third to the sheets. The various parts are as follow:

STANDING RIGGING No. 1	RUNNING RIGGING No. 2	No. 3
	HALYARDS	SHEETS
1. The *shrouds,* terminating in the deadeyes.	1. *Main* or *throat halyard.*	1. Main sheet
2. *Forestay*	2. *Peak halyard*	2. Foresail sheet
3. *Backstays*	These two are often included together under the name *main halyards.*	3. Jib sheet
4. *Topmast shrouds,* terminating in the *legs.*		4. Jib topsail sheet
5. *Topmast forestay*	3. *Topping lift*	5. Topsail sheet
6. *Topmast backstay,* often called the *Preventer*	4. *Foresail halyards*	6. Maintack-trice
7. *Bobstay*	5. *Jib halyards*	7. Maintack line
8. *Bobstay trice,* for drawing up the bobstay while at anchor	6. *Topsail halyards*	8. Topsail tack line
	7. *Jib-topsail halyards*	
	8. *Signal halyards*	
	9. *Flag halyards,* or *peaklines*	
	10. *Jib inhaul*	
	11. *Jib outhaul*	

Rigging out is fitting out or "dressing" a boat when she leaves the builder to be prepared for sea. The term is also used with respect to the fitting of her out for a cruise, or for a season after laying up, and consists in replacing in her all the rigging of which she had been denuded. Yachts are often laid up for a term, or during the winter, when all the rigging is taken down and the hull and mast are left naked; and in the spring they are rigged out again. The term rigging is practically equivalent to "dressing", and, indeed, has its origin in the Anglo-Saxon *wrigan,* to dress.

Rigging loft (in dockyards).—A loft in which rigging is stored for sale or prepared for ships.

Rigging screws.—Double-ended screws used for setting up shrouds, etc.

Right.—To *right a ship.*—To get her back to the perpendicular when she has careened too much over, by putting her head into the wind. When she comes again to the upright she is said to have *righted* herself; and a vessel which rights herself without difficulty is said to possess *righting power,* or, to use the more common phrase, to be *stiff.*

To *right the helm.*—To place the tiller of a rudder in a right line with the nose of the vessel so that the rudder ceases to act.

Right away.—An expression which, when used at sea, may imply "in a certain direction"; as when another ship may be sighted "right away on the port bow", etc.

Right-handed rope.—Rope with the strands twisted "with the sun"—*i.e.,* in the most usual manner.

Right knot.—Another name for the reef knot. (*See* KNOTS.)

Right on end.—In a continuous line; as a topmast on the lower-mast when elevated.

Right up and down.—Said of the wind when it is a dead calm.

Ring (of an anchor).—The ring or shackle at the lower end of the shaft. (*See* ANCHOR.)

Ring-bolt.—A bolt with a ring at its head. It is usually passed through one of the strong timbers of a vessel for the attachment of a tackle or rope.

Ring-ropes.—Ropes which were sometimes made fast at intervals to hempen cables so as to give them greater power in holding the ship against heavy seas. Hence a rope used in the same manner on any hawser may be called a ring rope.

RING BOLTS

Ring-sail.—Ring tail (*which see*).

Ring tail.—A sort of studding sail for fore-and-aft rigged craft. It is a narrow strip of sail set out beyond the leech of the mainsail of a cutter, or any similarly rigged boat. Its head is stretched on a small yard on the gaff, and its foot on another small spar called the *ring tail boom* (on the main boom), both of which rig in and out as do the booms of the studding sails on square rigged ships. This sail was seldom seen except on racing yachts, when running before the wind. (*see* fig. p. 237).

2. A small sail set at the stern of a vessel, sometimes as an aid to steering.

Rip.—Tide rip. (*See* RACE.)

Ripping-iron.—An instrument used to rip the copper off the bottom of a vessel.

Rising.—*Rising floors.*—In shipbuilding, the floor timbers which, gradually rising from the plane of the midship floor of a ship, give the shape to the lower parts of the bow and stern.

Rising line.—In shipbuilding, a line drawn on the *sheer plan* to determine the height of the ends of all the *floor timbers* throughout the length of a vessel.

Rising wood.—In shipbuilding, that portion of the keel which rises through the floors.

Rivers.—Rivers, as sailing-grounds, have certain advantages, to amateurs, over the open sea. Boats are more easily got at than on the coast; there is less wear and tear, and more days on which one may go out. At the same time winds are more variable, sailing is in some of its branches more difficult, as well as more dangerous.

Rivet.—A metal pin clenched at both ends (usually while hot).

Roach, or **roaching** (in square rig).—The curve in the foot or leech of a square sail. It is so cut to keep it from the futtock plates and ropes about the mast (*see* fig.).

Roadstead, or **road.**—A place of anchorage at a distance from the shore. Thus we have the Yarmouth Roads, the Margate Roads, and others.

A *good road* is one well protected from gales, etc.

An *open road* is one open or unprotected.

Roadster, or *roader.*—A vessel lying in a road.

Roarer.—A name sometimes given to a vessel which makes a loud roaring noise as she moves through the water. This is the case with some yachts, and is generally to be traced to some peculiarity of formation about the bows.

Roaring Forties.—The latitudes between 40°S and 50°S, where strong westerly winds prevail.

Roast-beef dress.—Full uniform.

Robins (*i.e.*, *rope-bands*).—Part of the gear of a square sail. Small ropes, used in pairs, one leg of each pair being longer than the other, to attach the head of the sail to its yard. The long leg of each is taken two or three times round the yard and then lashed to the short leg.

Rockered.—Rounded, as the keels of some boats are rounded, when they are called rockered or drag keels. It is mostly seen in small boats or racing yachts (*see* fig. p. 238).

Rocket.—Rockets are used at sea, by night, as signals. A red rocket sent up alone, every few minutes, is a signal of distress.

Rocket apparatus.—Consists of line-carrying rockets and lines, for firing over a stranded vessel. When a rocket-line has been received

on board a block and end-
less whip can be hauled
on board from the shore
and a breeches buoy used
to rescue persons from the
wreck.

Roger's blast (at sea).—
A sudden disturbance of
the atmosphere, resem-
bling a small whirlwind.

Rogue's yarn.—In rope
manufactured for the Royal
services, it is the practice
to interweave one yarn of
a colour different from
the rest. This is called the
rogue's yarn, because it
can be identified if stolen.

ROCKERED, OR DRAG KEEL

And, moreover, since each dockyard may have its distinguishing
colour, a rope may be traced back to the place at which it was made,
which is a wholesome check upon defective manufacture.

Roll, rolling.—The oscillation of a vessel from side to side in a
heavy sea. The result of heavy rolling may sometimes be to throw
sails over to windward and back.

Rolling tackle.—A tackle used in square rigged vessels to hold a
yard to the mast when rolling to windward.

Rollers.—1. Heavy seas (waves) setting in without wind; sometimes of enormous size and length, as may often be seen on the
Cornish coast or along the shores of the Bay of Biscay. 2. On
shipboard, revolving timbers placed where constant friction of ropes
occurs.

Room.—*Room and space.*—In shipbuilding a purely technical
term referring to the space supported by each rib of a vessel.

Rooming (old term).—"To leeward" (*which see*).

To *go rooming.*—To bear down upon anything.

Roost.—"A phrase applied to races of strong and furious tides
which set in between the Orkney and Shetland Islands; as those of
Sunburgh and the Start."

Rope.—Generally speaking, cordage above one inch in circumference. A rope, technically, is a twist of a certain number of *strands*
of hempen fibre; a strand being a number of *yarns,* and a yarn a
certain proportion of twisted fibres. Three strands form a rope;
though four-stranded manilla is sometimes used.

Rope is of several kinds.

Italian hemp is the best, and when worn out is always saleable.

Manilla (from the fibres of a species of wild banana), being of a
softer nature, is very suitable to yachts, but it is expensive, and to
take its place, *fash rope,* an inferior kind of manilla, is occasionally
used.

Coir rope is made of the fibrous husk of cocoanut. It is not so strong as manilla, but is sufficiently light to float.

Bass warp is very light with strands interwoven.

Synthetic fibres.—*Polypropylene,* generally used for marine purposes; *polyamide (nylon),* very strong and very elastic; *polyester (terylene),* very strong and less elastic than nylon; *polythene,* about as strong as hemp, and will float.

Steel wire.—Used in rigging, mooring, etc. Usually of six strands twisted round a hemp heart, each strand consisting of wires also twisted round a hemp heart; this makes it flexible. Standing rigging need not be flexible, and the strands of such wire are made entirely of wire.

Rope is either *hawser* (sometimes called *shroud*) laid—when it is made up of three or four strands; or *cable* (*cablet or water*) laid—when it has three great strands, each being made up of three small ropes, twisted left-handed.

The size of rope is designated by its circumference expressed in inches; as a "9 in rope", which is one 9 in round. It is issued in *coils*; sold by the lb weight; and its length measured in fathoms. (The breaking strain of hemp rope is, in tons $= \frac{\text{circumference}^2}{5}$ about. Its weight in lbs per fathom $= \frac{\text{circumference}^2}{4}$ about. "Rope is either white or tarred, the latter being the best if liable to exposure to wet, the former if not exposed. The strength of tarred rope is, however, only about three-fourths that of white rope, and its loss of strength increases with time."

In rigging, the *standing part* of a rope is the part fixed; the *running part,* that part which is hauled upon.

A *bight* is a bend in a rope whether in making a knot or for any other purpose. Rope when wet swells in diameter and shrinks in length; this should be allowed for when tightening up dry ropes which are to be left standing for any length of time, or even for one night. New rope is stiff. This may be taken off to some extent by steeping in boiling water and stretching while hot. When a rope gets partly worn through it is said to *fret*; when its end becomes loose it *frays.*

Rope bands.—(*See* ROBINS.)

Rope end.—A punishment. The infliction of a whipping with a short rope.

Rope of sand.—A thing without cohesion. A people who cannot combine, but who at critical moments separate and thus lose their object; the principal failing of many communities of seamen, more especially, perhaps, of coast men. "A term borrowed from a Greek proverb signifying attempting impossibilities."

Rope yarn.—The smallest component part of a rope. (*See above.*) It also means the untwisted yarn of old rope (*junk*), for which there are a multitude of uses on ship-board.

On the high ropes.—Ceremonious, puffed up, proud, etc.

Rose box, or **Strum box.**—A perforated box fitted around the lower end of a suction pipe to prevent the pump from becoming clogged.

Rose lashings.—Fanciful or decorated lashings with rope.

Rough.—Unfinished. Hence:—*Rough knots* (properly "rough *nauts*", abbreviated from "nauticals"), unsophisticated seamen.

Rough spars.—Those in an unfinished condition.

Rough tree, or *rough tree timbers.*—The *stanchions* supporting the rough tree rail, also the tree out of which a spar is to be made.

Rough-tree rail.—The topmost rail round a vessel's bulwarks. Also, an old term used on trading ships for almost any long piece of timber placed as a rail above the ship's side.

Round.—To *round in*—to haul in. "To round in generally implies to pull upon any slack rope which passes through one or more blocks in a direction nearly horizontal", and is particularly applied to the braces. It is apparently derived from the circular motion of the rope about the sheave through which it passes. "To *round up* is used in nearly the same sense, only it is expressed of a tackle which hangs in a perpendicular direction without sustaining or hoisting any weighty body." (Falconer.)

To *round to.*—To bring a vessel "head to wind".

Round turn.—The passing of a rope once round a timber or post so as to be able to stop some motion, or temporarily hold on.

To bring up with a round turn.—To check with a sudden jerk.

Round house.—Apparently so called because it was possible to walk round it. On old ships it was a square cabin on the after part of the deck, and in men-of-war was sometimes called the "coach". Later, it was built abaft the main mast.

Round robin.—"A compact or agreement entered into by seamen, when they have cause of complaint against their superior officer, to state their grievances to the Admiralty or commander-in-chief, and to endeavour to obtain redress without subjecting any one individual more than another to be thought the leader or chief mover." The term comes from the French *rond* "round", and *ruban* "ribbon". "Their complaints are generally stated in a circular form, and the signatures written all round them, so that none appear first."

Round dozen.—Thirteen. In old days a round dozen meant thirteen lashes with the cat.

Round ribbed.—Spoken of the shape of a vessel when her sides are very much curved.

Rounding a rope.—*Serving* it. Much the same as *keckling* (*which see*).

Roundly.—Quickly.

Rounds or *rungs.*—The cross pieces forming the steps of a wooden ladder. At sea the rounds forming the steps up the shrouds of a vessel are called the *ratlines,* or rattlings.

Roust.—(*See* ROOST.)

Rovens.—1. A pronunciation of the word robins (more properly rope-bands). 2. Ravellings of canvas or bunting.

Rover.—A pirate or freebooter.

Rovings.—(*See* ROBINS.)

Row.—*Rowing.*—The propulsion of a boat by *oars,* not by sculls, that being, in the language of boating men, called *sculling.* The art of rowing is not easily learned. The best schools are the universities, but the various rowing clubs of the Thames also produce very perfect oarsmen.

Row dry.—To row without splashing; just as to row *wet* is to splash a good deal.

"Row off all!"—The order to rowers to cease rowing, and lay upon their oars; but the term *"easy all"* is much oftener employed.

Row in the same boat.—Equivalent to riding in the same curricle with another person; that is, being in the same situation or holding the same views.

Rowl.—A single block or pulley. "The iron or wood shiver or wheel for a whip tackle."

Rowlock (pronounced "rollock").—The rowlock, as the name implies, is a *lock* or holding portion for a *rowing* machine, *i.e.,* an oar; it is, in fact, the fulcrum from which an oar obtains its leverage. There are fixed rowlocks, sometimes called *tholes* (but not correctly, because tholes, properly speaking, are pins), and swivel-rowlocks, which revolve upon pivots, turning in holes made to receive them in the gunwale of a boat. The swivel-rowlocks have certain advantages over the fixed in that a longer stroke may be taken by their use, and that sculls or oars may be brought alongside a boat instead of lifted out or shipped when passing very close to any object They are nearly always found in boats with a gunwale, but in such skiffs as those built on the Upper Thames, the absence of a gunwale necessitates an arrangement of fixed rowlocks, in consequence of which the oars and sculls made for use on these waters are nearly always square in the loom. There can be no doubt that the fixed rowlock is more elegant than the swivel, and to up-river men the sound of the measured rattle as the square oars fall to the feather is very musical. For rough rowing, however, use has to give way to appearance, and the swivel is undeniably the more useful. Sailing boats have often the rowlocks cut out of the washstrake, so

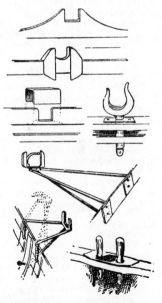

VARIOUS FORMS OF ROWLOCKS. The third is closed with a *poppet,* shown above it; the fourth type is a *crutch,* and the last are *thole pins.*

that they may be out of the way of all sails, sheets, etc.; and to preserve the height of the freeboard a cover is usually fitted over them, when under sail. (*See also* THOLES.)

Rowse.—To pull on a rope without tackle.

"*Rowse away!*" "*Rowse away cheerily!*" etc., are encouraging exhortations on the part of an officer to men hauling on a rope.

Royal.—*Royal mast.*—The mast in a ship, bark, brig, etc., above and usually part of the top-gallant, and named according to the lower mast upon which it rises, as fore-royal, main-royal, etc. The royal mast is the highest ordinary mast in a ship, and carries the royal sail and sky sail, if any.

Royal sail.—The sail on the royal mast, and named accordingly—as main-royal.

Royal yard.—The yard which carries the royal sail. It comes down to the top-gallant yard when the sails are furled.

Rubber.—"In sail-making a small iron implement fixed in a wooden handle and used to rub down or flatten the seams of the sails."

Rubbing piece, or **wale.**—A beading of wood or rope running round the outside of a boat just beneath the gunwale to protect it against injury in touching quays, piers, or other boats. (*See* WALE.)

Ruck.—A measure of string.

Rucking.—Easing down a gaff sail rapidly, by lowering on the peak and throat halyards. It may be necessary in case of a sudden gust or to run before a squall.

Rudder (Anglo-Saxon, *steor-roper*).—That instrument by which a vessel is steered. Tiphys (the pilot of Jason's ship *Argo*) is said to have been its inventor. The rudder is hung upon the stern post of a vessel by means of *gudgeons* and *pintles*, otherwise called *rudder bands* or *braces*.

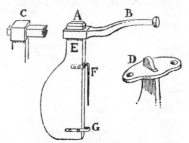

Its parts are as follow:—A is the *head* over which the *tiller* (B) fits; or into which it is inserted as at C; or the tiller may take the form of a *yoke* as at D. E is the *stock* or *neck*, F is the *pintle* or brace, and G the *gudgeon*, or *rudder band*; these last two (the gudgeon and the pintle) constituting what are sometimes called the *rudder irons*, or forelocks. The *rudder rake* is the shape of the aftermost part. The *bearding* is the fore-part.

In vessels of great draught the rudder is narrow—that is, extends but a little way from the stern post; in those of small draught it is proportionately wider (or extends further out), until, in flat bottomed vessels, such as barges, it is very wide. "When carried to a considerable breadth, as in the Chinese vessels, it is pierced with holes, which preserves an increased leverage with a diminished direct resistance from the water." (Brande and Cox.) This principle of boring holes in the rudder has occasionally been followed in certain English craft; but it is unusual. With respect to small sailing boats we find that rudders are larger and deeper on smooth waters than on the coast, for river craft carry a great spread of canvas, which lays them over to a very considerable extent; and were the rudder narrow or wanting in depth it would be brought so much out of the water that its command over the boat would be gone. So also in the case of very long row boats, such as the Thames skiffs, as well as in racing boats, the rudder is increased in width, both on account of the boats' length and the speed with which they are intended to travel.

BARGE RUDDERS (WIDE)

The rudder is worked by means of the tiller. The tiller is a handle or bar at the head of the rudder. It is one of the component parts of the helm. (*See* HELM.) In small craft it is moved by hand; in large, by a wheel; while in long row boats, where the steersman sits too far amidships to be able to give it the necessary sweep, it is worked by ropes, called *rudder lines,* or *yoke lines*; and in this case it ceases to be a bar, and becomes, as above mentioned, a flat plate, called the *yoke.* The lines are sometimes crossed, enabling the rudder to be pulled over to a greater angle, which, in a long racing boat, gives the steersman an increased command over his boat's movement. In certain small craft, having two masts, the mizzen stands before the rudder head and impedes the sweep of the tiller. It then becomes necessary to

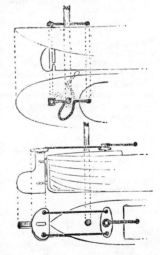

devise some means by which the tiller may be brought over without interference. The accompanying diagrams will best illustrate the means usually employed. In the first, the distance from the rudder head to the steersman is short, and the tiller is simply bent as shown. In the second, however, the distance is very long, and a double yoke is used—the first on the rudder itself, the second (to which a small false tiller is fitted) being placed before the impending mast.

Rudder chains and pendants.—Chains shackled to the rudder for preventing its loss in case of being carried away in a heavy sea. The chains terminate in short ropes, called the *pendants,* which are made fast to the stern of the vessel. We sometimes find these in barges. In vessels steered by a wheel, the chains by which the wheel works the tiller are also called *rudder-chains* or *tiller chains.*

Rudder case, or *rudder trunk.*—A casing of wood fitted round the *helmport—i.e.,* the hole through which the stock of the rudder passes when the boat has a counter.

Rudder chocks (at sea).—Wedges used in emergency to fix the rudder should it become unmanageable.

Balanced rudder.—A rudder whose stock is not on the leading edge, but some distance abaft it. The pressure on the fore part of the rudder then nearly balances the pressure on the after part, so that less power is needed to turn the rudder.

Rule of the Road (at sea).—The popular name for the International Steering and Sailing Rules included under Rules 5 to 19 of the Regulations for Preventing Collisions at Sea. They are to be found printed in full in Seamanship manuals.

Risk of collision.—If the compass bearing of an approaching vessel does not appreciably change, risk of collision exists. (Rule 7.) When risk of collision exists between two vessels one of the two is directed to keep out of the way, and the other, normally, stands on, (Rule 17); *except* when the two engine-driven vessels are meeting head-on, when *both* alter course to starboard, (Rule 14).

In principle, the more manoeuvrable vessel keeps out of the way of the less manoeuvrable; thus, "steam gives way to sail", (Rule 18). A "sailing vessel" with her engine running is classified as a "steam" or "power-driven vessel".

Power-driven vessels, i.e. those propelled by an engine, should, in general "Keep to the right", e.g. in narrow channels, and, when crossing, the vessel which has the other on her own starboard side keeps out of the way, (Rule 15).

Sailing vessels.—When two sailing vessels are closing and have the wind on different sides, the vessel which has the wind on the port side keeps out of the way of the other. When both have the wind on the same side, the vessel which is to windward keeps out of the way of the vessel which is to leeward, (Rule 12).

Manoeuvring signals.—When vessels are in sight of one another, power-driven vessels may make the following signals:

   1 short blast to mean "I am altering my course to starboard".
   2 short blasts to mean "I am altering my course to port".
   3 short blasts to mean "My propeller is going astern".

A vessel which is in doubt whether sufficient action is being taken by the other to avoid collision shall give at least 5 short and rapid blasts, which may be supplemented by short and rapid flashes of a light.

The Rules, of which the gist only is given above, are summed up in the following verses by the late Thomas Gray, C.B.:

Power-driven vessels meeting head-on
"When both lights you see ahead—
Steer to starboard; show your RED.

Two power-driven vessels passing
GREEN to GREEN—or RED to RED—
Perfect safety—go ahead!

Two power-driven vessels crossing
If to your starboard RED appear,
It is your duty to keep clear;
To act as judgment says is proper;
To Port—or Starboard—Back—or, Stop her!

But when upon your Port is seen
A steamer's Starboard Light of GREEN
There's not so much for you to do,
For GREEN to PORT keeps clear of you.

*All vessels must keep a good look-out, and power-driven vessels must
stop or go astern if necessary*
Both in safety and in doubt,
Always keep a good look-out;
In danger, with no room to turn,
Ease her! Stop her! Go astern!"

Two sailing vessels approaching
Wind on different sides? We ought
To keep clear if our wind's to port.
Wind the same for both? We say
The one that is to windward must give way.

Rumbowline.—Condemned or old rope, etc. Also the coarse rope which secures new coils of rope.

Rum gagger.—One who gags (tells improbable stories) in the hopes of getting rum for his trouble.

Rum-tum race.—A race among Thames rowing men in boats supplied to them by the clubs to which they belong. But few of the watermen are able to afford *best boats*; but by this method almost all can now enter for professional races. The boats thus supplied are not first-class racers, but are fitted with sliding seats and are full out-rigged. The practice of rum-tum racing was instituted within the last few years of the last century.

Run (in naval architecture).—The run of a vessel, occasionally called the *rake,* is the angle its under surface makes in running from beneath the greatest width of beam up to the counter: or, in other words, it is the backward sweep of

the under part of the hull. Much of the speed of a boat depends upon the run given her in designing.

To *run*, in sailing, or *run before the wind,* is to be sailing with the wind aft, or very nearly so. In centreboard boats the board is triced up when running before the wind. This is the time to be careful of *gybing* (*which see*).

To *run down* another vessel is to run into her.

To *run out* a warp or cable is to carry the end out away from a ship.

To *run the gauntlet.*—A species of punishment. (*See* GAUNTLET.)

To *let run* a rope, is to let it run quite loose.

In the rigging of a vessel:—

Runners.—The back stays of a mast, which, being fastened to pendants, or short ropes, are movable, and can, therefore, be *let run.*

Running moor.—Anchoring by dropping one anchor while the ship has headway and a second when she has gone further ahead. The first cable is then hove in and the second paid out until an equal amount is on each. (*See* MOOR.)

Running part.—1. (Of a rope).—The end which is not fastened. 2. (Of a tackle).—The part which runs in the blocks. (*See* TACKLE.)

Running rigging.—(*See* under RIGGING.)

Runner tackle.—A tackle applied to the running end of a rope or tackle.

Running the easting down.—Sailing in an easterly direction in high southern latitudes, where fair (or *running*) winds prevail.

Rung.—The step of a ladder.

Rung-heads.—In ship-building, a name occasionally given to the *floor-heads* of a vessel. (*See* under FLOOR.)

Runners.—(*See* under RUN.)

Rut (of the sea).—The breaking waves along the coast.

S

Saccade.—"The sudden jerk of the sails in light winds, and a heavy swell." (Smyth.)

Sack of coals.—"The seaman's name for the black *Magellanic clouds,* or patches of deep blue sky in the Milky Way near the South Pole." (Smyth.)

Saddle.—A rest for any spar, etc. A bracket or ring on the lower part of a mast, acting as a rest, or "saddle", for the jaws of a boom. (*See* BOOM-STAYS.)

Sag, sagging.—A dropping or depression; and therefore, in a keel, the opposite to "hogging" (*which see*).

To *sag to leeward* is to make considerable *lee-way.*

The *sag of a rope.*—Its bellying or drop, when extended.

Sail.—The following refers to the sails of a full-rigged ship. "Sails take their names from the mast, yard or stay upon which they are stretched. Thus the principal sail extended upon the main mast is called the *main sail*; the next above, which stands upon the main top-mast, is the *main top-sail*; above which is the *main top-gallant sail*; and above all, the *main royal.* In like manner, there are the *foresail,* the *fore top-sail,* the *fore top-gallant-sail,* and the *fore royal*; and similar appellations are given to the sails supported by the *mizzen* or after-mast. The *main stay-sail, main-top-mast stay-sail,* etc., are between the main and fore masts; and the *mizzen stay-sail, mizzen top-mast stay-sail,* etc., are between the main and mizzen masts. Between the foremast and bowsprit are the *fore stay-sail,* the jib, or *inner* and *outer jibs* and sometimes a *flying jib*; and the *studding sails* are those which are extended upon booms run out beyond the arms of the different yards of the main mast and fore mast." (Brande and Cox.) To the square sails on each mast may be added one or more, above all the rest, called respectively the *sky sail,* moon-raker, and jumper, or jolly jumper (but the two last are very rarely seen); and below the lower studding sails occasionally, another called the *water sail* or *save all.* Such canvas is commonly called, by seamen, *kites,* and the setting of them in a light breeze is called *flying kites,* from which we have an expression often used in general conversation, as when a man makes a great deal of show with paper money, he is said to be flying kites. (*See* under RIG.)

A *square sail* is one bent to a yard and balanced across the ship.

Fore-and-aft sails are those set in the direction of the length of a vessel.

Stay-sails are triangular (or jib-shaped) sails running on stays between masts or from a mast to a bowsprit.

Studding-sails (used only in square rig) are bent to short booms run out beyond the yards, to increase the lateral spread of the square sails.

A *gaff-sail* is one bent to a gaff. (*See* GAFF.)

A *lug-sail* is bent to a yard which is slung in a fore-and-aft direction. It is common to the open boat, and is of various forms. (*See* LUG.)

A *sprit-sail* is one extended by a sprit, which is a spar passing diagonally across it. (*See* SPRIT.)

A *spinnaker* is a racing sail for yachts, run out at right angles to the mast on the side opposite to that over which the main-sail stands; only used when running before a wind. (*See* SPINNAKER.)

A *leg of mutton* sail (in fore-and-aft rig) is a triangular sail, its foot extended on a boom and its apex attached to the head of a pole-mast: it is supposed to resemble a leg of mutton in shape. It is a sail well suited to small boats. (*See* MUDIAN.)

GAFF SAIL

A *lateen* sail is one extended on a yard of great length, which is made fast to the bow of the boat, and runs high into the air. It is common to the Mediterranean and Eastern seas, and was at one time much used in Norfolk and Suffolk. (*See* LATEEN.)

Headsails are those at the head of a vessel, as the fore-sail and jib in a cutter.

Storm sails are smaller and of stouter canvas than those in general use, and are often, even in small yachts, tanned. They are used in bad weather, in winter, or for rough work.

Trysails are small sails answering to storm sails. But when *the* trysail is spoken of it means a *gaff sail* without a boom. (*See* TRYSAIL.)

Flying sails are small head sails set out beyond those in everyday use, such as flying jibs, jib topsail, etc., in yachts; and the "*flying jibs*" in square rig.

A sail *set flying* (spoken mostly of headsails, jibs, etc.) is one stretched by its halyards alone, i.e., a sail not running on any stay. When it does run on a stay it is said to be *set standing*. (*See* SET.)

Battened sails are those on which battens (splines of wood) are fitted, both to keep them flat, as well, in some cases, as to assist in reefing. Junk sails are fully battened. (*See* under BATTEN.)

Balloon sails, used in yacht racing, are immense spreads of canvas, generally in the form of foresails and spinnakers. The complete racing equipment of a racing yacht constitutes that which is called her *balloon,* or *press canvas* (*which see*).

A sail is said to be *bent* to its yard or mast. To *make* sail is to set sail. To *spring* a sail is also to set it. To *shorten* sail is to take in some sail, or to reef it. To *loose* sail is to spread or to hang out in their places sails that have been furled, either preparatory to setting them, or to air them. To *strike* a sail is to lower its yard or gaff in token of salute. To *reef* a sail is to tie up part of it so that it may present a smaller area. (*See* REEF.) To *furl* a sail is to fold it entirely up on its yard or boom.

Sails are of canvas made from flax or cotton, or of terylene or other suitable material. "Sail-cloth is made in bolts, mostly 24 in wide, but also 18 in wide, and, for yachting purposes, frequently still less wide, upon the ground that the narrower the cloth the flatter and better will the sail stand to its work . . . As a rule, 4 yards in length may be considered as the average content of each bolt. It is generally made of eight different qualities in respect of thickness. Nos. 1, 2, and 3 are used for storm and other sails that have to do heavy work; the remaining numbers for the lighter descriptions of sails." ("Encyclopædia Britannica.") A *cloth* is one of the strips of canvas of which the sail is made; and the cloths are said to be *pricked* together, the instrument used in sewing up the seams being called a *pricker*. The several parts of a sail are as follows:—From the fact that sail cloth is made in *bolts,* we have the name *bolt ropes,* for ropes fastened all round a sail to strengthen its edges. At the head and foot these ropes are called the *head-rope* and *foot-rope* respectively; on the leeches, or sides, the *leech ropes.* The *bunt* or *belly* is the main surface of the sail. (*See* BUNT.) The *head* is the upper margin. The *foot* the lower margin. The *leeches* are the sides in general; but the weather

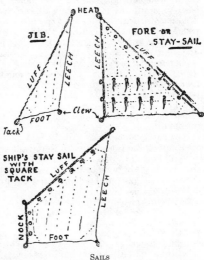

SAILS

side (that nearest the mast, in fore-and-aft rig) is called the *luff,* and the lee side the *after leech*; and when, as in yachts, the leech alone is spoken of, it always means the after edge. (*See* LEECH.) The *clews* are the lower corners: on a gaff-sail (as the mainsail of a yacht) the clew is the aftermost lower corner; the *tack* being the foremost lower corner. (*See* TACK.) The *peak* of a gaff-sail or sprit-sail is the aftermost upper corner. The *throat* of a gaff-sail is the forward upper corner. *Reef bands* are extra bands of canvas running horizontally across a sail. In these bands, holes are pierced and small eyes inserted, through which the *reef points* are rove. (*See* REEF.) A *balance reef* is a reef band running diagonally across a gaff-sail, so that the sail may be reefed in such a manner as to spread only the peak and upper portion. It is seldom seen in small craft. *Reef points* are short ropes hanging from the holes in the reef-bands. They are used to tie up the foot of the sail, which constitutes what is called "reefing" it. (*See* REEF.) *Reef cringles* are loops or eyes in the bolt ropes on the leech of a sail. Through these cringles short ropes called *reef pendants* are rove, so that the corner of sails may be drawn down and tied preparatory to reefing. (*See* REEF.) *Tabs* or *tabling* are strengthening pieces hemmed into the edge of a large sail where *bolt hooks* are employed. *Roaching* is the name given to the curve in the foot or sides of a sail; the side curve being called the *leech-roach*. This term is mostly applied to square sails. (*See* ROACH.)

Other terms relating to sails are:—

Sail burton.—A purchase for sending up sails to a masthead ready for bending.

Sail cover (sometimes called a *sail coat*).—A waterproof covering for a sail which is too large to be unbent and stowed away every time a boat is brought home from an outing. It is important to remember that a cover should not be put over a wet sail; if this is repeatedly done, or the wet sail left covered for any length of time, it will quickly rot.

Sail hanks.—(*See* CLIP-HOOKS.)

Sail hooks.—1. (*See* CLIP-HOOKS.) 2. A hook for holding the seams of a sail while sewing it.

Sail ho! (at sea).—The exclamation used on the first sight of another vessel.

Sailboard.—A buoyant board, fitted with a hinged mast, and sail, upon which the sailor stands.

Sailing.—"In navigation, the art of directing a ship on a given line laid down in a chart. It is called *plain sailing* when the chart is constructed on the supposition that the earth's surface (or rather that of the ocean) is an extended plain, and *globular sailing* when the supposition is that the earth is a sphere, the ship being then supposed to be sailing on the arc of a great circle." (Brande and Cox.)

Sailing free or *large.*—Sailing with the wind abaft the beam.

Sailing order, or *order of sailing.*—In the days of sailing fleets, "any determined order preserved by a squadron."

Sailing within 4 *points,* 6 *points, etc.*—Sailing within a certain angle of the direction of the wind. To explain the term it must be premised that the compass card is divided into 32 points (*see* COMPASS); and further, that a vessel cannot sail directly against the wind, but only within a certain angle of it, or, in nautical language, within a certain number of points of it. That is to say, if the wind be due North (*see* fig.), and the vessel sail within 6 points, she can only progress in the directions E.N.E. and W.N.W., those being respectively the 6th point on either side of the North. Six points is as close as a square rigged trading ship will sail under ordinary circumstances. Fore-and-aft rigged craft will, however, stand up to 5 points, and some to 4 points, still making good headway, while modern racing boats with centreboards may, under certain conditions, be brought even closer, though not to hold for any length of time.

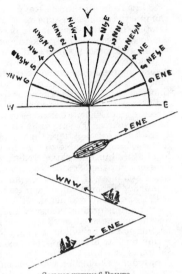

SAILING WITHIN 6 POINTS

Sailor.—"On shipboard, one who is making a long sea voyage other than his first, and who is qualified to go aloft and tend the sails. A sailor is not necessarily a seaman." (Brande and Cox.)

Saint Elmo's Fire.—(*See* CORPOSANT.)

Saint Lawrence skiff.—"In the *Century* (New Series, Vol. VIII) is an interesting article upon amateur canoeing and sailing under the heading of 'Camp Grindstone'. There is an instructive paragraph describing the St. Lawrence skiff and the way it is managed. The skiff as depicted is a row-boat built upon scientific principles, and capable of seating about six persons. It is furnished with a centreboard, and carries a spritsail on a mast stepped well forward. The peculiarity of the craft is that when under sail it is steered by neither rudder, oar, nor paddle, but is governed by a person distributing his weight either forward or aft and at the same time regulating the sheets." (Winn, *The Boating Man's Vade Mecum.*)

Saloon.—The main cabin of a merchant ship.

Salt.—*An old salt.*—An old sailor.

Salt Horse.—(*See* HORSE.)

Saltings.—Flat land generally lying outside a river or sea wall and sometimes covered at spring tides.

Salute.—In the Royal Navy salutes are made by the firing of cannon, the number of guns marking the rank of the person or object saluted. Thus the Royal salute is twenty-one guns, and the number decreases to seven, the salute to a consul or a naval commander. But in a more humble manner salutes are also performed by the dipping of colours. Thus a boat on passing or being passed by a vessel displaying the Royal Standard (which floats only above royalty) will dip three times; on other occasions, as to a naval officer's flag, to that of a yachting-club officer, or to a friend, once.

Salvage.—"Originally meant the thing or goods saved from a wreck, fire or enemies. It now signifies an allowance made to those by whose means the ship or goods have been saved.

"Salvage loss.—A term in marine insurance implying that the underwriters are liable to pay the amount insured on the property lost in the ship, but taking credit for what is saved." (Smyth.) It may be useful for the beginner to know that if any person find a boat he has a lien on it. If, therefore, a boat be lost or get adrift any person capturing her may deliver her up to the receiver of wreckage, who will, if she be not reclaimed, sell her at public auction. If an amateur have the misfortune to lose a boat he will do well to make some private arrangement with the finder, but he may conclude from the beginning that he will have to pay "through the nose".

Salvo.—"A discharge from several pieces simultaneously, as a salute." (Smyth.)

Salvor.—The person who saves a ship or any part of it from peril or loss. (*See also Wreckers* under WRECK.)

Sampan.—A boat of the Far East, often propelled by an oar over the stern, the larger ones carrying a mast and balanced lug sail.

Samson post.—A post; or short mast, which supports a derrick.

Sand.—*Sand bags.*—Canvas bags for use in boats to fill with ballast. (*See* BALLAST.)

Sand hopper.—A small crustacean, not unlike a shrimp, which abounds on some beaches. He is one of the "sessile-eyed" class.

Sand strakes.—Another name for the *garboard strakes* (*which see*).

Sand warpt.—"Left by the tide on a shoal. Also striking on a shoal at half-flood." (Smyth.)

Saraband.—"A forecastle dance borrowed from the Moors of Africa." (Smyth.)

Sasse.—"A kind of weir with a flood gate, or a navigable sluice." (Smyth.)

Saucer (of a capstan).—The part receiving the spindle upon which the capstan revolves.

Save-all, or **water sail.**—"A small sail sometimes set under the foot of a lower studding-sail." (Smyth.) (*See* under STUDDING-SAILS.)

Sawbones.—The surgeon on a ship was sometimes so called, as also occasionally on shore.

Saxboard.—The uppermost strake in an open boat. To it the *gunwale* is secured (upon which the rowlocks are fixed), together with the *inwale* and outer wale, or *rubbing piece.* It is some-

times called the *gunwale strake*.
(*See* under GUNWALE and SHEER-
STRAKE.)

Scandalising.—Applied to a gaff
sail (as the main sail of a yacht), it
implies that the wind is let out of it
by *tricing up* the *tack* and *settling*
the peak. It is often done when
coming up to moorings in a breeze.

Yards are said to be scandalised
when they are not squared.

Scant (or scrimp) (of the wind).—
1. A scant wind is a head wind, in
which a vessel will barely lay her
course. It therefore usually implies
also a very light or poor wind. 2. In
general conversation the word "scant"
implies "of short dimensions".

SCANDALISED

Scantling (from "scant", a measurement).—The dimensions of
any timber when reduced to its standard size. In shipbuilding the
scantling implies the measurement, or, more properly, the *proportion*
of the various constructive parts. A vessel is said to have *good
scantlings* when her timbers and all other parts of her are of such
dimensions as shall render her powerful and seaworthy. It need not
necessarily mean that these are very large, but that they are large
enough, and especially so proportioned, one to the strength of the
other, that they will all strain equally together.

Scarf.—A precipitous steep.

Scarfing or *Scarphing.*—The joining together of two timbers, by
sloping off the ends of each and fastening them together, so that they
make one beam of uniform size throughout.

Scarfed.—An old term for "decorated or dressed with flags".

Scaw.—A jutting point of land.

Scend.—An abbreviation of "ascend", as when a boat lifts herself
up to waves. It is, therefore, the contrary to the *pitch,* which is the
plunging of her head down; but in ordinary language a vessel is
always said to *pitch* in a heavy sea, the word "scend" being used to
describe only the upward movement.

Schooner.—There were two rigs of schooners common to our
waters: the first mostly applied to traders, the second more particularly to yachts: both had two masts, fore and main.

The merchant schooner, commonly a *top-sail* schooner, carried a
square top sail, sometimes *double* (*which see*) on the foremast, the
main mast being fore-and-aft rigged.

The schooner yacht is occasionally square rigged in so far as that
she may carry a square fore-topsail; but more often she is fore-and-aft
rigged on both masts. Schooner yachts were at one time extremely
popular, and the first competitors for the Americas Cup were of this
class; but the cutter and sloop have entirely superseded them in racing.

JACKASS   BARKENTINE

TOPSAIL SCHOONER   SCHOONER YACHTS

There is also another class of schooner, with three masts, each being fore-and-aft rigged. This is called the *three-masted schooner*. When it sets square sails on the foremast it is sometimes called *jackass* rigged. But the *jackass* rig must not be confounded with the barkentine, which, at a distance, it resembles; the barkentine having a *brig-foremast*, while the three-masted schooner has a schooner foremast.

Besides these there is also a beautiful class of schooner, having four masts, all fore-and-aft rigged. These vessels hail mostly from America. They were swift and close-winded.

Schooner mast or schooner *fore-mast.*—This is spoken of in contradistinction to the *brig-mast*. The schooner foremast is composed of two parts only, the lower and the top mast. The brig, on the other hand, has lower, top, and top-gallant masts, and this constitutes the difference between the schooner and the brigantine, and between the three-masted schooner and the barkentine. A two-masted vessel with a brig-foremast is either a brig or a brigantine; with a schooner foremast, a schooner. In like manner a three-masted vessel (setting square sails on the foremast only) is a barkentine if she have a brig-foremast, and a three-masted schooner if she have a schooner foremast. (*See* fig.; also BRIG and BRIGANTINE.)

Schuyt, or *eel schuyt* (pronounced "scoot").—A Dutch vessel, of one or two masts, employed in the eel trade between Holland and London. These vessels had those peculiar characteristics which mark the Dutch from other craft, and may for general purposes be included under the broad term "Dutchmen". (*See* fig.)

SCHUYT

Scoot.—A Dutch vessel.—(*See* SCHUYT.)

To *scoot* (slang)—to get out of the way.

Score.—The groove on the shell of a block which admits of the strop being tightened so that it will not move. (*See* BLOCK.)

Scope.—The length of cable by which a vessel is anchored.

Scotch.—To be *scotched up* is to be supported, as a boat may be when propped or "scotched up" against a quay by timber shores or legs.

Scotchman.—"A piece of stiff hide, or batten of wood, placed over the backstays fore-swifter of the shrouds, etc., so as to secure the standing rigging from being chafed. Perhaps so called from the skotch or notch where the seizing is passed." (Smyth.)

Scow.—1. "A large flat-bottomed boat, used either as a lighter or for ferrying. 2. In old Naval works the *scroll* is thus written. (*See* SCROLL.)

Scow banker.—A manager of a scow; also a contemptuous term for a lubberly fellow." (Smyth.)

Scrabble.—"A badly written log."

Scran Bag.—A bag, or compartment, in which articles of clothing left lying about were impounded.

Scratch.—1. The line from which a race is supposed to start. And in a handicap where the various competitors are given more or less start, the one who has no start is called the scratch man or *scratch*. 2. In another sense, a *scratch race* is one in which the crews are brought together by lot or without previous training together. It is, therefore, often understood to mean a race got up at short notice.

Screw.—*Screw bolts* or *screw eyes*.—Bolts which have an eye at the head and screw into the deck or elsewhere. In sailing boats they are very frequent, sometimes taking the place of *shroud plates,* sometimes acting as *fair leads,* etc.

SCREW EYES

Screw stretcher and *screw tightener*.—(See SET-SCREW.)

Screw propeller.—The propeller of a screw steam vessel.

Screw well.—An aperture into which a screw propeller may be lifted when connecting or disconnecting it.

Scrimp.—The same as *scant* (*which see*).

Scroll, or **scroll-head** (in old Naval works written "scrow").—A curved timber at the head of a ship by way of ornament. It is mostly seen in old vessels, but occasionally on schooner yachts.

Scud.—To run before the wind. It is usually, but not necessarily, understood to mean before a high wind.

To *scud under bare poles*.— To run before the wind without any sail set, the masts, yards, and rigging of a ship being sufficient to keep way on her, even in a moderate breeze. Vessels may occasionally be seen scudding to an anchorage in large estuaries, such as that of the Thames. That the practice

SCUDDING

is ancient is certain, for St. Luke speaks of it. (*See* under STRIKE.)

Scud.—Low, misty cloud, flying quickly.

Scud like a mudian.—An expression hurrying someone off—"Be off quickly"; the mudian rig of vessel being very fast. (*See* MUDIAN.)

Scull.—With rowing men, to scull is to row with two oars called sculls. (*See* under OAR.)

Single sculling.—Sculling by only one person.

Double sculling.—Two persons sculling; a plan very popular on the Upper Thames, and very much quicker than "pair oar" rowing. On rare occasions eight scullers are put in a boat and are found to "walk away" from eight-oared boats; but the plan is not common.

2. Sculling, is also performed with only one oar used at the stern of the boat, the sculler mostly standing to do his work, the blade of the oar being continuously in the water and moved transversely.

Scuppers.—Openings in the bulwarks of a ship to carry off deck water. They are usually fitted with swinging flaps or doors, some are mere holes cut in the waterways, which holes are often fitted with small pipes called *scupper hose* or *scupper shoots*—or if with leather valves the valves are called *scupper leathers*.

Scurvy.—An illness caused by deficiency of Vitamin C due to lack of fruit, or fresh vegetables, and once very prevalent on deep-sea ships.

Scuttle.—To sink, or founder. The meaning of the word scuttle is "a hole cut". Thus an opening in a vessel's sides or deck, whether to admit light or to allow of persons descending through it, is a scuttle;

as the "fore-scuttle", which is the name given to the forecastle hatchway when that consists of a mere opening in the deck without hood or companion.

To *scuttle a ship* is to cut a hole in her, below the water line, so as to sink her; and in the same sense to scuttle a deck, or any other part, is to cut an aperture in it.

To *scuttle down* is to close and, if necessary, batten down the scuttles.

A *scuttle butt* is a large butt (carried by vessels on deck and containing the water required for the constant use of the ship) into the top of which a hole, or "scuttle", is cut large enough to admit of a pail being lowered through it.

Sea. — "The sea was called *saivs* from a root *si* or *siv*, the Greek *sêiõ*, to shake; it meant the tossed-about water in contradistinction to stagnant or running water." (Max Müller.)

The *high seas* are that part of the ocean beyond the (three mile) limit over which the Government of a country claims jurisdiction.

The word sea is often used to describe the condition of the surface of the water, as a *heavy* sea when the waves are large, a *long* sea when there is a considerable distance between them, a *short* or *choppy* sea when they follow closely one upon the other, a *cross* sea when, in consequence of a change of wind or a run of tide, the waves meet each other from different directions. A single wave is often called a sea, and in the plural, the *seas* may mean the waves.

Sea anchor. — (*See* DROGUE.)

Sea board. — The sea shore.

Sea boat. — A ship's boat kept ready for immediate launching. Sometimes called *Accident boat*. A good sea boat generally means a boat which conducts herself well at sea: a bad sea boat one which sails all awash.

Sea borne. — Carried by sea. Brought from over the sea: as sea-borne coal, which comes round the coast by ship.

Sea breeze. — Wind from the sea which blows towards the land.

Sea cock. — A valve in a vessel's bottom which can be opened to allow the entry of water.

Sea craft or *scarf* (in shipbuilding), the scarfed strakes, called the *clamps.* (*See* next page.)

Sea devil. — 1. The fish known as the *angler,* also called the *fishing frog* and *wide gab* (*Lophius piscatorius*). 2. One of the tribe *Acanthopterygii.*

Sea dog. — The seal. 2. An old and experienced seaman.

Sea egg. — The sea-urchin; one of the *Echinodermata.*

Seafarer. — One who earns his living by service at sea, who "follows the sea".

Sea fardinger. — A name for a seaman.

Sea fret. — Morning mist.

Sea gate, or *gait.* — "A rolling swell: when two ships are thrown aboard one another by its means, they are said to be in a sea-gate." (Smyth.)

Sea girdles.—The common name for the seaweed *Laminaria digitata.*

Sea-going.—A sea-going vessel is one designed for sea work in contradistinction to one built for river or canal navigation. Hence we speak of sea-going barges, because there are various sorts of barges, not all of them sea-going.

Sea gull.—A term applied to any of the large family of Gulls, which are very common at sea and near the shore.

Sea hog.—The porpoise.

Sea holly.—"A harsh spiny-leaved seaside plant."

Sea horse.—The small fish hippocampus, the head of which resembles that of a horse: also the walrus.

Sea jelly.—A name for the *medusæ.*

Sea lawyer.—"An idle litigious long-shorer, more given to question orders than to obey them." (Smyth.) This gentleman is not a stranger a long way from shore.

Sea legs.—To have got one's sea-legs is to be able to move about the ship when she is rolling or pitching heavily.

Sea lion.—A large seal with shaggy mane.

Seamark.—A beacon erected in shallow water to be an aid to navigation.

Sea mew.—Another name for the *sea gull.*

Sea otter.—An animal the fur of which is much sought after.

Sea pie.—A dish at sea, consisting of fish, meat, and vegetables, with a layer of crust between each, from which it becomes known as a two or three decker.

Sea reach.—The reach in a river which stretches out seaward. But the term is also used as a proper name for reaches elsewhere.

Sea scarf (in shipbuilding).—A clamp or block of wood upon which some member of a vessel's frame is often fastened. (*See* diagrams under FRAME.)

Sea serpent.—A creature, "whether in earth, or fire, sea or air," which Science has not yet fully acknowledged.

Sea sickness.—A malady which, though originating at sea, receives but scant sympathy thereon.

Sea snake.—A creature belonging to the family *Hyorus* or *Hydrophis,* and distinguished from the land snake by the compression of the tail into a swimming organ. The genus exists and is even said to abound in some parts of the tropics.

Sea thongs.—One of the British seaweeds, *Éclonia buccinalis.*

Sea urchin.—The sea egg. (*See* above.)

Sea wall.—An embankment protecting reclaimed land from the sea or a river. It is kept in repair by those holding land through which it runs.

Sea way.—A navigable portion of the sea. It is also called *a fairway,* which term may answer also for the navigable channel of a river.

Seaweed.—Plants growing in sea water. Seaweed forms excellent manure, and may also be used in the building of sea walls. When thus used it is called:—

Sea-wrack.—The seaweed which is thrown up by the tide.

Sea-worthy.—Fit to go to sea.

Seam.—1. Of a sail, the stitching up of two *cloths,* which, among sail-makers, is called *pricking.* 2. In shipbuilding, the space between two planks of a vessel. Seams are *caulked* with oakum, and *payed* with pitch. The seams in the deck of a yacht are often very close together, the narrowness of the plank constituting not only a safeguard against warping but also a great beauty. For this latter reason it is often the practice, where, for economy, wide planks have been used, to make a sham seam down the middle of each. Though no fault can be found with such a method of decoration, it is well for the amateur, if he be buying a boat, to see that he is not deceived into the conclusion that narrow planks have been employed, when, in fact, they may have been but imitated.

Seaman.—A man who has been brought up to or served a certain number of years at sea. A complete seaman is called *able-bodied* and rated A.B.; one having served a less number of years, an *ordinary seaman;* one only beginning his career, a *landsman.*

Seaman's disgrace.—An old name for a foul anchor.

Seaman's pleasure.—Time spent by a seaman on shore.

Seamanship.—The practical part of working a ship; rigging her, etc.

Season.—To keep baulks of timber, or a vessel, some time in the water before making use of either.

Seat-pad.—A small piece of cloth, wool, or sheepskin, with a tape at each corner, for tying on to the thwart of a row-boat and thus making the seat less hard.

Second-hand.—On shipboard, but more particularly on small craft, such as fishing boats, the second in command (excluding the captain) is usually called the second-hand; the word "hand" meaning "man".

Section.—A drawing representing (in marine architecture) the internal parts of a vessel as if she had been cut straight down along any particular line, either longways or athwartships. In the designing of a large ship a great number of sectional drawings are made. In small craft two, with a plan, may be sufficient; one showing her cut along the line of the keel—*i.e.,* a side view of her interior, and called the *sheer plan;* the other showing her cut in half across the widest part, and called the *body plan.* And this latter one is generally so arranged that one-half shows the interior looking forward, and the other half the view looking aft. This will be better understood by a reference to the paragraph under *lines.*

Seel.—To suddenly lurch over, but quickly return to the upright.

Seize.—To secure; as to fasten two ropes, or different parts of the same rope, together, with a binding of small rope, or with yarn. The material used for binding is called the *seizing.*

Selvage, or **selvedge.**—The natural edge of any woven material, or of sail cloth.

Selvagee.—A ring of rope for fastening round a spar, so as to lift or move it.

Semaphore.—An instrument, as its name implies, (Greek *sema,* a sign, and *pherein* to bear), "carrying signs" or signals; and sometimes used at sea. In its most familiar form it is the railway signal with its post and arms. Semaphore signals can be made by a man's arms (usefully extended by hand flags) placed at angles from his body, and is a rapid system of communication within visual range.

Sennit.—A cord braided out of yarns.

Serve.—To bind up or cover anything. To serve rope, to bind it round with canvas and line; these materials being called the *service.* (*See* WORM, PARCEL, AND SERVE.)

Set.—*Set-bolts.*—Bolts used in driving others deeply into some timber.

Set a course.—To put the ship's head in a desired direction.

Set-screw, screw-stretcher, wire-stretcher, or *screw-tightener.*—An instrument consisting of a long shanked hook screwing into a frame, which may be turned round up it so as to increase or reduce the length of shank exposed. In small boats it sometimes takes the place of the *shroud tackle* (dead eyes, lanyards, etc.), and is found very convenient, as by a few turns of the frame the shroud may be rendered taut or slack. It may also be used with advantage on a *bob-stay* purchase, or with bow-sprit whiskers.

SET
SCREW

Set-flying.—A sail is said to be *set flying* when it has no stay, gaff, or yard to guide it up. And when it does go up on a stay or spar it is said to be *set standing*. Thus, in a cutter yacht, the foresail is attached by hanks to the forestay, which guides the sail up so that it cannot fly out in the wind. But the jib has no such stay to guide it; it is merely attached by its head to the halyard and by its tack to the traveller, and, being lifted, it flies about in the wind until it is hauled taut, and may, therefore, be justly said to be "set flying". (*See* fig.)

Set of the tide, or of a current.—The direction in which the tide or current flows, *i.e.,* runs up.

Set sail.—To haul up the sails preparatory to starting, synonymous with "*make sail*".

Set up.—Generally speaking, to tighten up, in contradistinction to *settle,* which is to lower. Thus, to "set up the peak" is to give the final pull, or *swig,* on it, so as

1. SET FLYING
2. SET STANDING

to bring the sail quite flat; to "set up the shrouds", to take in their slackness so that they may have the same strain as before.

Sett.—A particular spot in a river where nets are set. The word was frequently met with in Norfolk, where it was the custom for eel fishermen to locate themselves permanently in one spot. Here the eelman brought an old boat, which being converted into a house, afforded him shelter from the weather, and round it his gear might be seen hanging ready for baiting, forming a characteristic and picturesque incident in a very romantic landscape.

Settee.—A four-sided fore-and-aft sail with a very short luff and long leech.

Settle.—To lower, or to become lower. The word may be used in both senses; as "settle the peak", *i.e.,* "lower the peak"; or "the ship is settling", meaning she is lowering or becoming lower in the water, perhaps preparatory to sinking, as "she settled and sank".

Severe.—"Effectual; as, a *severe* turn on a belaying-pin."

Sewed (pronounced "sued").—A vessel aground is said to be *sewed* by as much depth as is still required to float her. Thus if she draws 12 ft and the tide leaves her in only 6 ft of water, she is sewed 6 ft.

Sextant.—The instrument used at sea for measuring the altitudes of the celestial bodies, and thereby determining the position of a ship.

Shackle.—A small U-shaped iron with the open end connected by a screw-pin. Shackles have various uses, *e.g.,* to connect lengths of chain, as in a cable; in which case the head of the screw-pin is countersunk so as to allow of the chain running free. They are also a good deal employed on the tacks or clews of sails, their principal advantage over hooks being that they cannot shake off; in a squall, however, or in any emergency, they are somewhat awkward to manipulate.

sail

Anchor

SHACKLES

When fitted to cables, shackles should be placed with the apex forward, so that the chain may pay out freely. Anchor shackle-pins are not screwed in, but tapered and slipped in, and fastened with wood or lead plugs.

A *shackle of cable*—is a length of wrought iron or forged steel studded anchor chain, 15 fathoms long. (In ships of the Royal Navy, before 1949, 12½ fathoms long.)

Shackle-crow.—A bar of iron (like a crowbar), but fitted with a shackle for drawing out bolts, etc.

Shadow building.—A term used to denote a method of building boats without regard to specially drawn plans (called "lines") or to intermediate calculations.

Shaffle.—A split collar: one of the fittings on a mast to receive its boom. (*See* GOOSENECK AND SHAFFLE.)

Shake.—To cast off or loosen, as:—To *shake out a reef.*—To let it out.

To *shake a cask.*—To take it to pieces and pack up the parts, which are then termed *shakes*. Hence the term, "No great shakes," expressing "of little value".

Shake in the wind.—A sail shakes or *shivers* when a vessel is brought head to wind; and this is sometimes called a *tell-tale* shake.

Shakes (in shipbuilding).—Cracks or rents in a timber.

"*Shaking a cloth in the wind.*"—In galley parlance, means "slightly intoxicated".

To *shake out a reef.*—To loose the reef points and re-set the sail.

Shallop.—1. A small, light vessel, schooner or lugged rigged, used for fishing or as a tender to large vessels.

2. A smaller ship's boat, rowed by one or two men.

Shanghaied.—Shipped on board against one's will.

Shank (of an anchor).—The main shaft. (*See* ANCHOR.)

Shank painter.—A rope which holds the shank of an anchor while on deck.

Shank of a hook.—That part above the bent portion.

Shanty.—(*See* CHANTY.)

Shape.—A verb used in connection with the course, e.g. to *shape a course* to reach harbour.

Sheave.—The wheel in a block; and sometimes in a spar, such as the bowsprit of a small yacht. (*See* note under BLOCK).

Sheave hole.—The hole in which the sheave runs.

Sheepshank.—A method of shortening a rope without cutting it or loosening its ends. (*See* under KNOTS.)

Sheer.—The word may be synonymous with "mere"; as "a sheer hulk" in the sense of a "hulk merely". (*See* HULK.)

In shipbuilding, the *sheer* is the straight or curved line which the deck line of a vessel makes when viewed from the side. When straight, she is said to have a straight sheer.

The *sheer-plan* is the drawing in which the sheer is delineated. It is a longitudinal section through the keel, and shows the position of every point with regard to its position fore and aft, as well as its height above the keel. (*See* LINES.)

Sheer battens are long rods used in shipbuilding to mark off the position of the planks called bends or wales before they are bolted on.

Sheer pole.—An iron bar lashed to the lower eyes of the lower rigging to prevent the deadeyes or screws from turning.

The *sheer strake* is the strake immediately below the sheer line. In ships it is often of thicker planking than the other strakes. (*See* diagrams under FRAME.)

To *sheer* or *sheer off* (in sailing), to bear away from.

2. *Sheers* are long beams or legs forming a sort of crane, used for lifting heavy weights into vessels or on to quays, etc. The apparatus is sometimes set up on old hulls, for dockyard use, pier building, etc.; these hulls being then called *sheer hulls* or *hulks.* (*See* HULK.)

Sheet.—The rope attached to a sail so that it may be *worked,* that is, let out or hauled in as occasion may require. Sheets take their names from the sails they work, as the *main sheet,* working the mainsail; the *jib sheets,* working the jib, etc.; and they will, accordingly, be found described under their specific headings. To *rally out* a sheet is to let it run out. To *overhaul* it is the same. When a vessel is close-hauled with sheets brought in and belayed, they are said to be *sheeted home*. In a ship, the ropes attached to *both* clews of those square sails which are above the courses are called sheets; in the courses (lower square sails) only the aftermost of these ropes is the sheet, the weathermost being called the tack. In poetry, we often find the word "sheet" used to designate a sail, as in the line, "the fresh breeze meets her dinghy sheets." This, of course, is often licence, taken for the sake of rhyme; and if the poet is to be excused for straining after rhyme, it must be passed over as such.

Three sheets in the wind.—A grade in drunkenness, verging on the incapable.

Sheet anchor.—The most powerful anchor carried by a ship, and popularly supposed to be used only as a last resource, in which sense the term is frequently used in general conversation.

Sheet clip (or *sheet slip*).—An instrument, the principal agent in which is a sort of drop pawl, by which sheets may be held, while necessary, and instantly released. They are of great use in single-handed sailing, and in small boats may often be used to hold the main sheet. (Illustrated under CLIP.)

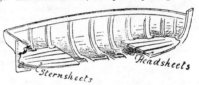

HEAD AND STERN-SHEETS

2. *Head-sheets, stern-sheets* (in open boats).—The floor-boards covering the space either at the head or the stern of the boat. (*See* fig.)

Shelf (in shipbuilding).—A longitudinal timber within the ribs of a vessel. (*See* diagram under FRAME.)

Shell.—1. A popular term for the remnant of a vessel after she has been completely stripped.

2. *Of a block.*—The outer casing of a block is its shell.

3. *Among rowing men,* and especially among journalistic litterateurs, a *wager boat,* or best racing boat, is sometimes called a shell.

Shellback.—An experienced sailor.

Shelve.—To slop down rapidly, as a shelving beach, which is a very steep beach.

Shifting.—*Shifting backstays.*—Those of the backstays of a vessel which may be shifted over from side to side when she goes about on another tack, and from which, therefore, may be derived the origin of the terms *in stays, missing stays, slack in stays,* etc. (*See* under BACKSTAYS and TACK.)

Shifting boards.—Boards erected in a wall in a ship's hold to prevent the movement of bulk cargo, such as grain, or ballast when the ship is rolling.

Shifting sands.—Such banks of sand as are soft and liable to alter their form. Also *quick-sands.*

Ship.—In general, a sea-going vessel, larger and distinct from a *boat*. In the last days of sail, a ship was a three-masted vessel, square-rigged on all three masts; a very few 4-masted ships were built, and one 5-masted ship, the *Preussen* built in 1902, was 408 ft long and had 47 sails with a total area of 50 000 sq ft. The largest sailing ship ever built was *France II*, 1911 (a five-masted barque) of 8 000 tons deadweight. Immensely larger ships have since been built, of course. The liner *Queen Elizabeth*, launched in 1938, was 82 998 gross tons, and a tanker of 484 000 tons was launched in 1976 in Japan, where others of 800 000 tons are proposed to be built.

To *ship*.—To put a thing into its proper position for working, as "to ship oars", to put them into the rowlocks preparatory to rowing. "To ship the rudder", to hang it ready for use, etc. And if to ship is to put a thing in working position, then to *unship* is to take it off. Thus to "unship oars" is to take them out of the rowlocks, and to "unship the rudder" to unhinge it. From this it will be seen that to *ship* is not *necessarily* to bring within the ship, but in most cases it is so, as to *ship a cargo*; to *ship hands* (men); to *ship stores*, etc., which is to take them on board.

To *ship a sea*.—To be overtaken by a wave, or to plunge into it so that it comes into or over the ship.

Ship breaker.—One who breaks up old or unserviceable vessels.

Ship broker.—One whose business is to buy or sell vessels.

2. An intermediary between a shipowner and a shipper of cargo.

3. One who acts as a ship's agent.

Ship chandler.—A tradesman dealing in ship's stores and equipment.

Ship's Company.—All the personnel of a man-of-war other than her officers.

Shipmate.—One who serves, or has served, in the same ship as another.

Shipshape.—Seamanlike in appearance.

Shipwright.—A man skilled in the repairing or building of ships.

Shoal.—1. Shallow. 2. A shoal is a shallow place.

Shoot the sun.—To obtain the angle between the sun and the horizon, by means of a sextant.

Shore.—The margin of the sea, or of a river. (*See* FORESHORE.) Those living close to the shore are called "shoresmen", to distinguish them from those living inland. So also a *shore raker* is a man who hangs about by the waterside. (*See* LOAFER.)

2. *Shores.*—Props placed under a vessel while building or in a dry dock, or it may be to keep a vessel upright when she is aground. She is then said to be *shored up*.

Shorten in.—To heave in the anchor cable preparatory to weighing it.

Shorten sail.—To take in sail.

Shot.—An additional cable's length. (*See* CABLE.) In fishing;

the nets which are put out at one time; also the catch which is hauled in.

Shot in the locker.—An old expression signifying money in one's pocket. The old motto is "Never say die whilst there's a shot in the locker".

Show a leg.—An exclamation meaning "Show that you are in earnest", or otherwise "Look sharp"! The term is derived from the old saying that if a man showed a leg out of his bunk it might reasonably be considered that he was about to rise.

Shrouds.—Strong ropes supporting a mast laterally; they are now almost always of wire rope. They take their names from the spars they support, as the *main* or *mizzen* shrouds, the *topmast shrouds*, the *bowsprit shrouds*, etc. In large vessels they are connected by small ropes to form ladders; these ropes being called *ratlines* or *rattlings* (*which see*). The shrouds of fore-and-aft rigged masts are fitted in the following manner:—One piece of wire rope is doubled so as to form two legs. A little below the bend these parts are seized together, forming what is called a *collar, i.e.,* a loop; and this collar being passed over the head of the mast, both legs come down on the same side of the vessel. Or if there be only one shroud, an *eye splice* is made at the upper end, which is passed over the mast in the same way. But the shrouds of large square rigged masts are not fitted in this manner. These communicate singly with a strong *spider hoop* beneath the mast-head,

COLLAR

EYE

TURNED IN

SHROUDS

and thence extend downwards to the sides of the vessel. And for small boats, or in case of having to rig up shrouds temporarily, a very simple method is employed by the fishermen. It consists in taking two ropes of sufficient length to span the boat from the mast-head; making a simple overhand knot in the middle of one; passing the other through it, thereby making a sort of slip knot of the two; and passing the loop thus made over the mast head (or if that cannot be done the loop is made round the mast head) in the manner illustrated under KNOT. At the end of each leg of the shrouds a *dead-eye* is turned in; and a *lanyard* (a small rope) passing through this dead-eye and another fellow to it on the *channel plate* allows the shrouds to be tightened (or *set up,* as it is technically termed) on each side. The dead-eyes are blind blocks—*i.e.,* they have no sheaves, and for this reason the lanyards are less liable to slip through them. In rigging them it is customary to pass the lanyard through one of the eyes and, by making a stopper knot at the end of the rope, thus prevent it from slipping through. The other end of the lanyard may then be reeved through the holes in both dead-eyes and the shroud "set up". (*See* DEAD-EYES.) The length of shroud from the dead-eyes on one side, over the mast and to the dead-eyes on the other side, is called *the span of the rigging.*

Such are the shrouds of a lower mast; others are fitted somewhat differently, as will be seen:—*Topmast shrouds.*—1. One a fore-and-aft rigged mast, or one carrying only one topmast, such as the main mast of a cutter or the mizzen of a schooner, etc., the shroud is passed over the head of the topmast and extended by means of a *cross-tree,* shortly below which it terminates; being then taken up by another length, or by a tackle with ropes called the *legs.* The reason for this is that when the topmast is lowered its shrouds may only just reach to the deck. For were they so long as to do this when the mast was up, they would be greatly in the way when it came down; whereas, the shrouds being short and the legs movable, these latter can be disconnected and stowed away when the mast is lowered. 2. On masts which carry more than one topmast, as the fore and main masts of a bark or a brig—in other words, on a brig mast—the method above described is impossible, for even if practicable, the cross-trees and side gear would prevent the yards of the square sails from traversing about the mast. Another system is, therefore, necessary, and it is carried out as follows:—Each mast head is furnished with a large plate of iron called the *futtock-plate,* to which, by smaller plates, dead-eyes are attached; and the shrouds which come down from the top-mast head also have dead-eyes, so that they may be set up in the same way as those of the lower mast.

Bowsprit shrouds are the ropes (usually of wire) which give lateral support to the bowsprit just as mast shrouds do to a mast. They are attached to a ring called the *cranse-iron* at the end of the bowsprit, and being taken up by tackles (like the legs of topmast shrouds) may be set up from the bow of the vessel. In small craft they are often attached to the bow by a *set-screw* or *screw-tightener* (*which see*) which, by being turned one way or the other, either tightens or slackens them.

Shroud knot.—A means of joining a parted hemp shroud. The ends are married and a wall knot then formed in each three strands.

Shroud plates, or *shroud irons.*—Irons fitted to the sides of small boats to take the shroud tackles. They take the place of the *channel plates* of larger craft. (*See* CHANNELS.)

Sick bay.—The place set apart in a ship for the treatment of sick and wounded.

Side.—*Side fishes.*—In a made mast, the convex pieces which form the rounded sides of the mast; to *fish* being to secure one piece of wood over another, usually for strengthening it.

Side lights.—The red and green lights displayed on the port and starboard sides respectively, and visible from right ahead to two points abaft the beam, of a vessel when underway at night.

Side kelsons, or sister kelsons (in ship-building).—Side timbers forming kelsons beside the actual kelson, for extra strength. (*See* under FRAME.)

Sight.—An observation of the sun, or other heavenly body, which will give a line of position.

Signals.—Communication between ships at sea and between ship and shore may be carried out by means of signals made by flags and shapes; lights; sound; semaphore; and radio.

Flag signals are made by hoisting from one to four flags as one *"hoist"*. The appropriate flags to be hoisted can be found in the *International Code Signal Book* (*see* INTERNATIONAL CODE). This signal book is issued in seven languages, so that, for instance, a Japanese vessel wishing to communicate with a Spanish vessel would look out the appropriate flags against Japanese wording, and the Spanish vessel would take out the meaning in Spanish wording.

Shapes are employed chiefly to denote the state of a vessel, e.g. whether she is fishing, at anchor, not under command, etc. On shore they are used for storm signals and for regulating traffic at harbour entrances, etc.

Lights.—Fixed lights are used to indicate the type of vessel displaying them, and the general direction in which they are heading. (*See* LIGHTS.) Intermittent lights which flash at different intervals and in different groups of flashes serve to identify different lighthouses, lightvessels, and buoys. Signal lamps are used to flash signals by *morse code* (*which see*), using either plain language or *International Code* groups of letters.

Sound signals are made with compressed-air or steam whistles or sirens, and are best confined to those presented by the *Regulations for Preventing Collision at Sea* and the Single Letter signals of the *International Code.*

Semaphore (*which see*), today confined to plain language messages made with hand-flags is effective over short distances.

Radio, on the contrary, has an enormous range, and signals can be made by using morse to send plain-language or coded messages by radio telegraphy (W/T), or by voice on radio telephone (R/T).

Distress Signals.—*The Regulations for Preventing Collisions at Sea* provide a large variety of Distress Signals, no doubt that any vessel in distress should be able to make *some* sort of recognisable signal of distress.

(*a*) A gun or other explosive signal fired at intervals of about one minute.

(*b*) A continuous sounding of any fog-signal apparatus. (But SOS made on the fog-signal apparatus would be more likely to attract attention.)

(*c*) Rockets or shells, throwing *red* stars fired one at a time at short intervals.

(*d*) A signal made by radio telegraphy or by any other signalling method consisting of the group SOS in the Morse Code.

(*e*) A signal sent by radiotelephony consisting of the spoken word "Mayday" (corresponding to the French pronunciation of the expression *m'aidez, i.e.* "help me").

(*f*) The International Code Signal of distress indicated by NC.

(*g*) A signal consisting of a square flag having above it a ball or anything resembling a ball.

(*h*) Flames on the vessel (as from a burning tar barrel, oil barrel, etc.) (Specially manufactured *red* distress flares are more likely to attract attention.)

(*i*) A rocket parachute flare showing a *red* light.

(*j*) A smoke signal giving off a volume of orange-coloured smoke.

(*k*) Slowly and repeatedly raising and lowering the arms out-stretched to each side.

An ensign hoisted upside down is an unofficial but widely under-stood distress signal.

Fog signals.—When underway engine-driven vessels blow one blast every 2 minutes, but if stationary, 2 blasts in succession every 2 minutes. Sailing vessels and vessels fishing or unable to manoeuvre freely sound three blasts in succession, namely one long blast followed by 2 short blasts every 2 minutes. A vessel at anchor shall at intervals of not more than 1 minute ring the bell rapidly for about 5 seconds, and, if of 100 metres or more in length, immediately after the ringing of the bell, beat a gong in the after part of the vessel.

Manoeuvring signals.—Engine-driven vessels may make the follow-ing signals: One short blast to mean "I am altering my course to starboard". Two short blasts to mean "I am altering my course to port". Three short blasts to mean "I am operating astern pro-pulsion". A vessel in doubt whether sufficient action is being taken by another to avoid collision may give at least 5 short and rapid blasts. All the above sound signals may be supplemented by using a light to make a similar number of flashes.

The Regulations for Preventing Collisions at Sea give more and fuller information about such signals.

Pilot Signals.—The International Codes provides the following signals for "I want a pilot". The letter G made either by flag, flashing light or sound; or a blue light, every 15 minutes; or a white light, shown at short intervals above the bulwarks for about a minute at a time. A pilot vessel on her station flies flag H, or a white and red flag divided horizontally.

Port Signals.—Many ports have their own code of signals for regulating the traffic in their area. It is always advisable to make sure about this matter when approaching a strange port. The careful navigator will study this matter before he arrives off the port; Brown's, Reed's, or the Macmillan and Silk Cut *Nautical Almanacs* contain such details.

Storm Signals are shown on the coasts of most maritime nations when gales are expected. On British coasts a *black cone* is usual. This is hoisted *point upwards* when a gale is expected from a N'ly point; that is from NW round by N to E. The cone *point downwards* means that a gale is probable, at first from the southward; that is from SE round by S to W. When the direction of the gale is expected to change from one side of the east–west line to the other, the cone is reversed.

At dusk, whenever a signal ought to be flying if it were daylight, a *night signal* consisting of three lanterns hung on a triangular frame, will be hoisted in place of the cone, point downwards (for south cone) or point upwards (for north cone) as the case may be.

Signal halyard.—The halyard used to elevate signals, burgees, or any other flags to a mast or topmast head. It is a thin rope rove through a small sheave hole in the *truck,* and in yachts, etc., is usually tied to the shrouds, a *clove-hitch* being a quick and secure knot to employ in fastening it. (*See* KNOTS.) By the *flag* halyard is generally understood (in fore-and-aft rig) that halyard which takes a flag (usually the ensign) up to the peak, and often called the *peak line.* (*See* under PEAK.)

Signal Letters.—Four letters allotted to a vessel for indicating her name and port of registry by International Code.

Silent deaths.—A name given by fishermen to screw steam vessels, and possibly not altogether without reason. Those who have found themselves accidentally in too close proximity to large steamers, more especially towards night, will appreciate the full meaning of the term, and will have discovered how silently these huge vessels creep along.

Single-banked.—Said of boats that pull one oar at each thwart, and of an oar pulled by one man.

Single up.—To take in all mooring lines except the minimum, preparatory to leaving a berth.

Siren.—A class of steam whistle with an undulating note.

Sister-ship.—A vessel built to the same plan.

Sixteen bells.—Eight double strokes of the ship's bell struck at midnight when the new year comes in: eight bells for the old and eight for the new year.

Skeg.—A short length of keel extending aft as a protection to the rudder.

Skerry.—A rocky islet or reef.

Skids.—Wedges or supports which fit under a vessel when launching. Athwartship beams upon which a boat is stowed.

Skiff.—An open boat usually employed for pleasure. It varies in form according to locality; thus on the Upper Thames, the long light-built pleasure boats with pointed stems and extending sides are called skiffs, to distinguish them from the gigs, of the same district, which are heavier and built with a straight sheer and upright stem. Lower down,

UPPER THAMES SKIFF

SEASIDE SKIFF

OYSTER SKIFF

on the same river, the gig, or something like it, becomes the skiff, while certain sailing boats go by the same name, and in commerce, an *oyster skiff* may become almost a fishing smack. The name is only another form of the word "ship".

Oyster skiff.—A boat used in the oyster fisheries of the Essex rivers, and occasionally elsewhere. (*See* under Tow-hauling.)

Skimming dish.—A slang name sometimes given to the modern form of racing boat which, depending for its stability upon its centre-board, is so designed as to lie almost entirely on the surface of the water.

SKIMMING DISH

Skin.—The skin of a vessel is the planking which covers her ribs. Where the planking is double, the *inner layer* is called the skin, the outer being the *case*.

Skipper.—The master of a merchant vessel; called, by courtesy, captain, on shore, and always so at sea. The man employed as captain in a yacht is also called the skipper.

Skirts (of a sail).—The main body of the sail. Thus a sail brailed up is sometimes said to "be gathered up by the skirts". (*See* Brail.)

Sky.—*Skylight.*—A framework of wood, often glazed and made to open, admitting light and air into the cabin of a vessel.

Sky sail.—The highest sail ordinarily set on a ship, though there can be others above it. It is only used in light winds, one on each mast, and the ship is then said to be "flying her kites". (*See* Light Sails.)

Slack.—*Loose or slow.*—The slack of a rope is the loose part of it.

Slack in stays.—A vessel is thus described when she is slow in coming round from one tack to another. (*See* Tack.)

Slack tide, or *slack water.*—That condition of the tide when it is nearly stationary. When it approaches its full it becomes slack and remains so until a short time after its turn. Likewise, but in a lesser degree, when it nears its lowest ebb it slackens, and remains slack until the full force of the incoming flood is felt. At the moment of its highest and lowest points, it becomes theoretically stationary.

Slammer.—A slang term meaning a very heavy squall.

Slant.—A favourable wind for sailing a desired course.

Slatting.—A term applied to the sails when they are alternately *filling*, and *spilling* the wind; as occurs when a vessel is rolling heavily during a calm.

Slew.—To swing round rapidly. Spoken sometimes of a boat under sail, if allowed to turn her head suddenly round to the wind.

Sliding.—*Sliding gunter.*—A short pole for extending a sail upon a pole-mast. It takes the place of a gaff and slides up and down the upper end of the mast, thereby reducing or increasing sail as may be required. In theory this principle is undeniably good; but for pleasure boats the practice has not become general, though at one time it was much used in the Royal Navy.

Sliding keel.—The old name for a *centre keel* (*which see*).

Sliding seats (in rowing).—Movable seats used in light racing boats to enable the rowers to increase the length of their stroke. They may either run on metal or glass bearers or be carried on rollers, the latter method being now usually the favourite. It has been said that racing records since the introduction of sliding seats have failed to prove their superiority over the fixed seats. This, however,

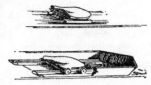

SLIDING SEATS

is a mistake: records are becoming lessened year by year; and though the best times made on fixed seats may not appear to be so very far behind those of to-day, it must be remembered that a matter of a few seconds often means a considerable distance when boats are travelling through the water at racing speed; while in comparing old records with those of to-day, conditions of wind, tide, and weather are too often left out of consideration.

Sliding ways.—In shipbuilding, the baulks upon which a vessel slides into the water when launched.

Sling.—1. In square rig, the sling of a yard is the middle point. (*See* YARD.) 2. In fore-and-aft rig, a rope passed under anything to go it support or lift it by. An instance may be given:—It is the practice in yachts to put sail covers over such sails as cannot be readily bent and unbent, when the boat has been out and may be required again shortly. Thus the mainsail is lowered, furled and covered with the cloth, which is also laid over the gaff. But to do this the peak halyards must be

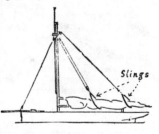

Slings

removed, or otherwise the cover could not be taken over the gaff. The blocks are, therefore, unhooked, and when the cloth is passed over they are attached to *slings* which pass under the boom and over the cover (see fig.). 3. The *topping lift* in some sailing boats, the "Una" more particularly, and in those carrying lug sails is sometimes called the sling.

Sling your hook.—A slang expression, meaning "Be off!".

Slip.—To let go a thing purposely, as to "slip the anchor"—that is, to let it go from the ship.

Slips.—In shipbuilding, the inclined plane upon which a vessel is built or repaired, the slope of which enables her to be "slipped" into the water when finished.

Slip stoppers.—*Slips* or *stoppers,* on shipboard, are ropes used in letting go the lashings of a large anchor.

Slipped his cable.—Died.

Slippery hitch, or *Snowball hitch.*—A hitch that will slip under strain.

Sloop (Dutch, *sloep*; French, *chaloupe*).—"A vessel with one mast like a cutter; but having a *jib stay,* which a cutter has not." This definition, which gives the foundation of the difference between the cutter and the sloop, necessitates that the bowsprit of the latter, if she has a bowsprit, be a standing (or fixed) one, and not, as in the cutter, a reeving one— *i.e.,* one ready at any time to be drawn inboard: for in the sloop, the jib-stay takes the place of the cutter's forestay in giving permanent support to the mast, which it could not do were it liable to be shifted in or out with the bowsprit. The structural difference between the two is, therefore, in the fixing of the bowsprit, while the result of this difference is seen in the arrangement of the head sails. In the cutter, the forestay is attached to the stem-head, and the foresail runs on this stay, the jib being set flying—that is, without a stay at all. In the sloop, on the other hand, the fore-stay (now called the jib-stay) is fixed to the nose of the bowsprit, and the jib is hoisted on this stay; and it is generally made sufficiently large to do entirely away with the foresail. It may possibly be said that this large sail has as much right to be called a foresail as a jib, and so, perhaps, from a certain point of view, it has. But a jib, in the usual acceptation of the meaning, is a sail run out on a boom at the head of a vessel, irrespective of the manner in which it is set; and as the sail in question answers to that meaning, it is properly called a jib. Moreover (though it is not customary), the sloop may have the two head sails common to the cutter, the jib-stay still remaining, and in such a case the confusion entailed by changing the names of sails would be very great. It will be understood from the above that the bowsprit of the sloop is usually shorter than that of the cutter; and, indeed, in some cases, it is so short as to become little more than a *bumpkin* or *jigger,* and today, is frequently not fitted at all.

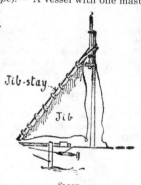

SLOOP

The Americans have a method of fitting some of their racing yachts with a short fixed bowsprit, over which is run out a sort of jib-boom. The fore-stay is carried to the head of the short bowsprit: this enables the size of the foresail to be greatly increased, while a jib is also set on the jib-boom. They call this *sloop rig,* and obtain very successful results with it.

Further reference to the differences existing between the cutter and the sloop will be found under the heading CUTTER, under which they are also illustrated.

The sloop rig is very usual on the Norfolk broads. It is very handy in single-handed sailing, and may be applied to craft of almost any size.

Sloop of war (old Naval term).—The general name at one time given to ships of war below the size of corvettes and above that of brigs. The term is still in use for a certain class of war vessels.

Slops.—"A name given to ready-made clothes, and other furnishings, for seamen, by Maydman, in 1691. In Chaucer's time, *sloppe* meant a sort of breeches. In a manuscript account of the wardrobe of Queen Elizabeth, is an order to John Fortescue for the delivery of some Naples fustian for 'Sloppe for Jack Green, our Foole'." (Smyth.)

Slot.—A groove or hole for a pin.

Sludge.—Mud deposited by a stream.

Slue.—(*See* SLEW.)

Slush bucket.—On ship board, the bucket containing the grease for the masts, etc.

Smack.—The name given indiscriminately to any sort of fishing vessel. But the fishermen distinguish between a smack and a *boat,* the smack being considerably the larger of the two and engaged exclusively in trawling. It is wholly decked, and often supplied with a steam engine for getting in the trawl, whereas the boat is often (though of perhaps from 20 to 40 tons burden) only half decked. The finest smacks in the world sailed out of Grimsby, Yarmouth and Lowestoft, and some from Brixham. Formerly a boat for mercantile or passenger service was

SMACKS

BOATS

called a smack, even though as high as 200 tons burden.

Smack smooth.—An expression signifying that nothing stands above the deck; or that everything has been carried away, leaving the decks absolutely bare.

Smart money.—The name given to the pensions of wounded men—calculated according to their rank.

Smart tackle.—An expression used by sailors for the necessary certificates to enable a man to obtain smart money.

Smelling the ground.—Said of a vessel when she is in very shallow water.

Smoke-stack.—The funnel and its pipes, on a steam vessel.

Snaffle, or **shaffle.**—A collar with open ends: one of the fittings of a boom to its mast. (*See* GOOSENECK AND SHAFFLE.)

Snag.—A submerged obstacle.

Snaking.—Much the same as *worming*, only usually done with larger stuff, as with a small line round a rope. It is said that the backstays of the ship "Shannon", when she engaged the "Chesapeake", were snaked with half-inch rope to prevent their falling asunder if shot away.

Snarled-up.—Entangled.

Snarley-yow.—A discontented person.

Snarl-knot.—A knot which cannot be drawn loose.

Snatch.—Any guide or block for a rope to pass through, so as to alter its direction.

Snatch block.—An iron block of one sheave which is fitted so that a rope can be slipped into it without passing the end through. (*See* BLOCK.)

Dumb snatch.—A snatch in which there is no sheave.

Snood.—The attachment of a fishing hook to its line; as the gut or gimp.

Snotter.—The support into which the foot of a *sprit* is placed so as to prevent it from slipping down its mast. In small boats it is usually a loop in a rope, in barges it is an iron ring. (*See* fig.; also under SPRIT.)

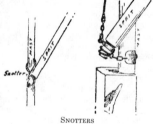

SNOTTERS

Snotty.—A nickname for a midshipman in the Royal Navy.

Snow.—"A vessel formerly much in use. It differs slightly from a brig. It has two masts similar to the main and foremasts of a ship, and close abaft the main mast is a trysail-mast. Snows differ only from brigs in that the boom mainsail is hooped to the main-mast in the brig and traverses on the trysail-mast in the snow." (Smyth.) The vessel is extinct.

Snubbing.—Bringing a vessel up suddenly with an anchor and short cable. Generally speaking, to *snub* is to check suddenly.

Snug.—Ready for a gale or for the night, etc.

Sny.—1. A diminutive *toggle,* often attached to a flag. 2. In shipbuilding, one of the timbers in the bow of the vessel. Also a slight upward curve in a piece of timber.

Soak.—A boat is said to soak up or down on

the tide when, in making her way across the tide, she is carried up or down with it.

Sod-bank.—A phenomenon sometimes seen in calm water. A multiplication of objects by refraction.

Soft plank.—An easy berth on board a ship.

Soft-tack.—Bread.

Soldier's wind.—A wind which serves either way—therefore, a side wind. It is undoubtedly so called because when a vessel is once under way with such a wind—there being no tacking required—even a soldier can sail her.

Sole (from the French *sol*—a floor).—A cabin deck is sometimes called by this name.

Sole of the rudder.—A piece added to make it level with a false keel.

Sole plate.—A plate of iron forming the foundation for a marine engine.

Solstice.—The time, about 21st June and 22nd December, when the Sun is farthest from the equator and appears to pause before returning.

Soul and body lashing.—Spunyarn passed round an oilskin to exclude water and wind.

Sound.—1. *Sound,* in perfect condition.

2. An inlet from the sea over which soundings may be taken, as Plymouth Sound. A deep bay.

Sounding.—Taking depth of water and the quality of ground, by the lead and line. Tallow being inserted into the hollow space at the bottom of the lead, will enable a small quantity of the ground upon which it descends to be brought up, and by this means an experienced navigator is enabled to judge his whereabouts in foggy weather, or if for any other cause he is unable to determine his situation.

Sounding line.—The instruments used in sounding. (*See* LEAD AND LINE.)

South.—*Southing.*—Distance southward. The opposite to Northing (*which see*).

Southing of the moon.—The time at which the moon passes the meridian at any place.

South-wester (pronounced "sou-wester").—A waterproof hat, with a large flap behind, much used by fishermen and sailors.

Span.—The span of a rope, or of the rigging, on shipboard, is the same as, in architecture, is the span of an arch—*i.e.*, the distance across its extremities. It follows, therefore, that to form a span, a rope must be bent. And since a rope thus bent may be used for a multitude of purposes, the actual meaning of the word "span" has become forgotten, and *the rope itself* has

SOU-WESTER

come to be called the span. The *span of the rigging* is, theoretically, the distance across the shrouds, from deadeye to dead-eye; but, for the reason above-mentioned, the span in practice is often, as described by Smyth—"The length of the shrouds from the deadeye on one side, over the mast, to the dead-eye on the other side." But, in proof that this is not the actual and true span, we have the expression "To *span in* the rigging", which is, according to the same authority, "to draw the upper parts of the shrouds together by the tackles, in order to seize on (attach) the cat-harpings", or, in other words, to reduce (span in) the *lateral span* of the shrouds on one side, at the point where the cat-harpings are secured. Our business, is, however, with practice, and the simplest definition which can be given of a *span* is, perhaps, *a rope bent so as to form two legs.* Thus, a short rope or chain with both ends secured to a spar so that a purchase may be hooked to the bight (middle) is a span; and this is the way in which the peak-halyards of

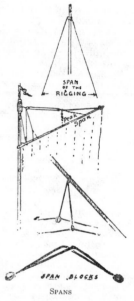

SPANS

a heavy gaff are usually fitted, whether in a yacht or in any other craft, thereby giving the peak a lift in two places. And, in the same manner, if a rope, having an eye or a block at each end, be attached by its middle to any portion of a ship's rigging, it forms a span; and this arrangement is sometimes made use of as a guide for leading sheets or any other ropes in a desired direction. Again, in square rigged ships we find short ropes with blocks seized (fastened) into each end, hanging from the mast caps, the blocks taking the main lifts, topmast studding-sail halyards, etc.; and these blocks, because attached to a span, are called *span blocks.*

Spanish burton.—A purchase with two single blocks and suitable only for a short lift.

Spanish reef.—1. In square rigged vessels, the yards lowered on the cap of the mast. 2. A method of reducing the size of (reefing) a jib sail, by tying the head of it into a knot.

SPANISH REEF

Spanish windlass.—A means of heaving together two parts of rope. A short bar is laid across the ropes and a small line passed round the two parts and over the cross bar. A marline spike is hitched to the line and used as a lever to tauten it.

Spank.—To *spank along* is to be carried briskly along by a fine fresh, or, as it is often called, a *spanking* breeze.

Spanker.—The gaff sail on the mizzen mast of a ship. It is also called the *driver.* It is not, however, the gaff sail on the mizzen mast of a bark: that is the mizzen; and the same on the barkentine. 2. The fifth mast, or after mast of a five-masted ship.

Spar.—A spar is one of the timber members of a vessel's gear disunited from the rest. A boom, a gaff, a yard, or any other such member, is itself a spar; and all these, taken collectively, form the spars of a ship. Thus we may come across a member of which we do not immediately recognise the purpose; but we know it at once to be *a spar.*

Spar ceiling.—Battens fitted in a hold to keep cargo off the ship's side, and promote the ventilation of the cargo.

Spar deck.—(Possible meaning "spare deck".)—(*See* DECK.)

Speaking trumpet.—An instrument used on shipboard for speaking to someone at a distance or in a high wind; and if the amateur proposes to take his boat to sea or to visit strange waters he will often find it useful. A *megaphone.*—The modern version fitted with an amplifier is a *loud-hailer.*

Spell.—Usually a period of work allotted to a man (*see also* TRICK), but it often implies merely a period; as "I shall take a spell on deck", meaning "I shall go on deck for a time". The word is much used at sea: in its old sense it signifies taking another's place, from whence may be derived the exclamation "Spell ho!" meaning "time to be relieved", "time to cease", or "time to rest".

Spencer.—In square rigged vessels, a fore-and-aft gaff sail introduced on the main-mast in place of the mizzen staysails. They are generally attached to the gaff by hoops (like the mast-hoops); and either drawn in along the gaff or brailed up like the sail of a barge.

Spent.—Broken or injured in such a manner as to be no longer serviceable. We often hear of a *spent mast* or any other spar; sometimes of a *spent sail,* when it is torn.

Spider Hoop.—1. In yachts, etc., a metal hoop round the lower part of a mast, fitted with belaying pins for the various halyards, and often with one or two shaffles, to take gooseneck joints. When there are two shaffles, one is aft to take the boom, the other forward for a spinnaker boom.

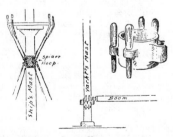

SPIDER HOOPS

2. In ships there is another spider hoop on those masts which are square rigged. It is placed under the futtock-plate and fitted with eyes to take the shackles of the *futtock shrouds.* (*See* FUTTOCK-PLATE and SHROUDS.)

Spile.—The name for a short wooden spike or pin.

Spill (of a sail).—To cause it to cease its action, whether it be by lowering it or by so bringing it to the wind that it no longer draws. It is found in practice, and more especially in large vessels setting square sails, that a sail will continue to hold wind for an appreciable time after the vessel has been brought up head to wind; and before a large sail is furled it is necessary to empty it, as it were, of the wind it holds. This may be done by bringing its side directly to the wind and letting it flap itself free of wind, or, in other words, *spill* itself. With small craft to spill is usually to lower, or partly lower, a sail.

Spindrift.—Spray swept from the crest of waves by strong winds.

Spinnaker (in yachts).—A triangular racing sail of immense spread, reaching from the topmast head to the end of the *spinnaker boom,* which is a spar set out to take it. The spinnaker is set on the weather side, that is on the side opposite to that on which the mainsail stands, and is kept in position by guys forward and aft. It follows from this that it can only be used in such a situation when running: but in some instances it can be carried forward when the boat comes on to the wind, and by taking the boom along the bowsprit the sail may thus be made to do service as a balloon jib; and in this manner it is now often employed in small craft. (*See* fig. under BALLOON CANVAS.)

Spinnaker topsail, more properly called the *big topsail.*—A topsail on the principle of a lug-sail, but the clew of which is extended on a short yard called a jack yard (*which see*). It has no connection with the spinnaker, except that it is often used at the same time.

Spirit compass.—The modern and improved form of mariners' compass, in which the card floats in spirit.

Spirkets, spirketting.—The inside strake between the water-ways and port sills of a wooden deck.

Spit.—A small projection of land, or a sand bank projecting at low tide into the water. The term is common where the shores of the sea are flat, or, again, as in "Spithead".

Spitfire.—A name sometimes given to the smallest jib-sail a boat carries, and used only in very bad weather, or alone to steer by. (*See* JIB.)

Splice.—A method of joining rope by interweaving the strands. It is a very useful art for an amateur to acquire, and though almost impossible to teach by description, can be easily learned. Any fisherman will be glad, for a few shillings, to impart the information.* (*See* under KNOTS for simple splicing.) When two ends of rope are joined by untwisting the strands of only a short part of each, the union is thick and is called a *short splice.* If a long piece be unravelled on each rope and the join made fine, and well beaten

---

* This was presumably so about the year 1900.

with a marling spike, or any other weighty tool, so that the join may be passed through the sheave hole of a block, it is known as a *long splice*. An *eye-splice* is made by turning up the end of a rope, and splicing it into the rope itself so as to form an eye at the end.

To *"splice the main-brace"* is one of the many metaphorical expressions used by seamen in old times. "The phrase", says Dr. Denham Robinson, "denotes an extra allowance of spirits in cases of cold or wet." (Brande and Cox.)

Splicing-fid.—A spike for opening the strands of a rope when splicing.

Spoil ground.—An area of the seabed where dredged or other unwanted material is deposited.

Sponson, or **sponsing** (in paddle-wheel steam boats).—The staging between the paddle box and the vessel's sides. It adds strength to the paddle-box, and forms a platform upon which the men may stand who work the springs (ropes) by which the vessel is held at the proper distance from a quay or pier.

Spoon drift.—Spray or moving foam from the top of waves. The result of a sudden squall, generally a white squall.

Spooning, or **spooming.**—Driving before a heavy gale.

Spray.—The foam of the sea thrown up by breakers or by the water dashing against rocks, etc.

Spring.—The name given to a rope attached to a buoy, pier, or dock, and by which a vessel is hauled in and held for a time, and which prevents it from surging ahead or astern. It is called after the position it occupies with regard to the vessel, as the "forward spring", which leads aft from foreward, and "back spring" which leads foreward from aft. A *spring pipe* is a short pipe through the bulwarks used as a fairlead for springs.

To *spring* is to crack or split, usually spoken of a spar, as to spring the mast, to to spring the bowsprit.

The *spring of a vessel* is her elasticity under sail.

Spring a leak.—A vessel taking water by any accident is said to spring a leak.

Spring stays are extra stays to assist the usual stays in any undue strain.

Spring tides.—The tides at full and new moon, when (the sun and moon being in a line with the earth and consequently raising the waters of the ocean to a maximum) the tides are at their highest and lowest. At these times the tide is high approximately at 12 o'clock, and low at 6 o'clock; when therefore we meet with the expression "between 12 o'clock high and 6 o'clock low water" we know that the spring tides are meant. Questions of law occasionally arise with regard to that portion of the foreshore which lies between the low water-mark of neap tide and that of spring tide. (*See also* LAGGING and MAKING OF TIDES.)

SNOTTER

FIG. 1

Sprit.—*Sprit sail* (often pronounced by the fishermen, as it is in Holland,—"spreet").— The word "sprit" is very ancient, and indeed, of Saxon origin, meaning "to sprout" (spoken of a pole). Hence, we have the *bow-sprit*, which sprouts out from the bow; and the sprit sail, in old ships, was set under the bowsprit, while, in the 17th century, a small mast rises from the bowsprit, carrying that which is described as a sprit top-sail. (*See* fig., p. 281.) The sprit, in modern sailing craft, is a pole set diagonally across a fore-and-aft sail to extend that sail by the peak. The heel of the sprit is placed in a loop, called the *snotter*, which is either suspended from the masthead, and held in to the lower part of the mast by a ring or *grommet*,—and this is the system followed on barges (*see* fig. 1, p. 279); or, in small open boats, it may consist simply of a grommet fitting closely round the mast, and over the end of the sprit, the tension preventing it from slipping down. (Both of these are illustrated under SNOTTER.) The head of the sprit fits into a cringle made to receive it at the peak of the sail, which is thus set up tighter as the snotter is brought nearer to or elevated on the mast, and *vice versâ*. The advantages of this rig are that the sail, having brails round it, may be gathered up almost instantaneously (fig. 2, also diagram under BRAIL); and that, when reefing, it may either be lowered, as with boom sails (*i.e.*, reefed down), or

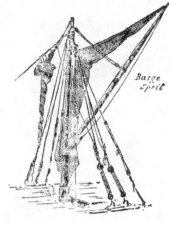

FIG. 2

FIG. 3

reefed upward, i.e., without lowering, as was often seen in hay barges and the like.

Sprit and foresail.—The sprit sail, as applied to small boats, is used in conjunction with a foresail, in consequence of which the combination is called the sprit and foresail rig (fig. 3). It was at one time very popular.

Sprocket.—An old name for the barrel or wheel of a capstan.

Sprung.—The state of a wooden mast or spar which is strained or partly fractured.

Spun yarn (pronounced by the fishermen "spunian").— The fibres of old rope twisted into yarns; in other words, a species of string. It is used for *serving,* etc. When tarred it is sometimes called *whipping.*

Spur.—1. A small cleat. (*See* THUMB CLEAT.) 2. *Spurs.*— Timbers used in the launching of a vessel.

Spurling, or **Navel-pipe.**— The pipe leading from the *windlass* to the *chain locker.*

Ship *c.* 1660, showing spritsail and spritsail topsail.

Squadron.—Part of a fleet under a flag officer. The principal yacht club in the kingdom is called the Royal Yacht Squadron.

Squall.—A sudden gust of wind, or a sudden increase in its force. There are white squalls, such as those met with in the Mediterranean and Eastern seas, and black squalls, such as we are familiar with in this country. If a beginner in the art of sailing be overtaken by a squall he should quickly put his boat up into the wind, and lose no time in taking in sail. On rare occasions it may be necessary to run forward and cut the halyards; such, however, is a last resource. Should he see it coming, however—and there is, usually, no mistaking its appearance when once seen—the boat may be luffed up and the sail lowered to meet it. It is a good rule for the amateur to follow the professional. If he be sailing in squally weather and within sight of beach or fishing craft, let him keep an eye on those to windward of him. If they take in sail it is high time he should do the same, for they know the temper of the elements better than ever he can hope to.

Square.—*Square rig.*—The name given to that method of disposing the sails of a ship in which they hang athwart the ship. They are then called square sails, in contradistinction to those which hang in the same line as the keel and are called *fore-and-aft.* The name "square-rigged" is given, as a general rule, to those vessels which carry square sails, notwithstanding that they carry fore-and-aft sails at the same time. Thus a bark, a brigantine, and a topsail schooner are square rigged, while a cutter, a yawl, and many schooner-yachts are fore-and-aft rigged. And yet the discrimination must be considered somewhat arbitrary, for there are vessels which carry square sails, and even square top-sails, and which are always described as fore-and-aft rigged. It was indeed at one time the practice on cutters, sloops, yawls, etc., all of which we now regard as purely fore-and-aft rigged, to set square sails for *running.* These, of course, are obsolete so far as yachts are

concerned, their place having been taken by the spinnaker. The ketch might
often have been seen with
a big lower square sail,
and on rarer occasions with
one or two square top-
sails. These are illustrated
under the headings KETCH
and BILLYBOY, and the ac-
companying figure illus-
trates a vessel setting both.
These are called the square
sail, or square top-sail, as
the case may be, the latter
being sometimes set alone
between the upper and
lower caps of the mast-
head, as described under
MIDDLE TOPSAIL.

KETCH SETTING SQUARE SAILS

Square stem and *square stern.*—A square
stem is one which meets the water at a
right angle, and a raking stem or bow that
which meets it at an acute angle. A square
or *transom stern* is a stern cut off square, that
is, having no counter, the rudder being
braced to the boat outside it. This is generally the build of bawleys and dredging boats;
it enables nets or dredges to be worked, if
necessary, over the stern. (*See* fig.)

SQUARE STEM AND STERN

Square knot or *right knot.*—Names, among
others, by which the *reef-knot* is sometimes
called.

Squat.—The increase in a vessel's draught caused by her movement through the water.

Squeegee.—A form of broom with a rubber edge, used for sweeping
water from a deck.

Squirm.—A twist in a rope is sometimes thus called.

Stability is the tendency in a boat to keep the upright, or to
return to it when careened over. Boats are designed in accordance
with the law of hydrostatics, that pressure exerted upon a liquid
surface is transmitted equally upon all parts of a body immersed.
Their form is, theoretically, such as to present a larger surface to
the pressure of the water when heeled over than when upright; and
they are constantly tending, therefore, to preserve or regain the
natural equilibrium. Breadth, of course, will increase this tendency;
depth furnishes a resistance to the force of wind upon sails; while
length decreases the tendency to lateral movement, called lee-way
(*which see*). It is in the proper application of such data that the

quality of stability—called stiffness by seamen—is obtained. (*See* STIFF.)

Stage.—A gang-board with side rails, to enable persons to walk on board a vessel alongside a quay, etc. A plank with cross pieces, slung by ropes over a ship's side, for men to work on.

Staith.—A landing place in a river. The term is very common in Norfolk.

Stanchion (sometimes called *stanchard*).—An upright post in the frame of a ship. Certain stanchions support the beams in a vessel, others are to be found along the bulwarks. (*See* FRAME.) The small posts sometimes seen running round the gunwale of a launch, yacht, or part of a deck, and supporting a man-rope, are also called stanchions.

Stand.—*Stand by.*—An order to be ready to do something; as "Stand by at the anchor", *i.e.*, make ready to let go the anchor.

Stand clear.—Keep out of the way; as "Stand clear of the cable".

In sailing:—

To *stand out*, is to be sailing out from the shore.

To *stand in*, to be coming in towards it.

To *stand on*, to continue on the course.

Stand up to within 6 *points*, 4 *points*, etc. (*See* under SAILING.)

A sail is said to *stand* when it is lifted. Thus it may stand well or ill.

Standing bowsprit.—A bowsprit which is fixed, such as that of a *sloop*, in contradistinction to one which reeves in and out as does that of a *cutter*. This is the distinguishing mark between those two rigs. (*See* diagram under SLOOP.)

Standing lug.—A lugsail without a boom, or its tack made fast by the mast. (*See* LUG.)

Standing part of a rope or tackle.—That part which is made fast, in contradistinction to the *running part,* which is the part hauled upon.

Standing rigging.—The ropes which support masts, and the disposition of which, therefore, is not continually being altered, constitute that which is called *standing* rigging, in contradistinction to those which, being attached to the sails, are constantly moving, and form the *running* rigging. Shrouds and stays constitute standing rigging. The standing rigging of a cutter yacht is as follows:—(*See* diagram No. 1 under RIGGING.) To the lower mast—1. The *shrouds,* which support it laterally. 2. The *forestay,* preventing it from being drawn backward. 3. The *backstays,* preventing it from going forward: these are sometimes called *runners,* because they may be slackened off as the boom swings over or when running before a wind. The *jib-stay* of the cutter is not, properly speaking, a stay, being a running and not a standing rope; but in the sloop it takes the place of the forestay. To the topmast—4. The *topmast shrouds* and *legs.* 5. The *topmast forestay.* 6. *Topmast backstays,* otherwise known as the *preventers,* used in large yachts which carry a great press of canvas. To the bowsprit—The *bowsprit shrouds,* to prevent it from bending sideways. 7. The *bobstay,* to bowse it down, in counteraction to the pull of the forestay and topmast forestay; and 8. The *bobstay trice.*

Standard.—*Standard knee.*—1. In shipbuilding, a knee or bracket placed *above* the object to which its horizontal arm is bound—*i.e.,* in an inverted position.

2. *Standard.*—In heraldry, a large square flag bearing the whole of the achievements of the monarch or nobleman, as seen in the Royal Standard of England.

Standard compass, or *Azimuth compass.*—This is the master magnetic compass of a ship. It is mounted so as to be as far as possible from local magnetic influences, and free of all obstructions for the taking of bearings.

Starboard.—The right-hand side of a vessel when facing forward.

Starboard tack.—A vessel is on the starboard tack when the wind blows from the starboard or right-hand side. Sailing vessels with the wind on the port side give way to those with the wind on the star-board side. (*See* RULE OF THE ROAD.) This may easily be remembered from a common expression among sailing men generally: the phrase has a double meaning, as will be seen; it reminds one at the same time which is the starboard side and which is the safest tack to be on:—"When you are on the star-board tack you are on the *right* (hand) tack." When the wind comes from abaft the beam on the star-

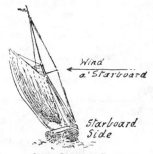

ON THE STARBOARD TACK

board side a vessel is sometimes said to be on the *starboard gybe.*

Starboard the helm, helm a'starboard.—Put the tiller over to the right, or starboard, side. Previously to 30th June, 1931, steering orders were, in British ships, invariably directions in which the *helm,* or *tiller,* was to be moved. At the order "starboard the helm", the *steering wheel* would be turned to *port* and the tiller would move to starboard, the rudder, and consequently the ship's head (providing she had headway), would move to *port.* Since that date, steering orders, in ships of every nation, refer to the direction in which the wheel, rudder, and ship's head are to be moved.

Starbowlines (pronounced "starbolins").—The old name for men on the starboard watch. (*See* WATCHES.)

Start.—To move or loosen. Also to become injured or to break. Thus a plank which it may be desired to take out of a vessel is said to be started when it is loosened. And if it should crack or break through some accident, while at sea, it is said to have started.

Starting bolt.—A bolt used to drive out other bolts from a timber, etc.

Station.—A man's place or post for a special duty, e.g. for leaving harbour; or the allotted place for a ship in a squadron or convoy or flotilla.

Stave.—To break a hole into anything. Also to fend or guide off some one object from another. Thus a vessel may be in collision and have her bows or side *stove in*. Or she may be fortunate enough to evade the threatened danger by pushing, or *staving*, it off.

Stays.—Supports. Strong ropes, mostly of wire, supporting spars, and more especially masts in a fore-and-aft direction. They form part of the *standing rigging* of a vessel. Those leading aft become *back-stays*. Other supports answering various purposes may also be called stays, as *boom stays, counter stays, stay-pieces,* etc. (*See* below.) Stays take their names from the spars they support or from the direction in which they run, as the *top-mast-stay* supporting the topmast; the *back-stays,* running backward, etc. The stays of a cutter yacht are described under the heading RIGGING. Those of a large vessel are according to the number of masts she has; and they may be variously disposed. Thus in old ships the *fore stay* runs to the end of the bowsprit; the *main stay* through a collar half-way up the foremast to the stem head; and the *mizzen stay* to a collar on the base of the main-mast. In more modern vessels the fore-stay extends only to the stem and the main stay to a collar at the base of the foremast; while in two-masted vessels a *triatic stay* often takes the place of the main stay.

Boom stays.—The support of a boom to its mast. This may be either a collar (the *shaffle*) on the *spider-hoop* to take a *goose-neck* joint (*which see*); or it may be a *bolster* upon which a boom with jaws may rest.

Counter stay.—A timber supporting the counter of a vessel. (*See* diagram IV under FRAME.)

Preventer stay.—An additional stay fitted to back up another, a more usual name for *spring stay*.

Spring stay.—In large vessels, an accessory to a principal stay, and running nearly parallel with it.

To *stay forward* (of a mast).—To rake or lean forward, the result of being pulled forward by *stays*. By *raking* masts is understood to mean those which lean slightly backwards. To be stayed forward is the opposite to this. (*See* RAKE.)

In the working of a ship there are certain stays (shifting back-stays) the positions of which require altering every time the vessel comes about from one tack to another. (*See* TACK.) And from this circumstance a number of expressions employed in seamanship, having reference to the tacking of a ship, have been derived. They are as follow:—

To *stay* is to tack, or go about. To be *in stays,* or *hove in stays,* is to be in the act of going about. To be *slack in stays,* to be slow or unhandy in coming about, as some vessels are. Or if the vessel comes round quickly and without trouble, she may be called *handy,* or *quick in stays*.

To *miss stays* is to fail in getting about; the result being that the

K

boat becomes "hung up in the wind", as it is called. This is an accident which may occasionally happen to very long boats, especially when the wind is light; but it may also be the fault of the helmsman in having put his tiller too rapidly down, or in having failed to get sufficient way on the boat before putting her round. When, therefore, it is desired to go about the tiller should be put over steadily—not slowly, but deliberately, and, as it were, to *feel* the boat round. This is an art which requires a little experience, more especially as boats vary, some coming about much more quickly than others.

To *refuse stays.*—Much the same as to miss stays, except that some boats literally cannot be got round at any time. This will hardly be the case with a sailing vessel, though she may occasionally miss stays; but with steam-boats under sail, as for instance with launches rigged for occasional sailing, the engines may have to be used to get the boat about.

Stay-sails.—Those which are set on the stays between the masts of a ship, or as head sails. They are mostly, therefore, jib-shaped (triangular); though not necessarily so, for in old ships they were often four-sided in shape; and being sometimes *roached* head and foot, presented a very curious appearance. Even in the present day it is not uncommon to see them shaped as a jib with the nose cut off, the luff running on the mast. This luff is called the *nock* (under which heading its appearance is also illustrated). The great use of stay *sails* is to enable a vessel to sail *full* and yet *by* the wind; *i.e.,* with her sails full, and yet close-hauled. (*See* FULL AND BY.) The foresail of a cutter or yawl, inasmuch as it runs on the fore stay, may be equally correctly called the *forestay sail,* just as the sail more commonly known as the jib topsail is actually the *topmast forestay sail*; and besides these the schooner may set staysails between the fore and main masts. But we often see, in certain fore-and-aft rigged coasting craft, sails answering precisely the same purpose as stay-sails, though unconnected with stays. The ketch type, for instance, sometimes sets a large triangular sail ahead of the mizzen mast (*see* figure under KETCH); while even a barge may occasionally be seen with a small one set on her little jigger mast.

Steady.—To keep a vessel steady is to keep her on her course without deviation. If a helmsman receive the order "Steady!" it will often mean that he is to keep the boat from yawing about, as she may be liable to do in a heavy sea.

Stealer.—In shipbuilding, "a short length of plank worked in among the other strakes to facilitate rounding off in parts of great curvature." (Brande and Cox.) A strake is a line of planking along a vessel's side; and one of the planks which form the strake, if short and not reaching either stem or stern post, may also be called a stealer.

Steam launch.—(*See* LAUNCH.)

Steer.—To steer is to guide a boat, whether under sail, steam, or oars. To do this properly a steersman must be acquainted with the theory of the helm, and should know the rule of the road. (*See* HELM and RULE OF THE ROAD.) No better rule for steering could be given than that contained in the following comparison of helmsmen:—"A good helmsman opposes in time the tendency of the ship to deviate from her course by a small motion, which he relaxes as soon as the effect is felt, thus disturbing her sailing as little as possible. A bad helmsman gives her too much helm, and keeps her perpetually yawing from one side to the other." (Brande and Cox.) (*See* STARBOARD THE HELM.)

Steerage way.—Way sufficient to enable a boat to be steered. (*See* WAY.)

Steerage.—In a steamship. That part of the vessel having the poorest accommodation, and occupied by the steerage passengers or those paying the lowest fare. The word seems to be derived from the circumstance that these passengers were, in earlier times, placed in the after or steerage part of the vessel.

Steeve.—The steeve is the angle a bowsprit makes with the horizontal. In very early ships this member was so lifted up as to become almost perpendicular; in each succeeding design, however, it continued to be lowered until it now almost approaches the horizontal.

The bowsprits of schooner yachts have often a steeve, and large vessels nearly always; but it is rare in small craft, the bowsprit in them usually lying along the deck.

Stem.—*Stem, stem post, head post,* or *fore post.*—The foremost timber of a vessel. The stem post is united to the keel inside by the *deadwood,* and outside by the stem band; and at its head the *breasthook* binds the upper strakes of the vessel firmly to it. Just as there is a keelson to the keel, and a sternson to the stern, so there is, in large vessels, a *stemson* to the stem, which gives to it an additional support; and the whole is connected with the *apron,* which also secures the forward end of the strakes, thus rendering the bow, as it needs to be, a very powerful construction. (*See* diagrams under FRAME.)

Stem band, stem iron, or *keel band.*—A band of iron connecting the keel and stem post. (*See also* under KEEL.)

Stem head.—The head of the stem post.

To *stem* a tide or current. To face it; or, in other words, to meet it stem-on. Hence the meaning of the term in every day conversation.

Step.—A block of wood, with a hole or recess in it, to receive the heel of a mast. It is placed on the keelson of a vessel. Its object is not only to take the heel of the mast, but to distribute its weight over the keelson as much as possible; and in large vessels, where the masts are very heavy, the step stands upon an iron plate.

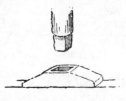

MAST STEP

Stern.—The after part of a vessel.

Stern board.—1. Sometimes a progress backwards, the result of an accident, and occasionally dangerous to small craft. (*See* STERNWAY, below.)

2. The term is also used as follows:—In making way against the wind a sailing vessel is bound to proceed in a zig-zag course; the distance she travels between each turn being called a *board*. (*See* TACK.) There are occasions— as, for instance, when navigating a channel—when she may go a long distance on one board; but, having to turn at last and finding the wind dead in her teeth, will be obliged, so as to gain the other side of the channel once more, to travel in a somewhat backward direction, thereby losing ground; and her progress in this backward direction is therefore

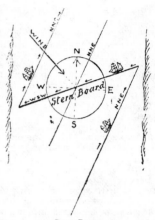

STERN BOARD

called a stern board. In the diagram the vessel is endeavouring to make a course due north with the wind north-west, and she sails *within six points* (in explanation of which last term *see* under SAILING). She therefore proceeds forwards in a direction N.N.E. (*i.e.* 6 points from the wind), until she comes so near shore as to be obliged to turn, when her next course must be in a direction W.S.W. (6 points from the wind), which is actually going backwards, or, in other words, she then makes a "stern board".

Stern-chaser.—A gun, carried in the days of sailing navies, used to fire directly astern at a pursuing ship.

Stern fast.—A rope holding a vessel by the stern, just as a *head fast* is one holding her by the head.

Stern post.—The post or stanchion at the stern of a vessel. It is kept in position by the transom, and on it is hung the rudder. This member, like the keel with its keelson, and the stem with its stemson, is further strengthened, in large vessels, by an inside timber called the *sternson*. (*See* diagram under FRAME.)

Stern sheets, in an open boat, are the boards covering the floor space of the stern, just as the head-sheets cover the fore part. These boards are sometimes kept together by under pieces and lifted as one. Where cost is no object they are made in the form of gratings. (*See* diagram under SHEET.)

Stern-way.—The way (distance) a vessel makes if carried *stern first*, as in a calm or in a current, or having missed stays. But sternway is not *lee*-way: if a vessel sailing across the run of the tide be carried down on it ever so far, she makes considerable lee-way, but no stern-way.

Stevedore.—A man whose business it is to undertake the stowage of cargo in ships.

Stiff.—*Stiffness* is the quality of stability possessed by a boat, or, in other words, the capability of a boat under sail to keep the upright or to return to it when heeled over. (*See* STABILITY.) It is an exceedingly necessary quality in any vessel, for upon it depends the safety of those who venture in her. Seamen have various ways of expressing their admiration of a stiff craft, *e.g.*, "stiff as a house", "as stiff as a church", etc.

Stirrups.—In square rig, short ropes hanging from the yards of a square sail and holding the horse or footrope. (*See* HORSE.)

Stock.—1. Of a rudder, the upper part, upon the head of which the tiller is set. (*See* RUDDER.) 2. Of a bowsprit, that part at the foot of it which is held by the *bitts*. (*See* BOWSPRIT.) 3. Of an anchor, the cross-piece at right-angles to the flukes, which causes them to lie vertically so that the lower fluke bites into the sea bed.

Stockholm tar.—A weather-resisting preservative largely used in rope-making. It was supposed by sailors to possess curative properties.

Stomach-piece.—Another name for the *apron* (*which see*).

Stools.—The channel plates of the backstays. (*See* CHANNELS.)

Stop.—A short rope used to confine a sail when furled or *stopped*. (*See* TIES.) It may also be a small projection, as on a mast or any other spar, to prevent anything from slipping down.

To *stop.*—To tie anything up temporarily, as:—

To *stop a sail.*—To tie it up preparatory to setting it. Sails which are set flying, such as jibs, are often tied up with a thin yarn before hoisting; and when halyards, outhauls, etc., are all belayed a sharp pull on the sheets will snap the yarn and the sail unfolds itself. Sometimes the sail is stopped and hoisted, but not unstopped until required.

To *stop a flag.*—To tie it up. Sometimes this was done to make it resemble a wheft for use in signalling (as in the fig.); and very generally a flag sent up on a tall mast is stopped before hoisting, by securing a bight of the tack line around it to prevent its becoming entangled in the rigging as it ascends.

Stopper.—*Stoppering* is to check or hold fast any rope.

Stopper.—A short length of rope, one end of which is firmly secured, for temporarily holding another rope. *Stoppers* for wire hawsers are of chain with a rope tail.

Stopper knot.—A knot made at the end of a sheet or any other rope to prevent it from flying out of its lead. Thus the jib and fore-sail sheets of a small yacht, which run aft through fair leads, are usually stoppered with figure-of-8 knots. (*See* KNOTS.)

Storm.—A wind whose average speed lies between 48 and 63 knots, *i.e.* force 10 and 11 of the Beaufort Scale. A disturbance of the atmosphere. Among seafaring men the term has but little reference to wind, but is generally understood to mean rain or thunder and lightning.

Storm sails.—Those for use in bad weather. Such, on a yacht, are the *storm-jib*, the *trysail*, etc.

Storm signal.—A signal, consisting of a cone, made at the various stations of the Meteorological Office in forecast of weather to be expected. (*See* SIGNALS.)

Storm wave.—A wave which comes rolling in without wind. It is said to mark the recent occurrence of a gale in some distant locality.

Stove.—(*See* STAVE.)—A vessel is *stove in* when she has been *bilged* or broken into.

Stow.—Stowage is the room in a vessel for cargo, and to stow the cargo is to pack it so that it will not shift as she rolls.

To *stow away* anything is to put it in a safe place for future use.

To *stow away a boat* is the same as to *trim her down* after a sail; that is, to take in her sails, furl them, or stow them away, and to do all that will leave her in a condition ready to be taken out again at short notice.

Stowage factor.—The number of cubic feet required for stowing one ton (or other unit quantity) of any specified sort of cargo.

Stowaway.—One who hides himself on board a ship with the object of fraudulently obtaining a passage.

Stow-boat fishing, commonly called *stow-boating.*—A method of taking sprats in large quantities once much practised in the estuary of the Thames and along the East Coast. The fish thus taken were sold at prices varying, according to demand, from five or six shillings to as low as 4½d per bushel, the smaller sums being paid for those sold as manure, for which they were at one time largely used, especially for hops. The stow-boat net goes with two beams, which are kept square by anchors. To these a huge bag net is fixed, the mesh of which is extremely small. The fishermen say they have sometimes taken as many as 300 bushels of sprats in a tide.

Strain bands.—Extra bands of canvas, usually only seen on large square sails, to give the same support to the *bunt* of the sail as the *bolt-ropes* do to the leeches.

Strake (often pronounced "streak", from which, indeed, it is not impossible that the name is derived).—A strake is a line of planking extending the length of a vessel. It is needless to say that a single plank cannot extend the entire length of a vessel, and that a continuous line of planks must, therefore, be employed to effect this: it is this line of several planks which forms *one* strake. Strakes are variously named according to their position, as, for instance—

Garboard strakes.—The lowest strakes of a vessel, being on the outside, next the keel. In small boats, the keel and garboard strakes are sometimes of one piece. (*See* FRAME.)

Limber strakes.—The lowest strakes on the inside, running, therefore, beneath the limbers.

Sheer strakes.—Those immediately below the sheer; they are of thick planking.

Thick strakes are placed at different heights on the sides.

Black strakes run along the flat sides of the vessel, outside.

Wash strake.—The name sometimes given to a *weather board* (*which see*).

The uppermost strake of a vessel is stronger than the rest, and is called the *wale*. In an open boat it is the *saxboard*.

In clinker-built boats the strakes overlap; in carvel, they meet in a smooth join. There is not much to choose between the two styles of building, each having its own advantages in its proper place; but with many amateurs carvel is the more popular, and instances are not altogether unique in which a person having a clinker-built boat for sale has filled in the over-lapping of the strakes so as to imitate carvel—a process called *doubling*. Doubling is useful enough in renovating old boats, but the beginner in boat-buying will do well to assure himself that a doubled boat is not being palmed off on him as a carvel-built one.

Strand (of a rope).—Fibres of yarn twisted into a loose string. Strands compose ropes, just as the yarns compose strands. Three strands form a rope, though more may be employed.

Stranded.—1. (Of a ship.) Aground. Said of a vessel when she has been left by the tide. 2. (Of a rope.) When one or more strands are broken, or worn through.

Strap.—An iron bar, forming a break to any machine in work, as a capstan. The grommet or band round a block, whether of rope or iron, is sometimes called the strap, but more often the *strop*.

Stratus.—A low cloud usually hanging in horizontal bands over the horizon.

Cirro stratus, a cloud of the same description as the above, but lying much higher. (*See* also CIRRUS.)

Stream.—The most rapid part of a tide or current.

Stream anchor.—An anchor carried by large vessels, less than the *bowers,* but more powerful than *kedges*. It evidently derives its name from the fact that it is sufficient to hold the ship against the run of a stream without the necessity of dropping the bower anchor.

To stream.—To place in the water, *e.g.* the log rotator, or an anchor buoy.

Streamer.—A very long and narrow flag.

Stress.—Hard pressure. The word is an abbreviation of "distress", and from this a vessel may be said to put into a harbour under *stress of weather*.

Stretch.—Another name for a *board,* in tacking. (*See* TACK.)

To stretch.—To reach; or, in other words, to sail *by the wind—i.e.,* with the wind ahead of the beam, but it may also mean to sail thus under a great crowd or stretch of canvas.

Stretcher (in a row boat).— The movable piece of board, or it may be only a stick, against which a rower presses his feet. These are of various forms, according to the class of boat in which they occur. No. 1, in the figures, shows a simple and very common method employed in open boats round the coast. No. 2 is a style often found in Thames skiffs, up-river. No. 3 is the practice followed in best boats (racing outriggers): the sculler slips his feet, sometimes without taking off his shoes, into the large boots (which are a fixture), and laces them loosely up. But the beginner may sometimes find himself in a rough boat without stretchers. In such a case a useful substitute may be fashioned by taking a clove-hitch with the painter, at the right distance, round almost any piece of wood or iron (No. 4

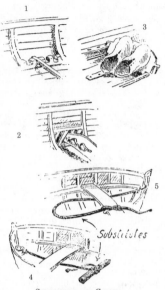

STRETCHERS AND GUIDES

in the fig.). Or if nothing can be found, the painter itself may do duty by simply bringing it under and taking a clove-hitch with it round the thwart, allowing, of course, sufficient length in the bight for the legs to get a purchase (No. 5).

Stretcher guides.—The notches, grooves, or any other agents, by which a stretcher is held in place. These guides are so designed that the rower may move the stretcher forward or back as required. Their form will be understood by reference to the figures.

Strike.—To take down. Spoken of a mast or sail, as to strike the topmast—*i.e.,* to lower it.

To *strike the flag,* also to lower it, but permanently; not simply to lower and re-hoist as in saluting:—that is *dipping.*

To *strike sail.*—The term is used by St. Luke, "and fearing lest they should fall into the quicksands they *strake sail,* and so were driven" (Acts. xxvii. 17). Thus they "scudded" before the wind under bare poles.

String.—Sometimes the highest strake *within* the ship. (*See* STRAKE.)

Stringers.—Strengthening timbers running along the inside of a vessel at various distances up the sides. Their true office is to assist in bracing the heads (ribs) together. The extra stout stringer upon which the thwarts (seats) of an open boat are placed is called the *wiring* or *rising*. (*See* diagrams under FRAME.)

Strip.—To dismantle.

Stripped to a gantline, or *Stripped to the girt line.*—An expression signifying that a vessel has been completely stripped of her rigging, with the exception of a gantline left aloft to enable new rigging to be hoisted and placed over the mastheads.

Strip to the buff.—Among rowing men and athletes, to completely undress down to the waist. Professional scullers usually "strip to the buff" for their matches during hot weather.

Stroke.—In rowing, the force used in propelling a boat through the water is called the stroke: and this action may be divided into two motions, 1. The stroke proper, and 2, the recovery; the first being the pulling of the oar through the water, and the second the thrusting of the arms forward in preparation for snother stroke.

Stroke.—In a boat, the sternmost rower, and he who sets the stroke for all the others, is called the stroke. In an eight-oared boat he is No. 8, but is never spoken of as such, his title being "Stroke", and as such he is always addressed. So, likewise, the headmost rower, though his position is No. 1, is always known as "bow"; but all the others answer to their numbers only. Thus the composition of an eight-oar is as follows:—*Bow* (1), 2, 3, 4, 5, 6, 7, *Stroke* (8), *Coxswain.*

Stroke side.—The side upon which the stroke man puts out his oar; that is, on his right-hand side. The terms starboard and port are never used in rowing; the *bow-side* and *stroke-side* being spoken of instead. The stroke side is, therefore, the port side. (*See* figure under BOW.)

Strongback.—The detachable spar running fore-and-aft across a lifeboat, over which the canvas cover is stretched.

Strong breeze.—A term signifying a wind blowing between 22 and 27 knots: force 6 of the Beaufort Scale. (*See* under WINDS.)

Strop.—An iron or rope band or grommet. Sometimes it is a rope for hitching a tackle to, but usually we hear of the *strop of a block,* the band round the shell of the block which holds the entire thing together.

Strum.—(*See* ROSE-BOX.)

Stud.—A short bar through the link in a *stud-link chain,* which is a species of chain much used by large vessels because of its great superiority of strength over other kinds of chain. (*See* figure under CHAIN.)

Studsail, or *ringtail* (pronounced "studs'l", evidently only an alteration of "stuns'l", itself an abbreviation of studding sail).—A narrow sail like the studding sail, run out beyond the leech of the mainsail of a racing cutter. (*See* fig., p. 294.) It forms part of the *press canvas* (*which see*) of a large yacht, but is not often employed.

Studding-sails.—"In square rig, narrow supplementary sails run out on small booms beyond the leeches of the principal square sails. Although not of great power from their size, they exert considerable force on the ship's movements from the leverage which their distance from the mast, as centre, gives them." (Brande and Cox.) (*See* fig.)

Sugg.—To rock heavily on a bank or reef.

Suit (of sails).—A set of sails. Thus a yacht may have several suits, as a suit of racing canvas, of cruising, or of storm sails.

Sujee; suji-muji; soo-gee-moogee.—Soap or cleaning powder mixed with water. To wash paint-work with sujee.

Sullage.—Garbage or rubbish.

STUDDING AND STUDSAIL

Sun over the yardarm.—An expression indicating that the sun has risen sufficiently for it to be time for the first drink of the day.

Supercargo.—A person superintending transactions relating to a vessel's cargo.

Surf.—The breaking of the sea into short quick waves over shallow places.

Surge.—The swell of the sea.

To *surge a rope.*—To slacken it suddenly, where it goes round a capstan, windlass, etc.

Surge ho!—Notice given that a rope is about to be surged.

Sutiles.—Ancient cobles made of strong staves sewed together and covered with leather or skin. (*See* CORACLE.)

Swab.—A mop.

Swagg.—Synonymous with *sag—i.e.,* to sink down by its own weight. (*See* SAG.) The *sag of a rope* is the bellying or drop when it is extended.

Swallow.—The score in a block in which the sheave runs. (*See* BLOCK.)

Swallow-tailed.—The shape of the flag called the burgee (*which see*), though not that flown by the ordinary members of a yacht-club. It ends in two tails.

Swallow the anchor.—An expression meaning to settle on shore.

Swamp.—To be swamped is to be filled with water; but not necessarily to sink.

Swap.—A mop. The same as a swab. Also to exchange.

Swash (often pronounced "swatch").—A shoal in a tideway, usually found at the mouth of a river.

Swash way.—A channel across a swash or among several shoals. It is the result of a peculiar set of the tide, which also keeps it from silting up. There is an important swash way between the Goodwin Sands. Another runs round the Nore Sand in the estuary of the Thames, and is sufficiently deep to admit of the largest vessels entering by it into the river Medway, and on the opposite shore again there is a permanent swash way not less than two miles in length, navigable for fishing craft, even at the lowest tides, almost up to the town of Leigh. A swash *way* is often called merely a swash or swatch, as the "Leigh swash" just mentioned.

Swathe.—The entire length of a sea wave.

Sway.—To hoist. To sway a yard or any other spar is to haul it up.

Sweat.—To *sweat up.*—To haul up tight, or to *swig* upon, as halyards are swigged upon or "sweated up". (*See* SWIG.)

Sweater.—A thick jersey or vest used by rowing men when in training. Being very warm it conduces to perspiration or sweat; and it is by this means that men get down superfluous fat.

Sweep.—*Sweeps* are very long and heavy oars, for occasional use on board a sailing boat, as, for instance, to get her round should she "miss stays", or to get her along in a calm. River lighters are mostly steered by sweeps, as they are carried up or down on the tide; and this is called "sweeping"—hence, to *sweep* up or down a river. Until comparatively recent years, even tolerably large sailing vessels, such as brigs and schooners, carried sweeps, more especially, it would appear, in case of being chased by an enemy. Thus the combined oars and sails of the ancients may be said to have survived almost to our own day. But the introduction of steam has completely altered the entire system of the sea. (For the names of the various parts of a sweep *see* OAR.)

The *sweep of the tiller.*—The circle it describes when brought from one side of a vessel to the other.

To *sweep* for anything lost at the bottom of the water, is to drag for it with a rope. Usually two boats are employed in doing this, each taking one end of a rope, and a weight being attached to it about midway to sink it.

Swell.—An undulating motion of water, at sea always felt after a gale. A swell must be distinguished from a *wash,* as from a passing steam vessel and from *sea,* caused by the wind then blowing, which the *swell* is not. (*See* GROUND SWELL and WASH.)

Swell in, or *take up.*—To become water-tight. Spoken of the planks of a boat which will let in the water when she has been laid up for any length of time, but which will, when she is returned to the water, swell in after a few days.

Swift.—To tighten up, as to "swift in the shrouds".

To *swift a vessel.*—1. To ground her preparatory to careening her for examination. 2. The art of careening her over. Either of these, or the whole operation, appears to answer to the term swifting.

To *swift* a ship by the hull appears to be something akin to the ancient *"frapping" (which see)*. It consists in passing cables round the hull. Smyth describes this as the "undergirdling" spoken of by St. Paul, while Falconer and others place that under frapping.

Swifters.—Extra stays, usually forward of those which they assist, as the *backstay fore swifters* in a big ship. Certain ships are found to require an extra pair of shrouds, set forward of the usual ones, and these are called swifters.

Swig.—To give an extra pull on a purchase. Thus halyards, when the sails have been hauled up, are *swigged upon* by men laying all their weight upon them in sudden jerks and thus getting them a little tighter. This is also called *sweating* them up: it is always done in yachts. It is important to the beginner to know that the halyard of a lug-sail should not be swigged upon after the tack of the sail has been drawn down.

Swing.—Sometimes this has the same meaning as to *sway*; as, for instance, to "swing a yard", which is the same as to "sway" or hoist it.

Swing on the tide.—A vessel at anchor *swings* when she changes her position at the turn of the tide.

Swing (in rowing parlance).—The swing of a crew is the motion resulting from the long, steady stroke-and-recovery of all the rowers together in good *time*. It is thought that nothing tends to increase and retain the speed of a boat so much as a good swing. A jerky stroke destroys the swing, and consequently reduces the speed.

Swinging boom.—"The spar which stretches the foot of a lower studding sail; in large ships they have goosenecks in one end, which hook to the foremost part of the forechains to iron strops fitted for the purpose." (Smyth.)

Swinging ship.—Putting the ship's head through all the points of the compass in order to adjust it, or to determine the compass error.

Swivel.—An instrument consisting of a pin revolving in a link. Swivels are fitted between lengths of chain to prevent the chain from kinking. They are used in cables to connect two or more anchors with the main cable in the manner described under HAWSE. They have also a number of uses on shipboard. (*See* fig.)

Swivel-rowlocks.—Those working in a swivel. (*See* fig.)

Syren.—(*See* SIREN.)

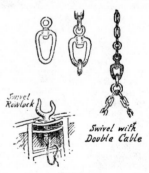

Swivel Rowlock

Swivel with Double Cable

SWIVELS

T

Tab (of a sail).—The tab or tabling is a broad piece of hemming on the edge of the sail, to strengthen it where bolt-hooks are situated. (*See* diagrams under SAIL.)

Tabernacle.—A housing or case on the deck of such vessels as have lowering masts. They are to be seen in barges, and occasionally in river yachts; and have sometimes been employed to lengthen a mast by stepping it on deck instead of on the kelson. (*See* diagrams under MAST.)

Tack, stay in stays, wind, go about, beat, beat to windward, or work to windward.—All these terms are to a certain extent synonymous; but under the term *tack* is included several meanings.

To *tack* (in sailing) is to perform the evolution called "Tacking" (*See* below).

The *tack of a sail* is the forward lower corner; also called the *weather-clew* (*See* under SAIL and CLEW.)

A *tack* is also a small rope by which this same weather clew is held down. On a balance lug sail it is fitted to the boom some way aft of the foremost end; in other cases it may be attached to the tack of the sail itself.

Tack line.—A length of signal halyard inserted between two groups of signal flags when hoisted on the same halyard.

Tack purchase or *gun tackle purchase.*—The tackle applied to the tack of a fore-and-aft mainsail.

Tack pins or *jack pins.*—Belaying pins in a *fife rail*, etc. (*See* PIN.)

Tack trice or *tack tricing line.*—The rope which *trices* up the tack of a sail.

To *tack* (in sailing) is to change the course of a vessel from one direction, or tack, to another, by bringing her head to the wind and letting the wind fill her sails on the other side; the object being to make progress against the wind. It follows, then, that to tack her must be to turn her round, or, in other words, to *go about*: and as this must be done by bringing her head to wind, the operation is also very often called *winding*. To perform this, in large vessels, it is necessary to alter various stays, and hence, as the ship comes about, she may just as correctly be said to be *staying,* or *in stays,* while, if she fail to come round, she will be said to have *missed stays.* If a vessel miss stays, and cannot be *cast* one way or the other, she is said to be *in irons,* or *hung up in the wind.* To *go about, tack, wind, stay,* or be *in stays,* are, therefore, terms all signifying the same act of bringing a vessel from one tack to another, *head to wind,* which is the direct opposite to *wearing* her. (*See* WEAR.) A vessel, then, is said to be *tacking* when she keeps changing her course from one tack to the other; and the distance she makes each time she stands on one tack (that is each time she continues in a straight line without coming about) is called a *board* or *stretch*. This she will only do when the wind is against her; and, therefore, if tacking, it follows that she must be beating against the wind, or, in other words, *beating to windward*. And as this is a performance often attended with difficulty, and always in a manner entailing a good deal of *work* on board, it is, as often as not, called *working to windward* or *pegging to windward*. To *beat* or *work to windward,* or to *beat up against the wind,* are, then, practically the same as *tacking*. Now, there can be but two tacks (as there are but two sides to a vessel, viz., the *starboard* or right-hand and the *port* or left hand), called Starboard-tack or Port-tack according to the side upon which the wind blows. (*See* STARBOARD TACK and PORT TACK.) It is, therefore, upon these tacks that the *Rules of the Road* are founded, and with which every person intending to take up boat-sailing should become familiar.

A boat when tacking will not bear anything like the same press of canvas as when sailing large. It is necessary, therefore, in a stiff breeze, before coming round to tack, to shorten sail.

Tackle (Dutch *takel*; and pronounced by us "tay-kle").—A purchase formed by the combination of a rope with two or more blocks.

The various parts of a tackle are as follow:—The rope is termed the *fall*; the pulley wheels are called *sheaves*, and the case which contains these the *block*. When a tackle is in use one end of the fall (rope) is made fast and called the *standing end*; the other is hauled upon and called the *running end*; but in every-day conversation that part of the rope which is hauled upon is often called the fall. Where a tackle is applied to a halyard (which is often the case), that part of the rope which hangs between the blocks is called the *pendant,* and the part hauled upon the fall. (*See* under PENDANT.)

A simple tackle consists of one or more pulleys with a single rope. The chief simple tackles are:—

The whip.—A purchase consisting of only a single pulley, and therefore not, properly speaking, a tackle; but when whip is placed upon whip then it becomes a true one. (*See* WHIP UPON WHIP.)

Gun tackle.—"A system of pulleys consisting of *two single blocks,* one movable, the other fixed, the standing end of the fall being made fast to the movable block. It increases the power three-fold."

Luff tackle.—A tackle consisting of *one double* and *one single block.*

Gyn tackle.—"A system of pulleys consisting of a *double and threefold block,* the standing end of the fall being made fast to the double block, which is movable. It increases the power five-fold."

But besides these there are many combinations in use, such as a *threefold*, with two threefold blocks, and *fourfold* purchase for heavy lifts, and the *jigger* tackle, which is one with a movable tail-block; and *luff* tackle, used on various occasions to assist other tackles, and on ships to "succour" the tackles attached to the tacks of square sails, and others.

Tackle upon tackle, or a combination of tackles, is the application of a simple tackle to the running end of another as often as necessary, the result of their combined actions being found by multiplying together the values of the several simple tackles.

Overhauling a tackle is separating the blocks after they have been *fleeted;* that is, brought close together, and their action thereby rendered void.

Taffrail, or **taffarel.**—The sternmost rail of a vessel; that is, the rail round the stern. Hence the stern-most part, or rim, of the vessel is often understood when the taffrail is spoken of.

TAFFRAIL

Tail.—*Tail block.*—A block having a rope strop (band) which is extended into a "tail" so that the block may be tied on to anything. It is sometimes called a *jigger-block.* One leg of the tail is usually longer than the other.

Tail on.—1. To attach; as to clap on a rope to some other. 2. A ship aground by the stern is said to be tail on.

Tail up or *down.*—Spoken of a ship at anchor, and describing the direction in which she lies. Thus if she be at anchor in a river and the tide be rising she will lie *tail up* because her stern, or "tail", will point up.

Take.—*Take charge.*—A boat is said to take charge when she suddenly runs up into the wind, or can no longer be kept from doing so. To be out of control.

Taken aback.—Surprised: a sailing vessel is taken aback when the wind strikes her sails on the wrong side.

Taken by the lee.—Said of a sailing vessel when her sails are thrown aback by a sudden shift of wind.

Take in sail.—To reduce sail, either by reefing or by taking some sail altogether off. The latter meaning is more generally understood by the term.

Take up, or *swell in.*—When a boat has been laid up for any length of time she may, when first put into the water, be leaky, if she does not nearly sink. This will be the result of her planks having shrunk; but in time they will *swell in* or *take up,* as is sometimes said, and she will become watertight.

Taking off.—Said of a tide or wind which is getting less.

Taking off tides.—Lessening tides: *i.e.,* the tides as they occur after full and new moon. (*See* MAKING AND LAGGING OF THE TIDES.)

Tallant.—"The upper hance or break of the rudder abaft." (Smyth.)

Talurit Splice.—A method of putting an eye in the end of a wire rope. The wire is passed through a metal collar and then threaded back to form the eye. The collar is then compressed tightly round both parts of the wire by a hydraulic press.

Tally.—To count; particularly items to be loaded or discharged from a vessel. A word properly used in commerce, and very generally at sea. To agree with the account of another person, on comparison with one's own (generally with regard to numbers), is to tally. The ancient practice of cutting notches in sticks, one stick being given to each party to a transaction, is regarded as the origin of our system of tallying.

Tally (on shipboard).—To haul both sheets aft, as for running before the wind, thus—"Taut aft, the sheets they tally, and belay." (Falconer's "Shipwreck".)

Tan (for the preservation of sails).—A decoction of kutch or catechu with ochre, or some other colouring matter, strained after boiling. Sails may be steeped in this for several hours, after which they are washed and dried. The process of tanning is said to give several years of extra wear to sails.

Tang.—A metal fitting on a mast to which a stay is attached.

Tanker.—A vessel specially constructed to carry liquid cargoes in bulk.

Taper (of a rope).—Rat-tailed: that is, diminishing towards a point. Ropes may be tapered and whipped so as to enable them to pass easily through eyes, etc.

Tar.—This material is obtained in the distillation of various organic matters. There are three sorts of tar—wood, coal, and Stockholm. The residue from the distillation of tar is pitch.

Tarpaulin.—Canvas well covered with tar or paint. The water-proof clothes worn by fishermen and sailors in foul weather (*see* OIL-SKINS) are often called tarpaulins, and rightly so, for they are often saturated with tar or paint instead of with oil.

Tarpaulin muster.—Passing round a hat (originally a tarpaulin hat) for general contributions.

Taunt.—Spoken of the masts and spars of a vessel when very high. When all her light and long spars are aloft she is said to be *all ataunt*.

Taut, or **taught.**—The seaman's pronunciation of the word "tight". But it has a much fuller meaning at sea, and often expresses neatness; properly disposed; prepared for any emergency, etc.

Taut bowline.—A ship is described as sailing with a taut bowline when she is *close-hauled* to the wind, because in that situation her bowlines (being ropes which draw the leeches of square sails forward) are hauled tight.

Taut helm.—When a vessel carries much *weather helm*, she is said to have a taut helm.

Taut leech.—A sail well filled and standing flat is said to "hold a taut leech".

Tell-tale.—Generally speaking, an instrument by which a person can obtain certain records. Thus an inverted compass swinging on the ceiling of a cabin tells the tale of a ship's course; or a dial plate on the wheel shows the position of the tiller.

Tell-tale shake.—"The shake of a rope from aloft, to denote that it wants letting go." (Smyth.)

Tell-of.—To detail men for work.

Tend.—1. To have a tendency; as "she tends to bury her head". 2. The swing of a vessel on the tide is her tend; as "she is tending up".

Tender.—A small vessel employed to attend a larger one. 2. Said of a vessel which is easily inclined from, and slow in returning to, the vertical. The contrary to *stiff*.

Tenon.—Any piece of material so cut as to fit into a mortise. Thus the square tongue cut on the heel of a mast to fit into the *step* is the tenon or tongue.

Tew.—To beat hemp. (Smyth.)

Thames Conservancy.—The common appellation for the Conservators of the Thames, "a body of modern creation, representing the Imperial Government, the city of London and the commercial interest of the river, and exercising the general powers of harbour and conservancy board over the lower river and estuary, as well as those of conservancy on the upper river as far as Cricklade."

Thames Measurement.—A measurement for the tonnage of yachts, introduced by the Royal Thames Yacht Club in 1855, and still used to a certain extent, for example, in *Lloyd's Register of Yachts*. The formula used is:

$$\text{Tonnage} = \frac{(L-B) \times B \times \frac{1}{2}B}{94}$$

were L = length and B = beam, in feet.

Thick.—*Thick-and-thin block.*—A block taking two sizes of rope. (*See* also FIDDLE BLOCK.)

Thick strakes (in shipbuilding).—Strakes (lines of planking) along a ship's sides which are thicker than the rest. (*See* STRAKE.)

Thick stuff (in shipbuilding).—Thick timber.

Thimble.—A small metal eye or ring, concave on its outer diameter, so that a rope may be brought round it and spliced. A thimble is usually inserted into such loops as are liable to get quickly worn, as, for instance, where a lanyard passes through them; or in the *reef-eyes* of sails, through which the *reef-points* are rove. But thimbles are not necessarily round: they may be roughly triangular or "thimble shaped", when they are called *thimble-eyes,* which are also thimble-shaped holes in iron plates where sheaves are not required. They are often used instead of dead-eyes in small craft.

THIMBLES

Tholes (otherwise *thole-pins*, or *thowels*; Anglo-Saxon *thol*).—Pegs fitted into holes in a boat's gunwale, and between which oars are placed while rowing. They are, practically, but a form of *rowlock,* and are to be seen more particularly in sea boats; their chief advantage being that they may be removed when necessary. (*See* ROWLOCKS.) In some waters, more particularly abroad, only one thole-pin is employed, to which the oar is either loosely held by a grommet of rope, or the fulcrum of the oar is so enlarged that a hole may be bored through it, and this hole is dropped over the pin. (*See* fig.)

Thorough put.—"A tangle in the ropes of a tackle." It is, in fact, a thorough mess.

Thrapping.—A binding.

Thrash.—A boat is sometimes said to be "thrashing along" when she is ploughing through the water either at a high rate of speed, or apparently so, either close-hauled or reaching.

Three.—*Three-masted schooner.*—A rig which appears to have originated in America. Every mast is fore-and-aft rigged, which enables the vessel to sail very close to the wind, and to come about quickly. When square topsails are added to the foremast the rig is called

THOLES

jack-ass, and approaches the barkentine, but is to be distinguished from it by the composition of the foremast. (*See* under SCHOONER.)

Three-decker.—A ship which carried guns on three decks below the upper deck.

Three-island type.—A cargo ship with a raised forecastle, centre-castle, and poop.

"Three half-hitches are more than a king's yacht wants." An old expression. It signifies that in making fast by half-hitches, two are sufficient, and three, therefore, quite unnecessary. It is a hint to the landsman not to waste his time or his rope in making more knots than are required.

"Three sheets in the wind".—A very common expression for a man slightly intoxicated. It would appear that there must be definable degrees of drunkenness, and that, under the rule, the condition of three sheets in the wind is one degree less advanced than that of *half seas over* (which *see*).

Throat.—1. That part of a boom or gaff immediately behind the jaws. It is sometimes called the *neck*. To it, on a gaff, is attached the *throat halyard*, which elevates the throat while the *peak halyards* are lifting the *peak* (*see* below); and under the

THROAT

throat is attached another rope called the *tricing line*, which serves to pull or *trice up* the *luff* of the sail, so as quickly to reduce the area it presents to the wind. 2. The forward part of the head of a gaff sail is also called the throat. (*See* SAIL.) 3. The word *throat* is also used in shipbuilding to describe such parts of any timbers as are narrowed down to a neck.

Throat halyard.—The halyard which elevates the *throat* of a gaff. In fore-and-aft rig it is often called the *main halyard,* from the fact that it is the principal halyard on the main mast, just as "mizzen halyard" will mean mizzen *throat* halyard because it is the principal halyard on the mizzen mast. But when spoken of in the same connection with other halyards belonging to the same spar, the distinguishing term "*throat*" would be used, as, for example, the mainsail having been hoisted, the order might be given: "Belay the *throat* halyard and set up on the *peak*". Spoken of in conjunction, the halyards lifting the mainsail are called the *gaff halyards,* because they act upon the gaff. The throat halyard in small craft is fastened to a ring at the throat of the gaff, and after passing through a block at the mast head, comes down on deck and is belayed, usually on the starboard (right hand) side of the mast.

Throt.—On full-rigged ships, that part of the mizzen yard which is close to the mast is sometimes called the throt. It is equivalent to *throat.*

Through fastenings (in shipbuilding).—Bolts or treenails driven through both the planks and timbers of a vessel.

Thrum.—The material for thrumming. Any coarse woollen or hempen yarn.

Thrumming.—To stop a leak by working a portion of thrum well greased and tarred, and contained in a piece of heavy sail cloth, under the vessel by means of ropes, until it reaches the leak, when it is hauled taut and left. The pressure of the water forces the tarred thrum into any openings, and thus the leak is gradually filled, or at least sufficiently so to stop any serious ingress of water. But thrumming is often done with simple yarn, ungreased, and by some is held to be far more efficacious thus.

Thumb cleat.—A small cleat, resembling a man's thumb. These are often fitted to spars, masts, etc. (*See* fig. under CLEAT.)

Thwart.—Athwart means across; and in a boat the *seats* are called the *thwarts,* because they are placed across, or athwart, the boat. The thwarts are secured by knees to a *wiring clamp* (a short stringer) which lies on the bent heads (ribs) of the boat. Their office is somewhat akin to that of the beams of a ship, for they carry such weight as is placed on the upper part of the boat.

Thwartships.—Across the ship or boat.

Thwart-marks to a harbour.—More usually today called *Leading Marks.*—"Two objects on the land which, brought into line with each other, mark the safe course between shoals; as those on Southsea Common act for the Needles, swashways, etc." (Smyth.) Some suppose that the pinnacles which so often cap the corner buttresses of the square church towers of the 15th and 16th centuries have a like purpose. But although these may, and in some instances undoubtedly do, guide the coaster on approaching the shore, it appears improbable that they can have been erected for such a purpose expressly, since they are by no means peculiar to the sea board.

Tide.—The periodical rise (flood) and fall (ebb) of the sea, due to the attraction of the moon and sun. (*See* LAGGING OF TIDES, MAKING OF TIDES, SPRING TIDES, NEAP TIDES).

Tidal wave.—An exceptionally large wave, *not* due to tidal action, but usually following an earthquake or volcanic disturbance. A *tsunami*.

Tide rip, race, or *whorl.*—Short ripplings which result from eddies or the passage over uneven bottoms; also observed in the ocean where two currents meet, but not appearing to affect a ship's course. (Smyth.)

Tide-rode.—A vessel at anchor in a tide way is said to lie tide-rode, when, as is usually the case, she is heading into the tide.

Tide way.—The mid-stream of the tide.

Tide under the lee.—A tide running up against the lee side of a vessel when she is sailing across it. (*See* LEE.)

Head tide.—A tide ahead; that is against the course of a vessel.

Tide and half tide.—"The turn of the tidal stream off shore is seldom coincident with the time of high and low water on shore. In open channels, the tidal stream ordinarily overruns the turn of the vertical movement of the tide by three hours, forming what is usually known as *tide and half-tide*, the effect of which is that at high and low water by the shore the stream is running at its greatest velocity." (Lloyd's "Seaman's Almanac", 1897.)

Tier.—1. A species of fender, made up of old rope. 2. The hollow space in the middle of a coil of rope. 3. In old ships, the battery of guns on one side of a ship.

Ties, or **stops.**—Short ropes which are used to confine a sail to its yard or gaff when furled. They are also called *gaskets* and *furling lines.* (*See also* under STOP.)

Tiffin.—One of the meals once supplied to the officers on board a merchant or mail ship. It was a sort of "high tea", or a light lunch.

Tight.—Spoken of a boat, it means that she is free from leakage or watertight. In any other sense the word as used at sea becomes "*taut*" (*which see*).

Tiller.—One of the component parts of the helm. (*See* HELM.) It is the handle, or beam, at the head of the rudder, and by which that member is worked. In small boats it is a mere bar worked by hand; in large ones it is worked by a wheel; and in long open boats, where the steersman sits too

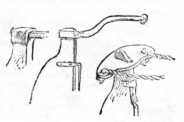

TILLER AND YOKE

far amidships to work it, it changes its form into a *yoke,* or plate, which is worked by lines, called *yoke lines* or *rudder-lines.* The tiller of small craft may be of iron or of wood, and is sometimes decorated with carving at the *head,* that is the end furthest from the rudder. It fits either over or through the rudder stock. If there is any impediment, on deck, to its sweep round it is bent either upwards or downwards; and sometimes, where a mizzen mast stands between the rudder and the tiller head, the tiller makes a deep bend and return so as to clear it; the form of these bends will be seen in the figure under RUDDER. The bar and yoke may also be combined in the manner shown in the same figure. It is a plan sometimes applied to boats, pointed bow and stern, in which a long space exists between the rudder and the helmsman's seat; its object being to do away with the necessity of handling rudder lines. It applies naturally to sailing boats (in which rudder lines are very awkward), and can only be carried out in those which are decked in fore and aft. The principle is very simple; the rudder retains its yoke, and a second yoke is fitted to a pivot on the deck near the helmsman, this second yoke being worked by a short tiller; but the rudder lines which connect these two yokes must in this case be of iron. For further remarks on the subject refer to HELM and RUDDER.

Sweep of the tiller.—The circle the head makes in travelling round.

Tilt.—This word, whether used afloat or ashore, generally means a cover of canvas or of some like material. So, the cover of a boat is occasionally called the tilt, as also may be the small awning over the well of a yacht.

Timbers.—This is a collective term applied to the various members employed in the building of a vessel, such as beams, ribs, floors, etc. But when "timbers" are spoken of without further specification the term often means the ribs only.

Timber heads.—The heads of the ribs of a vessel.

Timber hitch.—A useful knot for taking a hasty hold on some bollard, or post. (*See* KNOTS.)

Timber space (in shipbuilding).—Distance between timbers. The same as ROOM AND SPACE.

Time.—1. *Time allowance,* in yacht and sailing-boat racing, is the foundation for handicapping. A large craft allows time to a smaller one, so that they may compete on equal terms. This allowance is calculated, in seconds per mile, according to rules adopted by any particular club, or on the new system of linear measurement (1896). (*See* under RATING.)

2. *Time,* in rowing, is the space of time occupied between each stroke of the rowers. When all swing together they are said to keep *good time*; when they dip unevenly, that is, one before or after another, the time is called bad, and the crew may then be justly described as "wild". In this latter case, the coxswain or the coach would call out *"Time!"*—meaning this as an expostulation or as an order to *keep time.*

Tingle.—A patch put on over the outside (or inside) of a broken plank in a boat; it must be distinguished from a patch let in, which is not a tingle. Tingles may be of wood or lead; the first is more general, the latter more serviceable, except where the boat has much beaching, for it cannot split. Tingles are usually

TINGLES

nailed on over strips of thick paper or canvas previously saturated in tar, varnish or linseed oil.

Whelk tingle, otherwise called *dog whelk.*—A mollusc which bores through the shells of others. (*See* WHELK.)

Toggle and becket.—A *toggle* is a short piece of wood intended to pass through an eye at the end of a rope: it is grooved about the middle so that the rope may not slip off it. A *becket* is a small eye at the end of a rope, sometimes intended to hold a toggle, sometimes large enough for the toggle to pass loosely through. When a rope or lanyard is furnished with a toggle at one end and a becket (or eye) at the other, the combination is called a *toggle and becket,* and becomes a very useful

little agent, employed on numberless occasions, as, for instance, for hastily confining sails when furled, for holding a sail cover over a boom, for temporarily holding a tiller, etc.

A *sny* is a small toggle attached to a flag whereby it may be bent to its halyard without tying. (*See* SNY.)

Tom.—*Tom Collins, whether or no.*—An old expression of positive assertion. It may mean, literally, "Such is the case, whatever may be said to the contrary".

Tom Pepper.—"A term for a liar; he having, according to nautical tradition, been kicked out of the nether regions for indulging in falsehood." (Smyth.)

Tommed up.—To support, or shore up, with toms or substantial pieces of wood.

Tompion.—A plug placed in the muzzle of a gun to exclude water.

Ton.—*Tonnage*—The measure of a ship's internal dimensions, as the basis of a standard for dues, etc. The term appears to have originated from the *tun* cask of wine and to have meant the number of such tuns which the ship could carry. The *ton,* as a term of space, is 100 cubic feet.

Gross tonnage.—The number of tons enclosed in a ship.

Net tonnage.—The cubic capacity, in tons, of the *earning space* in a ship (*i.e.* cargo holds and passenger accommodation).

Deadweight tonnage.—The number of *tons weight* which a ship can carry.

Displacement tonnage.—The number of tons of water which a ship displaces, *i.e.* her total *weight.*

Tonne.—The metric unit of weight, of 1000 Kilogrammes, is increasingly used to measure displacement tonnage. The tonne (2204·6 lb) varies from the avoirdupois ton (2240 lb) by only 1·6 per cent.

Tongue.—1. In shipbuilding, the long tapered end of one piece of timber made to fall into a scarf at the end of another piece to gain length. 2. A low or sunken sand, as that in the Thames estuary (off Margate) marked by the lightship known as *The Tongue.*

Top.—1. That portion of a mast from the hounds upwards. 2. A sort of platform placed at the head of the lower mast.

To *top.*—To raise one end of a yard or boom by means of a rope called the *topping lift;* in old ships the free traverse of the square sails about the mast was often interrupted by stays, thus necessitating that the yards or booms should be topped as the ship came about. In the modern rigs, however, this is to a great extent obviated; and the topping lift belongs now, more particularly, to a gaff-sail, such as the main sail of a cutter, a yawl and other fore-and-aft rigged craft. In sails of this description a topping-lift is a halyard used to elevate the after end of a boom, which is called *topping* the boom, and is necessary under various circumstances, as in *reefing, tricing* up the sail, etc. (*See* diagram under RIGGING.) The standing end of a topping-lift is either permanently secured or simply *eye-spliced* and passed over the boom end; it then runs through a block, usually placed high up on the head of the mast, and comes down on deck to be belayed on the starboard side of the mast. In large vessels the topping-lift is double, one rope being on each side of the sail. In some sailing boats, more particularly in those carrying lug-sails or those una-rigged, the topping-lift is occasionally called the *sling.*

Top gallant (pronounced t'garn).—This term has a considerable use at sea. It is derived from top "garland"; a garland being originally a rope used for swaying a topmast. (*See* GARLAND.) In a ship we have the top gallant masts, yards, sails, stays, etc.

Top gallant forecastle (pronounced "t'garn fo'ks'l").—A small extra forecastle in certain ships, above the deck.

Top-hamper.—Weight aloft, that is, above the decks of a vessel. Thus her topmasts and yards constitute her top-hamper; and if these are too much for her, she is said to have too much top-hamper. In a ship the top-hamper is sometimes a rope for swaying a top or top-gallant mast—the ancient "topmast garland".

Topmast.—This is described under the heading MAST.

Topmast stays.—Topmasts, like lower masts, are supported by various stays, those keeping them forward being called fore-stays, and those keeping them back, the back-stays. In a ship each topmast has these stays, which take their names from that of the mast, as main stay, top gallant stay, fore stay, etc. In single masted craft the *topmast fore-stay* is a stay or rope running from the head of the topmast to the bowsprit end. Upon it is set the jib-topsail. *Topmast back-stays,* also called *preventers,* are only seen in yachts of tolerable size, being found unnecessary in small boats (except under extraordinary circumstances), and always a little difficult to work, since they have to be shifted as the boom comes over. (*See* diagram under RIGGING.)

Topsails.—In square rigged vessels the topsails are those set above the *courses,* taking their names from the masts, yards, or stays upon which they stand. Thus, in a ship, there will be the main-topsail, main-top-gallant, main-royal, main-top-studding-sail, main-top-gallant-studding-sail, main-top-stay-sail, main-top-gallant-stay-sail, etc. In modern days, the huge square topsail of the old ship having been found to hold too much wind to work rapidly, has been divided into two parts, called respectively the upper topsail and the lower or middle topsail; and this division constitutes what are known as *double topsails* (under which heading they are more fully described). In cutters, sloops, and other fore-and-aft rigged craft, the *main topsail* is that one set above the mainsail; here it is but an extension of the mainsail, and the two should work together as one. The *jib-topsail,* or, as it may be called, the topmast fore-stay-sail, is a jib sail standing on the topmast fore-stay.

A topsail extended on a gaff is called a gaff topsail; and the gaff topsails on a cutter yacht may be as follow (*see* fig.):—*Jib-headed topsail.*—That most usually carried, because by far the most handy for general cruising, and at all times the most easily manipulated. It takes its name from its shape, being a jib-shaped or triangular sail; its head draws up to the topmast head, and it may be either laced to the topmast or held to it by a rope, called the *jack-stay,* which is attached to a cringle in the middle of the luff. *Big topsail.*—A general name, given for want of a better, to the largest topsail a yacht carries under normal circum-

GAFF TOPSAILS

stances. Its head is extended on a yard, so that it becomes, in fact, a sort of *standing lug,* elevated above the mainsail, with its *clew* drawn up to the peak and its tack-line running down to the base of the lower mast. It is only used in light winds.—*Spinnaker topsail,* often called the *big topsail,* has no connection with the spinnaker, but being a racing sail only suited to *running* or *sailing large,* is often used at the same time as that. The peculiarity of this sail lies in the fact that its after leech is extended beyond the peak of the mainsail on a small boom called the *jack-yard.* It is difficult to determine whether this sail possesses any real advantage over the ordinary *big topsail,* but with certain boats it may, without doubt, be effective.

Jack topsail.—A topsail laced to a spar called the *jack-yard,* which yard is drawn up close to the mast and extends perpendicularly up beyond it. The foot of the sail is also sometimes extended on another small yard (also called the jack-yard), like the spinnaker topsail previously described.

Theoretically a topsail should be set to windward so that the tack may always lie down on the mainsail; but as this, of course, is impossible, it is usually hoisted on the starboard side.

A boat is said to *hold her topmast* when she can beat to windward under a topsail. This, as above noted, she cannot do with her big topsail if the wind be at all fresh, for that sail is liable to belly away from the mast and loose the wind, and is then said not to hold the mast. She holds her topmast best under a jib topsail. With barges and other heavily laden craft the topsail is often carried when the mainsail is double reefed or brailed up.

Topsail sheets.—The ropes which work topsails. In ships the ropes attached to both clews of all topsails (*i.e.,* all square sails above the courses) are called sheets, but not so with the courses. (*See* SHEETS.) In fore-and-aft rigged boats the topsail sheet is that rope which brings the clew of a topsail to the gaff. It is bent to the sail, passes through a sheave at the gaff end, thence to a block which is often suspended by a short rope or *tail* from the throat, and then downward to the deck, to be belayed in the most convenient position, for the belaying of this sheet varies in different boats. (*See* fig., p. 308.) This method of bringing the topsail sheet down may need explanation: the topsail, it must be remembered, usually (though not always) is set on the starboard side, and while the boat is on the starboard tack there is no reason why the sheet should not be brought straight down from the gaff end. But when the boat comes about on the other tack the mainsail will press very heavily upon the topsail sheet, and most probably overstrain, if indeed it does not break it. It is necessary, then, that this sheet should be relieved, and the best manner of doing this is to take it along the head of the mainsail as nearly parallel with the gaff as possible.

Topsail breeze.—A fine breeze in which a vessel may sail under topsails.

Topsail schooner.—The common name for a schooner carrying square fore-topsails. (*See* SCHOONER.)

Top sawyer.—A slang term. The chief man in any undertaking; he with the authority. A person who does anything in a first class manner may also be called a top sawyer, as also may a boat which has more than usually excellent qualities.

Top timbers (in shipbuilding).—The topmost futtocks of a vessel, sometimes called the *heads* or *head timbers.*—Above the top timbers are placed the *short timbers. (See* diagrams under FRAME.)

Tornado.—A violent whirlwind of small extent, occurring in West Africa, the U.S.A., and less frequently, elsewhere.

Torse.—A coarse kind of hemp usually called *cordilla.*

Torsion (of cables).—Twisting; the state of being spirally twisted. "All ropes formed by twisting have a contrary turn, and a disposition to kink from torsion." (Smyth.)

Tosh.—A slang term for a theft, more especially from dockyards.

Toss oars.—The expression is variously used, but especially signifies to throw the oars up to the perpendicular as they do in the Royal Navy in compliment to an officer, preparatory to shipping or unshipping.

Total loss.—A term in marine insurance, signifying that the underwriters (who insured her against loss) have to pay the whole amount for which a lost vessel has been insured, without deduction for salvage.

Touch (in navigation).—To touch at any port is to stop there for only a short period. (In sailing).—Sails are said to touch (meaning touch the wind), when they just begin to shiver as the vessel is put up to the wind.

Luff and touch her.—An order to the helmsman to sail the vessel so close as almost to touch the wind.

Touch and take.—"An old proverb which Nelson applied to a ship about to encounter her opponent."

Tow.—1. To *tow* is to draw a vessel along in the water. It may be done either from banks, by horses or men, or by another vessel in the water, as a tug takes a ship *in tow.*

A *tow-line* or *tow-rope* is the rope by which the vessel is towed; those employed by tugs are very large hempen ropes, seldom less than 9 inches in diameter, and very costly. On the Upper Thames a thin tow-line formed part of the inventory of every new skiff; and towing was a very favourite method of getting up against stream.

A *tow-mast* is a small mast used in canal barges and in skiffs to lead the tow-line clear of all impediments along the banks. The line is usually attached to the mast in such a manner as to form a sort of backstay on the side farthest from the bank.

A *tow* among tug and barge men signifies the vessel or vessels in tow.

To steer while being towed is not altogether easy. In an open boat a tow-line should never be made fast to the stem, the strain on the boat being too great; it should be passed round one of the forward thwarts. "As the vessel towed affects the motions of the other, much attention is required on her part to second the intentions of the towing vessel." (Brande and Cox.) This, of course, only applies to large vessels.

2. *Tow-hauling.*—A method, in the oyster fisheries of the Essex rivers, and occasionally elsewhere, of dredging for oysters in small creeks and under banks, where a sailing vessel cannot work. The work is done in large open boats called skiffs (oyster skiffs). Two anchors being placed at a convenient distance apart (say 60 or 80 fathoms), the dredges are put overboard and the skiff is "hauled" from one anchor to the other, and then back, thus "towing" the dredges along, and hence called "haul-towing" or "tow-hauling". If there be a fair breeze, a lug-sail is set, which assists the dredgermen at their work.

3. *Tow.*—By the material *tow* is usually understood the hard or coarser part of hemp or flax.

Track.—A vessel's wake upon the water.

Trade winds.—Those winds which, in and near the torrid zone, continue to blow more or less constantly from one quarter. The North East Trade Wind from about 30°N towards the equator in the Atlantic and Pacific oceans, and the South East Trade Wind from about 30°S towards the equator in the Atlantic, Pacific, and Indian oceans.

Trail boards.—In old ships the carved boards on either side of the stem, and helping to support the figure head.

Tramp.—A cargo ship that is not confined to any particular route but carries cargo anywhere that is convenient and profitable.

Transit.—When two objects are in line one behind the other they are said to be in transit. (*See* THWART-MARKS.)

Transom (*trans,* across).—In a ship the transoms are beams bolted across the sternpost to receive the after ends of the decks. In smaller craft the transom is either a solid piece, or a frame work, taking the form of the end of a boat, and secured to the after side of the sternpost. (*See* Drawing of up-turned boat under TINGLE, where the transom appears white.) In either case it gives the form to the stern of the vessel, though this may be concealed by the addition of a counter. (*See* FRAME.) In large ships and especially in old ones there are a number of transoms. The *deck transoms* are the highest, being those upon which the deck planks are rebated (recessed). The *helm transoms* are at the head of the sternpost. The *wing transoms* come next below and form the lowest part of the stern. *Transom knees* are knees which connect the transoms with the sides of a vessel.

Traveller.—1. A ring which travels along a spar; it is frequently connected with a hook or an eye to which a sail may be attached. The jib-stay of a cutter carries the jib-sail along the bowsprit by means of a traveller. A lug sail is also sometimes confined to its mast by the same means, though the plan is not altogether a good one, unless the traveller be made of two parts, when it is less likely to jam. A traveller is also sometimes used instead of a *clamp* on a boom, for reefing. Travellers are the better for being served (or bound) with leather, which must be kept greased.

2. *Travellers* (in the stays of a ship).—The *running backstays* are sometimes called by this name. (*See* under BACKSTAYS.)

3. *Travelling iron.*—A name sometimes given on ship board to that which in a yacht or sailing boat is usually called the *horse* (*which see*).

Traverse.—A yard traverses about its mast when it turns about. To put the yards *a-travers* (Fr. *à traverse*) is to dispose them in a fore-and-aft direction.

Traverse sailing (in navigation).—Sailing in different courses in succession.

Traverse Board.—A board upon which the points of the compass were marked and along which small holes were bored. Pegs were stuck into the holes to denote the direction and distance a vessel had been sailing.

Traverse table.—A species of table, giving the lengths of the sides of all right-angled triangles and the angles between them, employed in reducing the courses made in traverse sailing.

Traverse wind.—A wind setting directly against the course a vessel desires to take, as into a harbour, and thereby preventing vessels from getting out.

Trawl.—A large net attached to a heavy beam called the trawl-beam, used in bottom fishing. A vessel employed in the trawl fisheries is called a *trawler,* and if in the North Sea, a *North Sea trawler.*

Otter trawl.—Another form of trawling net used in estuaries and for inshore fishing.

Tread.—The length of a vessel's keel is her tread.

Tree.—The word "tree" is often employed at sea to mean "of timber" or "wooden". Thus we hear of the treenails, chess-trees, cross-trees, rough-trees, trestle-trees, waist-trees, etc. (all described under their respective headings), all of which are of wood.

Treenails (*i.e.,* *tree* or *timber* nails, pronounced, and often written, "trennels").—Wooden bolts of various forms, by which the strakes of a ship's bottom are secured to her lower timbers.

Treenail wedges.—Treenails of wedge-like shape.

Trench.—To trench the ballast is so to place it that a passage or trench is left, in case it may be necessary to get at any part of the vessel.

Trend.—The general direction.

The trend of a coast line is its direction, as south-west, north-east, etc.

Trestle trees.—A trestle tree is a flat piece of wood at a masthead supporting the cross-trees and topmast. In large vessels there are two; one each side of the mast. In small craft, one piece, having a hole in it to fit over the mast and another to form a *lower cap* for the topmast, takes the place of the two. Trestle trees are supported on the shoulders, or bibbs, as they are sometimes called. In old ships fitted with *tops* they carry the tops; and in all cases they support the entire weight of the topmast. (*See* under MAST.)

Triatic stay, or **jumper stay.**—This is a stay (or rope) running from the main to the fore-mast head in a schooner and acting as a forestay to the main-mast. Also, the horizontal stay between a mast and funnel, often fitted to carry signal halyards. It will be seen that the triatic stay precludes the possibility of setting a gaff top-sail on the foremast. In this case square top-sails are set (as in the fig.). When it is desired to set a gaff topsail a mainstay—running from the main-mast head to the fore-mast foot—is employed instead of the triatic

TRIATIC STAY

stay, the large boom foresail being "topped" over it each time the vessel comes about.

Trice.—To trice up is to draw up, shorten or tighten some sail or rope, and the *tricing line* is the rope by which this is accomplished.

Thus the main trice (also called the *tack trice,* or *tack tricing line*), in a fore-and-aft rigged boat, trices or draws up the tack of the mainsail towards the mast head (as in the fig.), the object of this action being to let the wind out of the sail without lowering it. This line is attached to the *tack* of the sail and, passing through a block beneath the throat of the gaff, comes down again on deck. The *bobstay trice* is a rope bent to the bobstay, and serving to pull it up beneath the bowsprit so that it may not

TRICED UP

chafe the cable while the boat lies at anchor.

Trick (at sea).—The time allotted to a man to be at the wheel or elsewhere. The word has somewhat the same meaning as spell, and may otherwise be defined as "a spell on duty".

Tricolor.—The national banner of France, adopted from the ancient standards, during the First Revolution. These colours are blue, white and red, the blue being first, or next the flagstaff. These are also the colours of Holland, conferred by Henry IV of France, but disposed lengthwise. Tricoloured flags have also been adopted by various other nations. (*See* INTERNATIONAL CODE, Flag T.)

Trim.—The trim is the position of a vessel in the water with respect to the horizontal. If she is level she is *in trim*; if on *uneven keel* or if lying over on one side she is *out of trim*. (*See* fig.) She is also popularly called "trim" when she presents a smart appearance, as in the old song, "Farewell, my

BOATS OUT OF TRIM

trim-built wherry," though this line might also mean that the boat was so built as to float level in the water, or "trim".

To *trim a boat* is, therefore, to balance her in the water so that she may lie both level and on an even keel. (*See* KEEL.) In a sailing boat or a yacht this will mean to properly dispose the ballast. In an open or row-boat it will be to place the people so that she is in trim; for passengers are often in the habit of moving about or of choosing such situations as put the boat quite out of trim.

To *trim sails* is so to dispose the sails of a boat that she will move at her best; and as sails are, of course, worked by sheets, to haul in a sheet to the required extent is called *trimming in* the sheet.

To *trim down* a boat is to take down and stow away the sails, etc., after a cruise, and to leave all things in proper order for future use.

Trimaran.—A vessel with a central hull and two floats, one on either side.

Trinity House.—The body responsible in Britain for lighthouses, lightships, buoys and other aids to navigation, the disposal of wrecks and the licensing authority for pilots, and other matters connected with navigation. This institution was incorporated by Henry VIII in 1515, and its powers were confirmed by James II and further defined in the reign of Victoria. Its members are called "brethren", the *Elder Brethren*, of whom there are thirteen, carry out the practical duties of Trinity House.

Trinity high-water mark.—The height of high water at any time or place, as marked by the Trinity House.

Trip.—1. A passage or cruise. 2. In sailing, a single *board*. (*See* TACK.)

The *anchor atrip.*—The anchor just as it leaves the ground. (*See* ANCHOR.)

Tripping (in yacht-sailing).—The striking of the boom of a vessel on the crest of a wave, as she is running before the wind. Should this occur with any violence, or in a heavy sea, the result may be that the sail will suddenly gybe, a possibility by all means to be avoided and often successfully guarded against by slightly *topping* the boom.

Tripping a yard.—Bringing it to the necessary angle.

Tripping a topmast.—Lifting it slightly so as to withdraw the *fid.* This is done by hauling on the—

Tripping line, a rope for lifting the heel of a top or top-gallant mast.

Trireme.—A Greek warship of pre-Christian times, propelled by three banks of oars.

Troll.—To fish by drawing bait through the water.

Tropics.—"The parallels of declination between which the sun's annual path in the heavens is contained, the distance of each from the equator being equal to the sun's greatest declination. The northern tropic is called the tropic of Cancer, and the southern one that of Capricorn, from their touching the ecliptic in the first points of those stages." (Brande and Cox.)

Trot.—A line of buoys laid out at regular intervals.

Trough.—1. (Of the sea.) The hollow between the waves. 2. A small boat broad at the ends. (Smyth.)

Trow.—A species of barge which, as with so many other forms of vessels, varies with locality. Thus, on the Severn River it is a *clincher-built* hull with a flat floor, while on the Tyne it is a sort of double boat with a space between, at one time used in the salmon fishery.

Truck (of a mast).—1. The wooden cap at the head of a pole or topmast. It is flat and circular, and generally has one or more small holes in it for flag or signal halyards.

2. The small wooden beads often threaded on the jaw rope of a gaff are sometimes called trucks or *parrel-trucks*, though more properly, perhaps, they are *parrel-rollers*. (*See* PARREL.)

3. The small wheels of a wooden gun-carriage.

Truckle.—1. To lower, or partly lower; spoken of a sail. The term is often used in general conversation, as to "truckle under". 2. A Welsh coracle.

MAST TRUCK

Trundle-head.—The circular head of a capstan into which the bars are fixed for turning; to trundle being to make ambulatory gyrations,* as in the saying "to trundle around".

Truss.—To truss or *truss up* (in sailing craft) was to brail up a sail quickly, which is done with a *truss rope* or *line*. (*See* BRAIL.)

Truss.—An iron fitting which held the yard to the mast of a square-rigged vessel, while allowing it to move.

Truss and parrel.—An arrangement, usually consisting of an iron ring, but sometimes a peculiar loop in a rope, by which a yard is held to its mast. Such an arrangement is generally required with lug sails. (*See* under LUG.)

Truss hoops.—Clasps which may run on masts or any other spar. A divided ring may be regarded as a truss and serves very well with lug sails.

Try.—To *try*.—To lie to, or heave to, in a heavy gale. This is always a somewhat difficult operation; but by a judicious balance of canvas, a vessel's bow may be kept to the sea without causing her to make great way; and this is called *trying*. Thus if, in a yacht or sailing boat, close-reefed, the helm be put down, the foresail belayed on the weather side, so that it lies aback, the jib to leeward, and the main sheet be close-hauled, the boat, if in proper trim, ought to lie to without difficulty. With respect to the old ships there were great discussions on the art of trying, which, with all the square sail they carried, was a very nice performance. It was said by Smyth that close-hauled and under all sail a vessel gained headway within six points, while in trying she might come up to five and fall off to seven. Falconer speaks of lashing the helm alee. Smyth, on the other hand, speaks strongly against it. "If a vessel be in proper trim," he says, "she will naturally keep to the wind; but custom and deficiency of seamanlike ability have induced the lazy habit of lashing the helm alee."

* In plainer English, to walk round.

Try back.—To *pay* back, or let go back. Spoken of a rope or cable which is being hauled upon, it means "let it go out again".

Trysail (a name derived, probably, from sails set when "trying").— The trysails, as part of a vessel's inventory, are small sails used in very bad weather, when no others can be carried, or, occasionally, for rough work. But in fore-and-aft rig, when *the trysail* is spoken of, it means a gaff sail (such as the mainsail of a cutter) without a boom. Such a sail is made of stouter canvas than the fair weather sails, and, the boom being absent, is very much better suited to rough winter work; for a boom-sail holds the wind when a trysail will readily shake it out, while the latter possesses the further advantage that it can be quickly brailed or triced up.

TRYSAIL

Trysail mast (in old ships).—"A spar abaft the fore and mains masts for hoisting the trysail." (Smyth.) They are now seldom seen.

Tsunami.—A wave caused by an underwater upheaval; commonly, but improperly, called a tidal wave.

Tuck.—That part of a vessel's stern immediately under her *counter* and terminating under the *tuck-rail*—which is a line of horizontal timbers forming part of the counter of a ship.

Tug.—A powerfully-engined vessel especially built for towing.

Tumble home.—(*See* FALL HOME.)

Tumbler.—A fitting between the jaws of a gaff to prevent its chafing the mast. Sometimes called a *clapper*.

2. A hinged pin fitting over a chain. When the tumbler is rotated the chain is released.

Turk's head.—An ornamental knot used on side ropes or wherever else convenient. Its name is derived from a supposed resemblance to a turban.

Turn.—To *take a turn.*—To pass a rope once or twice over a spar, etc.

Turn in.—1. Of a rope or rigging, to turn the end over and into the rope itself, thus making an eye, generally enclosing something. So to *turn in dead-eyes* is to secure the ends of the shroud round the dead-eye. This is the method in which dead-eyes are usually fitted.

2. To turn in, among seafaring men, means to go below; or if already below, to get into one's bunk.

Turn-turtle.—An expression sometimes used of a boat when she suddenly turns in the wrong direction, as up to the wind, etc.; but some use the same term when she capsizes.

Turn up.—To summon, as "Turn up the hands", an order on shipboard to summon all hands on deck.

Turret ship.—A ship of war in which the heavy guns are mounted on rotating and covered decks called turrets.

2. A merchant ship whose upper plating curved sharply inwards, forming a *harbour deck,* and then upwards to form a *trunk* or *turret.* With bulk cargoes such a vessel was self-trimming.

Twiddling line.—This term is now seldom heard because the thing itself is no longer in use. In old ships the twiddling-line was a small line employed to steady the steering wheel; and it was often of ornamental appearance.

Twig.—To twig, to pull upon a bowline (Smyth).

Twine.—Strong thread used in sail-making.

Two blocks.—(*See* CHOCK ABLOCK.)

Tye.—A rope or chain. In ships it is often part of a purchase, such as that used in hoisting topsail or top gallant yards.

Tye block and *fly block.*—Blocks connected with the lifting of heavy yards in square rigged ships.

Ties.—Ropes or bands of sail-cloth employed in tying up sails when they are furled.

Typhoon.—A violent storm in the Eastern seas.

L

U

U-boat.—(From German *unterseeboot*.) A German, or other enemy submarine, of the World Wars.

Ullage.—That part which a cask lacks of being full. A useless or lazy seaman.

Un.—*Unbend.*—To unlash or take off, *i.e.*, the direct opposite to *bend,* which is put up or tie up. So a sail is unbent when taken off its yard or boom, etc.

Unbitt.—To loosen the belay of a rope from the bitts. (*See* BITTS.)

Unclaimed.—Spoken of a vessel, it is the same as "derelict"; a vessel found without any living person or domestic animal on board, and if left unclaimed for a certain period, becomes the property of the finder, or if claimed he has a lien on it to the full extent of the salvage. But if any domestic animal is on board she is not derelict.

Unhandy (of a boat).—Not handy, slow in stays, etc.

Unreeve.—To draw ropes out from sheaves or blocks.

Unrig.—To take the rigging off a vessel, as for laying up, etc.

Unship.—To remove anything from its proper place. Thus the rowlocks may be looked upon as the proper place for oars; and, therefore, to unship oars is to take them out of the rowlocks.

Una rig.—A rig at one time very common in Norfolk, from whence it was to a certain extent taken up on the Upper Thames and other smooth water rivers. It consists of one sail only (whence the name), with gaff and boom, hoisted by a single halyard, the mast being stepped very far forward. The boat carrying the una rig is usually very shallow and beamy, the breadth being carried aft; and she is fitted with a centreboard. Her qualities come out when working to windward, for which she is peculiarly adapted; she is not suited, however, to broken water. "Una boats should be kept well down by the stern, as if they are down by the head they gripe or fly to windward, and no amount of weather helm will keem them away." (Davies.) This rule, indeed, applies more or less to every craft. Norfolk wherries are the origin of una rig, and on their own waters are unsurpassable. (*See* WHERRY.)

Under.—*Under bare poles.*—A ship is described thus when she has no sails set: and in this condition she sometimes runs before the wind, which is called *scudding under bare poles.* (*See* SCUD.)

Under canvas.—Having sails set; in contradistinction to being under bare poles.

Under-current.—A current under the surface of the water, and often in a direction contrary to that of the surface.

Under-manned.—Lacking the number of hands (men) necessary to work a vessel properly.

Under-masted.—When the masts of a vessel are too short.

Under-run.—To under-run a tackle is to separate its parts. To under-run a hawser or rope is to drop it underneath any object so as to clear it, or to put it over a boat and haul the boat along it for the same purpose.

Underset, or **undertow.**—"Wherever the wind impels the surface water directly upon the shore of a bay the water below restores equilibrium by taking a direction contrary to the wind. The *resaca,* or underset, is particularly dangerous on those beaches where heavy surf prevails." (Smyth.)

Under-shore.—To raise up by *shores* placed underneath.

Under the lee.—1. Under the shelter of any object.

2. The tide setting under the lee of a vessel. (*See* LEE.)

Under the wind.—To be sheltered by any object so as not to feel the force of the wind. The same as *under the lee* of anything. (*See* LEE.)

Under turns.—(*See* OVER TURNS.)

Under way.—"A vessel is *underway* when she is not at anchor, or made fast to the shore, or aground": she is making way through the water, or has way, when making progress. This term must be distinguished from the next, which is pronounced in exactly the same manner; the mistake being often made.

Under weigh.—To be in the act of weighing anchor. Thus a vessel may be under *weigh* without having *way* on her, or, in other words, "under weigh but not under way."

Underwriters.—"Parties who take upon themselves the risk of insurance, and so called from subscribing their names at the foot of the policy. They are legally presumed to be acquainted with every custom of the trade whereon they enter a policy." (Smyth.)

Uneven Keel.—(*See* KEEL.)

UNION, Union Jack.—The Union is the national flag of Great Britain. When hoisted on a Jack-staff it may be called the Union Jack; otherwise the latter name is incorrect. It is a composition of the flags of England, Scotland, and Ireland, or, in other words, of the cross of St. George

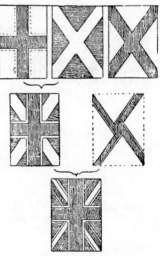

UNION JACK

(a red cross on a white field), the saltire of St. Andrew (a white saltire on a blue field), and the saltire of St. Patrick (a red saltire on a white field). From the date of the union of England and Scotland it consisted of the flags of these two countries only; when the union with Ireland took place, the Irish flag was also introduced. The manner in which this composition is obtained is purely heraldic, and may be to some extent understood by reference to the figures. Those who would know more of the subject may be referred to *Flags and Signals*; RYA, Gillingham, Dorset SP8 4LJ.

Up.—This word is often used at sea as an order meaning to raise up, as "up anchor", "up topsail", etc., just as the word "down" often implies "lower". To *up helm* is to put the helm *up,* that is *up to the wind,* or, in other words, against the wind. (*See* HELM.)

Up (of the tide).—The tide rising. In a river this is very easily remembered, for as rivers must have their source on high ground their waters must run *downwards* to the sea. The same applies with regard to the *stream* of a river where there is no tide. The stream is the water running down from the hills, and, therefore, to go up must be to go against the stream, and *vice versâ.*

Up river.—A name given to that portion of a river which is above the first lock: that is where there is no longer a tide. So we often speak of up-river boats, etc., meaning boats suitable to the non-tidal parts of a river. The expression, however, may often mean any part of a river up away from the sea, or where the water becomes fresh: and in this sense it is generally used by down-river men.

Up and down.—The state of an anchor cable when it leads vertically downwards from the hawsepipe.

Upper.—*Upper and lower caps.*—The rings at the head of a mast through which a topmast passes. The lower cap is often incorporated with the *trestle tree,* which supports the weight of the topmast, by its fid. This combination is occasionally called the *cap and yoke.* (*See* CAP and YOKE.)

Upper works (old term).—The same as *freeboard* when a vessel is loaded.

V

Van.—The leading ships of a fleet or squadron.

Vane.—A narrow strip of bunting at the masthead to show the direction from which the wind is blowing.

Vangs.—Ropes extending from the peak of a gaff, sprit, or lateen yard, to the sides of a vessel; their office being to steady either of these when hoisted without a sail, as is often the case in square rigged vessels and steam boats. In the Thames and sea-going barges they always exist, and serve the further purpose of main sheets when the vessel is hay laden or freighted with any cargo which necessitates the sail being reefed up so high that the sheet cannot be used. In lateen rig they also assist in working the sails.

Vail (old term).—To lower, as in dipping a flag.

Variation.—The difference in direction of the earth's magnetic pole from the geographical north pole, due to the former being at a considerable distance from the latter.

Veer.—To *veer* (in sailing).—To turn away from the wind. But the word is almost obsolete, having been replaced by the more familiar term *wear* (*which see*).

To *veer out* (of a rope).—To let out a hawser or any other rope by which a vessel is fast, or by which anything is fast to her. Thus, if a dinghy in tow be too close to a yacht's stern, her guest rope may be "veered out". Or, again, if a vessel ride uneasily for want of cable, the cable may be "veered out". So also if the cable be running out when it should be fast, it is said to be "veering".

Veer and haul.—Hauling on a rope and slackening up again alternately.

Veering and backing of the wind.—The *veering* of the wind is its change in direction with the sun, *i.e.* from E. through S. to W., etc. Its *backing* is its change in the other direction. (*See* WINDS.)

Vessel.—"Any ship or boat, or other description of vessel, used in navigation." (British Merchant Shipping Act.)

Vigia.—A rock or shoal that has been reported to exist, but has not yet been verified by survey.

Voyal.—"A rope used on shipboard to bring the pressure of the capstan to bear on the cable without the necessity of winding the latter round the barrel." (Brande and Cox.)

W

Waft.—A 16th century term meaning to convoy or escort. 2. A weft.

Wager boat.—A boat in which races are rowed. The name would appear to be derived from the fact that in professional racing wagers are laid by the competitors or their backers on the result of a meeting. The type of wager boat now in use is the improved "whiff", called the *best boat*. (*See* BEST BOAT and WHIFF.)

Waggon.—A place on board a ship where superannuated goods are stored. The term applies principally to old war-ships.

Waist.—That part of a vessel between the forecastle and the poop. The term, however, more particularly refers to those vessels which have quarter decks. In these it is that part of the main deck immediately forward of the quarter deck. A flush-decked ship can hardly be said to have a waist. In old ships with big poops the waist was just forward of the poop.

Waist anchor.—An additional anchor in a ship, stowed somewhat further aft than the main anchor, though not in the waist.

Waist cloth (old Naval term).—A painted covering for hammocks in the waist.

Waist rail.—In ships, a sort of channel rail or moulding on a ship's sides.

Waist-tree.—Another name for a *rough-tree,* in the vicinity of the waist of a ship.

Waister.—A name for a person who is no good. As an old Naval term it implies those green-hands or superannuated ones who, not being fit to send aloft, were relegated to the waist of the ship, where they might haul ropes and swab the decks.

Wake.—The track a vessel leaves behind her on the surface of the water. One vessel may therefore sail in another's wake.

Wale.—1. In shipbuilding, the *wale,* or outer wale, of a boat is the strake running beneath and supporting the outer edge of the gun-wale. (*See* fig.) It is sometimes called the *band,* or the *rubbing piece,* and is occasionally incorporated with the uppermost strake of the boat. The *inwale* is a corresponding strip running inside the boat. (*See* GUNWALE.)

2. *Wales* or *walings* are strengthening planks or battens laid down upon the ribs inside

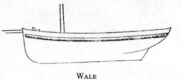

WALE

a boat to protect the skin. Those in the lowest part of the boat are called *foot walings*. (*See* diagrams under FRAME.)

Walk away.—To haul on a rope by holding it and walking. 2. One boat is said to walk away from another when she easily passes the other and leaves her a long way behind.

Walk back.—To keep hold of a rope or fall, but to walk back, allowing the weight hauled upon to control it.

Wall.—*Wall knot* ("Wale-knot").—The name of a knot raised at the end of a rope by passing each strand through the bight of the next one.

Wall-sided.—A vessel with perpendicular sides, as a barge.

Wardroom.—The officers' messroom in H.M. Ships.

Ware.—(*See* WEAR.)

Warm the bell.—To strike eight bells early at the end of a watch, and thus, in general, to do something unnecessarily or unjustifiably early.

Warp.—1. A rope by which something is dragged.

2. A light hawser (*i.e.,* a strong rope) by which a vessel is moved: this is called *warping*; it was an old method, before the introduction of tugs, of getting a ship out of harbour. Warps were made fast to buoys, and being heaved upon gradually brought the vessel along until she could make sail.

3. *Warp* (of timbers).—To curl up: the usual consequence of unseasoned timber being allowed to become wet and dry alternately.

4. *Warp and weft* (in sail-making).—The *warp* is the lengthwise measurement of sailcloth, the width being the *weft*.

Wash.—The commotion resulting in a wave, created by a vessel moving rapidly through the water. This is her *wash,* not her swell. (*See* GROUND SWELL and SWELL.)

Awash.—Wet. Gunwales under. Hence a boat is said to sail "all awash" when she heels over under sail so that her decks are washed by the water.

Wash board.—A planking fixed along the bows and sides of a boat to prevent the water she cuts from coming on deck. (*See* WEATHER-BOARDS.)

Wash port.—An aperture in the bulwarks which allow water on deck to flow overboard.

Wash strake.—The same as wash board.

Wash of an oar.—The blade is occasionally called by this name.

Wash (a measure).—In the shellfish trades one fourth of an oyster bushel, or "tub", the tub itself varying according to locality.

Watches.—The division of a ship's company into two, called the starboard watch and the port watch; these names being derived from the situation in which the hammocks of the crews are usually hung. "The crew are divided into two divisions, as equally as may be, called the watches. Of these the chief mate commands the larboard (port), and the second mate the starboard. They divide the time between them, being on and off duty, or, as it is called, on deck and below, every other four hours."

Watch and watch.—Four hours on, and four hours off.

Dog watches.—"They are to shift the watches each night, so that the same watch need not be on deck the same hours. In order to effect this, the watch from 4 to 8 p.m. is divided into two halves, or dog watches, one from 4 to 6, and the other from 6 to 8. By this means they divide the 24 hours into 7 watches instead of 6, and thus shift the hours every night." (Dana, "Two Years before the Mast.") The system of watches has somewhat changed since the introduction of steam vessels, upon which the 4 hours on and the 4 off has given way in some cases to 4 on and 8 off, or to day and night watches of 12 hours' duration. (*See* also under BELLS.)

Watch Bill.—A nominal list of men, giving their watch and special stations and duties.

Water.—*Water bailiff.*—A Customs official whose duties relate more especially to the inspection of vessels under weigh within certain boundaries.

Water ballast.—Water carried to increase the stability of a vessel, usually in double bottom, peaks or deep tanks.

Water borne.—Brought by water.

Water-laid (called by the stow-boat fisherman "stow-boat rope").—The same as *cablet,* or cable-laid, *i.e., left-handed* rope. (*See* ROPE.)

Water-laid coils.—Those laid left-handed or against the sun.

Water-line or *Waterplane* (in Naval architecture).—A section of a hull, taken parallel to the line of flotation. There are two cardinal ones; the *water-line* or *light water-line,* and the *load-water line.* The first is the line to which a vessel is designed to float; the second that down to which she may with safety be immersed when freighted. And between these two there may be, for purposes of calculation in the designing of a vessel, any number of water-lines. In the popular sense the water-line of a boat is the line of flotation. (*See* LINES.)

Water-logged.—A vessel is water-logged when full of water but still floating; she has then lost all her buoyancy and becomes the creature of every sweeping sea, under which circumstances she is often abandoned. The term relates, of course, only to wooden ships which do not sink. These freighted with timber occasionally become water-logged.

Waterman.—Generally speaking, one whose vocation is carried on by the waterside. But a distinction is to be made, for not one half of those men whose work is connected with the water are watermen. The Thames or Queen's waterman is one who has served his apprenticeship to some member of the Watermen's Company, and who is fit to navigate on the Thames.

Watermen's and Lightermen's Company.—One of the riparian authorities on the Thames. "The members have a monopoly of the navigation of craft plying between Teddington and Gravesend; and the court licenses and exercises certain jurisdiction over its members."

Water-proof clothing.—(*See* Oil-Skins.)

Water sail, or *save all* (in ships).—"A small sail sometimes set under the foot of a lower studding-sail." (Smyth.) (*See* STUDDING SAILS.)

Waterspout.—A whirling column of rain and spray, perhaps hundreds of feet in height, between low cloud and sea, and generally encountered in the tropics. Waterspouts are dangerous to small craft and a hazard to shipping. They are the ocean counterpart of tornados.

Water stang.—A pole or rod across a stream, or a system of such poles.

Water stead.—The old name for the bed of a river.

Water stoup.—A name sometimes given to the common winkle.

Water ways (in a ship).—The deck planks extending round the ship's sides, and usually having grooves or channels which carry off the water from the decks. In a small half-decked boat the narrow decking round the well is called the water ways.

Water war.—Another name for the peculiar rising of the tide which in the Severn is called the *bore,* or anciently, the *hygre.* (*See* EAGRE.)

Wattles.—Hurdles composed of withies woven together and often placed along a river bank at high-water mark to keep the banks from falling in.

Waveson.—Goods after shipwreck floating on the waves.

Way.—*Momentum.*—It is important to note the difference between this and the term "weigh", the two being often confounded. A vessel in motion is said to have *way* on her: and when she ceases to move, to have *no way.* But a vessel under *weigh* is one in the act of weighing her anchor, or having weighed it, during which time she has no way on her.

Fresh way is increased speed made by a vessel under sail. (*See* under FRESH.)

Head-way.—To make head-way is to make progress forward. (*See* under HEAD.)

Stern-way.—A vessel makes stern-way when she moves stern foremost. (*See* under STERN.)

To *gather way* is to make *fresh way.*

To *lose way,* to fail in making any progress and lose that already made.

Gang-way.—An opening in the bulwarks of a vessel, through which a gang-board may be pushed.

'Way aloft, or *'way up* (literally *away* aloft).—A command to the crew of a ship to go aloft to furl, reef, etc.

Ways.—Baulks of timber laid down for launching vessels upon, or for moving any heavy weight.

Wear (from "weather") or *veer.*—To *wear* or *wear ship* is to put a vessel on the other tack by bringing her round *stern to wind* (in other words by paying her head off before the wind); and it is, therefore, the opposite to tacking, which brings her round *head* to wind.

(Compare with TACK.) In fore-and-aft boats the practice is not general; but there are occasions, and more especially with slow turning craft, as for instance when from a heavy sea a boat refuses to "wind helm", upon which it is necessary to wear. The safest plan is then to *settle* the *peak*, trim in the main sheet, and press the helm up. As the boat gets stern to wind the sail will naturally gybe, and as soon as this has taken place the peak may be again hauled up, the sheet trimmed, and the boat brought on the other tack to the desired course. It would appear, from the accounts of fights between sailing ships, that wearing was a very common evolution in old naval warfare.

Wear bare.—Spoken of ropes that are thin and weak from constant friction and exposure. Ropes should always be renewed before they have worn bare.

Weather (Anglo-Saxon *woeder,* the temperature of the atmosphere).—The term as a nautical expression, says Smyth, is applied to all things to *windward* of some particular situation. Hence the following: The *weather side* of a vessel is the side upon which the wind blows, the other side being the *leeward.* To *weather* another ship (in sailing) is to pass her on the weather or windward side. To *weather a gale* is to lie to in a gale; that is with the vessel's head to wind; and she is said to have *weathered* the gale when she has lived safely through it. A *weatherly* vessel is one that points well up to the wind and makes little leeway, or, if a steam vessel, rides comfortably in a seaway.

Weather beam.—That side of the ship's beam presented to the wind.

Weather board.—That side of the ship to windward.

Weather boards.—Boards set up round the bows of a boat to prevent water from coming over her. They usually extend from the headpost to a point just forward of the shrouds. It must be admitted, however, that as a boat ships water at the shrouds quite as much as over the bows, and in some cases a good deal more, the weather boards are seldom taken sufficiently far aft. It would undoubtedly be better, therefore, to carry them from the headpost to the beam amidships, when that is possible.

Weather boat.—One which behaves herself well, or the reverse, in any weather. The one is a good weather boat, the other a bad.

Weather-bound or *weather-fast (*anciently *woeder-foest).*—Unable to proceed because of the condition of the weather. Also *windbound.*

Weather clew.—(*See* CLEW.)

Weather-cocking.—A term used of boats which have a troublesome habit of *running up to the wind* and refusing to pay off either on one side or the other. The position such a boat then assumes is supposed to resemble that of a weather-cock; whence the term. It may be caused through some mistake on the part of the helmsman (*see Miss stays* under TACK) or it may be the fault of the boat itself being too much down by the head; in which latter case, if a change in the disposition of the ballast does not cure the fault, a considerable increase in the size or weight of the rudder has been recommended. Very long boats will be more liable to this than short ones.

Weather coil.—"An expression signifying that a ship has had her head brought about, so as to lie that way which her stern did before, as by the veering of the wind, or the motion of the helm; the sails remaining trimmed." (Smyth.)

Weather coiling.—"A ship resuming her course after being taken aback; rounding off by a stern-board, and coming up to it again." (Smyth.)

Weather eye.—"Keep your weather eye open"—keep a good look out to windward. Hence in general conversation it usually means keep a good look out.

Weather gage is the distance of a vessel (or any object) from another on the weather or wind side; *e.g.*, a ship on the weather side (or to windward) of another is said to have the *weather gage* of her; just as that one to leeward is said to have the lee gage.

Weather gall.—(*See* WIND GALL.)

> "A weather gall at morn
> Fine weather all gone."

Weather helm.—A vessel is described as *carrying weather helm* when—her tendency being to run up into the wind—the helm must be kept over to the weather side. Therefore, to *give her weather helm* is to put the helm up, *i.e.*, over to the weather side. (Compare with *Lee helm,* under the heading HELM.)

Weather lurch.—A roll over to windward.

Weather ropes.—The tarred ropes (old term, before wire roping was brought in).

Weather sheets (in square rig).—The ropes attached to those corners of a square sail which for the time being are the tacks or weather clews. (*See* TACK and CLEW.)

Weather shore.—The shore to *windward*. (Illustrated under the heading LEE.)

Weather tide.—A tide running *weatherwards*; or, in other words, a tide which, running, contrary to the direction of the wind, presses a vessel, as she is sailing, towards the windward. (*See* fig. under LEE.)

Weather warning.—A forecast from the Meteorological Office. (*See* SIGNALS.)

Weather wheel.—"The position of a man who steers a large ship, from his standing on the weather side of the wheel." (Smyth.)

Weed.—To clear rigging of knots, seizings, etc.

Weekly account.—"An old name for a white patch on the collar of a midshipman's coat." (Smyth.)

Weeping.—Drops of water oozing through the seams of a vessel.

Weevil.—(Anglo-Saxon *weft*).—An insect resembling a maggot, found in old biscuits; it also perforates wood.

Weft.—In sail-making, the width measurement in a sail cloth, the length measure being the *warp*.

Weigh (Anglo-Saxon *woeg*).—To lift the anchor from the ground.

(*See* ANCHOR.) This term must not be confounded with "way", as is too often the case. (*See* WAY.) A vessel is *under weigh* from the moment her anchor is *weighed,* or off, the ground (or as soon as she has slipped her mooring), even though she may have no *way* on her.

Well.—That part of a yacht or sailing boat which is not decked or covered in: it is often called the *cockpit.*

Well room is the space in a half-decked boat which is open or undecked, and hence resembles a well. The deep part of a vessel, in which water accumulates, and from which it is pumped, or, in boats, baled out, is also sometimes called the well. North Sea and other fishing vessels are built with a large compartment in their holds, through which the water passes so that fish may be preserved alive for a considerable period. This compartment is called the well. It appears also in the old Thames peter-boat.

Well found.—A vessel fully equipped and with all gear in good condition is said to be well found.

Well grown, said of a spar or timber when the grain of the wood runs in the right direction.

"Well there!" usually *"Well there, belay!"*—Equivalent to saying "That will do, belay!"

Wending (another name for, though more correctly a local pronunciation of the term, *winding*).—Putting a vessel about. (*See* TACK.)

Wentle (old term).—To roll over.

West.—A cardinal point on the compass.

Westing.—Distance westward. The movement of the sun after passing the meridian.

Westward Ho!—This was one of the cries of the old Thames watermen. It signified a readiness to proceed westward.

West Country parson.—"The hake; from the black mark on its back, and its abundance on the West coast."

Wet.—*A wet boat.*—One which sails all awash, *i.e.,* gunwales under; or one which plunges her head, bringing water aboard.

Wet dock.—A dock in which vessels float.

Whack.—A seaman's term for his daily allowance of provisions.

Whaler.—A ship employed in the whale trade.

Whale boat.—A long boat used in whaling. It is sharp at both ends, swift and buoyant. Old whale boats may often be seen along the coast, having generally been picked up as bargains by the 'longshore men. Some of these boats reach to 56 ft in length, with a beam of 10 ft. *Whalers* used in the Royal Navy derived from whale boats. They were 27 ft long, pulled five oars and were yawl-rigged, and latterly fitted with engines.

Whale Catcher or *Whale Chaser.*—Small handy ship of trawler type, mounting a harpoon-gun, and working in conjunction with a whale factory.

Wharf.—1. A lading place for vessels.

Wharf dues.—Charges made for lading or discharging cargoes at certain wharfs.

Wharfinger.—One who owns a wharf.

2. A scar of rock, or a sand bank, as Mud Wharf, Lancashire.

What.—*What cheer Ho?* (often pronounced "whatchee" for what cheer?).—A greeting common in many localities; more especially in the Eastern counties.

What ship is that?—A signal expressed by the International Code, once often seen exposed at Lloyd's signalling stations. Hence, when a person uses an exceptionally long word, or some expression beyond the understanding of his hearers, the seafaring man may not unnaturally ask, "What ship is that?"

Wheel.—The wheel and axle by which the tiller and rudder of a vessel is worked. As well as in ships it is found in yachts, and steam-launches, even of the smallest size, are usually furnished with it, to enable one man to both steer and drive the engine.

Wheel house.—A covering over the wheel in large vessels.

Wheel ropes or *chains.*—The ropes or chains which communicate with the ship's tiller from the wheel.

Wheft.—1. (Sometimes *weft, whiff* or *waft*).—Any flag that has had a stop passed around it halfway along its length. It then has some special significance. 2. In sail making. (*See* WEFT.)

Whelk.—A mollusc, *Buccinum undatum,* much consumed in East London, and valuable as bait for fishing.

Whelk tingle, or *dog-whelk.*—A smaller whelk (*Purpura lapillus*), which have the power to bore through the shells of other molluscs, and is, therefore, the *bête noir* of oyster culturists.

Whelps.—The projecting ribs on the barrel of a capstan or windlass. They enable a cable to get a good bite.

Wherry (said to be another form of the word "ferry", from the fact that wherries were often ferry boats).—Wherries have been, in time past, of different builds and employed for different purposes, and they have, like skiffs, a different use according to locality. The old Thames wherries, were wide and long, with a high pointed

OLD THAMES WHERRY

bow ending in a sharp iron nose. (*See* fig.) They were the boats used by watermen, and often became ferry boats. Where the wherry is actually a ferry boat, it is often pointed both bow and stern, and rowed either way. Sometimes it is large and almost resembles a pontoon.

Norfolk wherry.—In Norfolk the wherry is a trading barge, of peculiar build and una rigged. (*See* under NORFOLK BROADS.)

Whiff.—1. A small flag. (*See* WHEFT.) 2. The name given on the Thames to a long, narrow, out-rigged sculling boat used for racing. It superseded the wedge-shaped wager boat, being made by the Claspers, and has, in its turn, been superseded for racing purposes by the *best boat* (*which see*) of the present day. But it is still used by scullers in practice, and in *rum tum* races. It is often *clincher* built.

Whiffler (old term).—One who blows a fife.

Whip.—1. "A rope and single block used in lifting light articles. If another block is added the medium is known as a *double whip*." (Smyth.)

Whip upon whip.—"One whip applied to the fall of another, and so on." (Smyth.)

2. To *whip*.—To bind up, as a rope *served* (or bound) with tarred twine is said to be *whipped*; from which we have—

Whipping.—A sort of string of spun yarn, saturated with Stockholm tar, and generally used in whipping the ends of ropes. (*See* under KNOTS.)

Whipper.—One who unloads *colliers* into *lighters* on the Thames.

Whipstaff.—A vertical lever operating on the fore end of a ship's tiller. It was used in the 16th and 17th centuries before the invention of the steering wheel.

Whirl.—Another name for a *rope-winch*.

Whiskers.—*Cross-trees* to a *bowsprit*; or in large vessels to a *jib-boom*. They are employed in small craft, where the bowsprit is long, or when the bows of the boat are narrow, to extend the bowsprit shrouds and give increased lateral support to the bowsprit, just as top-mast shrouds, extended on the cross-trees, do to a top-mast. (*See* fig.)

Whistle.—The older name for the boatswain's pipe, or call. Originally the badge of the English Lord High Admiral, worn round the neck on a silver chain.—*Whistling for the wind* is a practice so ancient and so constantly followed by a majority of the seafaring and fishing community, that it is difficult to believe that it can ever die out. And, indeed, if the amateur who has not yet tried the experiment is willing to do so on the next occasion upon which the wind fails him, he will very possibly return a partial believer in it himself.

Whistling psalms to the taffrail.—An expression signifying the throwing away of good advice upon some person who may be about as susceptible to its influence as is the taffrail of his yacht.

WHISKERS

Wet your whistle.—To drink. Chaucer's "Miller's Lady of Trumpington" had "Hir joly whistle wel ywette".

White.—*White boot-top.*—The white line painted round a vessel.

White caps or *white horses.*—Waves the crests of which break into white foam.

White lapel.—"An old term for a naval lieutenant, from the white lapel on his uniform."

White rope.—Rope which is not tarred. (*See* ROPE.)

White squall.—A sudden squall of wind, often unforeseen, covering the sea with a mass of foam called *spoon-drift*. It is common to the tropics and occasionally occurs in the Mediterranean.

Wholesome (occasionally written "holsom").—The behaviour of a vessel in a heavy gale. One which will "*try, hull,* and *ride*" safely and well is wholesome.

Wick (Anglo-Saxon *wyc*).—"A creek, bay, or village by the side of a river", as Hampton Wick, on the Thames; Walberswick, on the Suffolk coast, etc.

Widdershins.—A slang word signifying "in a direction contrary to that of the sun".

Widows'men.—"Imaginary sailors, formerly borne on the books as A.B.'s for wages in every ship in commission; they ceased with the consolidated pay at the close of the war. The institution was dated 24 George II, to meet widows' pensions; the amount of pay and provisions for two men in each hundred was paid over by the Paymaster-general of the Navy to the widows' fund." (Smyth.) Captain Basil Hall describes the system as "an official fiction by which the pay of so many imaginary persons was transferred to a fund for the relief of the widows of non-commissioned and warrant officers".

Wild (in sailing).—To steer badly. In rowing, to keep bad time, a bad stroke, and get excited.

Wimble (with shipwrights).—The boring implement worked by the centre-bit.

Winch (Anglo-Saxon *wince*).—In a ship, a machine consisting of a horizontal barrel rotated by steam or electric power, and round the drum of which a rope may be wound. Used for hoisting cargo and other purposes. 2. A species of small windlass with a crank, which in some small yachts takes the place of the *windlass.*

Winch bitts.—The posts which support the winch.

Wind.—Wind, in sailing, is described according to the direction in which it blows upon a vessel, or the compass point *from* which it blows. Reference to the accompanying diagram will best explain the following terms. A. Wind ahead. B. Wind abaft, or astern. (Sailing with the wind thus is called "running".) C. Wind on the port beam. D. Wind on the starboard beam. E. Wind on the port bow. F. Wind on the starboard bow. (A vessel with the wind on the bow is sailing "close-hauled".) G. Wind athwart the beam, port side. H. Wind athwart the beam, starboard side. (With the wind athwart the beam a vessel is "reaching".) J. Wind abaft the beam, port side. K. Wind abaft the beam, starboard side (With the wind in this direction the vessel is "sailing large" or "free".) L. Wind on the port quarter. M. Wind on the starboard quarter.

To *wind* is to go about head to wind as in tacking (*see* TACK); and a vessel having come round is said to have *winded*. To sail *in the eye of the wind* is equivalent to sailing very *close to the wind,* that is, as nearly against the direction of the wind as possible.

Windward.—That side of a vessel or of any other object upon which the wind is blowing. It is often called the *weather* side.

To *wind a call.*—To pipe a call upon the whistle, as a boatswain does the orders.

Wind banks.—Long clouds supposed to prognosticate wind.

Wind-bound.—Unable to proceed because of contrary winds.

Wind gall.—"A luminous halo on the edge of a distant cloud, where there is rain, usually seen in the wind's eye, and looked upon as a sure precursor of stormy weather. Also an atmospheric effect of prismatic colours, said likewise to indicate bad weather if seen to leeward." (Smyth.)

Wind lipper.—A very slight disturbance on the surface of the sea—the first effect of a breeze.

Windmill.—In rowing, lifting the oars so high out of the water each time a stroke is taken that their motion resembles that of the sails of a windmill. It is an art in which beginners are peculiarly adept. (*See* fig.)

Windmills (on ships).—There were sometimes seen on sailing ships, more especially on Scandinavian vessels. Their use is to work the pumps. (*See* fig.)

Wind-rode.—When the wind overcomes the tide so that a vessel lying at anchor rides with it (and therefore, against the tide).

Wind sail.—A tube or awning of canvas, employed in hot latitudes to convey a draught of fresh air to the lower parts of a ship.

Wind-taut.—"A vessel at anchor heeling over to the force of the wind." (Smyth.)

WINDMILL

Wind-vane.—A thin strip of metal mounted to pivot upon a masthead or elsewhere aloft, to show the direction of the wind.

In the eye of the wind.—Sailing very close to the wind.

In the teeth of the wind.—Making progress directly against the wind.

Head to wind.—The position of a ship when her stem points exactly in the direction of the wind. In sailing evolutions vessels are generally brought round head to wind. (*See* TACK.)

Winds.—"Currents in the atmosphere conveying air with more or less velocity from one part to another. A contraction or expansion in one part of the atmosphere, such as is caused by a variation in temperature, or by an increase or diminution in the quantity of aqueous vapour suspended in the air, will disturb the equilibrium, and produce a wind.... Winds may be divided into three classes:—1. Permanent winds, as the trade winds of the torrid zone. 2. Periodical winds, as the monsoons of the Indian Ocean. 3. Variable winds, as the winds of the temperate and frigid zones." (Brande and Cox.)

The tendency of winds has been found to be a *veering* round with the motion of the sun, that is, from north through east to south, and so through west back to north; and it has been observed that this circle may be traversed for several days continuously, though the circle in the opposite direction is very rarely, if ever, completed. (*See* BACKING OF THE WIND.)

The velocity of wind may vary from a motion almost imperceptible to one of upwards of a hundred miles per hour. The *Beaufort Wind Scale*, on **pp. 334–335**, is generally used to indicate this. The scale is a system of estimating the force of the wind by the amount of sail a ship could carry; or by observing the appearance of the sea. Devised in 1806, it has been used, with slight revisions, ever since. The author later became Rear Admiral Sir Francis Beaufort and a distinguished Hydrographer of the Navy.

A gale is a continuous storm; it ranges from a *fresh* gale to a *strong* gale, and lastly to a *heavy, hard,* or *whole* gale. (*See* GALE.)

Windjammer.—A sailing vessel.

Windlass.—The machine in the bows of a vessel, used for heaving in the anchor cable. When worked by hand in old, or small vessels, the wheel and axle was turned by either handspikes or a crank, by which the chain cable of a vessel (or any other weight) may be hauled in. To prevent the windlass from moving backwards, it has a ratchet wheel connected with it, into the teeth of which fall one or more *pawls*: the pawl being, of course, lifted when it is necessary to pay out chain, or, as they used to say on ship-board, to "freshen hawse". The uprights which support and take the bearing of the windlass are known as the *windlass bitts* or *chocks*; and the smaller head, which, in large windlasses, carries the pawls, is called the *pawl-bitt*.

Spanish-windlass.—"A machine formed of a hand-spike and a small lever, usually a tree-nail; or a tree-nail and a marling spike; to set up rigging, heave in short purchases, etc."

Wing.—The studding sails of a square rigged ship are sometimes thus called; as also, in sailing with the wind aft, may be the spinnaker and mainsail of a yacht. (*See* WING AND WING, p. 336.)

Wings (in large ships).—Passages below,

WING AND WING

BEAUFORT SCALE

Force on Beaufort Scale	Speed in knots	Description	Height of waves in feet	Deep sea criteria
0	0–1	Calm	—	Flat calm, mirror smooth
1	1–3	Light airs	$\frac{1}{4}$	Small wavelets, no crests
2	4–6	Light breeze	$\frac{1}{2}$	Small wavelets, crests glassy but do not break
3	7–10	Gentle breeze	2	Large wavelets, crests begin to break
4	11–16	Moderate breeze	$3\frac{1}{2}$	Small waves, becoming longer, crests break frequently
5	17–21	Fresh breeze	6	Moderate waves, longer, breaking crests
6	22–27	Strong breeze	$9\frac{1}{2}$	Large waves forming, crests break more frequently
7	28–33	Near gale	$13\frac{1}{2}$	Large waves, streaky foam
8	34–40	Gale	18	High waves of increasing length, crests form spindrift
9	41–47	Strong gale	23	High waves, dense streaks of foam, crests roll over
10	48–55	Storm	29	Very high waves, long over hanging crests. Surface of the sea white with foam
11	56–65	Violent storm	37	Exceptionally high waves, sea completely covered by foam
12	above 65	Hurricane	—	The air filled with spray and visibility seriously affected

OF WIND FORCE

Original criteria for "a well-conditioned Man-of-war"

—just sufficient to give steerage way.
Fishing smack just has steerage way.

—under all sail and clear full, would go in smooth water 1 to 2 knots.
Wind fills the sails of smacks which then travel at about 1–2 knots.

—under all sail and clear full, would go in smooth water 3 to 4 knots.
Smacks begin to career and travel about 3–4 knots.

—under all sail and clear full, would go in smooth water, 4 to 5 knots.
Good working breeze, smacks carry all canvas with good list.

In which the same ship could just carry close-hauled, Royals, etc.
Smacks shorten sail.

In which the same ship could just carry close-hauled, single reefs and topgallant sails.
Smacks have double reef in main sail: care required when fishing.

In which the same ship could just carry close-hauled, double reefs, jib, etc.
Smacks remain in harbour and those at sea lie-to.

In which the same ship could just carry close-hauled, triple reefs, courses, etc.
All smacks make for harbour, if near.

In which the same ship could just carry close-hauled, close reefs and courses.

With which she could only bear close-reefed main topsail, and reefed foresail.

With which she would be reduced to storm staysails.

To which she could show no canvas.

along the sides, to enable carpenters to get at any leak. The *lee boards* of barges are also sometimes called *wooden wings*.

Wing and wing is an expression invented long before the naming of that which we now call a *spinnaker*, and which shows its principle to be of some antiquity, for old works define the term as used of fore-and-aft vessels when running before the wind, "the foresail boomed out on one side, and the mainsail on the other": and this practice of making one sail serve the purpose of both balloon jib and spinnaker has again become very common in yacht racing. In square rigged vessels, when studding sails are set both sides (as in running), they are said to be wing and wing, and with lateen rig, a vessel with two masts often runs with the peak of the fore-sail on one side, and that of the main sail on the other. (*See* fig., p. 333.)

Wing transoms (in shipbuilding).—The uppermost transoms in the stern frame of a vessel. Or a transom supporting the stern of a square-sterned vessel.

Wind surfing.—(*See* SAILBOARD.)

Wire.—*Wire-rope.*—This is of steel or iron, and is now almost universally employed for standing rigging—such as shrouds, etc.; when the wires of each strand are wound round hemp hearts, and the strands themselves wound round a hemp heart the rope is flexible enough for general purposes, and is then termed *flexible wire rope*. It is often galvanised, though this is found to somewhat weaken it. Its cost, compared with that of hemp, is scarcely more than half. Stout wire rope may be spliced, but when thin it becomes considerably damaged, and therefore weakened by splicing.

Wire stretcher.—(*See* SET-SCREW.)

Wiring or **Rising.**—A stringer or batten upon which the thwarts (seats) of a boat rest: it is fixed to the ribs. The thwarts do not (or should not) rest upon the sides of the boat, but are fixed by knees to a short piece called a *wiring clamp,* and that to the wiring.

Wishbone.—A divided gaff or boom, joined at the fore end, which allows the sail to take an aeroform shape.

With the sun.—In the same direction as the sun's path—*i.e.,* from east through south to west. Often said when turning anything about clockwise.

Withe.—*A boom iron, i.e.,* an iron at the head of a boom, yard, or bowsprit with a ring on it through which another spar can run—or it may be a joint, like that of a fishing rod, by which the length of a spar is made up: this being a useful way, in small craft, of rigging out a spinnaker boom.

Within.—*Within* 4 *points,* 6 *points, etc.*—Sailing close-hauled at a certain angle with the direction of the wind. (*See* under SAILING.)

Within and *without board.*—The same as in-board and out-board (*both of which see*).

Withy.—A place where willows grow. Hence the willow itself, or a twig of it, is called a withy.

Wood.—*Wood ends.*—Another name for *hood ends* or *hoodings* (*which see*).

Woodlock.—A block of wood nailed near some movable object to prevent it from shifting; as those which sometimes keep a rudder down.

Wood sheathing.—The feathered planking used in *doubling* a vessel.

Wood wings.—The *lee boards* of barges are occasionally thus called.

Woolding.—The strengthening of a weakened spar by binding it up. "Winding a piece of rope about a mast or yard to support it when it is fished, or when composed of several pieces."

Work.—1. To *work* signifies to set and keep going, as—

To *work a vessel.*—To adapt the sails to the wind, steer, etc.

To *work the sheets.*—To haul in or let them out as occasion may require. 2. But in another sense we have—

To *work up* or prepare, as to train and exercise a newly-joined crew until they become proficient, or to work up a junk—*i.e.*, to draw out yarns, old cable, etc., and with it to make *foxes, points, gaskets,* sinnit or *spun-yarn,* etc.

Working.—1. This word as applied to the planks of a vessel signifies "to open" or "work open" as she strains in a sea, and the extent to which she works is called her *give* (*which see*).

2. *Working to windward.*—Beating to windward, or making progress against the wind. (*See* under TACK.)

3. *Working a day's work* (*at sea*).—Calculating a vessel's progress from noon on one day to noon on the next, and her then probable position.

The word *work* is also applied to certain sails, as—

Working foresail (in fore-and-aft rig).—A foresail which runs on a horse.

Working lug, the same as a standing lug; and it often has a boom. (*See* LUG.)

Working topsail (in fore-and-aft rig).—The most general form of big-topsail. It is, in fact, a working or standing lugsail elevated above the mainsail.(*See* TOPSAIL.)

And in various other senses; thus:

Working deck, sometimes called *spar deck.* (*See* DECK.)

Working up (old term).—Keeping men at work as punishment.

Worm—*Worm, parcel and serve.*—A method of protecting parts of a rope which are likely to be chafed. It is first *wormed,* by laying thin pieces of line (the worms) between the strands; next *parcelled* by winding strips of canvas (saturated with tar) over the part wormed; and lastly *served* or tightly bound with spun yarn. There is an old rhyme with respect to this proceeding which runs:—

> "Worm and parcel with the lay,
> Turn and serve the other way."

Wrack.—Sea weed and (perhaps) all else which has been cast by the sea on the ebb-dry foreshore.

Wreck (it is said that this term is derived from *wrack,* denoting all that the sea washes on shore as it does this weed).—A wreck is,—1. The destruction of a ship by the sea; or (as the insurance policies put it) by the act of God; 2. The ship herself (or the remnant of her) after this act. A vessel may, in a sense, be said to become a wreck when there is no longer any hope of saving her: but, in law, she is no wreck while any person or domestic animal remains alive aboard her; and this fact is said to have given rise, in times past, to acts which one might well feel ashamed to recount.

Wreckage.—"Goods cast up by the sea after a shipwreck, and left on land within the limits of some county." Goods jettisoned or cast overboard, and not stranded, do not come under this head. (*See* FLOTSAM, JETSAM and LAGAN.) Wreckage is now taken charge of by "receivers of wreck", who keep it a certain time, after which, if not claimed, it becomes the property of the Crown, and is sold in open auction.

Wreckers.—In times past, men who made it their business to gather up the spoils of wrecks, and who are said to have occasionally employed means to bring wrecks about. To-day the name is occasionally opprobriously applied to those fishermen and others who may always be found ready to risk their lives in going out to ships in distress, both to save other lives, as well as on the chance of earning that which very frequently turns out to be but a miserable reward for their labours: for which latter reason they are often called "grabbers" by those who sit at home, and, while risking nothing, are certainly not less eager after plunder. The nation may feel proud, however, that in the Admiralty it has a court which recognises the enormous risks these men run, and is always anxious to award them just compensation.

Wreck free.—Exempt from the forfeiture of wreckage. Under Edward I this privilege was granted the lords of the Cinque Ports.

Wriggle.—A projection over a port hole or scuttle to prevent water running in.

Wring.—To twist or injure by too severe a pressure.

Wrong.—To *wrong another* (in sailing).—To take the wind out of her sails by unfair means. Under some circumstances this may, in racing, constitute a *foul*.

X

Xebec (pronounced "*zebeck*").—A small three-masted vessel, lateen-rigged, but with a square sail on the foremast and with an over-hanging bow and stern, used in conveying merchandise in the Mediterranean and sometimes seen on the west coast of Spain. Once greatly used by the Barbary pirates.

Y

Yacht.—In its broadest meaning, a pleasure vessel, of any sort, size or shape, from the half-decked boats of the inland rivers to the three-masted "Sunbeam", the well-known ship which belonged to Lord Brassey. (From the Dutch *jacht,* chaser.)

Yard.—A spar suspended to a mast for the purpose of extending a sail. It is elevated by means of a rope; and this rope is accordingly called a *halyard* (*i.e.,* haul yard). In square-rigged vessels the yards go athwart the masts—*i.e.,* at right angles to the keel line. In fore-and-aft rig they run fore and aft, *i.e.,* in a parallel with the keel. Yards take their names from the sails they carry: on a full-rigged ship there will be five on each mast. On the main mast the main yard, main top-sail yard, main top-gallant yard, main royal yard, main sky-sail yard, and in rare instances a yard to higher sails called respectively the moon-raker and the jumper; and the same on the other masts, substituting for "main", the word "fore" or mizzen" as the case may be, with the exception that the lowest yard on the mizzen mast

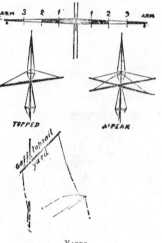

YARDS

is known as the *cross jack* (*which see*) or *crotched* yard. The yard of a square-rigged ship is divided into two parts, each part being again sub-divided into four. The middle is called the *sling*; the end the *yard arm*; and the distance between these, the *quarters.* Hence we have the 1st, 2nd, and 3rd quarters, and the 4th or yard arm, on each side. (*See* fig.) The *yard arms* are very frequently mentioned both at sea and in all literature relating to it. It is from them that punishments (keel hauling, etc.), said once to have been practised in the British Navy, and most probably so in the Dutch, were performed. To the yard arm the *braces* are attached, which work or *traverse* the yards about the masts, and beyond them run out small booms which carry the *studding sails,* when set in fair weather.

To clear one's yardarm.—To give an explanation of, or offer an excuse, for some action.

Brace the yards.—To *traverse* them about the masts so as to present the sails at a proper angle to the wind.

Top the yards.—To elevate one side by the *lifts* so that it is higher than the other. (*See* fig.)

Yards apeak.—The yards *topped* in such a manner as to resemble the letter X; this was sometimes a sign of mourning. (*See* fig.)

Yard tackles.—Tackles attached to the yard arms for lifting anything into the ship.

In fore-and-aft rig the word "yard" is less often used, but still there are several spars called yards; and rightly so, for they are both balanced to the mast and carry sails, and are swayed (lifted), moreover by *hal-yards.* Such are the:—

Topsail yard (or *gaff* topsail yard) which extends the head of a big-topsail.

Jack-yard.—This is, generally speaking, a small yard, and in fore-and-aft rig it extends the head or foot of a sail beyond some other sail or spar. The term "jack" is rather indiscriminately applied by seamen; its general meaning, however, is "small" or "extra". Thus in a jack top-sail, the jack-yard is a pole standing in a vertical position, its end rising beyond the head of the mast; while in a *big* or, as it is sometimes called, a spinnaker top-sail, the jack-yard is a small boom, at the foot of the sail, projecting beyond the guy-end of the gaff. (Both these are illustrated under the heading JACK.)

Booms and gaffs are not, properly speaking, yards; but a *sprit,* on the other hand, may be regarded as such. (*See* under SPRIT.) The spars to which the heads of *lug sails* are bent are also called yards.

Yards must be kept in to the mast, or otherwise they would lift, and their sails become practically useless. They are, therefore, kept in by various devices, mostly in the form of hoops of iron or rope, called *yard guides* or *parrels.* A sprit is kept in place by fitting its heel into a loop called the *snotter.*

Yarn.—Fibrous threads, which, being twisted together, compose the strands used in making a rope. 2. To converse.

Yaw.—*Yawing* (of a sailing vessel) is deviating from the true course. A person who is careless or ignorant of the method of steering, keeps a boat "yawing" from side to side. Great care should be taken, therefore, by beginners, not to fall into this fault, which is considered quite unpardonable by yachtsmen.

Yaw sighted.—Having a squint.

Yawl (Dutch *jol,* a skiff).—A vessel with two masts—main and mizzen, the mizzen being small and carrying usually only one sail. It is a serviceable rig for cruising yachts, the boom extending beyond the taffrail, which therefore allows of the sail being easily reefed. The mizzen sail, too, has many advantages—it helps the boat round when *in stays*; it keeps her steady in a rolling sea; it counteracts an overpress of head canvas; in going up to moorings, or in moving the boat only a short distance, it may be used with the aid only of a foresail; and, in a word, it renders the boat essentially a *handy* craft. But, on the other hand, the great loss of sail area sustained by placing a mizzen where, as in a cutter, the foot of the mainsail would extend beyond the taffrail, precludes it from being a fast

VARIOUS YAWLS

rig; and for this reason, perhaps, the yawl is no longer so popular as it was, the cutter and sloop having superseded it.

Yell (old term).—A rolling motion.

Yellow.—*Yellow flag.*—The flag carried by vessels in quarantine. Where this is seen it is wise to always pass to windward of it.

Yellowing.—The passing over of captains at a flag-promotion. An old term for a malpractice which, perhaps, may not be altogether obsolete.

Yellow fever.—An old term made use of in Greenwich Hospital, and denoting drunkenness.

Yoke.—A fitting binding two parts together, as the *yoke of a mast,* commonly called the *lower-cap.* The lower aperture (in the trestle trees), or, often, a ring through which a topmast runs. (*See* fig.; also CAP.)

YOKE

Yoke of a rudder.—The flat plate or tiller to which, in long, open boats, the *rudder* or *yoke lines* are attached. (*See* fig., p. 342; also under RUDDER.)

Yoke lines.—Another name for *rudder lines.*

Yulo, yuloh.—A long oar, or sweep, used by Chinese boatmen over the stern to propel sampans and small junks.

Young.—*Young gentlemen.*—On board a war-ship the midshipmen are thus termed.

Young flood (of the tide).—The first of the rising tide.

Youngster.—A fresh hand, or a young boy.

Yunker.—Another name for *youngster.*

Z

Zenith.—The point directly overhead of any person.

Zephyr.—The West wind: but in general conversation it often signifies only a light wind.

Zigzag.—To steer short courses on either side of the intended course to mislead submarines of the ship's true direction of travel.

Zone Time.—Time kept which is exactly a given number of hours ahead or behind Greenwich Mean Time. Easterly zones are labelled minus and westerly zones plus, and each is of 15° longitude, the distance the sun apparently travels in one hour.

ABBREVIATIONS

(The abbreviations used upon charts are too numerous to list here. They are printed on Admiralty Chart 5011 now also published as a booklet.)

A before capital letters	Associate Member of
A.A.	Anti-aircraft
A.B.	Able-bodied Seaman
A.M.C.	Armed Merchant Cruiser
A.1.	First class; the best
B.M.	Boatswain's Mate
B.O.T.	Board of Trade
b	Mainly blue sky
bc	Partly cloudy
C after 3 figures	Compass
C.P.O.	Chief Petty Officer
c	Cloudy
c before a date	About (Latin *circa*)
D.B.S.	Distressed British Seaman
D/F	(Radio)Direction-Finder
D.R.	Dead Reckoning
D.T.I.	Department of Trade and Industry
d	Drizzle
E	East
E.P.	Estimated Position
E.T.A.	Estimated Time of Arrival
e	Wet air
F before capital letters	Fellow of
FX	Forecastle
f	Fog
G.M.T.	Greenwich Mean Time
G.R.P.	Glass-reinforced Plastic
g	Gale
H.M.C.G.	H.M. Coastguard
H.M.S.	His, or Her, Majesty's Ship
H.P.	Horse Power
H.W.	High Water
h	Hail
I.A.L.A.	International Association of Lighthouse Authorities
I.M.C.O.	Inter-governmental Maritime Consultative Organization
I.M.O.	International Maritime Organization
K.H.M.	King's Harbour-Master

Kn	Knots
LASH	Lighter-aboard-ship
L.O.A.	Length Over All
L.S.	Leading Seaman
L.W.	Low Water
l	Lightning
M	Nautical, or Sea Miles
M before capital letters	Member of
M after 3 figures	Magnetic
M.N.	Merchant Navy
M.V. or M.S.	Motor Vessel/Ship
m	Mist
N	North
NE	North East
NW	North West
N.I.	Nautical Institute
O.D. or O.S.	Ordinary Seaman
o	Overcast
P.O.	Petty Officer
p	Passing showers
Q.M.	Quartermaster
q	Squalls
R.C.C.	Royal Cruising Club
R.D.	Reserve Decoration
R.F.A.	Royal Fleet Auxiliary
R.F.R.	Royal Fleet Reserve
R.I.N.	Royal Institute of Navigation
R.I.N.A.	Royal Institute of Naval Architects
R.M.M.V.	Royal Mail Motor Vessel
R.M.S.	Royal Mail Steamship
R.N.	Royal Navy
R.N.L.I.	Royal National Life-boat Institution
R.N.R.	Royal Naval Reserve
R.N.V.R.	Royal Naval Volunteer Reserve
R.O.R.C.	Royal Ocean Racing Club
R/T	Radio Telephony
R.Y.A.	Royal Yachting Association
R.Y.S.	Royal Yacht Squadron
Ro-Ro	Roll-on Roll-off ship
r	Rain
rs	Sleet
S	South
SE	South East
SW	South West
S.N.R.	Society for Nautical Research
SOS	International Signal of distress
S.S.	Steamship
S.V.	Sailing Vessel
S.W.L.	Safe Working Load

s	Snow
T after 3 figures	True
t	Thunder
USCG	United States Coast Guard
USN	United States Navy
USNR	United States Naval Reserve
USS	United States' Ship
u	Ugly, threatening sky
v	Unusual visibility
W	West
W.R.N.S.	Women's Royal Naval Service
W/T	Wireless Telegraphy
w	Dew
z	Dust haze

NOTES